WASHINGTON HALL AT NOTRE DAME

Washington Hall c. 2004, by architect Christopher K. Dennis.

WASHINGTON HALL

at Notre Dame

CROSSROADS OF THE UNIVERSITY, 1864–2004

MARK C. PILKINTON

Carol,
Thanks for the great
ND works article!
Mark C. Pilkinton
August 29, 2011

UNIVERSITY OF NOTRE DAME PRESS

NOTRE DAME, INDIANA

Manufactured in the United States of America

Library of Congress Cataloging-in-Publication Data

Pilkinton, Mark C. (Mark Cartwright), 1947–
Washington Hall at Notre Dame : crossroads of the university, 1864–2004 /
Mark C. Pilkinton.
p.   cm.
Includes bibliographical references and index.
ISBN-13: 978-0-268-03895-3 (pbk. : alk. paper)
ISBN-10: 0-268-03895-3 (pbk. : alk. paper)
1. University of Notre Dame—History.   2. University of Notre Dame—
Buildings.   I. Title.   II. Title: Crossroads of the university, 1864–2004.
LD4113.P55   2011
378.772—dc23

2011025681

TO

GEORGE AND LUTHER

The history of Washington Hall is a subject for reflection, as imaging forth the vicissitudes of human life.

—*Scholastic* 1:5, Oct. 5, 1867, 7

CONTENTS

Preface   ix

Acknowledgments   xvii

Washington Hall Timeline, 1845–2004   xxi

CHAPTER 1
The True Ghosts of Washington Hall   1

CHAPTER 2
Before the First Washington Hall, 1842–1864   13

CHAPTER 3
The First Washington Hall, 1864–1879   31

CHAPTER 4
Rebuilding After the Great Fire, 1879–1882   71

CHAPTER 5
The "New" Washington Hall, 1882–1895   99

CHAPTER 6
Growing Pains, 1895–1922   155

CHAPTER 7
The Ghost of Washington Hall, 1920–2004   205

CHAPTER 8
More Than the Home of the Lecture, 1922–1956   223

CHAPTER 9

Modernization, 1956–1984   263

CHAPTER 10

Renovation and Revitalization, 1984–2004   293

————————————————

Appendix   317

List of Illustrations   319

Notes   329

Works Consulted   385

Index   391

When I arrived at Notre Dame in the summer of 1984 to chair the Department of Communication and Theatre, I believed two absolutely eternal truths: first, that Washington Hall would remain the only performing arts center on campus throughout my career, and second, that I would never write a history of Washington Hall. With regard to the first truth, I knew Notre Dame had built Washington Hall a century earlier, and my dean and others at the time assured me that a new performing arts center would never be built, at least not in our lifetime. With regard to the second truth, I had been hired to help create the future of Notre Dame and so that was my entire focus. I had little interest in and less knowledge of the past. The senior professor in the department at the time, Fred Syburg, appropriately brought up historical precedent and reminded me that he had worked with students such as Phil Donahue who went on to become luminaries. But none of that piqued my interest then, perhaps because I had hit the ground running and had no time to think about the past. As I write this in the summer of 2009, things have come full circle: I am now myself the senior professor in the department, and clearly I am the one who tends to reminisce most about the past, often to the glazed-eye look of my younger, future-looking colleagues. In what seems like the blink of an eye rather than a lifetime the tables have turned.

My first visit to Washington Hall and indeed to the campus of the University of Notre Dame occurred on a very cold January day in 1984 when I arrived for an on-campus interview. The head of the Search Committee, Associate Dean of Arts and Letters Nathan Hatch (who later served as provost at Notre Dame from 1996 to 2005, before becoming president of Wake Forest University), gave me a tour of the "theatre" building—Washington Hall—still in the process of renovation. I asked if the department I would chair would have exclusive control of the space, a basic need if indeed theatre were to grow and prosper on the Notre Dame campus as the university envisioned. Hatch stated that exclusive control would be problematic and went on to outline the rather complex nature of administration of the building. He assured me the new chair would have "adequate" time in Washington Hall, but that time would have to be negotiated with other groups, and the precise mechanism had yet to be worked out. I explained that highly specialized theatre venues were the equivalent of laboratories for the sciences, and that the more the Department of Communication and Theatre had control of Washington Hall, the better the academic unit could become. Hatch understood and appreciated my perspective but nevertheless pointed out that the issues were real, in part because of the history of the building as an "exhibition hall" (although he never used the term) and the lack of any other purpose-built performing arts venues on campus at that time. I knew nothing about the history of Notre Dame then, but I immediately sensed from Hatch's comments that Washington Hall was a special place where nearly everyone wanted to stage nearly everything, including teaching large classes. I did not know then the uses for which the building was designed and had become historically accustomed to fulfilling, nor did I comprehend the psychological reliance the university placed on Washington Hall as a point of access and integration with the larger world. A major prestigious American university in the mid-1980s very much needed and required many performance venues, and until Notre Dame got around to building them Washington Hall would continue to be in very high demand.

I also assumed Washington Hall would remain the focus for theatrical production throughout my career at Notre Dame because I was told in no uncertain terms that a new performing arts building would never be built: Washington Hall must meet the university's theatrical programmatic and academic needs into the foreseeable future. The university band occupied space in the lower level of the north wing (rightfully so, since that was the original "Music Hall" portion of the building, although I did not then know that), but that meant the theatre unit within the Department of Communication and Theatre had little space from which to try to run an academic theatre production program. The department therefore operated out of four different buildings with Washington Hall only one of them. Not until the opening of the Marie P. DeBartolo Center for the Performing Arts in 2004 did the department at long last come together in one building.

In writing this history of Washington Hall, I have relied as much as possible on accounts closest to the events themselves in hopes of getting the most accurate sense of what actually happened. Especially valuable from the earliest years of the university have been the Minutes of the Local Council of the Indiana Province of the Congregation of Holy Cross. Called the Minor Chapter through the 1850s and afterward described as the Local Council of Administration or simply the Council, this executive committee assisted and advised the presiding father superior, and thus functioned as the decision-making and deliberative body of the fledgling University of Notre Dame. While terse and to the point, the Local Council Minutes greatly help to flesh out the early history of Notre Dame. The now student-written (but initially faculty-written and supervised) weekly journal, the *Scholastic*, survives nearly intact since publication began in 1867 and thus also provides an invaluable account of events over the university's history after the first quarter century. Before the creation of the school newspaper, *The Voice*, in 1963—which became *The Observer* in 1969—the *Scholastic* served in many ways as a weekly newspaper. When *The Observer* took over much of the *Scholastic* news function, the *Scholastic* reoriented more toward literature and issues of less quotidian immediacy. I have also relied on the student-written and produced annual yearbook, the *Dome*, which has provided since its inception in 1906 extensive and oftentimes unique photographs. The university's financial ledgers and journals from the Civil War period to the 1890s have been invaluable, too, as have other personal letters and documents available in the collections of the University of Notre Dame Archives.

As a professor in the Department of Film, Television, and Theatre at the University of Notre Dame, I recognize that my interest in Washington Hall—or any performance venue—is likely biased toward theatre. I have nevertheless sincerely tried to write a book about the building itself and the myriad events that have occurred there beyond theatre. As much as I would like to be able to agree with Hamlet that "the play's the thing," in fact this is far from true when it comes to Washington Hall. For the first eighty years of Washington Hall's history, the play was simply one component of a much larger, complex, and varied "exhibition" commemorating an important event in the academic year and accompanied by coequal musical concerts, declamations, and oratory. All the while, the building we know as Washington Hall provided space for classes, examinations, meetings, rehearsals, and recreation. Students lived in Washington Hall throughout much of its history, too, so the structure even functioned as a very small dormitory, sometimes housing as many as eight, although in two times of unusual need (1864–65 and 1879–80) the auditorium itself became a temporary dormitory for as many as eighty.

The most pleasant surprise for me in delving so deeply into Notre Dame's past has been to find unbridled optimism at every point of difficulty or hardship. From the pestilential marshes surrounding the two lakes before 1855 to the Great Fire of 1879, I have found always the most upbeat, optimistic sense that the path is right and true, and that providence will ensure that Notre Dame survives and prospers. Of course, it took a great vision both to believe a university of any kind could be carved out of the northern Indiana hinterland and that a French Catholic religious order could do it. When I arrived at Notre Dame in the summer of 1984, I accepted the conventional wisdom that Notre Dame had really become a "great" university only recently, and that Father Theodore Hesburgh had been instrumental in effecting that shift. In a very real sense that is certainly true, and in no way can we ever overvalue Father Hesburgh's huge contribution to Notre Dame and higher education in the United States. But in another sense I find it interesting that everything I have read in researching this book confirms Notre Dame from day one as a place of the greatest possible potential. Writing this book has taught me that Father Ted followed a path already well worn by his optimistic prede - cessors who intended always to build a great Catholic university. The vision of Presidents John W. Cavanaugh (1905–19) and James A. Burns (1919–22), for example, transformed Notre Dame into the fully modern national university we recognize today. It is well to remember so many others at every level, too, who shared the vision and worked tirelessly and often without fanfare or special recognition to realize the collective dream. The university owes its great prosperity and status today to the many past generations who both made things happen and made things better before handing the university over to the next generation, who then built on those achievements. Provost Timothy O'Meara reminded me often as a young department chair that as administrators we serve the future.

With sometimes several hundred events per year, the period covered within these pages includes thousands of entries, and thus it became obvious early in the process that a printed volume could not contain all the information and remain readable. With that in mind, I have taken on the responsibility of amending, correcting, and expanding the database of information in the theatre chronology website (accessible at http://archives.nd.edu/search/theatre.htm) to complement and supplement this book. By the time this book appears in print, my hope is that the expanded theatre chronology website will serve as an even more complete and important ancillary source for readers who wish to know more about the building so central to the history of the University of Notre Dame.

Each student generation staffing the *Scholastic*, a major source of information for this book, wrote that events they experienced in Washington Hall were "the best ever," or "the best in years." Sources such as these—always suspect qualitatively—are nevertheless very useful and generally quantitatively reliable. They often relate vital factual information reasonably accurately—the who, what, when, where. It remains outside the scope of this book to decide how the student production of *William Tell* at Commencement 1863 compared to Father Harvey's *My Fair Lady* in May 1964 or Fred Syburg's *Amadeus* in March 1988, or indeed whether any of these productions were truly up to the high professional standards the reviewers proclaimed. What matters is that each audience found the productions to be outstanding at that time, and an undergraduate writing about a transformative experience thus lets the reader know that these events really mattered. It is also well to remember that many of us view our undergraduate years through the rose-colored glasses of youthful exuberance and naïveté. Having taught university students since 1975, I remain amazed at the profound changes that occur from first to fourth year: in nearly every way, students truly "grow up" during that relatively short period of time. When students watch each other in plays, they inevitably value the productions they see very highly. And even we middle-aged professors, after spending half a semester in the rehearsal of a play, find ourselves feeling a special warmth and affection for the company's great progress made and are very likely to see the show, too, as "one of our very best, ever." Surely over the past century and a half every level of quality of lecture, play, and concert has undoubtedly occurred within the hallowed walls of Washington Hall. My interest as a theatre historian, rather than evaluating the quality of events within the building, has been instead to bring those events to light to put them into their proper context for the period they represent. We must remember that the administration gave a barrel of apples to students as a prize in 1878, and the students were thrilled. I can only imagine how our students today would react to such a bounteous autumnal gift! Just as the days are over when an orange in a Christmas stocking satisfies a child's desires, American life has become generally so prosperous and complex that expectations have moved far beyond the modest and simple. Much of Washington Hall's history occurred in a simpler age in a centered world, and it is well to remember that fact.

It turns out that a history of a building so important to the University of Notre Dame becomes, in a very real sense, a history of the university itself. Certainly, this study of Washington Hall helps expand our understanding of the cultural, intellectual, and artistic past at Notre Dame to give us greater insight into what has made Notre Dame special since its founding in 1842. The existence of "exhibition halls" at Notre Dame since 1854, and specifically one called Washington Hall since 1864, serves as a window on American history, too. To look at this microcosm closely allows us to understand better the macrocosm of our nation and world over the same period beyond issues solely related to Catholic higher education.

This book progresses mostly chronologically (but sometimes thematically within periods) from the earliest days of the university and explores and examines the central role the two buildings known as "Washington Hall" have played in the complex and varied history of

Notre Dame. Dividing up history into decades or periods is always arbitrary and never works completely satisfactorily, and that is the case here. The Great Fire of 1879, which one would think is a clear line of demarcation, in fact leaves Washington Hall standing and functional (but changes everything else): even the most cataclysmic event in Notre Dame's history denies a clean and complete break with the past.

A decade before the first Washington Hall existed, Notre Dame had a functional exhibition hall within the Main Building. But for the 140 years from the February 1864 dedication until the summer 2004 opening of the Marie P. DeBartolo Center for the Performing Arts, a building named after the father of the country served as the primary venue for secular assembly at the University of Notre Dame. On the National Register of Historic Places as part of the central Notre Dame campus since 1978, Washington Hall today stands as a jewel in the crown where communal assembly still occurs, even as society has changed so utterly. This book is a history of the building that perhaps more than any other has served as the community's crossroads, the place to access culture and integrate into it at America's premier Catholic university.

ACKNOWLEDGMENTS

For nineteen years, beginning in the summer of 1985 through the summer of 2004, Tom Barkes not only ably managed Washington Hall but also took an early and abiding interest in the building's past. His early recognition of the need for a history of the building was the inspiration for this book, one we initially thought perhaps we would coauthor. Tom's new duties related to the opening of the DeBartolo Center for the Performing Arts in 2004, however, put him on a different track. I immersed myself in the project when granted a research leave for the 2003–4 academic year, which coincided with the University of Notre Dame Press's desire to proceed with my proposal for this book. Tom has remained invaluable to me during the research and writing process; he especially has unique insight and knowledge into the period covered since 1985, much of which he directly influenced and nearly all of which he witnessed.

Successive managers of Washington Hall—Greta Fisher, Paul Peabody, and Ronald Grisoli—were wonderful, too, as was the building's technical director (and my former student), Kathleen Lane. On a moment's notice, they have granted me access into nooks and crannies of the building, including a vertigo-inducing visit to the bat-friendly south tower in the fall of 2006 where we viewed the timbers of the "temporary" tower roof as well as the remnants of the original 1894 Gregori/Rusca interior decoration on the balcony's domed ceiling, long concealed by the lighting booth.

I also owe a debt of gratitude to many other colleagues who happily agreed to share their thoughts and recollections about the role of Washington Hall in the history of the University of Notre Dame, including (in alphabetical order): Professor Emeritus Reginald F. Bain; Dennis Brown; Sister Kathleen Cannon, O.P.; Matt Cashore;

Walton R. "Walt" Collins; Professor Emeritus Donald P. Costello; the Reverend Paul Doyle, C.S.C.; Ted Fox; the Reverend David Garrick, C.S.C.; Michael Garvey; Brother Francis Gorch, C.S.C.; the Reverend Eugene F. Gorski, C.S.C.; M. Bruce Harlan; Professor Emeritus the Reverend Arthur S. Harvey, C.S.C.; President Emeritus the Reverend Theodore M. Hesburgh, C.S.C.; Professor William J. Krier; Professor William H. Leahy; President Emeritus the Reverend Edward A. "Monk" Malloy, C.S.C.; the Reverend Richard P. McBrien; Professional Specialist Karen Morris; Professor Emeritus the Reverend Marvin R. O'Connell; Dr. Harold L. Pace; Professor Emeritus Frederic W. Syburg; Kerry Temple; Provincial Superior the Reverend David T. Tyson, C.S.C.; and Robert Zerr. Among this group, my retired colleagues in the department, with whom I worked for many years, Reg Bain and Fred Syburg, have been especially helpful.

Alumni and alumnae who have contributed recollections and information for this book include: M. Clay Adams; Tony Bill; Daniel M. Boland, Ph.D.; J. Robert Costello; John "Jack" Gueguen; Jinny Porcari Keough; Vince LaBarbera; Lawrence A. Liebscher, M.D.; John F. Manion; James McKenzie, Ph.D.; Jim O'Brien; John K. Probst; James H. Roberts III; Erin Seng; Victor Shahan; Matthew Snyder; Barbara Benford Trafficanda; and John M. Walsh, Sr. I am indebted to alumnus Christopher K. Dennis for his architectural renderings and drawings of phases of Washington Hall now lost to history.

I wish to thank the University of Notre Dame Press, especially Associate Director Jeffrey L. Gainey, for his initial interest in and continued support of this project. Director Barbara Hanrahan later took over, and both she and Charles Van Hof have provided adept and supportive guidance, as have Assistant Provost Susan Ohmer and Interim Managing Director Harv Humphrey, both of whom I owe a special note of thanks. Managing Editor Rebecca DeBoer has also been invaluable to me, as has Manuscript Editor Margo Shearman, whose intelligence and attention to detail have improved the book enormously.

My colleagues in the Department of Film, Television, and Theatre have extended support and encouragement, especially Peter Holland, Jim Collins, and Don Crafton, who served as department chairs during the 2003–9 period when I researched and wrote. Bruce Auer -

bach, C. Kenneth Cole, Richard E. Donnelly, and Kevin Dreyer have offered insightful technical advice. Melody Kesler, Christina Ries, Christine Sopczynski, and Jackie Wyatt have provided exemplary assistance in the office.

President Edward "Monk" Malloy, C.S.C., and Provost Nathan Hatch approved my request for a leave of absence for the 2003–4 academic year, which proved absolutely critical to this project. In the College of Arts and Letters, Dean Mark Roche and Associate Dean Gregory Sterling granted (in addition to crucial support for the 2003–4 leave) research funds, which included very able undergraduate research assistants Lena Caligiuri Mucchetti and Meredith Ann Kaye. The Institute for Scholarship in the Liberal Arts under the direction of Agustin Fuentes, provided additional important funding.

In the Notre Dame Archives, Director Wendy Clauson Schlereth and her adept and involved colleagues, especially Sharon Sumpter, helped me immensely from day one, including Kevin Cawley, Elizabeth Hogan, Angela Kindig, Charles Lamb, and Peter Lysy. The Indiana Province Archives Office, headed by the Reverend William B. Simmons, C.S.C., and the Reverend Christopher A. Kuhn, C.S.C., has been especially helpful, including Brother Lawrence Stewart, C.S.C., and the Reverend John VandenBossche, C.S.C. Assistant Archivist Jacqueline Dougherty was my absolutely essential go-to person there who helped me to locate and understand important early primary sources. Since Dougherty's retirement in 2007, Deborah Buzzard has ably taken over. The faculty and staff of the Hesburgh Library at Notre Dame under the direction of Jennifer A. Younger also provided first-rate support throughout my work. At Saint Mary's College, Cushwa-Leighton Library Director Janet Fore and Archivist John Kovach have offered critical assistance, as did Penn Genthner, Archivist at Pasadena Playhouse State Theatre of California. I have also accessed the excellent resources of the St. Joseph County Public Library under the deft leadership of director Donald J. Napoli.

My wife, Carole, has endured and tolerated, as spouses of all academics do, the long periods of self-absorbed research and writing (and vacation-free summers) from 2004 through 2009, when my work was especially intense and preoccupying. As Electronic Resources

Librarian at the Hesburgh Library at Notre Dame, Carole enabled me to make good use of the abundance of information available electronically in this digital age.

William Farmer from the Office of University Architect, now retired, contributed much to this book initially by sharing his private collection of ground plans of the building and historical information related to it, including rare programs of events from the early twentieth century. His enthusiasm for Notre Dame's past rubbed off on me and, I hope, onto the pages of this book.

The Northern Indiana Center for History and its archivist, Scott Shuler, helped immensely, too, especially with questions related to early South Bend history.

Randy R. McGuire, Assistant University Archivist, and John Waide, Associate University Archivist at St. Louis University, as well as Joan Harris Zurhellen, Archivist of the Catholic Diocese of Memphis, assisted me with enrollment increases late in the Civil War. (Coincidentally, Dr. Zurhellen taught me both in eighth grade and in high school, so it was especially nostalgic to be in touch with someone who had such a positive influence on my life.) At Catholic University of America, Jane Stoeffler was very supportive.

The book reproduces photographs, illustrations, documents, and websites owned by others and gratefully acknowledges permission of the following to do so: the Archives of the University of Notre Dame, the Indiana Province Archives Center, Tom Barkes, Matt Cashore, Christopher K. Dennis, William Farmer, Greta Fisher, Ron Grisoli, M. Bruce Harlan, Lawrence H. Officer, and Samuel H. Williamson.

A history is always an interim report. I hope that those who notice mistakes or who come across new information will share their knowledge and insights so a subsequent edition can be even more complete and accurate.

WASHINGTON HALL TIMELINE, 1845–2004

1845	"Music Saloon" in Main Building I was used for performances.
1846	An amphitheatre (possibly outdoors?) existed, as did a Theatre (possibly indoors?).
1847	Performances took place "under the new shed."
1848	The Barn was used (possibly only one year) as a performance space.
1850	Performances took place outdoors, with the portico of Main I serving as the stage.
1852	A study room in Main I was used for performances.
1854	An exhibition hall was configured within the east wing of Main I after the additions of 1852, along with a freestanding building containing a "music room" and five practice rooms.
1857	Authorization was given to build a freestanding exhibition hall, but no evidence of construction exists.
1862	A purpose-built freestanding exhibition hall was completed (within the Senior Recreation Hall) probably over the summer of 1862, replacing the 1853 "exhibition hall" within the Main Building.
1864	An exhibition hall within the Senior Recreation Hall was dedicated as Washington Hall, on February 22, 1864, by Father Sorin.
1864–65	Washington Hall became a dormitory due to increased enrollment; no play took place this year at commencement, at which General William T. Sherman spoke.

1865	The Music Hall was erected (within the Junior Recreation Hall) north of Washington Hall (within the Senior Recreation Hall).
1866	Washington Hall was "renovated" and moved 90 degrees from north-south to east-west, to parallel the new Music Hall.
1867	A "large parlor" in Main Building II rivaled Washington Hall as a useful performance venue.
1871 & 1873	The first Washington Hall was deemed too small, with an addition proposed.
1879	The Music Hall was one of five buildings destroyed in the Great Fire in April, but Washington Hall survived and again became a dormitory until December 1879, at which time the rotunda in the new Main Building III (the interior under the Dome) became a performance venue. Seven buildings were under construction simultaneously to rebuild the campus, including a combined music and exhibition hall designed by Willoughby J. Edbrooke.
1880	The music faculty moved into the newly completed Music Hall (the north wing of the new Academy of Music) from the third floor of the Main Building, with the Junior Recreation Hall (including a handball court) on the lower level; the exhibition hall foundation (south wing) was laid but construction postponed, with the south wing foundation roofed over to provide a large dirt-floored, indoor winter recreation area for 1880–81 (see fig. 4.5).
1881	*William Tell* was the last commencement play in the first Washington Hall.
1882	Washington Exhibition Hall was demolished between May 23 and June 3, and for a little over three months Notre Dame had no Washington Hall. *Oedipus Rex* (in Greek) was the first commencement play in the new Academy of Music at the June 1882 dedication, although the Thespians' *Pizarro* and the St. Cecilians' *The Outcast* and *The Office Seekers* were produced a week or so earlier. Students referred to the new Academy of Music un-

officially as "the new Washington Hall" by September 1882, and the name was thus preserved. Seating capacity claims were 1,200. There were wooden steps at both the south Washington Hall and the north Music Hall entrances.

1883   Gas lighting was installed in the new building, replacing oil lamps. (General illumination of the auditorium was always by electricity.)

1884   There was extensive interior decorative painting of trim and the proscenium arch, and the creation of faux wood-finish doors by Brother Frederick. Professor Ackermann designed and painted wings and drops for the new space, and a new chandelier was installed in the house, followed by double-glazed windows, and a brick portico on the north entrance.

1885   Demonstrations took place of the pre-filmic phenakisto-scope and stereopticon in the hall. The first interior pictures were taken of casts on stage. A new Jacob Ackermann act/valence curtain (used through 1895) was installed.

1886   Canine pillars and iron stairs replaced wooden stairs on the north Music Hall entrance (and on the west entrance to Washington Hall as well). Additional electricity was installed, but gas footlights remained.

1887   Seats were placed in the gallery (balcony), and the tower construction was completed.

1889   Windows were installed in the tower, and stone steps replaced wooden steps on the south Washington Hall entrance, remaining until 1933.

1892   Additions were called for as Washington Hall was deemed too small a decade after its dedication.

1894   Gregori/Rusca interior auditorium murals with trompe l'oeil niches and columns were completed, replacing the ten-year-old efforts by Ackermann and Frederick, whose stage drapes upstage of the proscenium remained in use for another year. Electric footlights replaced gas.

1895   Ackermann wings and drops were replaced by Sosman & Landis (Chicago) professional box sets.

1907	The only addition to the footprint of the building occurred in the northeast corner of the exhibition hall to accommodate scene storage.
1908	An indoor toilet was installed.
1912	The first interior photograph of a Washington Hall theatre audience was taken, as seen from the stage.
1914	Film screenings began, a tradition that continued through the 1980s.
1916	A projection booth was likely installed in the balcony lobby soon after the first photograph of a Washington Hall film audience was taken, as seen from the screen.
1921	In early January, the first accounts of the ghost of Washington Hall appeared, with no connection to George Gipp (who died in the fall of 1920) until 1925.
1922	The last regular spring commencement was held in Washington Hall due to expansive growth of the university.
1930	A projection booth equipped for sound projection was installed (updated in 1937).
1933	The exterior south stairs were moved to the interior, with first-floor access; new interior staircases replaced two meeting rooms occupied at this time by Bill's Barber Shop and the Western Union office. The east fire escape probably was added soon thereafter.
1956	A major interior renovation was completed under Father Harvey with the Gregori/Rusca allegorical murals painted over in shades of gray, and with a new Lightolier (chandelier) and eventual removal of footlights. Seating capacity was reduced in the auditorium to 848. Audience restrooms were added.
1976	Most of the Department of Music moved from Washington Hall into the rededicated Crowley Hall of Music (originally constructed in 1890 as the Mechanical Engineering Hall where Albert Zahm taught aeronautics).
1984	A major renovation took place, with a new lab theatre on the third floor of the north wing, and with an elevator installed to access the auditorium, and improved backstage

access and amenities for performers. The seating capacity was reduced to 615, and later to 571.

1987   Central air-conditioning was installed.

1989   The name "Washington Hall" was placed on the south exterior of the building.

1990   When the band moved into its new purpose-built building, the Department of Music ended a 110-year residential presence in Washington Hall.

1997   Windows were replaced, and the east fire escape was removed.

2004   The Department of Film, Television, and Theatre and three Department of Music faculty moved to the Marie P. DeBartolo Center for the Performing Arts on the south perimeter of campus, Notre Dame's first new performing arts center since 1882. The theatre program thus ended a 122-year residential presence in Washington Hall.

CHAPTER 1

THE TRUE GHOSTS
OF WASHINGTON HALL

Flanking the Administration Building (the "Golden Dome") on the east as Sacred Heart Basilica does on the west, the building known today as Washington Hall served from its dedication in June 1882 until the summer of 2004 as a prime venue of communal assembly at the University of Notre Dame. Named in honor of the father of the country, Washington Hall for nearly a century and a half has physically reflected Notre Dame's ideology as the university's first performing arts center.

But nothing is ever as simple, clean, and neat as it might first appear to be. Today's Washington Hall is not the first Washington Hall in Notre Dame's history, and indeed the first Washington Hall was not the first exhibition hall at Notre Dame. An exhibition hall where all could assemble had clearly been essential since the inception of the University of Notre Dame in 1842—as indeed at any university—and by 1854 the first freestanding "exhibition hall" appeared in the surviving records (after some interesting fits and starts). The structure provided appropriate space in which to stage plays and concerts, hear lectures and debates, conduct graduation exercises, revere great personages, and celebrate important feasts. It functioned as a theatre, assembly hall, lecture hall, and multipurpose space where communal assembly could occur, where transformative rituals such as commencement could take place. Eight years later in 1862 a structure went up through the generosity of the Phelan family which the Reverend Edward F. Sorin, C.S.C., the founder and first president of the university, officially dedicated as "Washington Hall" at the conclusion of Washington Day celebrations in February 1864. In 1865 the university constructed a complementary Music Hall, and the two buildings together formed what was Notre Dame's first performing arts precinct. The Music Hall burned utterly in the Great Fire of 1879, and rather than retain separate buildings, the university decided to combine the functions into a single structure—a performing arts center called the Academy of Music—and, in so doing, made the first Washington Hall redundant. As the dedication of the new combined exhibition hall and music hall approached in the spring of 1882, there was talk of converting "old" Washington Hall into a gymnasium, but instead it was demolished (an entirely new gymnasium was built), thus freeing up the name "Washington Hall" just as the new building opened. By the fall of 1882 students began unofficially to refer to the Academy of Music as the "new" Washington Hall. The name stuck, and the building we know to this day as Washington Hall has stood southeast of the Main Building—the Golden Dome—since then (see figs. 1.1 and 1.2).

Inextricably linked to the history of Washington Hall on the campus of the University of Notre Dame is the actual or imagined ghost said to haunt the building, and I would be remiss if this book failed to address fully the "Ghost of Washington Hall." Indeed, in the early fall of 2003 when I first learned the University of Notre Dame Press had approved this book proposal, I happened to see President Emeritus Father Theodore M. Hesburgh, C.S.C., in the library named for him and where he has an office. As we rode the elevator together to our respective floors, I excitedly told Notre Dame's esteemed former president about the book. He immediately said something like "The ghost! You've got to write about the ghost!" I assured him that I would and that indeed no history of Washington Hall would be complete without a chapter devoted to the ghost. As interesting as the ghost stories from the 1920s to the present day may be, however, my task in this book has been to chase down what I consider to be the true

Figure 1.1. The triumvirate of three major "original" buildings, the Main Building or "Golden Dome" (1879), the Basilica of the Sacred Heart (begun 1871), and Washington Hall (begun 1879), which form the central core of the University of Notre Dame to this day. Aerial view of Main Quad—Color, Oct. 1994, Notre Dame Copy Negatives Collection (hereafter GNEG) 09A/41, UNDA.

ghosts of Washington Hall, the fleeting shadows of myriad ephemeral events that have occurred over time. The athletic fields of Notre Dame have provided the communal settings for the creation and perpetuation of great sports traditions that continue to this day. The church (the Basilica of the Sacred Heart since 1992) is at the center of a dynamic parish that has served as the communal spiritual center of the campus. The Main Building, with the statue of the Virgin Mary atop the Golden Dome, has always been the brain of the campus's central nervous system and today in restored glory continues as a fully functional administration building. But it has been Washington Hall, the building that contained the university's purpose-built "Exhibition Hall," where the University of Notre Dame has conducted the transformative ritual of commencement, recognized beginnings, middles, and ends of academic years, and affirmed American patriotism by celebrating the birthday of the father of the country and the flag that emblematically represents it. There the university has experienced

Figure 1.2. Close-up of Washington Hall, from fig. 1.1. The poster above the entrance to Washington Hall advertises the Department of Communication and Theatre's *Waiting for Godot*, directed by the Reverend David Garrick, C.S.C., and produced Oct. 12–16, 1994. Aerial view of Main Quad — Color, Oct. 1994, GNEG 09A/41, UNDA.

the creation of the ephemeral arts of theatre and music both as freestanding events and as part of commemorative celebratory "exhibitions," absorbed in stunned silence early "photoplays," and witnessed oratory, elocution, and debate from both the youngest students and the world's movers and shakers. As Father Hesburgh so insightfully pointed out, "Washington Hall has always functioned as the crossroads of the University."[1] At those many times when the university has gathered there for secular communal assembly, usually with visitors from the larger community, it must have seemed to those present that they were not merely at the crossroads of the university but at the very center of the world.

From its dedication in 1882 until 2004, Washington Hall served Notre Dame as a multipurpose building that accommodated many of the communal assembly needs of students, provided a home for the lecture, the play, and the film, housed practice and performance spaces for music, offered classes, meetings, and examinations, and (until the university outgrew it utterly in the early 1920s), was the setting for graduation commencement exercises. It was the place new students first assembled to receive their orientation and where as seniors they last congregated to receive their degrees. But as the university expanded rapidly and the society around Notre Dame changed, Washington Hall could no longer serve its many intended functions. A series of freestanding gymnasiums went up to handle indoor rec -

reational needs, music faculty and students shifted to other existing and some newly created spaces, and even the theatre program eventually split itself among multiple venues on two campuses. Recognized as being too small in 1892 just ten years after it was built, Washington Hall had long been inadequate to the needs of a vibrant university by the time the Marie P. DeBartolo Center for the Performing Arts opened in 2004.

While this book deals with the bricks-and-mortar of Washington Hall and its predecessors, my interest as a theatre historian centers also on the social history and the human ideology behind the decisions at Notre Dame to build, to maintain, and to program "exhibition halls" for over a century and a half. If institutions create physical spaces that reflect their ideology, as Louis Althusser suggests, then the history of a structure and its use can provide valuable insights into the culture of the institution itself.[2] Since 1854 places designated as "exhibition halls" have been central to communal assembly at Notre Dame, especially in the decades before electrical and electronic transmission and storage of information was possible. When Robert Tittler refers to the early modern English town hall as the "Doorway to the Community," I am reminded directly of Notre Dame's exhibition halls at least until the 1920s where students assembled communally both to access their culture and integrate into it.[3] The exhibition halls like Washington Hall served the ancient function of providing "the Public Realm as the sphere of revelatory personal deeds," which as W. H. Auden points out contrasts to the modern world with its dominance of the private realm.[4] Washington Hall was very much the primary communal venue that was not seriously challenged until the mid-twentieth century by the burgeoning and ultimately pervasive electronic media (radio, television, and the Internet). While the Basilica and the athletic fields have of course provided communal assembly and are no less worthy of serious academic study, Washington Hall has served uniquely as Notre Dame's "town hall."

In understanding Washington Hall's role as doorway to the community and crossroads of the university, I have come to realize that this charming building reflects the history of communal assembly both at the University of Notre Dame and in American Catholic higher education, and in so doing serves as a microcosm of American history. French immigrant Father Edward Sorin's decision to name the exhibition hall after the father of his adopted country is itself interesting ideologically. The only building ever named for a U.S. president on the Notre Dame campus is indeed Washington Hall. In the dedication year 1864 during the Civil War, only sixty-five years had passed since the death of the country's first president, the same time between 2010 and the death of Franklin Roosevelt in 1945.

We academics usually think of the library as doorway or crossroads of a university, but in terms of access to culture and integration into it, the structure that most closely parallels the town hall or guild hall in a university setting is the building that fosters a critical mass of persons collectively coming together to witness events, to participate in transformative rituals, and to be entertained. The church at a religiously affiliated institution such as Notre Dame fulfills the vital, sacred role in communal assembly, to be sure, but the secular equivalent of the church is the assembly hall, or, to use the nineteenth-century term, the exhibition hall.

The communal assembly function of Washington Hall manifested itself in many different ways, from the lecture to the play, from the concert to the class, from the minstrel show to the travelogue, from Washington's Birthday festivities to the celebration of Saint Patrick's Day. The 1877 recognition of the golden jubilee of Pope Pius IX, for example, combined great American patriotism with unswerving Roman Catholicism. This melding of affection and loyalty was constantly repeated in events in Washington Hall, confirming repeatedly that good Catholics and good Americans were one and the same.[5] The Catholic nature and heritage of Notre Dame remains palpable to this day, but in the early decades of the university's history the records often reflect a concern that being a good Catholic could somehow be perceived by the majority culture as not being a good American.[6]

During the entire history of the university, it was within the walls of Washington Hall that the university most often publicly revealed to the world what mattered most to it, in some cases nobly, but in others, not. The great lectures by G. K. Chesterton in 1931, the visit of Cardinal Pacelli in 1936 (who three years later became Pope Pius XII), the appearance of Tom Dooley in the late 1950s, and the Mario Cuomo speech in 1984 all show the university at its best as a reflection of the times. In contrast, the high praise of the film *The Birth of a Nation* at its first screening in Washington Hall in 1916 and the student minstrel shows that continued into the 1930s (with attempts to revive them as late as the 1940s) stand as testament to the university's affirming past attitudes our society has subsequently rejected.

As technological innovations have brought rapid and massive changes to daily life, including changing our sense of community by reducing our need for public ephemeral assembly, they have also affected the role of an exhibition hall such as Washington Hall in college life. The electronic revolution has permitted us to connect to the world without physically having to assemble. The new paradigm is virtual; we find ourselves constantly in touch with people, products, and information distant from us. No one must physically go to a cinema house to screen a film (although purists would argue otherwise), and with today's recording technology we can watch or hear whatever we wish to watch or hear whenever we wish to watch or hear it, and we can fast-forward, back up, or pause at any time as we manipulate time itself. Campus life has changed dramatically since the presentation of the first "exhibition" in Washington Hall when being physically present for an event was the only way to experience it. The telegraph permitted for the first time a lot of complex information to travel very quickly—at the speed of light—even though transcription and reception slowed things down at the beginning and ending points.[7] The larger world thus became part of the smaller community in a very direct and urgent way never before possible, and that change undoubtedly altered the way humanity viewed the world. For the first time, a telegrapher spent his day communicating with another telegrapher a great distance away—an action hitherto unknown in human history—in the same way today we can communicate on the Internet or by telephone seamlessly and easily with our children in Los Angeles or Luanda. The emergence of ubiquitous e-mail in the last twenty years has made letter writing obsolete and has extended our sense of community in such a way as to reduce greatly the demand to meet spatially and proximally.

Lifestyle changes made possible by new technologies have lessened historical requirements for proximity in relationships whether public or private. We no longer absolutely require communal assembly to perform many of our transformative rituals—to learn, to inform, to convince, to persuade, or to entertain—nearly all of which can be done virtually and, indeed, wirelessly. But our growing numbers have also been a huge factor; constant human population growth has made it increasingly difficult to include everyone in any activity and still retain a genuine sense of intimacy or community, and so groups split into specialized or "niche" audiences. Thus the combination of rapid technological change and unbridled growth have made largely obsolete the ideology behind the university exhibition hall.

Our culture also differs from the past in that we no longer communally celebrate holidays such as the birthdays of presidents except as a springboard for commercial sales. (When Notre Dame began in 1842, there were persons for whom the father of the country was a living memory, for example.) The feasts and holy days of the year that helped to keep a seemingly centered world glued together have become less celebrated, as our growing heterogeneity has at the same time enriched nearly every corner of American culture. We today seem to move quickly past all holidays with little time for communal reflection. But this is not all bad. We are today much less sexist, racist, and ethnically illiterate than we were when Washington Hall was functionally at its peak. We must remember always that the vast majority of audiences in Washington Hall throughout much of its history were white and male.

In the twenty-first century, we rarely need to gather in one place to experience an event in time and space. Even electronically transmitted events, such as sports on television, can be recorded and watched later. The ubiquitous cell phone means most people we see on the street, in shops, and driving cars are talking not to persons near them but to someone unseen and far off. For generations, we have been able to bring the greatest orchestras into our living rooms via vinyl records, tapes, CDs, and now iPods. Because of Edison, we have even coined the expression "live music," quickly forgetting that for the millennia before the advent of devices that could record, store, and transmit sound, music existed only ephemerally in time and space. With the exception of a handful of mechanical devices (such as player pianos, music boxes, and chiming clocks), all music in the 1840s when Notre Dame was founded had to be generated "live" by living, breathing musicians for it to occur at all.[8] If one wished to hear a specific piece of music, or to have music accompany an event, a musician had to play an instrument. There was simply no way to record and reproduce sound before 1877, and, indeed, recorded music did not become practicable and affordable for most people until the 1930s. Film and television have largely replaced live theatre just as recordings have replaced live music; the introduction of the videocassette recorder and later the DVD enabled us to bring nearly any film or television program throughout history into our living rooms to be watched precisely when we wish. The current incredible ability we have to freeze time, to create slow-motion, to reverse events, and to move frame by frame are very recent. The very nature of film editing permits almost anything to appear to happen, so the illusion of an event happening live is very different from the illusion created on a recorded medium, for example, seeing the play *Peter Pan* versus screening the film. To gain knowledge in the past, we attended lectures; today we go to our computer and "Google" a topic where, in seconds, we can access more information than we can possibly process in a lifetime. The myriad electronic databases accessible through our libraries have turned every laptop computer into a world-class reference library whose stacks can be browsed wirelessly from nearly any location. When it was built, Washington Hall served an absolutely vital function. As the world has changed and we have been able to experience great art and communicate great thoughts electrically, mechanically, and electronically, we have increasingly had less need for communal assemblies. As a result, venues such as Washington Hall necessarily have taken on more specialized functions for more specialized audiences as our culture became decentered, as Jim Collins points out.[9] So in a very real sense, the decentering of culture and the replacing of communal events by ones for niche audiences is one of the stories of Washington Hall. By the end of the nineteenth century, the "exhibition" in all its complex and varied glory had become outmoded and had fallen from favor, replaced instead by smaller groups doing highly focused activities for audiences especially keen to witness a particular event.

The need for a physical exhibition hall related logically to the ideology of the exhibition, a celebration connected to a centered cultural event, such as a holiday or a commencement exercise, which the entire community attended, and showcasing its varied talents and abilities. While the word *exhibition* today can connote a static display such as an installation in an art gallery, the word had a much wider meaning in the nineteenth century, including a "public examination or display of the attainments of students."[10] Thus an exhibition hall was a space for any sort of public, dynamic display by students, including concerts, plays, debates, and oratory, and could be connected to a transformative ritual such as commencement or any celebratory event. The exhibitions produced at the University of Notre Dame for at least its first half century were three-hour marathons of music, drama, and oratory, nearly always topped off by a speech by the president of the university, and ended with a recessional march by the band. If we think of an exhibition today as merely a play or a concert, we are off the mark. It is much more accurate to think "extravaganza" when we see the word *exhibition,* an afternoon or evening of up to two dozen unique events or acts that showcased talent while affirming respect and obedience to dominant and centered cultural norms.

The increasing size of the university also played a key role in changes that included the creation of niche audiences. As the community of students, faculty, and staff grew, it became increasingly difficult to find spaces large enough to accommodate everyone at once, even if everyone had wanted to continue communal assembly in ways unchanged from the 1840s. At the dedication of the current Washington Hall in 1882, the faculty and student body numbered 450, and all the students could be seated in the balcony alone. When the awarding of degrees ended there at the 1922 commencement, that number was just over 1,900, and the building could no longer accommodate students and faculty, much less guests. In 2004, with the opening of the DeBartolo Center for the Performing Arts with just over 1,700 seats in all five of its venues, students and faculty totaled around 12,000, meaning that no indoor facility on campus can currently accommodate everyone at once, the Joyce Center being the largest with seating of 9,800.[11] To retain the ability to bring students and faculty together in one place at one time, the university relied over time on the gymnasium, the Drill Hall, the Fieldhouse, the Joyce Center, and, of course, the only constructed venue on campus today that can accommodate all students, faculty, staff, and a modicum of visitors: the outdoor football stadium. For a variety of reasons both economic and ideological, the 1882 Washington Hall was never expanded, and Notre Dame built no direct replacement for it throughout the entire twentieth century; thus, one of the building's prime original functions—to permit the faculty and student body to assemble for an event (with room for guests and dignitaries)— was rather quickly lost and never regained. The growth of the university thus forced changes in the function and role of Washington Hall just as assuredly as did emerging technology.

Washington Hall has been more than just a theatre or a place for concerts in the history of Notre Dame. It has been for most of its history a focal point of secular communal activities, festivities, and celebrations for the entire Notre Dame community. Along with the Main Building and Sacred Heart Basilica, Washington Hall's location at the heart of the campus was purposeful and meaningful, symbolic of its central role in the life of the university. Time eventually made Washington Hall obsolete as other larger buildings took over so many of its original functions, and thus the story of Washington Hall parallels the story of Notre Dame in the public sphere where communal assembly occurred. This crossroads on the campus of Notre Dame has in its own very special way served as a crossroads to the world.

CHAPTER 2

BEFORE THE FIRST
WASHINGTON HALL,
1842–1864

Although the University of Notre Dame du Lac existed for twenty-two years before the official dedication of a place called Washington Hall, the need for such a space was always present, and the university took steps to provide venues for communal assembly from the earliest days. Buildings (like laws) nearly always result reactively rather than proactively, and the ultimate creation of a freestanding exhibition hall in 1862 (which Father Sorin proclaimed "Washington Hall" two years later) was a reaction to demand for such a space over the previous twenty years. From its inception, the University of Notre Dame required an exhibition hall, a place for all to assemble for events related to access to information, integration into the larger culture, and transformative rituals such as commencement. Annually recurring special events at Notre Dame included but were not limited to Founder's Day (October 13—Saint Edward's Day), Christmas (students in the early days did not go home for the holidays), Washington's Birthday (February 22), Saint Patrick's Day (March 17), and commencement (between mid-June and early August). Interspersed in this calendar, of course, were the many lectures, classes, meetings, speeches, debates, and demonstrations that encouraged maximum attendance by the entire community of students and teachers, and all of which required an assembly or exhibition hall.

The first known indoor assembly or exhibition hall at Notre Dame was a large room apparently in the main building (Main I) known as the "music saloon," which had been fitted out for the first commencement in August 1845 (but with no degrees yet awarded). In the earliest surviving printed record of performance at Notre Dame, the author "M. R. K." described the experience to the editor of the Philadelphia *Catholic Herald*:

> *Mr. Editor*—I attended the public distribution of premiums to the students of the University of Notre Dame du Lac, which took place on the first of this month, and being the first thing of the kind which ever took place in this section of the country, the numbers who attended the novel scene were large and respectable. About 9 o'clock in the morning, the entire vicinity of the University was crowded with all kinds of traveling vehicle; while the different apartments of the University and its vicinity, were scrutinized and examined according to each one's taste. . . . All were deeply engaged . . . when the warlike sounds of the big drum of the South Bend band was heard booming through the woods. Shortly after the band came into view, drawn by four horses, and accompanied by a number of ladies and gentlemen; on their arrival, the *music saloon* [my emphasis] was thrown open, and was soon crowded to a complete jam: how many remained outside I cannot tell, as I made sure to be among the "ins." As soon as all the apartment could contain were admitted, the students commenced a play, which for the space of an hour, kept the audience in a roar of laughter; after which the great work of the day—the distribution of premiums commenced.[1]

With no freestanding music hall, exhibition hall, or Washington Hall, visitors gathered in a room within the main building to be entertained and to witness the bestowal of "premiums" on the students (see fig. 2.1).[2] This account reinforced the need for a larger, purpose-built space, since clearly the overcrowded music saloon could not accommodate everyone who wished to attend.

FIRST COLLEGE BUILDING—1843.

Figure 2.1. Main Building I—Engraving, 1843, GNEG 11A/01, UNDA. This building very likely contained the "music saloon" described at the 1845 commencement.

By summer 1846, the words *amphitheatre* and *theatre* first appeared in the written record when the Local Council of Holy Cross priests and brothers who advised the presiding father superior made it clear that Mr. Kabel "shall also make a table for the large Boarders & shall prepare the amphitheatre."[3] We cannot know whether this "amphitheatre" is an interior venue in Main I or a new outdoor structure, or whether its function was artistic, athletic, or martial. A week later when the Council of Professors recorded that Father Cointet "will give the people their places in the theatre,"[4] it is reasonable to assume that the "amphitheatre" and "theatre" are the same venue for the event related to commencement.

We know from M. R. K.'s description that music played a key role in the 1845 commencement, and certainly by the 1846–47 academic year the university began to take serious steps to create and upgrade its own band and orchestra, even though the South Bend Band also performed at Notre Dame well after the university created its own. Music mattered from Notre Dame's creation, and the administration found new funds to purchase instruments. In June 1847 the Local Council paid "a bill of two hundred and seventy five francs ($55) for getting Instruments of Music . . . as those Instruments were deemed necessary for the completion of our Orchestra."[5]

For the Fourth of July celebrations in 1847, the university produced Shakespeare's *Henry IV* (or a portion of it), the first Shakespeare play in Notre Dame's history.[6] Brother Gatian described the event in his "Journal" and, in so doing, opened up another can of worms with regard to the assembly and performance venue he called a "shed":

> To attract the attention of the population great preparations were made for the celebration of the Fourth of July which falling on Sunday was observed on Monday. The theatre was magnificently painted for Mr. St. Mar under *the new shed* [my emphasis] where a number of seats were prepared for the spectators. The celebration was announced in the three newspapers of Niles thru the kindness of Judge Brown. A comic piece representing the youthful days of young Henry IVth, according to Shakespeare was played by the pupils. The performance was preceded by gymnastical exercises. Between the acts of the play, our band of Music, lately formed purposely for the Fourth of July, discoursed excellent music for the first essay. The concourse of people was as great as last year. There were about 80 carriages and four stages, upwards of 700 persons.[7]

The term *new shed* is intriguing; it is not at all clear whether this is a temporary structure, a more substantial freestanding building, or an addition to a pre-existing edifice. In the nineteenth century, the word *shed* could mean either a temporary or a substantial structure, usually attached to a larger structure, similar to the word *wing*. The influence of French in these early years and issues of translation may be factors, too.[8] We also cannot know whether the shed was the place Mr. St. Mar did his work, with the performance in the theatre from the previous year, or, more likely, an entirely new performance venue for the university. But it was clear from the Fourth of July celebration that space would have had to be found to accommodate communal assemblies far beyond the limitations of any existing interior music saloon. There was a huge need for a proper exhibition hall.

College musicians got officially assigned space in which to rehearse as early as fall 1847, a big step forward for the performing arts at Notre Dame, when the Local Council decided that "one of the classrooms will be used by the Musicians."[9] This entry confirmed the need for rehearsal as well as performance spaces very early in the life of the university. Perhaps no issue is more important to the success of artists than spaces in which they can prepare for performance. Not only do performers require a hall in which to showcase their work before audiences, but they also need spaces in which to practice and perfect their art. No sooner was this classroom assigned, however, than an absolute need for acoustical isolation must have also arisen—as it inevitably does when musicians practice in close proximity to nonmusicians—all the more reason to build, as soon as possible, a separate music building where practice could occur at some auditory distance. Indeed, this happened by 1854 when a separate music practice room was built.[10]

Also by the fall of 1847, the university had made the supremely important and practical decision to build the church near the main building instead of "at a distance."[11] This decision to place the church immediately west of the main building, essentially where it stands in relation to the main building today, increased the chances that additional buildings would ultimately stand east of the main building to balance the church, which is indeed where both the first Washington Hall and Music Hall went up in the 1860s. This decision proved a visionary step forward in the creation of the central core of buildings: (1) the main building where students lived and studied, (2) the church where the community assembled in the sacred sphere, and (3) the Exhibition Hall area where the community assembled in the secular sphere. This triune juxtaposition defined the core of the university throughout its history, and it is difficult now to imagine any other choice ever being considered, although clearly it was, with a more distant church foundation already laid but utterly abandoned.

With the need for a larger indoor venue for commencement where hundreds of persons would attend, the administration must have asked itself, "What is the largest indoor space on the campus?" The obvious answer was the barn, one of the first buildings "put up" and apparently still standing in 1869.[12] With the "music saloon" in the first Main Building proving inadequate, the barn was used at least one year for the commencement exhibition. The Local Council confirmed that for the 1848 commencement "it was proposed that the Distribution of premiums should take place in *the barn* [my emphasis]. Some objected, fearing that the barn might be burnt on such an occasion . . . Still the proposition was adopted. . . . [signed] E. Sorin."[13] This discussion regarding the barn indicated the continuing need for a purpose-built exhibition hall, one that displaced neither hay nor overwintering sheep and if destroyed by fire would not jeopardize the future of the university.[14] This discussion also demonstrated that the music saloon within the main building, which had been used previously for the assembly and distribution of premiums, was simply not big enough to accommodate students, faculty, and visitors.

The barn commencement of 1848, according to Brother Gatian, did not go well. He recounted in his "Journal": "Rev. Wm. Nightingale has the direction of the Play and Speeches. He did not get along very well, he was often or thought he was vexed. The apprentices, being disgusted with the nature of the piece they had to play, refused to learn it and it was not learned nor played." Things got worse: "The Right Revd Bishop Purcell of Cincinnati was present at the Distribution and gave Confirmation on the following day, July 5th at 9 o'clock A.M. There were very few persons at the distribution and it had never passed off so badly. It rained the whole morning and in the afternoon nothing was ready. The Musicians would not play and Mr. Nightingale, disgusted, left his boys to play alone." But the unmentored boys did as well as they could: "The boys though abandoned, to their credit be said, played the piece alone. Again when the Premiums were distributed, the boys were absent. In fact, the whole was botched. The Apprentices, who had several times threatened to run away on the fourth of July, could and would not do anything when the day came." But all was not lost, and there were standouts: "For the first time, several speeches were delivered and some of them were very good, especially Mr. McGean's. Mr. Neal H. Gillespie distinguished himself and got several premiums."[15]

By the 1848–49 academic year, exhibitions were regular events, often not related to commencement ceremonies, as seen when the Local Council reported, "The Musicians Bands of South Bend, Mishawaka and Niles shall be invited for our next monthly Exhibition, and a supper shall be prepared for them."[16] We do not know the venue for the 1849 commencement, which was, as Hope points out, the "first commencement in the real sense of the word,"[17] since degrees were awarded for the first time, one of the recipients being the exceptional student of the previous year, Neal Gillespie, whose stepfather and mother, Mr. and Mrs. William T. Phelan of Lancaster, Ohio, were benefactors.

Generally, an outdoor venue for a summer commencement could work in South Bend climatically, and that seems to have happened in 1850. A fire on November 18, 1849, consumed workshops, the kitchen, and other outbuildings, which were quickly rebuilt "no longer behind the college, but alongside the Grand Avenue, four hundred feet from the college."[18] The Local Council ordered, "The yard of the College shall be filled up near the Portico, and the Portico itself repaired, and fixed for the exibition [sic],"[19] perhaps indicative of the portico on the main building being used as the stage or dais for an outdoor commencement.

When Neal Gillespie wrote his mother to tell her about the Washington's Birthday celebrations of 1852, it is clear that the complex and varied exhibition occurred in the "Study room":

> But we had a celebration to day so I have something to write about—We celebrated Washington's Birthday on this day [Saturday, February 21, 1852] as tomorrow is Sunday & on Monday we begin the 40 hours.—The Exhibition commenced at 2'o'clock P.M. Immediately after dinner carriages & omnibuses began coming from Niles S. Bend & Mishewaka [sic]. The Study room was crowded—The Band, which is now much better than when you were here opened the Exhibition.—Then followed a very good

speech from one of us—of the Novices—afterwards three different speeches from as many students of the College—between the
speeches there was Music either on the piano by the young Woodworth or Mr Girac—or pieces by the Band—then we had a fine
song—the skaters chorus—Then a French play—some scenes
from "L'Avocat Patelin"—afterwards a quartette—"The Good
old Colony Times"—Then an English play—and the exhibition
closed with one piece from the Band and the evening Hymn—
and it being 5 o'clock the people started home being well pleased
at the idea of getting home before dark and having a cup of strong
tea, after having stamped the soles of their shoes at the speeches
& lost some buttons when laughing.[20]

As early as 1852, then, Notre Dame had celebrated Washington's
Birthday with a three-hour exhibition that included plays, music
from an improved band, and speeches before a town-and-gown
audience.

Gillespie's letter also made it clear just how early the Americanization of Notre Dame had occurred. Father Theodore Hesburgh has
said that five minutes after Father Sorin arrived in the United States
he became an American 110 percent. This letter by the future Father
Gillespie confirms Hesburgh's assessment of Sorin's clear patriotism
for his new country. Father Sorin wanted to create a great American
Catholic university, and by 1852 he had already made strong head-
way on the American part, the Catholic part being assumed and never
in doubt. It would take a bit longer before Notre Dame would become
an exceptional national university, but Sorin had begun to achieve
the vital and seamless fusion of American patriotism to devotion to
the pope in Rome. His earliest instincts and continued efforts juxta-
posed God and Country in ways always to reaffirm that good Catholics were also patriotic Americans, especially in a time of religious
discrimination as exemplified in the anti-Catholic, anti-immigrant
"Know-Nothings" who were rising in power and influence.

An incredibly useful inventory from October 1854 has survived
confirming that the university had designated space in a new east
wing of the main building for an exhibition hall, the first so described
at Notre Dame, as well as a separate music room in a nearby out-

UNIVERSITY OF NOTRE-DAME-DU-LAC,

ST. JOSEPH COUNTY, INDIANA.

UNDER THE DIRECTION OF THE PRIESTS OF THE HOLY CROSS.

Figure 2.2. Main Building I—Engraving as part of ND advertisement, GNEG 11A/003, UNDA. This must be around 1854 because of the additional east and west wings and a new façade. The 66' x 40' east wing (on the right) contained the university's first "exhibition hall" occupying the second and third floors with a recreation hall underneath on the first (or ground) floor. This east wing configuration of the Main Building served the needs of the university until the 1862 opening of the free-standing 100' x 50' Senior Recreation Hall, which contained an exhibition hall that would be named Washington Hall in 1864.

building (see figs. 2.2 and 2.3). This inventory provides valuable details regarding the first purpose-built exhibition hall at Notre Dame, one that precedes the first Washington Hall by nearly a decade, and one that came about as a result of the first addition to the Main Building, a clear indication of the need for such a venue. The inventory describes the east wing of the newly expanded main building as 66' x 40' by 4½ stories high, and containing a recreation hall on the first floor, a two-story exhibition hall (with "Paintings & Scenery"

Figure 2.3. Panorama of Notre Dame Campus—Engraving, c. 1856, GNEG 09A/05, UNDA. This engraving shows clearly the new east and west wings on Main I in context with the entire university, including the lower freestanding structure northeast of the Main Building (to the right) which was likely the building that included a "music room," three classrooms, and one piano-equipped practice room on its first floor. The second floor contained four dormitory rooms and one more music practice room.

valued at one hundred dollars) occupying the entire second and third floors, a museum and armory on the fourth floor, and a "Garret not occupied." The 1854 inventory goes on to describe a separate two-story building, 75' x 15', northeast of the Main Building which contained on the first floor a "Music room" with an assortment of instruments and supplies (including strings, brass, woodwinds, percussion, and sheet music) and five practice rooms, one of which housed a pianoforte valued at two hundred dollars. Upstairs were three double and two single sleeping rooms.[21]

Thus by the fall of 1854—within twelve years of the founding of the university—performers had purpose-built places for practice and performance at Notre Dame both within the east wing of the main building and in separate, well-equipped spaces in an adjoining building. In May 1856 the university added to its musical inventory when the Local Council authorized "that some instruments of music should be procured before the exhibition."[22] In January 1857 the

Local Council ordered that "the big stove of the large study room will be moved to the Exhibition hall, as soon as the furnace is fixed, that the Boarders might practice music there."[23]

By the 1857–58 academic year, however, plans had been made for a completely separate freestanding exhibition hall not within the Main Building, with dimensions for the first time indicating that the new structure might not be any larger than the exhibition hall currently in use: "It was decided that Mr. Taylor's propositions concerning his properties should be accepted, and that a wood shed 100 feet long by 25 should be built by Mr. Hudson in such a manner as to be used for the public Exhibition $60 to be paid in cash, the rest in trade [space] and the Lumber requisite to be got from Mishawaking [sic] also by trading."[24] In spite of authorization, no building went up until 1862, with the earliest recorded payments for the construction of an exhibition hall made in June 1862 for $533.16, plus $19.00 for "Lumber and Hauling."[25]

The university planning for commencement 1861 included the following oxymoronic warning regarding student actors and beer: "Our Exhibition will take place on the last Wednesday of June [26] at 3°ᶜˡ· P.M. but the play only after supper . . . Common beer (2 barrels) from Chicago will be procured for the dinner of the students and distributed with great caution to the actors in the play."[26] Evening plays by students who had consumed beer was an obvious recipe for disaster then as now and, indeed, would be the custom for only two more years at Notre Dame.[27]

The Dramatic Society performed *The Rivals* for commencement in 1861, the last year before a new detached exhibition hall opened.[28] Space needs propelled by rapid growth made the year 1862 an important one in the history of the physical campus: no fewer than four buildings went up, including the new Senior Recreation Hall, which contained within its walls on the second and third floors an exhibition hall nearly twice as large as the pre-existing venue in the main building.

The first real planning for the new freestanding exhibition hall occurred by May 1862, when the Local Council reported that "a new shed serving both as a play room and as an exhibition hall is in contemplation but no decisive conclusion is taken."[29] The decision to move forward with an exhibition hall came quickly, however, when a week later the council decided not only to proceed but to realign the entire recreational area of the university: "An exhibition hall shall be built immediately in the yard of the senior's and that the yard of the junior's shall be moved in consequence near the senior's yard."[30]

By late spring and early summer 1862, the decision to lay the stone foundation "as far as possible" also occurred, and the Local Council issued rules regarding exhibitions which showed that their huge popularity had drawn the wrong crowd: "Means will be taken to prevent strangers stopping at the college on the night of the Exhibition but only for next year." In addition, the council laid down particulars for managing the festivities: "On the day of the exhibition Mr. OBrien and Mr. Stanton will receive the tickets of adm. in Br. Peter's office. beer will be distributed by Br. Isidore to the students acting in the play Brs. Maximus and Gabriel will keep the door."[31] The Local Council passed some interesting resolutions related to exhibitions at commencement in late June 1862: "Then it is resolved in future there will be no play at night on the day of the Exhibition, and that all the premiums and accessits awarded to any student will be proclaimed at once so as not to call twice the same student."[32] Not calling students' names more than once, of course, helps to speed up the process, so that is simply a new efficiency, but the "no play at night" rule, while we cannot know with certainty, is likely related both to strangers on campus and to the boys having beer at dinner. By moving the commencement play to earlier in the day, students were more likely to be completely sober, and events ended early enough to be sure strangers did not loiter overnight on campus.

The records suggest that the new Exhibition Hall went up over the six-week period from the time the council approved it in mid-May to its first use at the late June commencement. On June 28, 1862, a payment for lumber was made, but it was paid with a note—not cash—to C. Shaefer, a very strong indication that there was insufficient cash on hand at that time, a reason Father Sorin would soon call on the consistently generous Mrs. Phelan to fund the building project. In early July the university paid for nails and in late August for "17700 Bricks" for the Exhibition Hall.[33] Indeed the *Scholastic* in a historical piece on the building a decade later confirmed that the new Exhibition Hall of 1862 "arose . . . like the palace of Aladdin . . . from the sandy desert of the Senior play-ground."[34] With the opening of the new Exhibition Hall by commencement 1862, the pre-existing facility in the Main Building ceased to be the only theatre on campus after eight years of use. The new Exhibition Hall constructed in 1862 would be the university's prime performance venue until 1882.

The construction of the new building occurred so rapidly that apparently Father Sorin had neither approval nor sufficient funds in hand to pay for it. As a result, he called on Mrs. Phelan in the summer of 1862 to fund the building project, pleading to the woman whose earlier bequest in 1855 had saved the university:

> The new Exhibition hall has been put up without any Consultation of the Mother House; there will be undoubtedly a charge made against me for the undertaking unless I am able to Show that I can pay for it otherwise than with the funds of the Institution Now I can cover the whole of it with $1200—& I write precisely now to beg of you the favor to donate in that amount on yr acct with the Institution. If you were to suffer in any way by it I would not ask any thing of the sort but I trust you will not & it will be for me quite an act of Kindness—
> In haste very truly
Your devoted friend
ESorin csc[35]

We know Mrs. Phelan responded in a most positive way because of Sorin's grateful letter of August 4, 1862, in which he thanked her for her $1,200 donation and noted that $170 of the amount was being used to credit "Thomey's bill," for a net donation to the University of $1,030.[36] Mrs. Phelan thus paid for the building that would become the first Washington Hall.[37] The financial ledger confirmed on January 10, 1863, the cost of the Exhibition Hall at just under $1,300, so Father Sorin's estimate six months earlier had proved reasonably accurate.[38]

By fall 1862 the new Exhibition Hall within the Senior Recreation Hall had been in use since the previous commencement, but it was still a work in progress. The Local Council reported in September that, perhaps in anticipation of winter and the need for indoor recreation, the "billiard room shall be fixed in the new hall plastered inside and boarded outside."[39] A week later the council actually approved the purchase of the billiard table for two hundred dollars "bought and paid by yearly installment."[40] This seemed to indicate a billiard room with one table, but one table was better than none. The tradition of a billiard room on the ground level below the audience in Washington Hall would persist well until the 1950s, which means this combined configuration that has its genesis in the east wing of the Main Building by 1854 continued for a century.

By Christmas 1862 the council recognized the perhaps dour simplicity of the framed clapboard structure and moved to spruce it up: "The windows of the first story of the exhibition Hall not appearing to any advantage, it was resolved to put ornamental caps on them."[41] These are very likely the same caps seen a decade later in the earliest surviving photographs taken of the exterior of the building during the Lemonnier presidency (see fig. 2.4).

The Local Council proudly recounted the great leap forward in 1862 in terms of new construction, including the desperately needed exhibition hall, which became immediately indispensable: "Considering the increasing [enrollment] of the college we hardly understand now how we could delay so long procuring such a hall." The Phelan gift seemed to have permitted the building to have three stories rather than two, which not only helped with scale and balance in relation to other buildings, but made it possible to create a new exhibition hall on the top two floors while still retaining a recreation hall on the ground floor: "Now in order that this building should agree with the other Buildings and not disgrace the place, it was found necessary to give it a decent elevation."[42]

The university continued its growth curve with regard to music by setting aside five hundred dollars per annum in February 1863 to hire "a good professor of music if one can be found,"[43] even though the realization of a freestanding music hall comparable in size to the new Exhibition Hall was two years away.[44] Work continued on the Exhibition Hall through June 1863, a year after it had opened to its first event, and an offer had gone out to a professor in music. The

Figure 2.4. Cast outside Washington Hall at a first (ground) floor entrance, probably on the "short" or west side of the building. Father Lemonnier in the center front row dates the photograph to his two years as president, 1872–74, in what may be the earliest photograph of Washington Hall. The ornamental caps over the windows probably date to 1862. The reverse of this photograph says "III-40 1874 Exhibition Hall in Background, front row (left to right) A. Stace, J. A. Lyons, A. Lemonnier, unidentified [Marcellinus], and J. Edwards." Thomas J. Schlereth Photographs (hereafter GTJS) 6/9, UNDA.

council reported that "the part of the Exhibition hall where the scaffold stands shall be painted over, and that the stage front shall be finished. . . . Mr. Frenay shall be offered 300 dollars per annum."[45] The minutes also related particulars of administering the exhibition hall, indicating a charge for tickets: "Mr. O'Brian and Mr. Campion shall sell the tickets for admission to the Exhibition hall,"[46] all in time for the 1863 commencement, where *William Tell* was produced for the first of many times as one event of many in the complex and varied exhibitions of the day.[47]

In preparation for the official dedication of the new Exhibition Hall as Washington Hall, the final interior work done on the building seems to have been 1,300 yards of "Lathing & plastering," including extra payment "for plastering between rafters," a likely indication of the treatment to the underside of the vaulted ceiling in the two-story-high auditorium.[48]

By February 1864, then, the finished Exhibition Hall occupied the top two floors of the Senior Recreation Hall and was ready to become Washington Hall, as the *New York Tablet* reported on the "time-honored custom to celebrate the birthday of Washington at Notre Dame." After the delivery of Washington's 1796 Farewell Address at noon and an afternoon of patriotic music and celebration, "the new hall was filled by a large and intelligent audience from the surrounding towns and country. The College Band, under the excellent leadership of Prof. Basil, gave sweet utterance to the soul of music, while the stage, decked with the Star Spangled Banner, and adorned with the gorgeous scenery painted by the master-hand of Prof. La Chassaigne, filled the eye with equal pleasure."[49] The program included an overture by the college band, an oration by Professor Howard (secretary of the faculty), performances of the farce *Furnished Apartments* by the Philopatrian Society and the drama *Pizarro* by the Thespian Society, and "the audience seemed well pleased with the entertainment." In his closing comments, Father Sorin then took the stage and

> in a short speech, returned the thanks of the audience to the students for the pleasant evening they had spent, and then adverted to the satisfaction all felt at the completion of the new hall, which would be the scene of so many delightful reunions like the present. He felt great pleasure in dedicating the hall on such an auspicious day, and hoped all would be pleased to know that hereafter it should be called Washington Hall. A burst of applause followed this announcement, and the well-pleased audience retired, wishing all America had received as much pleasure and new hope as they from this anniversary of Washington's Birthday.

The celebration continued a second day and included a lecture by the bishop of Fort Wayne, after which "Washington Hall is now fairly inaugurated, and we may expect many pleasant days and evenings there, which will make Notre Dame still dearer to its inmates, and more admired by friends and visitors."[50]

With this inauguration Notre Dame had a performance venue known as Washington Hall which provided for the next eighteen years a singularly vital space for secular communal assembly on campus. Father Sorin's decision confirmed the direct connection between being a good American and a good Catholic. Sorin's was a supremely patriotic act that also had positive political consequences; over the next century and a half, Notre Dame would serve both God and Caesar seamlessly. Washington Hall, the only building at Notre Dame ever named in honor of an American president, was created during the Civil War, which had ripped apart the country. From February 1864 onward, the name of the exhibition hall made it clear that Notre Dame, a Catholic university founded by French priests, was first and foremost "All-American" long before the gridiron successes of the 1920s.

CHAPTER 3

THE FIRST WASHINGTON
HALL, 1864–1879

What do we know about the first Washington Hall? Both the *Guide* of 1865 and the *Annual Catalogue* of 1864–65 provide the earliest engravings of the building in its context on campus along with detailed prose descriptions.[1] These engravings confirm the original north-south configuration of the building; the Charles Shober lithograph more accurately illustrates where buildings actually were in relation to each other (see figs. 3.1, 3.2, and 3.3), before the subsequent construction of the Music (Junior Recreation) Hall necessitated rotating Washington Hall ninety degrees into a parallel east-west configuration. The engraving of the Exhibition Hall that accompanies its description (see fig. 3.4) depicts an upper tier of windows that were likely double-length to accommodate the auditorium portion of the building. The engravings suggest the long side of Washington Hall had seven window bays while the short side had three.

The written description of the Exhibition Hall in the *Guide* of 1865 tells us a great deal about the newly dedicated Washington Hall:

This building is one hundred by fifty feet. The first floor, as you perceive it, is sufficiently spacious to afford the students abundant

NOTRE DAME UNIVERSI

RE I

1 The College.
2 The Church of the Sacred Heart.
3 The Washington Exhibition Hall.
4 The Manual Labor School.

5 The Infirmary.
6 Kitchen & Vestiary.
7 St. Joseph's Lake.
8 A Steamboat.

9 The Mis
10 The Chape
11 The Broth
12 The Priest

Figure 3.1. *A Guide to the University of Notre Dame, and the Academy of St. Mary of the Immaculate Conception, Near South Bend, Indiana* (Philadelphia: J. B. Chandler, 1865), frontispiece, GNEG 09A/03-04, UNDA. Note the north-south disposition of building 3 (the Washington Exhibition Hall). The artist's exaggerated perspective appears to place the Manual Labor School parallel to

JOSEPH CO. INDIANA.

CES

Home.
ly of the Angels, or the Portioncula.
osephites, Noviciate.
valorists, Noviciate

13 The Holy Sepulchre.
14 St. Mary's Lake.
15 The Farm Buildings.
16 The Road to St. Mary's Academy, 1 Mile from University—west.

and southwest of Washington Hall, when in reality it was much farther south. This engraving reflects the 1862–65 period because it precedes the building of the Music Hall in 1865 and the subsequent removal of Washington Hall south and ninety degrees into an east-west disposition to make the two buildings parallel.

Figure 3.2. Enlargement of fig. 3.1, frontispiece, GNEG 09A/03-04, UNDA, of the central campus, with the Washington Exhibition Hall building 3. Note the elongated window bays on the west front, perhaps to reflect the two-story height of the interior auditorium.

room for their amusements when the weather is unfavorable to out-door sports. The whole length on that side is railed off for a bowling alley, similar to the one in the Juniors' Playroom. Both are erected with care and skill, and afford most agreeable pastime. To your right is another room, neatly fitted up for billiards, if eye and hand are practiced and accurate, stranger, you may meet your match among some of these amateurs. The floor above is set apart as an Exhibition Hall, where the concourse of friends and strangers at the Annual Commencements may be accommodated during the interesting exercises which mark those occasions. In the galleries alone two thousand persons can be easily seated. You will

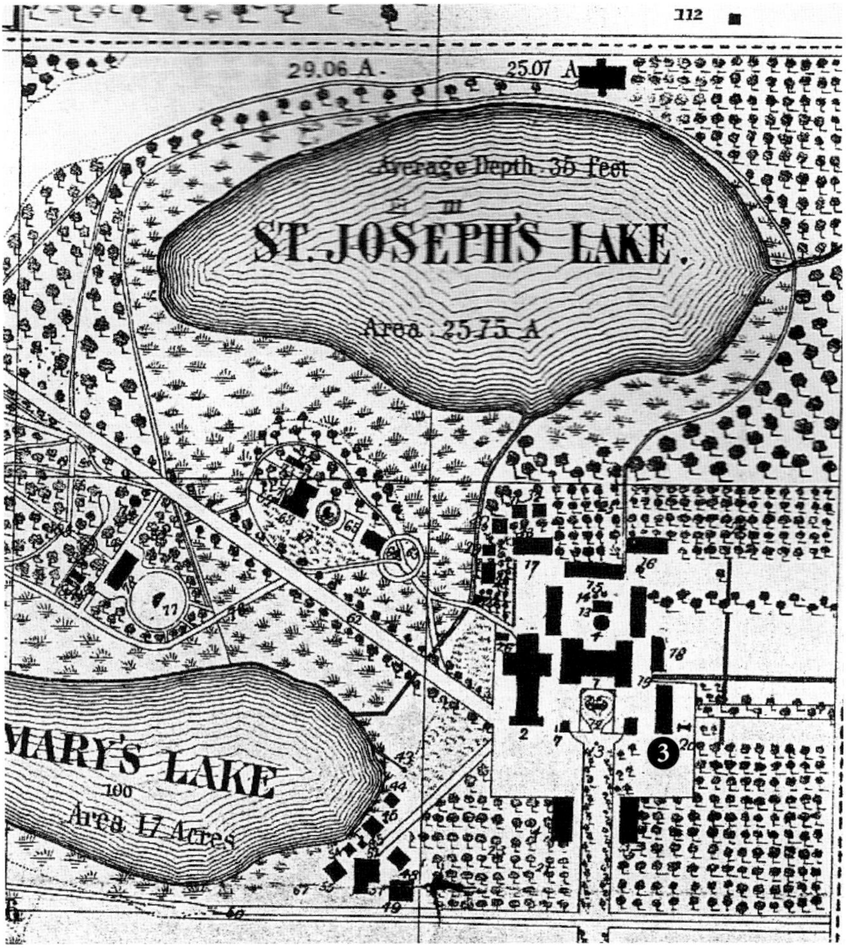

29.06 A.   25.07 A.

Average Depth 35 feet

ST. JOSEPH'S LAKE.

Area 25.75 A

77

77

75
74
73
7

78

79

2   7

3

100

MARY'S LAKE

Area 17 Acres

43
44
46

45
19

67

Figure 3.3. Blowup of Charles Shober lithograph 1865, shows the original north-south configuration of Washington Hall (before the complementary Music Hall was built) with Washington Hall (number 3) complementing the church just as it does today. This lithograph is a rare topographical map from a very narrow period in Notre Dame's history, after the Exhibition Hall was built in 1862, but before both the Music Hall went up by the end of 1865 and the Exhibition Hall was moved ninety degrees in 1866 from a north-south configuration to an east-west one, the position it would stay in until it was demolished in 1882. To achieve the point of view of the *Guide* engraving in figs. 3.1 and 3.2, the observer would be directly south of Saint Mary's Lake looking northeast toward the center of campus. Notre Dame Printed and Reference Material Dropfiles (hereafter PNDP) 10-Aa-05, UNDA.

EXHIBITION HALL AND SENIORS' PLAY ROOM.

Figure 3.4. *A Guide to the University of Notre Dame, and the Academy of St. Mary of the Immaculate Conception, Near South Bend, Indiana.* (Philadelphia: J. B. Chandler, 1865), 27, engraving of Washington Hall in its original north-south configuration. Note seven bays on long west front and ground floor entrance with portico in the middle of the building.

notice that the whole floor is an inclined plane from the stairway of entrance to the foot of the stage, thus affording as good a view to those at a distance from the young candidates for honors as is usually the case in regard to those much nearer the scene of action. This spacious Hall is, however, frequently called into requisition throughout the year. The Thespian Society of the University on festival occasions, present the numerous inmates of Notre Dame with most gratifying theatrical entertainments, where costume and scenery unite with dramatic talent of no mean order to please and instruct their appreciative audience. These entertainments are found to act beneficially by stimulating the capacity or talent for eloquence of word and gesture, and by giving that self-reliance so necessary to success. When the incidents of College life require, as they not unfrequently do, a special commemoration, or peculiar notice, the Hall affords a convenient place of assembly, and Greek, Latin, French and German Orations, awe the ignorant, and gratify the learned who listen to their sonorous periods. It is intended to complete this building by the addition of two stories, to serve as an observatory and laboratory.[2]

The building, of course, never added stories, and indeed this description raises as many questions as it answers. The capacity of two thousand in the gallery (or balcony) seems extraordinarily large, even keeping in mind the different building code and fire regulations of the time. Possibly the writer meant the entire "house" or audience area and not just the balcony, but we cannot know for sure. In a printed development appeal, Father Sorin praised the added capacity and beauty offered by the new balcony:

The late improvements made at Notre Dame for the comfort and convenience of our pupils, have met with universal approval. The large Exhibition Hall, of one hundred feet in length, and fifty in breadth, dedicated to-day [February 22]—"*To The Father of His Country*"—has been embellished in various ways, to render it, as far as possible, worthy of the occasion. Among other additions, a fine Gallery around the Hall, has been recently built, capable of seating a large number of persons, enlarging its capacity and much increasing its architectural beauty.[3]

Although we do not know with certainty, the entrance to the building was very likely through exterior stairs leading up to the second floor, a technique that conserved valuable interior space and one Notre Dame continued with its next generation of buildings. While the surviving early engravings show no exterior stairs to the second level, later photographs confirm them (see fig. 3.5), as well as a portico entrance to the first or ground floor (see fig. 2.4). We also do not know the angle or "rake" of the auditorium floor. The current Washington Hall has a rake of five degrees from the back of the house to the edge of the stage, an angle that the 1862 building also could have easily accommodated based on its dimensions. Furthermore, we do not know which end of the building housed the stage, much less where actors dressed and how they entered and exited the stage. We know from later discussions there was no fly space (the

Figure 3.5. *Dome* 1920, 145, showing exterior stairs on the first Washington Hall leading to the second (auditorium) level, probably on the "long" side of the building. Date and play are unknown, but Father Colovin in the center front row dates the photograph to his years as president, 1874–77. The elevated entrance to Washington Hall was added in 1871, probably on the north side with exterior stairs accessing the second floor. This is the best surviving picture of the exterior entrance to the first Washington Hall. Note the platform at the top of the stairs above the portico, almost certainly to access the auditorium directly.

area above the stage to bring in and take out scenic effects and "fly - ing" actors), and little is known about the wing space (the area on either side of the stage where scenery could be shifted on and off).[4] The first Washington Hall was much more of an assembly hall than a real theatre, then, and likely had very little backstage support. Despite these structural limitations the building was in constant use, adding hugely to the communal cultural life of the university.

Money to paint the Exhibition Hall and to buy canvas (to construct scenery for plays) came from the Thespians as early as the 1863–64 academic year.[5] The canvas became painted drops of scenery by May 16, when the Local Council recorded that "the Exhibition

Hall shall be painted and two frames of scenery made at the expense of the Thespian Society. . . . Twenty-five dollars will be advanced to the Thespian Society."[6] All of this was in anticipation of commencement 1864 at which the Thespian Society produced the first Shakespeare play in the newly dedicated Washington Hall; to no one's surprise the production was the ever-popular *Henry IV.* In an 1872 historical article, the *Scholastic* looked back and noted that "in 1864 appears the 'Thespian Society' under its proper title. Whether it be its first appearance as such we cannot tell, for want of the Catalogue of 1863. . . . The Falstaff of this occasion was Prof. M. T. Corby, who also took the principal part in the comedy of 'Rory O'More,' which followed."[7] We cannot know if the play done was part 1, part 2, or a combined and truncated version as was common at the time and therefore likely.

For the first academic year after the building's dedication as Washington Hall, 1864–65, the university deferred its intended use from exhibition hall to dormitory, as ever-increasing enrollments forced the university administration to find space. Beds replaced "benches . . . removed to the basement of the Church," and the stage itself became a storage space for musical equipment.[8] Father Sorin confirmed in a letter to Mrs. Phelan that "there are now over 80 beds in Washington Hall."[9] By fall 1864 the Exhibition Hall thus had a new use for which it was not designed. In September 1864, when the Local Council Minutes reported that "Bro. Gabriel will sleep with the Boys in the Exhibition Hall," Washington Hall was clearly being used as a dormitory.[10] In 1907 Timothy Edward Howard attributed the unexpected but rapid increase in enrollment later in the Civil War to "the great influx of students from the border states," but more recent work by St. Louis University archivists Randy McGuire and John Waide noted that Notre Dame's pattern paralleled that of St. Louis University at the time, where a significant percentage of the new students came from Tennessee, not a border state. Joan Zurhellen, archivist of the Diocese of Memphis, pointed out that the early Catholic immigrants to West Tennessee tended to be skilled workers, often stonemasons (and thus outside the plantation system), and they most likely would have sent their offspring north where Catholicism flourished and the temptation to join in the fighting was minimal.[11] It is important to note that the Conscription Act of 1863 seemed not to have been a causative agent for these increased enrollments, since the act involved men aged twenty-one and over, well beyond the age of typical students at Notre Dame at the time. But whatever the cause, Notre Dame was bursting at the seams with students in the final year of the Civil War.

During the dormitory year of 1864–65 the Local Council included the first official reference in their minutes to the building as "Washington Hall" in relation to major changes in music on campus with the empowering appointment of Father Lemonnier as "sole Director of the Brass Band and the Choir." The minutes proclaimed that

> by virtue of this new appointment, he may receive, either in the Band or the Choir, any Student, apprentice, or Brother he please, without being controlled in his choice by the respective Music teachers; it shall also be his duty to assemble the Members of the Band and Choir twice a week for rehearsal—on Wednesday, and Sunday, if he finds these days convenient; it shall also be his right to direct the Music teachers when there shall be Brass Band or orchestral Entertainments in the *Washington Hall* [my emphasis], and also vocal and instrumental Music in the Church during the public Religious offices. As it is desirable to have a permanent musical Association established in the College, the Director of Music shall organize one under the Style of St. Cecilia's Society.[12]

The university would have to ensure that adequate rehearsal and storage spaces existed to support an ambitious music program and so moved forward with its plans for a junior recreation hall that would contain a much-needed music hall to complement Washington Hall, in spite of the designated "music rooms" that had been constructed by 1854 but which had very likely proved inadequate. The Financial Journal records suggest that construction of the Music Hall likely occurred over a period of almost two years, from the first payment for "Music Hall Brick" on November 4, 1864, to settling a final bill of $105 for interior plastering on August 11, 1866, a strong indication that the building had been completed.[13]

With Father Lemonnier firmly in charge of an expanding and ambitious music program, plans for improvement and growth continued apace. The Local Council resolved on November 14, 1864, that "an effort shall be made to establish the musical Dept. of the College on a better footing; to attain this much desired end, a complete set of brass instruments for a juvenile Band shall be procured and the services of Mr. Overmayer, a Prof. of Music, from Laporte, shall be, if possible, secured. Six hundred dollars may be offered him as a fix [*sic*] salary for the scholastic year." In spite of the initial purchase of brick, the weather got in the way: "The musical Hall is postponed till the spring by reason of the cold weather."[14] After the Financial Journal included the costs for the joists for the Music Hall on January 28, 1865, payments stopped for eight months.[15] These construction delays, however, did not keep the university from offering merit scholarships to talented students at Notre Dame for the fall of 1865. The Local Council confirmed that "the Langen boys are to be received free in consideration of the service they can render by their musical talents etc."[16]

By February 1865 Father Lemonnier had clearly made his presence felt; as he reorganized band instrument storage, there is every reason to believe he got permission to convert at least part of the stage of Washington Hall into a band instrument storage area, at least until the new building became available. The Local Council reported that "Father Lemonnier having requested that boxes should be made for the drums etc of the Junior band, it was found objectionable to have these instruments in the College as a source of confusion. & Father Superior suggested that the Stage in the Exhibition Hall could be used for that purpose. It was agreed to, & orders were given to fix a place there for those instruments. & for the band to practice in."[17] The nature of the confusion is not clear, but anyone who has ever lugged bulky instruments across campus or, indeed, endured drum practice sessions can commiserate. While the issue could have been as simple as having band instruments dispersed all over campus and not being able therefore easily to assemble and practice, it is more likely related to the din created when musicians practice and the need to separate and isolate their activity from the main building. Whatever the case, clearly the council authorized the band both to store its instruments on the Washington Hall stage and to practice there. A music hall with proper storage and practice spaces was desperately needed, and it was only because Washington Hall had become a dormitory for the 1864–65 academic year that the stage was therefore available during the delayed construction of the new Music Hall.[18]

It was also during the 1864–65 "dormitory year" that John Wilkes Booth shot Abraham Lincoln on Good Friday, April 14, 1865, and the president died a day later. The Local Council tersely recommended quiet caution and keeping heads low: "In regard to civil affairs the council was of opinion that all the members should be extremely cautious in saying anything that might compromise the house in the opinion of the public."[19] Nothing else exists in the Local Council Minutes regarding the Lincoln assassination; indeed, Howard's *A History of St. Joseph County Indiana* fails to mention the sad event, which may signify the utter shock the country generally felt at the time. It is well to remember, however, that numerous Holy Cross priests served as chaplains in the Union Army, including Fathers Corby and Carrier, and General Sherman had close ties to the university at this time.

In spite of Washington Hall's being converted into a dormitory, the Local Council planned fully for the commencement exhibition of 1865 for Thursday, June 22, at 9:00 A.M., with preparation for "the Exhibition Hall" on May 29 and on June 19 "the tickets for the Exhib. Hall to be sold at 50 cts."[20] Commencement had included plays in the programs for 1862 (*Columbus*), 1863 (*William Tell*), and 1864 (*Henry IV*), but there was no play in 1865. Was it because the auditorium had become an eighty-bed dormitory during 1864–65 and the stage had been turned over to music practice and storage, thus making adequate rehearsals impossible? Did the mood of the country, still grieving the recent death of Lincoln, make drama seem especially frivolous?

In spite of the 1865 commencement including no play, the exhibition nevertheless contained a varied program of musical pieces by the band, the field band, and the orchestra, songs by the quartette, four speeches, and the valedictory, all interspersed in and around the awarding of premiums and the conferral of degrees. General William Tecumseh Sherman (who was forty-five years old), strongly tied to South Bend and Notre Dame, gave the address then described as "Closing Remarks."[21] His short speech called "upon the young men here to be ready at all times to perform bravely the battle of life,"[22] but he also never directly mentioned Lincoln's assassination. His niece, Ellie Ewing, a student at Saint Mary's College, wrote to her mother about the day. She confirmed that "they had no plays They only had speeches addresses music by the band and distribution of premiums Uncle Comp [Sherman] was there and he signed his name on the graduates' diplomas."[23]

With the new Senior Recreation Hall, which included the Washington Exhibition Hall, up and running, the Local Council turned to the needs of both the juniors (boys thirteen to sixteen) and the music program, and a building that would include proper spaces for both. Right after commencement 1865, construction had commenced on the transformation of Main Building I into a much larger Main Building II, and by that fall, the Local Council had agreed to move forward on the freestanding Music Hall as well.[24] Extensive payments related to the Junior Recreation/Music Hall occurred during the fall and early winter of 1865, with payments to as many as twenty workmen as well as for the purchase of lumber.[25] Initially, the plan was to have a new east-west running Junior Recreation Hall very close (possibly adjoining but perpendicular) to the north-south Senior Recreation/Washington Hall. This plan, interestingly enough, prefigured the building we know today as Washington Hall, with the exhibition hall running north and south, and with an adjoining music hall attached to it on the north end.

By September 1865 we know more about the plans for the Music Hall and for music rehearsal spaces in the infirmary. The Local Council related, "As a play room becomes necessary now for the Juniors, the council all agree to have one built running east and west in the rear of the Exhibition Hall."[26] A week later, we learn the size of the new building and that Holy Cross House had been considered for music rooms:

As the Professed Brothers prefer to remain where they are at holy Cross house, and as the administration is in great want of rooms for the musical department, the present rooms on the first floor of the Infirmary are to be converted to that purpose, at least three of them. A play room for the Juniors is finally resolved upon 100 ft by 40—having a trunk room above & below a room for Bro. Adolphus' department at one end and, two rooms at the other for the Field Band.[27]

The same length as Washington Hall, the Music Hall would be ten feet narrower, thus making each floor 4,000 square feet rather than the 5,000 square feet in Washington Hall. We know a bit more about the Music Hall from a calculation made after it was destroyed in the Great Fire of 1879. A pencil-written record of the loss states that the Music Hall measured 100' x 40.6' (likely 40' 6'') with a girth of 287' and was 24' high. It had forty-three windows 6½' x 3½' and nine windows 4' x 5½' (a total of fifty-two windows). There were two flights of stairs (we do not know whether they were interior or exterior), three double (probably exterior) doors, and twenty (probably interior) doors on three floors of 3,800 square feet each, although one floor was "double," likely meaning that the large space in the Music Hall had a high ceiling appropriate to a rehearsal and performance venue.[28] The specifics of this calculation provide great insight into our understanding of the physical properties of the 1865 Music Hall, although it is not clear at all to what degree these characteristics parallel those of the first Washington Hall.

In October 1865 the Local Council Minutes confirmed the need for order and that the new Music Hall would be built of brick: "Mr. Burns is to take charge of the Music rooms to preserve order there" and "the playroom for the Juniors is proposed to be built in brick as Carpenters cannot be had & that the work must be done."[29] In November the council authorized water closets to serve both buildings "should be built between the music hall & the Exhibition hall."[30] So it looks as if both the Music Hall and Washington Hall were both fully operational by late fall 1865, although the Music Hall would not be completed fully until August 1866.

With the Music Hall largely functional by fall 1865, the Local Council authorized hiring a musician "from Fort Wayne . . . to teach the brass instruments," and upgraded the seating in the Exhibition Hall, thus replacing the original benches, which had been stored in the church basement during the dormitory year, with custom-made seating in early 1866: "The music hall is to be finished at once. . . .

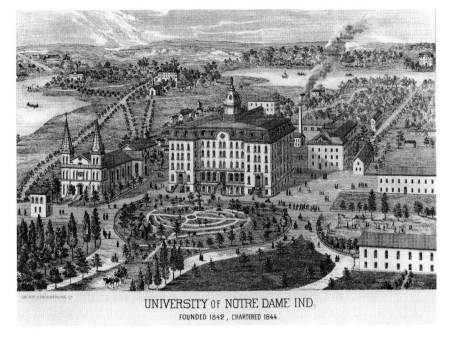

UNIVERSITY OF NOTRE DAME IND.
FOUNDED 1842, CHARTERED 1844.

Figure 3.6. The first Washington Hall, c. 1866, on the lower right side with the new Main Building II and parallel Music Hall to the north. Note the long curved-top upper-floor windows. This configuration would last until the Great Fire of 1879. Notre Dame Life Photograph Collection (hereafter GNDL) 06-16-02, UNDA.

Seats for the Exhibition hall are ordered to be made."[31] By late February, Mr. J. O'Neil had accepted an offer to teach music and "would arrive in the commencement of March,"[32] and he continued at Notre Dame through 1869 as professor of music.

Soon after the new Music Hall opened, the Local Council decided that the Exhibition Hall "should be removed" physically, and it was, a full ninety degrees, from a north-south to an east-west elevation, so the buildings sat parallel rather than perpendicular to each other (see fig. 3.6).[33] (This shift may have also been related to the summer 1866 construction of the new Main Building, in effect adding a "doughnut" of new construction around a preexisting structure.) The 1866–67 academic year is thus the first to have both parallel Music and Exhibition Halls in operation next door to the new Main Building II, a configuration that survived until the Great Fire of

April 1879 destroyed both the Main Building and the Music Hall and forced the Exhibition Hall once again to become a temporary dormitory as the university rebuilt. Also in the fall of 1866 both the Music Hall and Washington Hall had rectors assigned to them, with Brother Anthony in the Music Hall and Brother Isidore in the Exhibition Hall under the Local Council directive that "the Prefects are required to prepare the fires in their respective play rooms,"[34] making it clear that the administration intended to exercise proper control over and require decorum in campus spaces while revealing the method of heating these new buildings at that time.

Also in fall 1866, the Local Council approved either the creation or the repair of "shutters inside the windows of the brass band room and a case to put the instruments in," and two weeks later "a place to put the brass instruments was ordered to be prepared in the Exhibition Hall."[35] They also hired a teacher capable of painting scenery for plays. The Local Council resolved "that a proposal be made to the artist Mr Ackermann for $500. per annum to teach drawing & paint."[36] With a new music hall and overall expansion of the university, the hiring of a fine artist "to teach drawing & paint" indicated the early importance of the discipline of art in the curriculum at Notre Dame, as well as the likelihood that this was Jacob Ackermann, who would be inextricably involved in scenery for the Washington Hall stage for the next thirty years.

Almost as soon as they were up and functional, the two new halls, however, still seemed unable to provide all the recreational needs for the growing community, and so plans moved forward for a free-standing and separate gymnasium. It is well to remember that South Bend, Indiana, with an average annual snowfall of seventy inches, lends itself to indoor recreational opportunities for much of the regular academic year.[37] The Local Council resolved in the fall of 1866 that "gymnasiums should be increased & repaired," with the justification as follows: "A large Main building was spoken of for a gymnasium where the students could during winter exercise themselves & not suffer from the bad weather. It was agreed to build one 25 ft by 40." A week later, the council approved a larger building of 40' x 60' and, at the same time, postponed it, stating that "the music hall is to be heated by steam" (confirming that steam was not the method of heat before this time).[38] Almost two years later, interest returned in the building, and the Local Council authorized "that a gymnasium 60 feet by 30 should be erected," as well as painting "the fences and the Exhibition Hall."[39] Although more indoor recreational outlets were clearly needed by the 1860s, Notre Dame did not construct its first purpose-built, freestanding gymnasium until soon after the dedication of the building we recognize today as Washington Hall in 1882.

The first volume of the *Scholastic* accompanied the opening of the 1867–68 academic year, and the new weekly publication immediately criticized the work ethic of the Thespians, the drama group composed of members of the Senior Department (boys seventeen and older). Students in the Junior Department (boys thirteen to sixteen) who wished to create theatre did so as members of the St. Cecilia Philomathean Society. The minims (boys under thirteen) acted through their society, the Columbians. The *Scholastic* reported in September:

> Our Dramatic Society seems to be behind the times—instead of behind the scenes—as it should be, practising for the coming festival. It is in the Thespians we put our chief trust for an evening's entertainment, and they should not only feel honored by the confidence reposed in them, but should endeavor to increase and strengthen it by keeping up their reputation.[40]

Music had always been very important at Notre Dame, and by the 1867–68 academic year a separate "vocal department has been established in the University and would like to see, with the parents' consent, a very large number taking lessons in that branch which is of great advantage in any state of life in which one could be placed."[41] It is interesting to note the affirmation of vocal training as a life skill.

On the ground floor of the Senior Recreation Hall, the area below the stage and auditorium of Washington Hall, the year 1867–68 saw the creation of a "dancing floor" 25 feet square (625 square feet).[42]

In October 1867 the *Scholastic* compiled what is very likely the first history of Washington Hall, probably prompted by the recent removal and impending renovation of the building:

Washington Hall.—This time-honored, and much-put-about building, is going to be fixed up in Sunday-go-to-meetin's, by the same able and efficient corps of painters and grainers who transformed our college walls from plaster into wood. A new coat is generally worn outside, but Washington Hall prefers to take it internally, as the rheumatic patient said when the doctor ordered him to rub his knee-joint with Bourbon whiskey. Washington Hall's new coat is to be of white, gold and blue in glorious combinations. The ceiling pale pink—"sunset on the lake"—with natural stars. The white panels are to be frosted, so that the new coat may be called a frieze coat. All this is to be done in time for the coming festival. We beg to remind our Thespian friends that what did very well in the frowzy looking hall, as it used to be, won't be sufficient for frosted panels and gold stars. The stars on the stage must rival, if not surpass, the stars on the ceiling. That splendid new comedy of which they speak of in our present number, must be done up brown. That same old stage has been graced by many a talented amateur, from the time when it first suddenly started into existence, just in time for the Annual commencement of 1862, up to the present epoch, when it has scarcely settled itself in the position it was shoved into by the innovations of 1866. The history of Washington Hall is a subject for reflection, as imaging forth the vicissitudes of human life. Its foundations laid and left so, till the project of erecting it seemed to be abandoned—its sudden rise in a few days—its long unfinished state for a year and a half before the galleries were erected—its removal last year to the place where it now stands—its occasional evenings of splendor contrasting with its usual faded appearance by daylight, like the gleams of light and warmth in a gloomy lifetime—its assembled throng of hearts beating with varied emotions on commencement days—all combine to make the memories that hang around that building more interesting, perhaps, than those of any other at Notre Dame. It is now commencing a new era in its existence. We hope it will be an era of brilliancy commensurate with the increased prosperity of the University. The Thespian and musical societies must make this their chief care. They have an opportunity of causing their names to be remembered by their fellow-students for many coming years.[43]

We cannot know from this 1867 assessment whether the building was already showing signs of wear and tear so soon after its construction, or whether indeed it simply had never been properly completed. With the Silver Jubilee imminent, redecoration and renewal were certainly in order for this important facility that would be at the center of the celebration.

While completing the painting of the Washington Hall interior was critical, at this time we learn that the "large parlor" in the new Main Building II remained a useful alternative performance venue:

> The painting of the interior of Washington Hall has added a great deal to the effect of our exhibitions, and the finishing touches that are needed about the stage are promised by the talented artist as soon as the labors of his many duties allow him time. But Washington Hall itself has found a rival in the large parlor, which as a room for entertainments, is certainly more comfortable, though not capable of accommodating so extensive an audience. To Prof. Corby's Philharmonic Association we owe the discovery of the available facilities of the parlor for exhibitions.[44]

This revealed high demand for more performance spaces as early as 1867. Why else would Professor Corby use this space at all? If the Philharmonic Association had all the access it desired to Washington Hall, it likely would have performed there.

By the end of the first semester of the 1867–68 academic year, the *Scholastic* reported on "The Semi-annual Exhibition":

> Long deferred by a concatenation of untoward circumstances, an exhibition took place on the evening of the 4th inst. to celebrate the termination of one session and the beginning of another. The Thespians, as they should, took the management of this entertainment, under the able and efficient direction of Prof. E. A. McNally, A.M., the sister societies being admitted to a fair participation in the display, and taking the subordinate parts assigned them, with great improvement to the harmonious effect of the whole. The Cornet Band obligingly filled up the interval between the general assembling of the students in the hall and the arrival of the principal invited guests, by some pieces of excellent music,

in addition to the entrance march promised on the programme. The music of the Band is ever welcome to our audience, well chosen and well appreciated; we say the same of our orchestral performances, which are very grand, scientific and "classic."[45]

The two-act comedy performed, *Born to Good Luck, or An Irishman's Fortune,* was too short and was deemed not as good as the October exhibition due to lack of scenery and costumes, but it was still declared "a decided success. A comedy always does much better than a tragedy on our stage." The Father Superior's closing remarks, in addition to the usual praise for the evening, contained the important announcement for the future that "Prof. Griffith would arrive on the following day to begin a course of elocution for the students. The great elocutionist will have to work if he undertakes to surpass the doings of our amateur dramatic society, and make improvement upon what we had the pleasure of witnessing last night."[46]

By February 1868 and the Washington Birthday celebration, everything seemed to have been in place to showcase Professor Griffith's accomplishments in the classroom. The *Scholastic* reported that the celebration included a thirty-six-piece brass band (Professor O'Neil's "heavy artillery") playing Washington's "Grand March," directly in front of the college, followed by the flag raising from the dome, then "Hail Columbia" and "Yankee Doodle," all in preparation for the "literary entertainment" in Washington Hall. Carriage after carriage arrived from South Bend, Niles, and Elkhart, an important aspect of the Washington Day celebration always being the connection between town and gown. At 2:30 the cornet band "struck up a grand Entrance March" for a "sea of bright and beaming faces" in Washington Hall, where the orchestra was also present. The curtain rose to song and chorus led by Professor Girac, followed by the Junior Department's display of "practical elocution" from Professor Griffith's class, including the pantomime, "its object being to discipline the mind and lend grace and energy to the movements of the body." Afterwards, there was "a rather serio-comical colloquy," a debate between the value of mime versus elocution, and a presentation of elocution exercises and examples, followed by the orator of the day talking about Washington. Griffith performed on stage in "the greatest event of the afternoon . . . amid a perfect storm of applause, which fairly shook the Hall." The Reverend Father Superior had final comments, as was the custom, ending an extraordinary event "combining instruction and amusement with the gratification of the taste of the public for novelty."[47]

For the June 1868 (seventh) commencement in the building, the *Scholastic* published the program, including the play done by the "preps" of the St. Cecilia Philomathean Society, *The Recognition*, and two weeks later played up the newly painted scenery in Washington Hall:

> The newly painted proscenium and drop curtain executed by Prof. Von Weller, specially for this exhibition, added much to the *éclat* of the performances. The refined taste and judgment which pervade all the Professor's works was evident here. Our hall is henceforth and unmistakably a national institution and worthy of the name it bears.[48]

This commentary reflected on the name of Washington Hall, dedicated four years earlier, as the university prepared for the 1868–69 Silver Jubilee.

Celebrating a quarter century of success for Father Sorin's vision for a new Catholic university in the American Midwest, the Washington Exhibition Hall served as a focal point for the Silver Jubilee year of 1868–69. Beginning in October 1868 with the patronal festival of Father Sorin and ending with the June 1869 commencement, the entire year honored the university's charter of 1844. Virtually all current students at Notre Dame had been born after the university was established; the vast majority of them could not recall the campus without a place called Washington Hall.

The students created a unique Silver Jubilee Club, composed of Thespians and other interested participants, to see things through the year, which began with the Thespian-produced Saint Edward's Day (October 13) exhibition in honor of Father Sorin. On Saint Edward's Eve events began with the ringing of the bells when the Guard of Honor, headed by the Notre Dame University Cornet Band, escorted Father Sorin to Washington Hall, "where the greater portion of the students were assembled." The program's first part showed great variety: "Grand Opening March," by the cornet band; Allegro and Haydn's Fourth Symphony by the orchestra; a march and chorus by the Philharmonics; the Latin address; the Greek address; "Land of Light," by the Philharmonics; the Senior Department English address; the French address; the German address; the "Doretten Polka," by the orchestra; music by the cornet band; the Junior Department English address; Minims' address; music by the cornet band; a song, "The Founder of Notre Dame," by the Choral Union; and "Kalif de Bagdad," by the orchestra. For the second part, the program included the following: *The Ghost*, a comedy in three acts, by the Thespian Society, with the orchestra performing after act I, the band after act II, and the orchestra after act III; and concluding with a march for retiring, and closing remarks by Father Sorin, as was the custom.[49] No fewer than two dozen separate events composed this complex and varied exhibition.

While the Thespians produced the Founder's Day exhibition, the Silver Jubilee Club produced its first exhibition on the Washington Hall stage in April 1869, with Professor A. J. Stace serving as "the highly imaginative director." The exhibition was memorable, it seems, in its inclusion of very complex lighting and staging techniques that mimicked the sun and astrological events, with the added bonus of Mr. Noisy, who played the role of the Dog Star and who was very likely "the first quadruped that ever made his appearance before a Notre Dame audience." After the play, the afterpiece *The Mistake* (a shortened version of Sheridan's *She Stoops to Conquer*), with a cast of five men, plus a song-and-dance man between the scenes, was performed, followed by closing remarks and the march for retiring by the cornet band.[50]

In late May 1869 when Father Sorin returned from Europe, the Notre Dame University Cornet Band and university dignitaries met him at the depot and escorted him to campus, where after mass and dinner with the Senior Department, he went to Washington Hall "to receive the addresses prepared by the various bodies of the University," with interludes of pleasing vocal music, and the subsequent "play of the 'Prodigal Law Student,' being performed by the St. Cecilia Philomathean society . . . under the direction of Prof. J. A.

Lyons." Sorin's closing remarks "were very feeling and impressive." Father Sorin left for New Orleans the following Tuesday afternoon, but returned in time for the June commencement celebration of the "Silver Jubilee of the institution he founded and presided over so long and so successfully."[51] The commencement play, *Richelieu,* a drama in five acts "suitable to male characters only," by the Thespians under Father Corby and the band and orchestra under Max Girac, provided entr'actes, and the St. Cecilia Philomatheans reprised *The Prodigal Law Student,* with afternoon entertainments and conferring of degrees: "The celebration of the Silver Jubilee was all and even more than the warmest friends of the University could have anticipated."[52]

Professor Girac was in charge of original sacred music, masses, and the choir at this time, while Professor Corby directed the Philharmonic and Thespian societies, and Father Gouesse still conducted the cornet band he had founded in 1846.[53] The *Scholastic* praised their efforts, noting that "public opinion of Notre Dame now exacts a very high order of musical and dramatic talent in every one that ventures upon the stage of Washington Hall." The *Scholastic* further commented on events outside the building: "On emerging from the hall, the crowd found the college buildings illuminated with Chinese lanterns; and a display of fireworks closed the amusements of the evening."[54] All of this occurred just seven years after the building opened and within five years of its being named Washington Hall. Universities create traditions very rapidly, due to the constant turn - over of the student population, and the description of this event made it seem as though things had been done this way for a century. In addition, it is clear that those present felt that they were indeed at the very center of the world and attended the very best university with the best faculty. Optimism prevailed as it always had during Notre Dame's early history.

Other Washington Hall events in 1868–69, while perhaps not directly connected to the Silver Jubilee, nevertheless confirmed the constant use of the building that year. They included in the Christmas exhibition the play *If I Were King,* with a cast of forty, as well as "a Moot Court . . . by the united St. Aloysius Philodemic and St. Edward Societies . . . and the business attending the trial of the case before the house was carried on in a truly court-like style."[55] For New Year's night, Professor Stace wrote and produced the play *The Prince of Portage Prairie, or The Burning of Bertrand* "to relieve the monotony of the holidays, or rather to substitute for monotony a variety of innocent amusements," since many students at the time did not go home for Christmas.[56] For the Washington's Birthday exhibition in 1869, nine performance events preceded the five-act tragedy *Count De Moor,* with music and dance between each of the acts followed by "Hail Columbia," an overture, and the one-act comedy afterpiece *A Race for a Dinner.*[57] For today's niche audiences who select a particular play or concert by a particular group or artist, the exhibitions of the nineteenth century would seem like endless variety shows.

The Philomatheans and the Thespians

The St. Cecilia Philomathean Society (Junior Department) and the Thespians (Senior Department) were two of the earliest Notre Dame student organizations to produce plays on the campus generally as part of larger celebrations. Members of the Junior Department (the preparatory students aged thirteen but not yet seventeen) could join the St. Cecilia Philomatheans, while students in the Senior Department (those seventeen and older) made up the ranks of the Thespian Society. The extant Philomathean Constitution from the early days of Washington Hall provides great insight into the structure of extracurricular performance at Notre Dame in the early days. (The Thespians may have operated in a similar matter, but their constitution has not survived.) The constitution emphasizes not only the objectives of the organizations, but also the level of input and control over the society held by faculty members. This 1858 printed document, having been edited and containing the signed approbations of Fathers Sorin (1868) and Lemonnier (1874), thus in a very real sense bridges the period 1858–74.[58]

The purpose of the St. Cecilia Philomathean Society was "the advancement of its members in vocal culture, public speaking and singing, history and general literature," and the faculty officers of 1858 included Father Gillespie as director and Professor Lyons as president.[59] The director's duties included assisting "the Society in its deliberations by his advice. He shall authorize the choice of all subjects for public entertainments, and promote the welfare of the Society by every means of his power." The president should attend "all meetings of the Society, and perform the usual duties of a Chairman. He shall choose all subjects for Public Entertainments or Society Exercises. He shall give the final decision in matters of dispute, from which there shall be no appeal ['except to the Director' added in margin]. . . . He shall give decision at the close of literary and historical subjects." The constitution included the position of dramatic instructor—today's stage director—who "shall attend all rehearsals and conduct the same, and shall when called upon give dramatic readings." The first vice president

shall have charge of the Public Reading. The Second Vice President shall assist the Dramatic Instructor. The Historian shall produce a written historical essay once a month. . . . The General Critic shall give his views on the Drama, Historical Essays, Declamations, etc., and lecture twice a year on Political Economy before the members. The Promoter shall assist the Association by every honorable means to the utmost of his ability [in] both the Association Room and the Exhibition Hall and shall see that the members are properly costumed before appearing in Dramatic Exercises.[60]

Additionally, the St. Cecilia Philomathean Constitution of 1858–74 lists annual festivals the society helped to celebrate as follows: Saint Edward's Day (October 13), Saint Cecilia's Day (November 22), Washington's Birthday (February 22), the Anniversary of the College Dedication (May 31), the Festival of the President of the University (whenever it may occur), the Festival of Saint Aloysius (June 21, on which the annual reunion of the society will take place), and the Annual Commencement (last Wednesday in June). The constitution guaranteed the society "some public demonstration . . . on St. Cecilia's Day, by an entertainment in Washington Hall," but at the other times "this Society will take the place assigned it, among the other Societies of the College, by the general committee of arrangements."[61]

The "Draft for Prospectus for Notre Dame. August 15, 1868" also reveals important information regarding the St. Cecilia Philomathe - ans and confirms much of what the constitution contains while also providing an early history of the organization:

> This society is designed to embrace not only the literary, but also the eloctionary, dramatic and musical talent of the Junior Collegiate Department. It was first organized by Professor J. A. Lyons, in 1859, and is therefore one of the oldest societies in the College. Many of the names of its first members . . . are well known as old students of the University, passing afterwards into the Senior Department, and finally reaching the goal of graduation. On Professor Lyons' withdrawal to St. Mary's of the Lake, Chicago, then under the control of the Fathers of Holy Cross, the Society passed under other direction, and changed its original name of "Philomathean" to "Philopatrian." On Rev. Father Lemonnier's installation as an officer of the College, he conceived the idea of forming a Field Band, among members of the Junior Department. A number of Juniors were formed into a society, wore a red-and-blue Zouave uniform, and soon acquired great proficiency with their drums and other musical instruments. A dramatic element was next introduced, and on the restoration of Washington Hall to the purposes for which it was originally designed [1865, at the end of the Civil War], the St. Cecilians, as they were now called, were the first to appear on the stage. . . . Finally, within the last two years, the literary element was added, and the drums and Zouave Uniform dropped. The Society joined its old name of Philomathean with its new one of St. Cecilian, and returned to the protecting care of Prof. Lyons as President. Their meeting-room, No. 4, is the most stylish one in the house. They have weekly meetings, debates, essay, and moot courts. They appear on the stage on their patronal festival of St. Cecilia [November 22], and on other occasions during the year, choosing dramas of such a character as tends to combine instruction with amusement.[62]

It is noteworthy that music (the field band) is inextricably associated with the St. Cecilians.

While music had been from the university's earliest days a discipline recognized as independent and worthy of advanced study and training within the academy, theatre was from the first an extracurricular activity supported by societies run by faculty. Before today's drama and theatre courses, the university offered classes in elocution and oratory certainly by the 1860s through the work of Professors Lyons and Griffith. The production of plays, however, occurred from the very first years of the university, so that even by the 1850s the faculty-directed, student-acted societies that produced plays had formal constitutions that governed their operation. We know that students were fined for misbehavior coming to or from the study room and exhibition hall as well as for missing meetings, with even higher fines prescribed if a rehearsal was part of the meeting.[63] But A. A. Griffith's arrival in 1866 also underscored the importance of debate as pedagogically important, and both formal debating and persuasive speeches (sometimes labeled as "lectures") filled Washington Hall as often as musical and theatre events. The St. Aloysius Philodemic Literary Association began in 1851 as "essentially a debating society" and hosted debates by the 1860s on topics such as "Are Lawyers beneficial?"[64] Oratory, elocution, and debate, then, were as central to the exhibition hall and Notre Dame from the earliest years as drama and music, and the major societies served as umbrella organizations to promote them. Debate was always an important part of the entire declamatory, oratory, and elocution triad of education, and as early as the 1872–73 academic year, official student debates occurred at Notre Dame, sponsored by St. Edward's Society (sometimes known as St. Edward's Literary Association). The *Scholastic* described a debate in Washington Hall on compulsory edu-cation as "the finest literary treat of the year" attended by a "select and exceedingly well mannered audience."[65] The *Silver Jubilee* pointed out that the St. Cecilia Philomathean Association, "a debating, dramatic and musical association," also showed a strong early interest in debate and elocution, while even the theatre itself served a powerful pedagogical function: "The plays acted on the stage for the purpose of bringing out the elocutionary powers of its members are written especially for them, and are intended to increase the love of virtue and righteousness."[66] The university ideology of the time clearly saw debate, drama, and music as overlapping parts of an integrated approach to pedagogy and inquiry. By contrast in today's world university students who wish to explore music, drama, and debate often must find the appropriate departments or units where they can pursue their niche interests. A student today ordinarily can do only drama, only music, or only debate, while avoiding the other disciplines almost entirely. That was clearly not the thinking in the 1860s, a time before niche audiences when varied and complex exhibitions demanded students with equally varied and complex skills and training.

The sheer number of students involved in these regular exhibitions is significant. For the summer entertainment (in May 1871), for example, the band and orchestra offered a "noble band of vocalists, numbering about sixty, thoroughly drilled by Professor M. T. Corby," who himself sang beautifully and "with perfect facility."[67] The play was *The White Knight* by the Philomatheans with a cast of forty-two:

> The play itself was an excellent one. . . . If it was not fully appreciated on this evening, the fact was due to the lateness of the hour and the exhausting heat; not to any lack of interest in the play itself or to any deficiency in the rendering. . . . The entire scenery for the play was the finest beyond comparison that we have yet seen in Washington hall, and the audience, I am sure, felt indebted to Prof. Von Weller, to whose artistic taste and skill those beautiful scenes, which added so much to the play itself, are due.[68]

Father Lemonnier as director of studies had the general supervision of all public exhibitions and "deserves the highest praise," but Professor Lyons got a paragraph too as head of the St. Cecilians, and there was commentary regarding the disposition of the audience: "The students also who were unoccupied during the evening deserve commendation for their excellent behavior and their politeness in resigning their places to lady visitors and taking inferior accommodations themselves on the gallery."[69] A quick calculation reveals that the proportion of the entire student body actually involved in an exhibition such as this could be as high as 25 percent. One in four students thus took the stage routinely by the 1870s to the acclaim of the other three out of four students who watched from the house. This was indeed a close-knit communal event with a direct connection between performer and audience member. We do not know whether performers joined members of the audience to witness those many events of the evening in which they themselves were not directly participating, in the way that many recitals operate today. Having given "the French Address," for example, could the student in 1871 then join the audience to watch the rest of the evening, or was that student required to stay backstage (or go back to the green room or its equivalent in silent isolation) for the duration of the evening? Knowing that students would very much want to witness as much as possible, I suspect there was considerable movement between house and stage for these exhibitions that directly involved so many members of the student body.

Hall Too Small

No sooner had the university painted and completely fitted out the interior of Washington Hall in time for the Silver Jubilee year of 1868–69 than it became obvious the venue was too small. The two recreation halls so recently completed provided neither the performance nor recreational venues needed for a growing student body, and the university began in earnest to play the game of architectural "catch-up" throughout its long history (as have all successful American universities). Clearly at play was the nagging issue of "architectural lag," the notion that by the time a building opens it is often already obsolete or inadequate. And so it was with the first Washington Hall: just eight years after its opening, the university recognized the need for an expanded exhibition hall, as recorded by the Local Council when "the Subject of an addition to the Exhibition Hall, was brought up, but the question postponed till a bill of costs would be presented by the Carpenter."[70] Nothing happened for two years, however, when the Local Council again prioritized the need but also postponed action: "An addition to Washington Hall was spoken of. All agreed that it was necessary, but the building was postponed by reason of other Work more urgent."[71] Thus the need for a bigger Washington Hall was obvious long before the Great Fire of 1879. Needs had outgrown the space by 1873 when concurrently the *Scholastic* noted for Washington's Birthday that town and gown "flock to Washington Hall and fill it to overflowing."[72]

In late fall 1874 the *Scholastic* confirmed plans (never carried out) to add desperately needed dressing rooms and other spaces to the building: "The rumor has reached us that the upper part of Washington Hall is to be used as a recreation-room. We understand that at first it was intended to build small wings in the rear of the building, the upper stories of which were to be used as dressing-rooms and the lower as recreation-halls."[73] By commencement 1875, the Wednesday morning awarding of degrees occurred "in the unfinished church, it affording better accommodations than Washington Hall," a clear indication that the building could no longer fulfill one of its prime functions.[74]

Gender and Race

Lyons's *Silver Jubilee* tells us that the Thespian Society "has for its object the celebration of all our festivals by dramatic representations. It also aims to cultivate in the students of the University a taste for the classical drama, by presenting the plays of the most able writers, whenever they can be adapted without too great a change of plot, to male characters only."[75] The early official university attitude toward female theatrical roles was simply not to include them. In addition to the outright elimination of female roles, however, a convention existed of changing certain female roles into male characters of color, clearly reflecting the notion that it was more acceptable for a young white man at Notre Dame to portray an ethnic male than it was to portray a white woman. With regard to the 1870 Summer Entertainment (also called the late April exhibition), the *Scholastic* claimed that " 'Le Bourgeois Gentilhomme,' or 'The Upstart,' translated from Molière by Prof. A. J. Stace for the Philomatheans, and containing the largest cast of characters brought before an audience at Notre Dame,"[76] transformed the female roles into Dervishes, Turks, Terpsichoreans (dancers), and two "Culled Pussuns" (not in the original Molière, to be sure!) who "suddenly burst like two black clouds of personified ugliness upon our astonished gaze."[77] The ethnic performances won high praise and thus illustrate the endemic insensitivity in majority white culture to race at the time. This 1870 event seems to be the earliest record of blackface roles on the Washington Hall stage, the popularity of which eventually produced by the end of the nineteenth century full minstrel shows, which reached their peak of popularity in the 1920s.[78]

Changes to the Building

We cannot really know whether the *Scholastic* statement that "the side entrance to Washington Hall, from the Seniors' recreation ground, is a great accommodation" refers to a new addition in June 1871, even with the admonishment to the students that "the platform out side the door is not a good place from which to see the stage. 'Keep off the Platform!'"[79] (see fig. 3.5). A proper orchestra pit was indeed added, however, by the end of the 1870–71 academic year: "The change made in front of the stage, which gives spacious room both to the Orchestra and Band, is greatly to be commended. We believe it is due to the exertions of the Rev. Director of Studies, who frequently expressed his regret that the instrumental music had not, in our exhibitions, all the accommodations due its excellence."[80] One can only guess what changes this addition brought to the stage and the first rows of seating: to accommodate space for the orchestra, was the apron (or forestage) reduced, or were rows of seats eliminated, or a combination of both?

By early 1873 the Local Council formalized ticketing for events in the Exhibition Hall: "It was decided that tickets should be issued for the various Exhibitions & that 50 cts should be charged to all those not having a ticket to present. This is to do away with the noisy fellows who whistle & annoy the audience."[81] Ticketing clearly could help improve the quality of the audience, it was felt, and even perhaps control the number of audience members more readily than the "open-house" policy that must have been in effect previously.

The *Scholastic* reported, "All persons not receiving regular invitations to the Exhibition on Tuesday night next, will if they wish to attend, be required to pay an admission fee of 50 cts. for front seats, and 25 cts. for back seats and gallery. The students, of course, are not required to pay an admission fee."[82]

Deaths of Fathers Lemonnier and Gillespie

The fall of 1874 brought the unexpected deaths of both Fathers Lemonnier and Gillespie, who died two weeks apart and are buried beside each other. Lemonnier and Gillespie were Renaissance men, whose catholic interests (as well as Catholic ones as priests) at Notre Dame in the early years made them true giants of their age. The premature deaths of both especially affected the arts, although Professors Lyons and O'Mahony (and others) ably and quickly took up the slack. As with any functional bureaucracy, things moved forward. Lyons had come to Notre Dame as an orphan in 1848 and had been involved in exhibitions since the 1850s, so he was completely prepared and ready to take over from his fallen colleagues and mentors.

It is clear by the comments in the *Scholastic* on the St. Cecilians' first exhibition after the deaths of these two university patriarchs that the show had indeed gone on. Their exhibition included all-male versions of Molière's *The Miser* and *A Cure for Dumbness or Doctor Nolens* (a farce in one act), with the music especially receiving high praise.[83] The annual Christmas entertainment, the first Thespian exhibition after the two deaths, went on successfully in 1874.

Gillespie's death seemed also to have been the impetus for the creation of the Notre Dame Glee Club organized, along with vocal class and orchestra, by December 1874: "A glee club will be orga - nized to-morrow. Prof. Paul will be leader."[84] By January 1875 the newly named Gillespie Choral Union had "a number of fine glees, choruses, etc., in rehearsal."[85] The idea behind a glee club goes to the intellectual and pedagogical value of singing over elocution. Singing was thought especially good for the body and the soul. While today Notre Dame is understandably very proud to claim that its Glee Club has operated continuously since 1915 (although 1919 is a more accurate date), real and genuine efforts began in the fall semester of 1874 when Notre Dame certainly had a glee club performing in Washington Hall.

In the late winter and early spring of 1875, examples of continued vitality in the face of grief abound. In Washington Hall in February 1875, "last Saturday, the 13th inst., we were favored with a visit from Mi-na-gi-shig, the great chief . . . of the Otchipwe Indians . . . He was accompanied by three minor chiefs. . . . In the evening they gave an exhibition in Washington Hall, consisting of Indian war-dances, Indian games, etc."[86] This real Native American event was parodied soon after in the Washington Birthday exhibition in 1875 with a "Washington Hall . . . festooned with evergreens" serving as the setting for "the Grand Modoc War-Dance . . . a good take-off on the Indian war-dances of the week before." The president gave a few remarks, and it was clear that Professor Lyons had taken over the reins: "Too much praise cannot be given to Prof. J. A. Lyons, who had charge of the Exhibition."[87] And Professor O'Mahony received notice for his work on the Saint Patrick's Day exhibition in March: "Mr O'Mahony is entitled to the highest praise for his endeavors on the eve - ning" to bring actors on the stage for the first time.[88]

By the Summer Entertainment of 1875, the *Scholastic* commented on the ideal length of the varied and complex exhibitions. Two and a half hours was considered acceptable, although it was clear that many had gone on for a much longer time: "The Seventeenth Annual Summer Entertainment of the St. Cecilia Philomathean Society was the excitement Tuesday evening, June 8th." Persons of honor were Father Granger, Father Sorin, and Father Colovin: "When the curtain went down on the final tableau, Very Rev. Father Granger rose and gave the closing remarks in his kind, unostentatious way." The admonition was that "nothing is more wearisome than a long Exhibition."[89]

Pio Nono's Golden Episcopal Jubilee

Like the rest of the Roman Catholic world in 1877, Notre Dame celebrated Pope Pius IX's Golden Episcopal Jubilee, and Washington Hall played a prominent role, showcasing literary, musical, and dramatic exercises beginning Tuesday evening on June 5, 1877.[90] The *South Bend Herald* described Pio Nono as "the grandest man the century has produced," and the *South Bend Register* not only recorded the events of the day but also related much about Washington Hall itself. The *Register* of Wednesday eve, June 6, 1877, stated that the play of the evening, *Major John Andre,* was "an historical drama in five acts, recently written and prepared for the stage, by a Catholic priest, and played for the first time at Notre Dame, last evening."[91] The *South Bend Herald* reported, "The tableau at the end of the fifth act was positively grand, reflecting the highest credit on Prof. Lyons whose wonderful taste in arrangement and scenic effect made it such a success." The *Herald* also disclosed that the dressing rooms were beneath the stage in 1877: "On the stage and in the dressing rooms below were gathered the young gentlemen of the St. Cecilia society who with their able director Prof. Lyons, had charge of the entertainment." We also learn the exhibition was on Tuesday, the day

> best adapted for exhibitions at Notre Dame, as the Wednesday following, being recreation day gives the students opportunity for relaxation and rest. . . . Washington Hall was decked in beauty for the occasion. Wreaths and streamers of evergreen twined round the columns and hung in graceful curves from each of the four corners, meeting in the center in an immense floral sphere from which gaily floated the flags of all nations, a type of the universal Catholic church, which is broad as the earth and boundless as Time, all meeting as one to extend honor and homage to the spiri - tual ruler of the world.

The long and varied program included a great deal of music, declamations, and a farce, and ended with President Colovin's closing remarks "to one of the most interesting and best managed exhibitions ever held at the University."[92]

The *South Bend Daily Tribune,* Monday evening, June 4, 1877, in announcing the play for the next day certainly saw the effort as patriotic:

"Major Andre" is a play which introduces us to all the notables of revolutionary times, and is full of startling situations, soul-stirring words and patriotism of the kind in vogue before whisky rings and the like were known. Songs, declamations and music by the band and the orchestra will assist in serving to make the evening pass agreeably.[93]

The play's epilogue also made that connection with

one of the most momentous circumstances in American History. In this great action we see that the severest justice may be the greatest mercy as well as the greatest wisdom. Had Washington faltered in his stern duty American life Liberty and happiness would have been the sport of British misrule and the sufferings of unborn generations and the shame of a dishonored nation would have been the legacy left to us by the father of his country. We may pity Andre. He was young . . . but his sense of honor should never have allowed him to aid the traitor in bartering a generous people for filthy gold. May we learn this lesson both from the error of Andre and from the firmness of Washington to do our duty under all circumstances regardless of consequences.[94]

This huge event honoring Pio Nono in absentia very directly connected American Catholicism to American patriotism, and in so doing confirmed Father Sorin's philosophy of complete and unconflicted devotion to both church and country.

Telegraphy and Telephonics

The exhibitions produced in Washington Hall functioned as communal assembly in ways parallel and complementary to such events since the dawn of humanity around campfires. The nineteenth century, however, brought significant technological changes that forever changed the way we humans both access information and integrate ourselves into society. Morse's work in the 1840s brought telegraphy to the Notre Dame campus by the 1869–70 academic year: "Telegraphy will be taught at Notre Dame next session, and a telegraphic line to run between the College and St. Joseph's Novitiate across the lake, is already projected."[95] This localized installation prefigured a transformation of American life, one in which for the first time words moved at the speed of light instead of physically as inscriptions on media such as clay tablets, papyrus, or paper. There was clearly not yet any sort of telegraphic network that went beyond campus, but there soon would be, and this was the start of the electrical connection of Notre Dame to the larger world, one that prefigured the ultimate interconnectivity we take for granted today.[96] By fall 1873 the telegraph revolution had fully transformed Notre Dame. The *Scholastic* reported that the telegraph class was both fully equipped and "one of the most interesting Classes in the College," and that "we hope yet to connect our wire with the main line at South Bend before long." By the following fall semester, the university had hired "Mr. Ruddiman, teacher of Telegraphy," who achieved clear success by February 1875: "We paid a visit to the rooms of the telegraphers, the other day, and were pleased to see how well the students can manipulate the key, and read the sounder. Mr. Ruddiman is doing well with his class."[97] Telegraph day books from November and December 1875 included transmission fees to cities such as Chicago, Indianapolis, St. Louis, Cleveland, and New York.[98]

Not long after telegraphy took off in a big way at Notre Dame and indeed became an ordinary—as opposed to extraordinary— technology, the telephone was introduced, using the newly installed telegraph lines. The earliest telephonic event at Notre Dame seemed to have involved both speech and music, which then were accessed remotely, something new in the history of humanity. By spring 1878 the *Scholastic* reported the following technological milestone involving the transmission:

> On Thursday last a telephone was attached to the telegraph wires at Notre Dame connecting with South Bend. Conversation was freely carried on, and music played at Notre Dame was distinctly heard at South Bend. In the evening a concert was given in the telegraph-office and the music was listened to by a large audience of ladies and gentlemen.[99]

This remarkable experiment occurred at Notre Dame just two years after Bell invented the telephone.[100] Accessing music remotely in alternative venues thus became a reality for the first time in 1878 at Notre Dame; music created at one place could be accessed and enjoyed at another (although no one claimed the fidelity of reproduction to be of exceptional quality). The technological revolution was upon the country, and with Edison's invention of the phonograph and the creation of the Edison Phonograph Company in 1887, it was possible not only to access music remotely, but also to "store" it on devices that permitted its reproduction later and repeatedly (in effect to "time shift"). Human access to music had changed permanently. While the new telegraphy and telephonics seem not directly to have involved Washington Hall, the technological revolution of the late nineteenth century created a new model for communal assembly never before experienced, where instantaneous distance communication occurred and hitherto ephemeral information could be saved and accessed at will. To hear an orchestra play, throughout history, had required communal assembly at an appropriate venue that would house both audience and orchestra, and the unique event occurred only at a specific time. With telephonic transmissions and, ultimately, recording and playback devices such as the phonograph, an audience member of one could remotely experience an orchestra in complete privacy. With the coming of wire and then wireless transmission, access to our culture's formerly ephemeral arts could occur, for the first time, remotely and privately without having to assemble in a place like Washington Hall.

1878–1879: Just Another Year . . .

The academic year that ended with the Great Fire of April 1879 began just as so many academic years had before; until that fateful spring day when the university would be largely destroyed, things moved along much as they had for decades.[101] The production schedule for *The Hidden Gem* began at the fourth regular meeting of the St. Cecilia Philomathean Association on October 2 when the play "was read, and the parts were assigned to the members."[102] After only ten days of rehearsal, the play, performed on October 12, had "seven in number—scarcely enough—yet the acting of the young gentlemen showed that they benefited themselves greatly by the instruction of Prof. Lyons," called "the veteran manager of entertainment at Notre Dame." The *Scholastic* added, "Between the acts of the drama the University Band played. The music during the play was furnished by the Senior Orchestra."[103]

But exhibitions were also multifaceted variety shows, bordering on extravaganzas: "The hall itself was finely decorated; indeed we do not remember having ever seen so much taste displayed in the arrangement of the wreath, etc."[104] The actual program included the following: the first music (band) and second music (orchestra), the French address, the Greek address, the Latin address, the third music (orchestra), the address from the Junior Department, the German address, the address from the Senior Department, a song and chorus, an address from the Minim Department, the fourth music (orchestra), a prologue, the fifth music (band), the play with musical entr'actes between acts 1 and 2 by the band, a tableau, an epilogue (incorrectly labeled prologue in the *Scholastic*), closing remarks, and the last music (band). The twenty-one events of the evening rival even the best efforts of the eighteenth century, and all after only ten days of rehearsal. This form of entertainment was to celebrate an event, in this case Saint Edward's Day, in honor of the patron saint of the founder of the university, Father Edward Sorin. The *Scholastic* report of the evening said that the audience was engrossed and involved in nearly every event; indeed, they assumed very active roles in the proceedings. We know Washington Hall had recently acquired improved lighting for the stage, so there was a relatively high level of intensity,[105] but we do not know to what degree the audience area was (or could be) darkened during an event. We often credit the great actor and theatre manager Sir Henry Irving with popularizing the "dark house" during a performance in the early 1870s, so the whole idea was something of an innovation at the time.[106] Materials and methods of the period made controlling and regulating light sources problematic, and so there is a very long tradition in the theatre of the audience being as fully illuminated as the actors on the stage. The model of performance and entertainment on the Washington Hall stage in 1878, then, was probably closer to eighteenth-century traditions than to our own today. With a relatively "lit" house, there is inevitably more audience interaction.

So the St. Cecilians provided public entertainments for Saint Edward's Day in October and planned to do so again at the end of May. The Thespians prepared for Washington's Birthday with plans for commencement. The Philopatrians got ready for January 5, and the Columbians for Saint Patrick's Day in March. The Euglossians, although restricted to the use of their own study hall for performances, nevertheless received enthusiastic approval from their older peers, who questioned why the "Little Princes" of the campus did not perform in Washington Hall itself.

Thus the academic year 1878–79 was indeed a very good year up through the third week of April. Before then, there was no indication whatsoever that a total rethinking of buildings and functions would of necessity occur. On Tuesday night, April 22, 1879, everyone went peacefully to bed, not realizing, as is the case with all sudden and transformative historical events, that the next day the young university would be reduced to a mountain of ash, out of which a new Notre Dame would rise.

CHAPTER 4

REBUILDING AFTER THE GREAT FIRE, 1879–1882

The *New York Times* headline A UNIVERSITY DESTROYED described the circumstances and consequences of the Great Fire of April 23, 1879:

> The University of Notre Dame, two miles north of South Bend, Ind., was destroyed by fire today, with the Infirmary, Music Hall, Old Men's Home, Minum's play-house, and part of the contents of all. The origin of the fire is involved in doubt, but spontaneous combustion, caused by the rays of the sun on the pitch and gravel on the roof, is the generally-accepted theory. The fire was discovered soon after 10 o'clock, in the base of the dome which surmounted the University building, and vigorous steps were taken to check its headway. The dome burned like tinder, and soon the statue of the Virgin Mary, weighing a ton, and a gift of the Emperor Napoleon of France, fell, crashing through the roof and opening a passage to the interior for the now raging flames. By 12 o'clock the college and four adjoining buildings were a mass of ruins, and in the excitement that prevailed, much valuable property was sacrificed. The college and circulating libraries,

containing in all 25,000 volumes; the museum which cost $10,000; 17 pianos and other musical instruments were destroyed. This college boasted of the largest bell on the continent, the gift of the Brothers of the Sacred Heart, in Paris, France. President Corby estimates the loss at not less than $200,000, and states that the college will be rebuilt at the earliest possible date.

The insurance is as follows: Hartford, $15,000; Underwriters', $5,000; North British, $5,000; London and Liverpool and Globe, $5,000; German-American, $5,000; Imperial, Northern, Commercial Union, and Springfield, $5,000 each; Maine and North German, $3,000 each. The Rev. Father Sorin, Superior-General, started for Europe yesterday, but was recalled by a telegram at Montreal, and will return. The jewels in the dome, surrounding the Virgin Mary, were all destroyed. Their loss alone is estimated at $20,000. Owing to the distance from South Bend, no steam engines could be had until after 12 o'clock.[1]

After that fateful conflagration, construction commenced almost immediately on ultimately as many as seven buildings, including the Main Building (the Golden Dome), and over the ensuing months replacements for the buildings destroyed by the fire rose phoenix-like with a new architectural unity not present in earlier iterations of the university. The rebuilding of the Music Hall/Junior Recreation Hall, where band and orchestra rehearsals occurred and where students stored instruments and took lessons in numerous practice rooms, was a top priority. In addition to the "17 pianos and other musical instruments" mentioned above, additional priceless musical academic and creative output had disappeared:

Our musicians are grieved over the loss of a large number of manuscript Masses, cantatas and sacred hymns, the original compositions of a late director of our Musical Department, Prof. Max Girac, Mus. Doc., LL. D. It was the intention of this maestro's friends to have his works published in suitable form to hand down to posterity as a monument of the Professor's genius, but the fire destroyed in a few minutes those works, which were the fruits of a long and active life.[2]

Figure 4.1. A single stereopticon frame of the burned university soon after the Great Fire in April 1879. The gabled building on the right is the burned-out masonry Music Hall (Junior Recreation Hall), built in 1865. GNEG 11A/15, UNDA.

The Senior Recreation Hall, which contained Washington Hall, was sufficiently distant from the fire's fury and had survived (see figs. 4.1, 4.2, and 4.3).

The three-year period from the Great Fire of April 23, 1879, to the formal dedication of the new Academy of Music (which would become the "new" Washington Hall) on Saturday, June 17, 1882, thus saw the University of Notre Dame transformed into the physical

Figure 4.2. A close-up of fig. 4.1 showing the destroyed Music Hall. GNEG 11A/15, UNDA.

campus recognizable to this day. The Great Fire changed the university forever and perhaps provi - dentially improved it almost beyond description.

The quick rebuilding of a new Main Building—the "Golden Dome" that graces the campus today—over the late spring and summer of 1879 is legendary in the history of Notre Dame, but equally significant is the achievement of rapidly rebuilding the entire campus for reopening in the fall of 1879. The university began construction on the building we identify today as Washington Hall, as well as other ancillary buildings, almost as soon as it began rebuilding the Main Building. By fall 1879 construction on the north Music Hall wing of a new Academy of Music had begun, with the band and orchestra moving into this new space by May 1880, two full years before the south Exhibition Hall wing was dedicated and just a little over a year after the Great Fire. The urgency and need to rebuild the university transcended simply the massive Main Building, the center of campus, and actually included seven buildings under construction by fall 1879. While we all like to repeat and to cling to the notion that rebuilding happened very quickly—because indeed students forced to leave the university after April 23 returned to fresh, new living spaces in a new building, with the beginning of a slightly delayed fall term just four months later in September—it is well to remember that no new construction had actually been completed in

UNIVERSITÉ ᴅᴇ NOTRE·DAME.(IND.)

Figure 4.3. An engraving of the burned-out campus of Notre Dame, c. 1879, which shows how the prevailing wind from the southwest destroyed the Music Hall but skipped Washington Hall (lower right), out of range of both the direct firestorm and its radiant heat. "Donations from France for Rebuilding Main Bldg 1880 (Reconstruction de l'Université catholique de Notre-Dame du Lac)," UNDR 3/06, UNDA.

the fall of 1879. The Main Building would not get its dome until 1883, and while the Academy of Music (the "new" Washington Hall) would be partially occupied by spring 1880 and formally dedicated officially in June 1882, its exterior south tower was completed five years later in 1887. Although a great amount of reconstruction did in fact occur, much of it was incomplete and partial.

The Reverend Father Corby, president of the university, affirmed publicly his optimistic commitment to immediate rebuilding in the succinct Local Council Minutes' singular comment regarding the fire: "A petition was respectfully made to the Very Rev Father Provincial and his council to take [into] consideration the granting of extraordinary Expenses necessary to rebuild Notre Dame University destroyed by fire on the 23rd of April last the Amt asked is $58000.00."[3] Father Sorin reinforced the view he had expressed only a month earlier, when he had written Corby regarding his great fear of fire, that rebuilding with masonry construction and fire-retardant materials should occur, with other systems in place to reduce elements of chance and carelessness to help prevent a recurrence, such as centralized steam heating.[4] An even bigger factor, however, was the functional loss of the Junior Recreation Hall (the Music Hall), a structure that would absolutely have to be replaced as soon as possible. Thus the university gave serious consideration to constructing an entirely new building that would combine the functions of both the destroyed Music Hall and the surviving Washington Hall, the latter of which was already bursting at its seams when communal assembly occurred within its walls: it had been too small by 1871 and additions had been called for in 1873. A new building would also have the advantage of being designed literally from the ground up by the same architect in charge of the Main Building, the distinguished British-born Chicago architect Willoughby J. Edbrooke (see fig. 4.4), and thus the juxtaposition of buildings at the core of the campus could for the first time in Notre Dame's history take on a homogeneity of style deemed attractive and desirable both then and now.

The *Scholastic* confirmed in its report of the fire that Washington Hall had not only survived but also of necessity would become a dormitory for the second time in its history (the first time being the last year of the Civil War, 1864–65, when the auditorium contained eighty beds to accommodate the greatly increased enrollment). The *Scholastic* reported that "the Church, the Presbytery, Science [Phelan] Hall, the kitchen, the steam-house, and the printing office are left, as is also Washington Hall,"[5] and added that "the dormitories are located in Washington Hall, now known almost exclusively as the 'Hotel de Washington.'"[6] Indeed, Washington Hall had been forced into service as a dormitory the night of the fire, and not a month later the *Scholastic* reminisced: "On the night of the fire, the students camping in Washington Hall and on the campus beguiled the early hours of the night away by singing snatches of old familiar songs."[7] During the reconstruction period and well into the fall 1879 semester when students had returned, Washington Hall housed workmen and "mechanics . . . at work on the new buildings."[8]

But the times were serious; in its appeal for relief, the sober reaction reflected in *McGee's Illustrated Weekly* highlighted the very perilous threat posed to the future of the university:

Figure 4.4. Willoughby J. Edbrooke (1843–96), architect of the new Main Building (the Golden Dome), Academy of Music (Washington Hall), Science Hall (LaFortune), and Sorin Hall (the first freestanding dormitory). Edbrooke also served as architect for the U.S. Treasury in Washington, D.C., and the state capitol in Atlanta. Notre Dame Portraits Collection (hereafter GPOR) 4/8, UNDA.

The almost total destruction of the buildings of the University of Notre Dame is a real misfortune to the Catholics of the United States. Notre Dame is the centre of education and culture in the West, and anything that may impair its usefulness, even for a time, is much to be regretted. The insurance on the University buildings scarcely covered one-fourth of the loss, and the loss to the Church and the cause of education, by even a temporary cessation of the workings of the University, cannot be estimated, and can hardly be repaired. We are glad to learn that the office of the *Ave Maria* was unscathed. The *Ave Maria,* the *Scholastic* and their reverend editors have many friends. It is hoped that these friends will hasten to assist, by their contributions, in restoring the University of Notre Dame to it former usefulness. The mere mention of this institution, as the one dearest to the heart of Father Sorin, ought to cause a flood of contributions to flow westward.[9]

Also just a month after the fire, the *Scholastic* reported that the surviving Washington Hall would change functions, too, since a new music hall would be built to replace the destroyed one. With a bigger and better facility planned, the *Scholastic* reported that the building that had been the Senior Recreation Hall since 1862, with the (Washington) Exhibition Hall on its second and third floors, would be remodeled into a combined junior/senior gymnasium: "Our students of '79 and '80 will be pleased to learn that Washington Hall is to be used hereafter for a grand gymnasium—one story for the Juniors, the other for the Seniors. It will be fitted up with all modern gymnastic appliances."[10] This plan to convert Washington Hall into a gymnasium remained an option never acted upon right through the construction of the new Academy of Music—the building known today as Washington Hall—with the university ultimately deciding, however, to demolish rather than to move the old structure in favor of a new purpose-built gymnasium for the juniors and seniors to be built instead east of the new Academy of Music. While we theatre historians do not routinely deal with the counterfactual, had the first Washington Hall been moved and converted into Notre Dame's first freestanding gymnasium, the new Academy of Music would never have acquired the name.

Replacing the Music Hall

Two months after the Great Fire, the *Scholastic* remarked that "the rubbish has not yet been cleared away. . . . Where the Music Hall stood you can see the harps of the burned pianos, in regular order, on both sides of the building, as they stood in the rooms before the memorable 23d of April." With the heap of ashes still visible, the *Scholastic* published the first full description of the new building and commented on its secular juxtaposition to the sacred church in relation to the main building: "Very Rev. Father Sorin has drawn the plans for the Music Hall, a large building 200 by 80 feet, which will be a counterpart to the Church of Our Lady of the Sacred Heart. It will contain two music halls, the exhibition hall and two large recreation rooms."[11] The *Scholastic* related more detailed information three weeks later:

> The Music Hall.
>
> This is the name given to a large and most important building which will be immediately erected on the east and front of the College building—matching the Church on the west front. The main College as a centre will thus be flanked on the right and left by the Church and the Music Hall, the three buildings matching most perfectly and forming one picture, the garden fronting the College and lying between the Church and the Music Hall. The total frontage of these three buildings will be some 500 feet.
>
> The Music Hall will be 200 feet north and south, by 50 feet east and west, and three stories high. The first story will be divided into two playrooms, each 50 feet by 100. On the second floor will be the new Exhibition Hall, 150 feet long by 50 feet wide, and two stories in height. This will leave two music rooms, one on the second and one on the third floor, each 50 feet square. The play rooms, Exhibition Hall, and music rooms will thus all be larger and more convenient than before. Washington Hall will be devoted to gymnasiums. An observatory in front of the Music Hall will receive the fine telescope presented by the late Emperor of France.[12]

The programmatic plans for the building replicated and combined both the senior playroom space on the ground floor of Washington

Hall and the junior playroom space in the recently destroyed Music Hall. While the Senior Department (boys seventeen and older) in this new structure would gain no additional playroom space, the Junior Department (boys thirteen to sixteen) would gain one thousand square feet, a 25 percent increase.[13]

There seems to have been no thought in 1879 of carrying the name Washington Hall over to the new building because, of course, a building named Washington Hall had survived the fire and continued to be at the center of communal assembly at the university. Indeed, in February 1880 the *Scholastic* remarked that other colleges named buildings for generous donors and wondered whether the same plan might work with regard to the new building: "There is a great deal in a name, and if the trustees of Notre Dame could only get one with a few thousand dollars to tack onto, and christen, the projected Lecture and Exhibition Hall here, we think they would agree with us that there is something in a name."[14] We know funding the new building was a continuing problem, with the university holding a raffle in March in the rotunda for an "elegant gold watch . . . to aid in the erection of the new Music Hall."[15]

In August 1879 the *Scholastic* reported that Professor Arthur J. Stace had "surveyed the site for the new Music and Exhibition Hall, which will be a *pendant* to the Church of Our Lady of the Sacred Heart,"[16] a clear indication both that the plan was current and the project was a "go." The Local Council reported its formal acceptance in September: "The plan for the Music Hall and Exhibition Hall were examined and a new Budget for their erection requested. . . . At the same meeting it was decided to petition the Very Rev Father Provincial and his Council for an extraordinary grant of $ [blank] for the building of the Music Hall and Exhibition Hall."[17] The blank indicated that the amount of funding was unavailable or unknown or both, and it was clear just a week later that $15,000 would not be enough for the entire structure or that $15,000, while authorized, was simply not available at that time. In October 1879 the Provincial Council authorized building the Exhibition Hall foundation, with the rest having to wait until funds were on hand:

A meeting of the Provincial Council was held under the presidency of V. Rev. Father Provincial all the members being present.

The application of the Local council of Notre Dame for a grant of $15000.00 for the building of an Exhibition Hall was considered. After some deliberation it was decided to allow the foundations to be made and postpone the erection of the building until there are funds on hand to build it.[18]

Since all the funds needed were not on hand at this time, it made sense to build the structure in two parts, first completing the desperately needed Music Hall wing, whose function had been lost in the fire, and then moving on to the south Exhibition Hall wing, whose function could still be carried out by the existing and operational Washington Hall. Most importantly, spaces had to be found by September 1879 to replicate or reproduce the incinerated spaces; with the utter destruction of the Music/Junior Recreation Hall, it was clear its functions would have to be recreated immediately. The university had dedicated space to music practice, rehearsal, and performance since the 1854 additions and then built the Music Hall by 1866 to complement the Exhibition Hall, so it would now have to find a way to continue this vital program.

In the meantime the *Scholastic* reported that for fall 1879 the "musical faculty have for the present taken up quarters on the third floor of the College [the new Main Building].... The musicians will perhaps have to put up with some slight inconveniences in their temporary quarters, but let them wait with patience for a short time and the new Music Hall will more than repay them."[19] Until the new music hall could be built, then, the third floor of the new Main Building provided temporary space for a music faculty who had lost their freestanding Music Hall utterly in the fire; it was clearly not solely the music faculty putting up with inconvenience and who needed patience, but also their colleagues in other disciplines who had to endure the cacophony inherent to the practice of the discipline. The music faculty, the first occupants of this section of the third floor of the new Main Building, would stay there until May 1880—that is, throughout the entire 1879–80 academic year.

The *Scholastic* also emphasized that Father Corby had been true to his word, in spite of almost universal misgivings at the time. When he suspended classes following the fire on April 23, 1879, he promised that by September 1 things would be bigger than ever, and indeed they were,[20] but the necessity to convert Washington Hall once again into a dormitory, this time primarily for workmen rebuilding the campus, put the only theatre on campus in the same awkward position it had experienced in 1864–65: "We regret that we cannot have a public exhibition this year on our Very Rev. Father General's feast [Saint Edward's Day, October 13], because Washington Hall is now occupied by the mechanics who are at work on the new buildings." With seven buildings simultaneously under construction, there was a lot of activity:

> There are perhaps 300 men here and elsewhere working solely on these buildings. The masons and their help are but a small part of the force. Carpenters have every piece of timber waiting as soon as the walls are ready; stone dressers and workers in galvanized iron in Chicago have their carloads at the station here before the new story is reached; the factories in South Bend have the door and window frames on the ground looking up for their places on the walls; carloads of lime arrive every day; brick kilns in South Bend and Bertrand are connected with the building by a constant line of teams,—but these are not enough, and the cars are pressed into service to bring brick from more distant places. By the way, it is interesting to see how many varieties of brick are packed into the interior walls; not only the brick of the old College, but every color of new brick, from the pale Milwaukee to dark-red pressed brick, hand-made and machine-made. The face-brick is, however, of a uniform light cream color. To raise all this material, three double elevators worked by horse-power are in constant use, besides numerous pulleys worked by hand to lift iron pillars, joists, etc., to their place. Meanwhile slaters are getting out material to be ready to lay the roof at the earliest time possible. Nor are these all the workmen employed, but we have perhaps mentioned enough to let our readers know how it is that the work has advanced so rapidly, and why it is that the utmost confidence may be had that the building will be ready on the first Tuesday of September. Our readers will further bear in mind that it is the *College part* of the building that will be first completed—dormitories, study-hall, and class-rooms will be roofed, finished and dried long

before the front [administrative office] extension or other less needed parts will be completed. Have no fear but all things will be ready.[21]

Construction also moved quickly on the north Music Hall wing. By October 1879 "the first story of the northern part of the Music Hall is now well advanced, and it is expected that this end, or the Music Hall proper, will soon be ready for the roof. A portion of the foundations of the south section are laid, much of the material necessary is already on the ground, and from present appearances the workmen seem determined to have the entire building under roof this fall. Every one who has seen the plan of the building speaks of it in terms of the highest praise." The *Scholastic* continued:

> We had lately a peep at the elevation plan of the new Music Hall that is now in course of erection. When completed it will, in our judgment, be the most ornate building, at least exteriorly, on the premises. The style of architecture will be modern Gothic, slightly modified,—in keeping with the pointed Gothic of the Church, and the University Gothic of the College. The building will be 170 long, with a width varying from 40 to 80 ft. It will occupy a position southeast of the main building, designed to balance the Church on the southwest. When the Music Hall is completed, and the old garden replaced by a fine lawn, the appearance of the three buildings will be really imposing.[22]

Since Washington Hall was a dormitory for workmen during the fall semester of 1879, the university searched about for a space in the new Main Building in which to celebrate Saint Edward's Day and found quite unexpectedly that the spacious rotunda was a great venue, perhaps even superior to the exhibition hall: "Washington Hall—or as it has been known since the fire, 'Hotel de Washington'— was occupied by the workmen, who use it as a dormitory, and there was no other place in which an exhibition could be conveniently given; consequently the students had to limit themselves in their exercises." Father Sorin "was particularly glad to meet them in the rotunda, where he could hear and see all of them so well, and which he thought was an improvement upon the Exhibition Hall even for the purpose for which it was temporarily used." In spite of the rotunda's clear value as a performance venue, Sorin assured students that the new Music and Exhibition Hall would be completed by Easter of 1880.[23] The *Scholastic* added that the "rotunda and the corridors leading to it make a fine place for public exercises," in what seems to have been a completely unexpected and unanticipated turn of events.[24] Who would have known or guessed this would be the case? To this day, the rotunda is used for receptions and concerts and is a marvelous setting for many events.

The optimism related to the rapid rebuilding of the campus soon waned when the brick supply ran out. The *Scholastic* reported that by October 1879:

> The supply of white bricks having given out, work had to be suspended for a few days on the new Music Hall. We are scarcely sorry for this, however, as it gave the masons an opportunity to lay the [stone] foundations of the grand new Exhibition Hall. This last building promises to be one of the finest around Notre Dame, and we trust that the work on it will be pushed forward with such rapidity as to allow us to have an exhibition on Washington's Birthday [1880]. Work will be resumed on the Music Hall on Monday next, and we hope to see it ready to be occupied by the first of December.[25]

An adequate supply of face bricks and funding to purchase them would not be found until January 1880, when "several friends of President Corby have donated various sums of money to be used in purchasing brick for the completion of the Exhibition Hall. Consequently Mr. Cavanaugh, of the Bend, is busily engaged in hauling the fine cream-colored brick for which this manufactory is so famous."[26]

The building was being built on two foundations in two phases, with the construction of the rectangular north Music Hall wing preceding the multiangular south Exhibition Hall wing. By November 1879 slaters had installed permanent roofing over the north Music Hall wing: "The slating on the new Music Hall was nearly completed on Wednesday last. Although the work is not going on with extraordinary rapidity, it is probable that the building will be ready to be occupied in the course of a few weeks."[27] The Local Council confirmed the desire to finish the Music Hall too; in late November "it was also decided to finish the hard finish and moldings of the College Chapel before the scaffolds are removed and also to finish the Music Hall."[28]

Clearly, heating was always an important concern, and as winter approached in 1879 the *Scholastic* reported that the Music Hall would combine both steam and wood-stove heat: "The steam-fitters will soon begin operations on the new Music Hall. The lower story [ground floor], or Juniors' play-hall, will not be heated by steam, but by stoves. . . . The Juniors' play-hall is at last ready to be occupied."[29] The ground-floor recreational space was up and running by December 1879, even though the upstairs rooms and offices would not be available for music faculty and students until the following May: "The Juniors play hand-ball with such gusto that there is great danger of their knocking the north end out of their play-hall."[30]

The workmen apparently had stopped living in Washington Hall well before Christmas, since we know that by early December "the Columbians and Thespians gave a *soirée dansante* in Washington Hall, Saturday night."[31] Washington Hall had thus served as a dormitory for about seven months, from late April through late November 1879. The *Scholastic* continued with regard to the December exhibition: "Washington Hall was opened for college purposes on Tuesday evening. The sight of the well-remembered scenes, and of the old stage dear to so many generations of Thespians, Columbians, Cecilians and Philopatrians, evidently recalled to all present the most pleasant recollections of the good old times gone by." The Euglossians produced the first exhibition in Washington Hall since the fire and included a march by the cornet band, the string quartet, a performance of "The Pound of Flesh" (the fourth act of *The Merchant of Venice*), accompanied by assorted declamations and recitations, with closing remarks by the Very Reverend President Corby and concluding with the grand march by the band. Washington Hall was thus fully back in operation within eight months of the Great Fire of 1879 and had regained its central function as the premier performance venue on campus. The St. Cecilia Philomatheans followed fast on the heels of the Euglossians with a celebration of Founder's Day, postponed from October 13.[32] The minims appeared "on the boards of Washington Hall" for the first time, most likely because their own hall and playroom had not survived the fire.[33]

For Washington's Birthday and other events in the spring of 1880 "Washington Hall presented a very neat appearance," but there was great anticipation that "the new Music Hall when finished will be the handsomest building around Notre Dame," and Washington Hall was clearly not big enough to meet the university's needs, since "on the night of the Exhibition it was found necessary to bring in a large number of chairs from the class-rooms, study-halls, etc., for the accommodation of visitors."[34] Every effort was made, however, to maintain high production values, in spite of the anticipation of a new building. For Saint Patrick's Day, the Columbian Dramatic Club produced *The Corsican Brothers,* directed by Professor J. F. Edwards, who, the *Scholastic* said, "deserves special commendation for the excellent manner in which everything connected with the Entertainment for the celebration of St. Patrick's Day was presented—tableaux, sceneries, costumes, etc., were the richest and best we have ever seen at Notre Dame."[35] The Glee Club was also up and running at this time:

> Our friends of the "Glee Club," will, we trust, be heard from at the coming Exhibition. The few pieces which they have already sung in public have established their reputation, and given everyone a desire to hear them again. Vocal music has not been a drug in the market at Notre Dame for some years past, and the "Glee Club" is principally relied on to supply a long-felt want.[36]

The band and orchestra moved out of their temporary quarters in the Main Building and into the Music Hall in spring 1880: "The Band and Orchestra will in future have their rehearsals in the new Music Hall. The rooms on the upper floor of the College [Main Building] will probably do service as a museum."[37] This got the noise out of the Main Building and began a 110-year tradition of the band and orchestra in this space, which they occupied until 1990.

For the 1880 June commencement, the first with the new Main Building, the university continued to use Washington Hall as it had since 1862. For the Wednesday morning awarding of degrees, "Washington Hall was completely filled, and many were forced to abandon the idea of entering it at all."[38] In its history of the class of 1884, the *Class Annual* revealed that the original 1862 building was "long in the tooth" by the end of the 1879–80 academic year:

In '80 Notre Dame had hardly recovered from the effects of the fire which happened the year previous. There were then few of the advantages possessed by the students of to-day. No spacious gymnasium with its splendid collection of physical appliances invited the student, at recreation, to step in, and send the sluggish blood coursing through his veins. But only old Washington Hall, with its low and cob-webbed ceilings, and that never-to-be-forgotten old iron stove, around which during the winter months all would crowd, eager to gain the warmth of kindly fires. Indeed, this hugging of the old iron stove became such a habit with the majority of boys that even though the stove were as cold as a northern iceberg, you would find as large a crowd gathered around, pushing and jostling each other, in their eagerness to be near it. Every old student will remember this stove and acknowledge its magnetic influence. A tribute to thy memory old Washington Hall, long since torn down, and in thy place substituted a more modern structure; and it seems to us that associated as thou were with the recollections of many close friendships formed beneath thy roof, many happy hours spent in conversation and pastimes within thy walls, many pleasant walks upon thy old worn-out floors, thou shalt live forever cherished in the memories of those whose lot it was to be united with thine. No grand Music Hall, with its elegant interior and its excellent stage, was ready to harken to the strains of our instrumental music, nor view thy dramas then enacted. No cozy reading rooms nor billiard halls awaited the pleasures of whimsical minds. . . . It [our class] watched their building—the building of the Academy of Music and the Gymnasium—and had the honor of opening and of giving the first exercises in these different institutions.[39]

Members of the class of 1884 had entered the university in the fall of 1880 and experienced their first year with the original Washington

Hall. By the end of their second year, the new building had been dedicated and the original Washington Hall had been demolished.

For the functional, newly completed north Music Hall wing, Father Sorin urged the hiring "of a competent Music Teacher for vocal and Instrumental Music and suggested that advertisements be inserted in the papers for one."[40] A piano had to be purchased, too, since all of them had burned in the Great Fire, along with "a Potatoe Digger, and Extension Ladders."[41]

By fall 1880 the north Music Hall wing had been essentially completed as designed and was occupied and in use, but construction on the south wing stopped as the Local Council decided "to build the walls of the Exhibition Hall as high as the water table and roof it for the Juniors Play Room,"[42] a configuration that must have created an extraordinary looking building (see fig. 4.5). To get below the frost line in northern Indiana, the foundation footings must go down at least forty-two inches, so the dirt-floor basement circumscribed by the foundation would have been approximately four feet below grade. (Today, the crawl space under the ground floor of Washington Hall varies from twenty-two to fifty-five inches.) The brick cap at the "water table" was approximately three feet above grade which would have made the indoor ceiling of the roofed-over south wing no less than seven feet high around its perimeter. While no pictures or drawings or descriptions have come to light of this phase of the building's construction, it is likely that the roof would have been pitched to defend itself against the heavy lake-effect snowfall of the area. If the temporary roof-over had the same pitch as the newly completed Music Hall (as the architect's rendering in fig. 4.5 indicates), a huge indoor recreational space of over 5,600 square feet would have been created. The Music Hall destroyed in the fire had provided 4,000 square feet of first-floor recreational space, and the still existing Washington Hall contained 5,000 square feet of recreational space on its ground floor beneath the stage and auditorium. With the new north Music Hall wing having already allocated its ground floor to recreation (about 2,500 square feet), by the winter of 1880–81 students had not merely regained the recreational space lost in the fire, they had vastly increased it: the university provided just over 13,000 square feet of recreational space in the new building and in the existing Washing-

Figure 4.5. Architect Christopher K. Dennis's rendering of Washington Hall, winter 1880–81, with the north Music Hall wing completed and occupied by the Music Department, but with the south Exhibition Hall wing constructed above grade to the "water table" and roofed over to create a large, indoor, dirt-floor recreation area.

ton Hall, a 40 percent increase over prefire numbers. This roof-over also means that the building we know as Washington Hall today was in a very real sense "open" during the winter of 1880–81 as a large dirt-floor playroom or gymnasium two years before the dedication of the Exhibition Hall in June 1882. But the roof-over was temporary; by February 1881, as the end of winter was at last within sight, it was time to complete the Exhibition Hall with haste and determination. The Local Council generated "proposals for Contracts of Mason and Carpenter work for the erection of the exhibition Hall . . . as soon as possible."[43]

The construction of the new exhibition hall, even though moving more slowly than the administration had intended, would soon make the old Washington Hall obsolete. With indoor recreation spaces always in great demand, a freestanding gymnasium was on the short list of buildings needed, even though the new Academy of Music incorporated recreation spaces on the ground floor of both its wings. Since the ground floor of the Washington Exhibition Hall had always been recreation space, the logic existed to convert the building entirely into a gymnasium, which the *Scholastic* reported in June 1881: "Next year Washington Hall will be converted into an armory and a gymnasium."[44] Having missed the 1880 opening date, the plan was now for an 1881 completion date, which might explain why "1881" was inscribed on the east and west faces of the tower.

In June 1881 an accident occurred during the construction of the new south Exhibition Hall wing. The *Scholastic* reported that "one of the masons engaged on the addition to the Academy of Music fell while at work on the walls, Saturday last, and broke his leg. Rev. Dr. Neyron set the broken limb."[45] Although this accident resulted in a treatable injury rather than a fatality, it may possibly be the source of the unsubstantiated assertion that a steeplejack's fall in the 1880s related in some way to the appearance of the ghost of Washington Hall in 1920–21. With the new south Exhibition Hall wing still under construction, the first Washington Hall continued in use as it had always been. The *Scholastic* reported: "The entertainment given in Washington Hall, last Saturday evening [June 11], by the St. Cecilia Philopatrian Association was a success in every sense of the word. At seven o'clock, the Hall was well filled. Soon the officers of the University made their appearance, when the Band struck up a lively air." The report added that Mrs. Rea of Chicago sang beautifully and had an encore, and *Major John Andre* was "a fine drama, and was greatly enhanced by the almost perfect manner in which it was rendered by the young gentlemen of the Cecilia Association." Apparently, the evening was so overscheduled that the afterpiece was dropped: "Time would not permit the playing of the 'Virginia Mummy.'"[46] There was additionally the customary praise for the director: "As usual, the Exhibition was under the supervision of Prof. J. A. Lyons, whose well-known ability in conducting entertainments is too patent to need notice from us."[47]

Thirteen months after the music faculty had moved into the north music hall wing, the interior received its final plaster finish: "Material was allowed, the plastering of the Music [H]all finished."[48]

With the south Exhibition Hall wing not yet completed, the 1881 commencement exercises relied heavily on the newly discovered use of the impressive rotunda within the new Main Building, beginning with the assembly "in the Rotunda of the University," but ending with "the Entertainment in Washington Hall, the conferring of degrees, distribution of premiums, etc.," the last year the first Washington Hall would host these events.[49] The play was *William Tell,* preceded by overtures by both the university cornet band and the university orchestra. From fall 1879 onward, the rotunda quickly and unexpectedly became a new venue for communal assembly. When the minims celebrated the thirty-ninth anniversary of the Very Reverend Father General Sorin's first mass at Notre Dame in November 1881 in their newly constructed St. Edward's Hall, the exhibition was so exceptional that the *Scholastic* recommended future efforts be "either in the Rotunda or in Washington Hall," the two current more appropriate venues.[50] The new rotunda in the Main Building rivaled the old Washington Hall as a performance venue.

As the university moved into the 1881–82 academic year, there remained one last series of delays in August. The *Scholastic* said, "Work is, owing to the scarcity of workmen, for the time being suspended on the Academy of Music," even though clearly materials had been purchased: "What with bricks and lumber, the Juniors' campus has the appearance of a vast brick and lumber yard."[51] By mid-September, however, "masons, carpenters and plasterers are busy finishing up the printing-office and Music Hall."[52]

In stark contrast to the near silence surrounding the Lincoln assassination in April 1865, the university publicly memorialized President James A. Garfield after his death on September 19, 1881; he had been shot and mortally wounded on July 2 by Charles J. Guiteau. In this its last year of operation, the first Washington Hall hosted a memorial honoring the slain president. The *Scholastic* lamented:

At Notre Dame the services were solemn and impressive. The College and Washington Hall were hung in mourning, and at 2 o'clock p.m. the Faculty and several hundred students assembled in Washington Hall to attend the memorial services in honor of the lamented dead, and we question if in any part of the country a service was held in which the assemblage was more deeply impressed than at Notre Dame. The deep silence among the students, and the quiet and subdued manner in which all spoke, every action was indicative of a feeling far beyond the common, and to everyone it was an apparent fact that, in loyalty to country, in love and obedience to her laws, and in deep and filial respect for her rulers, Notre Dame has no superior in the land.[53]

Quoting from the *South Bend Tribune,* the *Scholastic* continued:

This forenoon many funeral decorations were added to those previously displayed at Notre Dame. Tasteful symbols of mourning for the departed President were shown on the University building, the Church of the Sacred Heart, the Music Hall, and, in fact, on all the buildings about the University grounds. At 2 o'clock this afternoon, a memorial service in honor of the dead Chief Magistrate was held, and was attended by all the Brotherhood, the Faculty, and the several hundred students gathered there from nearly every state and territory in the Union, and from foreign countries. Indeed, it is doubtful if a service was held to-day in this State, in which every part of our broad country was represented as it was at Notre Dame, or where the participants were more profoundly impressed with the loss which the nation has sustained. The fact that Garfield was once a college student, a college professor, and a college president bound him to the young men of this University by the closer tie of college brotherhood. The memorial services consisted of a dirge by the Notre Dame University Cornet Band and addresses by Rev. T. E. Walsh, President of the University, and Rev. D. E. Hudson, Editor of *The Ave Maria.* Both gentlemen spoke most feelingly and paid the highest tribute to Garfield's manhood and statesmanship. Addresses were also made by several of the students. Minute-guns were fired, and the great bell of Notre Dame, the largest in the United States, tolled a *requiem* for the statesman resting in peace in the cemetery by the lake.[54]

After the campuswide memorial for President Garfield, the first full-scale exhibition in Washington Hall in the fall of 1881 was

Founder's Day. The play, *The Expiation,* "as rendered by the members of the Euglossian Association, was a decided success, and the members, individually, are to be congratulated for the earnest and able manner in which each one performed his part. We have never witnessed, at Notre Dame, a more decided success than was the play, as rendered by the Euglossians, on Wednesday [October 12, 1881] evening last."[55] The *Scholastic* described the varied program of "The Thirty-eighth Annual Celebration of the Feast of St. Edward, Patronal Festival of Very Rev. E. Sorin, C.S.C., Superior-General of the Order of the Holy Cross, and Founder of Notre Dame University," as including a "Musical and Dramatic Entertainment" incorporating an opening march by the Notre Dame University cornet band, a Greek address, a Latin address, a German address, a French address, a declamation, an address from the minim department, an address from the junior department, an address from the senior department, an overture, the play *The Expiation,* with thirteen major roles (with a tableau and epilogue), closing remarks, and the "March for retiring."[56] There is certainly no indication in this last year of use of the first Washington Hall that anyone has decided to cut back on activity.

Electrification

Also in the fall of 1881, electrification experiments under the direction of Father John Zahm brought excitement to the campus. The reaction to an early electrical demonstration in Phelan Science Hall was typical of human responses to the new technology: "The light is so intense as to be almost blinding, and gives to kerosene and gas-light a dark and murky appearance in comparison. . . . [It is] a dazzling white light, resembling that of a miniature sun."[57] Father Zahm, who housed a steam-engine generator in the printing office a hundred feet away from Phelan Hall, clearly planned to move beyond experimentation to practical illumination as soon as it was feasible to do so in both the new Main Building and the Academy of Music.[58] He brought electric lighting initially to the Main Building in November 1881, where, for the annual celebration of the

Festival of St. Cecilia, the rotunda was "brilliantly illuminated by the electric light."[59]

By November 1881 the *Scholastic* praised the nearly finished new structure: "The new Music Hall is fast approaching completion. Workmen are busily engaged in finishing the interior. When finished it will be the handsomest and most complete building of the kind in this part of the country. A full description of the building and its appointments will be given in a future number."[60] Word had reached Denver regarding the new building at Notre Dame. In anticipation of the theatre opening in the Academy of Music, Alex Comparet lobbied Father Sorin for a job as a scene painter and dropped a lot of names in the process, all perhaps with the ulterior motive of getting home:

Rev Sir.

Mr. Edbrooke has employed me to do the scenic work in the Tabor Opera House here, and having nothing more for me to do; I would like to know whether or not I could get the scene painting to do in the New Music hall at Notre Dame. I have got letters of recommendation from Mr Edbrooke and Mr Bouvier. I feel certain of giving satisfaction if employed and I will work at a very reasonable price. I have been sketching and painting mountain scenery here in Colorado for two years past and I have a great many pictures and sketches which I wish to bring back with me, and which I can use in scene painting. If you have not already given the contract to other parties, I would like to have a chance to do the work, If you will send me a pass, ticket or the fare from here to South Bend, which is $32.00 I will come immediately. I refer you to Mr. J. F. Studebaker or Mr A. Coquillard. I am not able at present to raise money to get home on and that is why I asked you for the fare. If I don't get this work to do, I will pay you when I get home, and if I do get to work I can pay you.[61]

The job went to Jacob Ackermann, who, with Brother Frederick, built and painted scenery for the new building over the next fifteen years.[62]

By December 1881, in anticipation of the opening of the new building, the *Scholastic* published a history of the St. Cecilia Philomatheans that is one of the last contemporary commentaries on the old Washington Hall:

> Cast your eyes about you and behold this once handsome hall now in its decrepitude, and soon to be replaced by one more fitting and commodius. Observe these boards on which I now tread, worn by the feet of generation after generation of Cecilians, Philopatrians, Thespians, Columbians. Yet, when Washington Hall was new—when the first burst of its splendor flattered the blushing East, the St. Cecilia Philomathean Association was already hallowed by age—already had her children, graduate at their *Alma Mater,* gone forth into the busy haunts of men, the marts of trade, the courts of law and equity, and the tented field of patriotism. In those days their audiences assembled beneath the shade of the locust trees that then surrounded Notre Dame, and sat entranced at the mellifluous accents that made a temporary elysium of their surroundings. Three colleges have in succession appeared on the spot where now stands Notre Dame, and each of the three has witnessed the triumphs of the St. Cecilia Philomathean Association. . . .
>
> Washington Hall is soon to go; but the St. Cecilia Philomathean Association has not passed away. Her flag still waves from the proud pinnacles of our new palatial home, and when the new exhibition hall is finished and dedicated, her children will burst with renewed enthusiasm upon the astonished gaze of the audience there assembled.[63]

But as early as January 1882 there was concern about the shortening human attention span:

> We have had quite a number of very successful entertainments during the first session [semester], and not by any means the least of the many excellences which commended them to favorable notice was the fact that they were not protracted to unreasonable length. Long exhibitions, however excellent the programme, are as much out of date as long sermons or long editorials. Something short, pointed, and snappy is what most men want nowadays;

and few care for more amusement at one instalment than can be crowded into a two hours' programme.[64]

Indeed, finishing the Exhibition Hall took precedence over a wing on the Main Building, so important was its function to the overall functioning of the university: "It was decided to build but one wing of the College [this] year, and to finish the Exhibition Hall."[65] Competing needs required prioritization.

The Thespians produced their last exhibition in the old Washington Hall in February 1882:

> The Thespians bade their last farewell to Washington Hall on the evening of the 20th ult. So many generations of students have "trod the boards" and "faced the foot-lights" in the old hall, that few will see its day of glory eclipsed without a feeling of regret. Its memories are of a quarter of a century. Its scenes from the brush of various artists—Lachassaigne the melancholy, Louis Gosselin the sanguine, Von Weller the inimitable, not to speak of Prof. Ackermann and others still present amongst us, are souvenirs of the old college. These scenes will hardly bear transposition to a new stage. Each has its little history, and the best among them were painted from designs selected by the lamented Father Lemonnier, whose artistic and dramatic taste was one of his prominent characteristics. He would even wield the artistic pencil himself, when the work was to be hastened on, and some of his handiwork will perish with the old scenes.[66]

Change was in the air, and even the scenery painted by Father Lemonnier very likely would not make the transition to the new venue with the revered old building, which was to be "removed and converted into a gymnasium."[67] Nevertheless, the Columbian Literary and Debating Society celebrated the Annunciation (March 25), their founding day, in a reunion in Washington Hall, and the university honored Gregori there, even though by the end of April the *Scholastic* reported that "work on the new Music Hall is progressing rapidly. If the weather continues favorable it will soon be completed."[68]

The first Washington Hall continued to be used right up until the dedication of the new venue, such as the late April 1882 Mignon

Club reunion and reception,[69] as expectations simultaneously ran high for the future: "The new Music Hall, which is to be one of the finest in the State, will be completed about the 12th of June, when it will be dedicated with the production of a Shakspearian play, by Prof. Lyons. The work of painting the scenery begins next week. The hall, with all modern improvements and conveniences, will have a seating capacity of 1,200." The new Exhibition Hall would easily accommodate the entire student body of 437 students and the faculty of 38, with room to spare for townspersons and other guests.[70]

Plans to move and convert Washington Hall to another use continued well into May 1882, when the Local Council "decided to move the old Exhibition Hall to a line between the Juniors and Seniors Play Grounds for a Gymnasium."[71] Clearly, the days of Washington Hall as an exhibition hall were numbered as the university put the finishing touches on the new venue. The last official meeting held in Washington Hall seems to have been the "32d regular meeting of the St. Cecilia Philomathean Association" on May 21, 1882.[72] A week later "the Philopatrians had the distinction of giving the last entertainment in old Washington Hall," followed by demolition within days: "The work of demolishing the Old Exhibition Hall was begun on Tuesday. It was found impracticable to remove it. A new brick building 150 by 60 feet will be erected for a gymnasium."[73] Washington Hall was demolished during the twelve-day period from the end of May to June 3, 1882, just over twenty years after it went up.[74] After eighteen years, there was no longer a Washington Hall at Notre Dame, and there would not be one until the following September when the Exhibition Hall within the grand new Academy of Music acquired the name unofficially.

CHAPTER 5

THE "NEW" WASHINGTON HALL, 1882–1895

By June 3, 1882, the clapboard Senior Recreation Hall built in 1862 and dedicated as Washington Hall in 1864 had been demolished, as the university prepared to open its grand new Edbrooke-designed Academy of Music, a jewel in the crown of the almost entirely new campus erected since the Great Fire of 1879. Bigger and better in every way, the new building combined all the functions of the first Washington Hall and the adjacent Music Hall to form the first performing arts center on the campus of Notre Dame. This chapter is the story of the dedication and completion of this new structure from 1882 to 1895, a building that within three months of opening had unofficially taken on the name Washington Hall.

The formal dedication of the Academy of Music at Notre Dame over commencement week, June 17–22, 1882, culminated a thirty-year tradition that began with the construction by 1854 of the first exhibition hall within the enlarged Main Building I. Although the new Academy of Music opened officially at the end of the 1881–82 academic year, the university did not complete the building's exterior architecture and interior aesthetics until 1895 (with the north portico and iron stairs by 1885, the south tower by 1887, and the south entrance stone steps directly replacing the "temporary" wooden steps

Figure 5.1. Architect Christopher K. Dennis's rendering of the exterior of Washington Hall c. 1885 from the southwest, with the "temporary" tower (replaced in 1887) and wooden stairs (replaced by stone in 1889).

by 1889), so it probably looked very much like figure 5.1. Inside, the stage's initial oil lamps gave way to gas footlights in 1884 and ultimately to electric lamps in 1894, while Professor Jacob Ackermann and Brother Frederick provided a highly decorated interior, both upstage and downstage of the proscenium arch. Although Ackermann's upstage act curtain and wings and drops briefly survived this new setting, his downstage house decoration did not, and the grand interior of Gregori and Rusca in 1894 filled the theatre interior until Father Harvey's modernization in 1956. The new Academy of Music combined exhibition, music, and recreational needs for the first time into a single structure; at its dedication in 1882 the building had a value of about 75 percent of the church, 19 percent of the Main Building, or 10 percent of the entire university.[1] In terms of functionality, Washington Hall in 1882 supported what in 2009 required all of the DeBartolo Center for the Performing Arts, Crowley Hall, the Ricci Band Rehearsal Hall, and major elements of the Joyce Center and LaFortune Student Center.

Dedication

The campus excitedly prepared for the commencement week 1882 dedication of the new Academy of Music. The plan for the Saturday through Thursday commencement week encompassed a multitude of events, including the St. Cecilians' productions of *The Outcast* and *The Office Seekers* on Saturday (June 17), both as a diversion from examinations and because so many guests had already arrived: "The St. Cecilians had the first rehearsal in the new Hall last Saturday evening." In addition, the distinguished journalist Donn Piatt was scheduled to deliver the first lecture "in the new Hall," the first time the structure was described as such.[2] *Oedipus* by the Hellenists was on for Tuesday evening (June 20) after exams had concluded.[3] The Thespian Society would present *Pizarro* on Wednesday evening (June 21) after a day of events for alumni in the new hall and a speech by Colonel Piatt. The Thursday (June 22) closing exercises would include, all in the new hall, music, orations, distributions of premiums, awarding of class honors and diplomas, and conferring of degrees.[4]

Students rehearsed *Oedipus Rex* (in Greek) in the new Exhibition Hall of the Academy of Music for a Tuesday evening (June 20) performance, one of many events that would be produced:

The Rev. Professor of Greek is sparing no pains to make the occasion a grand success, and to put before the audience as faithful a representation as possible of the ancient stage. Special scenery and costumes have been designed by Prof. Gregori; the choruses are receiving the most careful attention from the directors of the musical department. . . . The "Oedipus Tyrannus" has, we believe, never yet been produced west of the Alleghanies [sic], and the Notre Dame students are determined to produce it creditably, if hard work can ensure their doing so.[5]

Indeed, work on the costumes for the production was already at full tilt: "The costumes for the Greek play, on which Prof. Gregori and the Rev. Professor of Greek have been so hard at work for some weeks past, are gorgeous."[6] The Thespians were also preparing *Pizarro* for the day after the Hellenists' *Oedipus*: "The interesting play of *Pizarro*, which the Thespians will bring out on Wednesday evening [June 21], has been slightly remodelled to suit the occasion. As the society is composed of members of the Senior Collegiate department, a very creditable performance may be expected."[7] Additionally, the innovative electrical illumination of the new structure included a total of six lamps: "So far, three lamps have been put up to light the interior of the Academy of Music, one over the main entrance, one over the west side entrance and one suspended from the College portico."[8]

The program for this the twenty-fourth annual "Summer Exercises of the St. Cecilia Philomathean Society" in conjunction with the opening of the new hall included multiple music and choral events, addresses in English and French, a recitation, and the play, *The Outcast* (translated from the French by President Walsh), with a cast of fifteen plus the orchestra and a duet. The afterpiece (second play) was *The Office-Seekers,* a farce in one act, with a cast of thirteen accompanied by the cornet band. The *South Bend Times* praised the new building in June 1882, and the St. Cecilians got credit for being the first:

Opening of New Music Hall at
Notre Dame

The new music hall at Notre Dame university, was formally opened on Saturday evening [June 17] by the St. Cecilian Philomathean society. The entertainment commenced with music by the Notre

Dame cornet band. Next was a well rendered song and chorus by several musical members of the society. Mr. G. Rhodius then read an original poem for the occasion, speaking of the good times the students had had in the old Washington Hall, and commending the new hall to the students of the institution, present and future. Mr. J.V. O'Donnell delivered a French address, and the first part of the programme closed with music by the university orchestra. The second part consisted of a three-act drama, "The Outcast," and a farce, "The Office Seekers." Both pieces were played in the good style proverbial of the Philomatheans, and were received with pleasure by the audience.

The new hall is a most elegant structure, and admirably adapted for presenting entertainments. The stage is large, roomy, and fitted up with fine scenery. The building is octagonal in shape, and large windows on the east and west sides give ample light for day exhibitions. It is fitted up with electric lights for evening, and will be tastefully ornamented. The gallery is capable of seating 500 persons, and is reserved for the use of the students. The seats in the body of the hall are arranged in raised tiers in the shape of a horseshoe, and slope down from the rear to the stage. About 700 people can be seated here. Altogether the new hall is one of the finest in the state.[9]

The same newspaper credited *Oedipus* with the official opening the following Tuesday, June 20, 1882:

"ŒDIPUS TYRANNUS"

A Greek Play at Notre Dame, Opening of the New Hall

The new college hall at Notre Dame was opened by the production of Œdipus Tyrannus by the Hellenists of Notre Dame, complimentary to Right Rev. Joseph Dwenger, Bishop of Ft. Wayne, right Rev. Francis S. Chantard, Bishop of Vincennes, right Rev. John A. Watterson, Bishop of Columbus, O. A large and intellectual audience was present. Distinguished people from all sections of the country, both clergy and laity, greeted the Hellenists, and the applause that was given testified the appreciation of the audience.

This is the first time that a Greek play ever was produced west of the Alleghanys [*sic*]. Its success is owing to the indefatigable efforts of Rev. Fr. Stoffel, professor of Greek at the university. The costumes were designed by Signor Luigi Gregori, the renowned artist. The music was composed expressly for the occasion by Mr. Nobles, professor of music at Notre Dame. The professors were ably seconded by the Hellenists in their efforts to make the drama a success. . . .

The play commenced at eight o'clock and occupied an hour and a half in its presentation. During this time not one word of English was spoken (the play being in Greek.) but the audience was so interested that not the least impatience or fatigue was shown.

Mr. A. Zahm's personation of Œdipus was perfect; his acting is beyond praise. W. Bailey as Creon was a grand success. W. O'Connor's rendition of Jocasta, the queen, was immense. The other parts were ably sustained by T. F. Clarke, W. Cleary, J. Walsh, N. Ewing and W. Arnold. The chorus was grand, M. T. Burns, chorentes. The singing was the finest ever heard at Notre Dame, especially duets by Masters, Florman and Shaeffer. The play was a success in every particular. Without a doubt this is the grandest commencement ever seen at the university. Fr. Stoffel is well known in the west as a Greek scholar of the first order. His untiring efforts are rewarded by success, and he will ever be remembered by the students and friends of Notre Dame as a scholar, a gentleman, a good priest and true friend.[10]

The Financial Journal confirms late June 1882 carpenter costs of over three thousand dollars related to the Exhibition Hall, as well as just over six hundred dollars for chairs undoubtedly used at this first commencement held in the new building.[11]

While the building was generally praiseworthy, clearly all the wrinkles had not yet been ironed out. The *Scholastic* commented, "There was just a *leetle* too much tramping in the corridors and stairways of the Exhibition Hall, during the oration. The absence of matting in aisles, etc., was a great oversight. It must be said, however, that the general order during Commencement week was never better." The efforts to bring electricity to the building proved positive: "The electric light turned out to be a great success, thanks to the energetic efforts of Rev. Father Zahm. The College buildings and grounds were brilliantly illuminated every evening, from Saturday to Thursday." Overall praise such as the following was typical, as the *Scholastic* noted in this *South Bend Tribune* reprint, saying, "The new Music Hall at Notre Dame was formally opened with a literary and dramatic entertainment by the St. Cecilian Association. It has all the modern improvements, with a seating capacity of 1,200, and its exterior is a fine piece of architecture."[12] Visitors who knew of what they spoke had favorable comments: "Among visitors at Commencement exercises was Mr. Gregory Vigeant, of Chicago, one of the most celebrated architects in the West. Mr. Vigeant thinks our new Music Hall a gem of architecture, and says a better plan for such a building could hardly have been adopted. Such testimony from a rival architect is a very high compliment to Mr. Edbrooke and his work."[13] The *Scholastic* gushed about the larger "new" iteration of the university: "The new University building is so much larger than the old, and its corridors and Rotunda so spacious, that a brigade could encamp in them without being crowded. Besides this there are the new Music Hall and a half dozen other magnificent buildings, so all in all, there is no lack of accommodations."[14]

There was specific praise for the acoustics of this new space from the *South Bend Daily Tribune*: "It contains the very best of acoustic proportions, the faintest speech on the stage being distinctly audible in the remotest part of the auditorium."[15] The *South-Bend Evening Register* continued the high praise and made the point that work remained to be done:

> Our readers must take an early opportunity to see the Music Hall at Notre Dame. It is certainly one of the most attractive rooms in which to give public entertainments to be seen anywhere. It is octagonal in form and the acoustic properties are unusually good. Large, tastefully-designed windows on the east and west afford ample light for day performances, and at night three electric lamps make a noonday radiance in every part of the auditorium, stage and gallery . . . The stage is well provided with scenery, and altogether Notre Dame has a public hall of which it may well feel

proud. The interior is still to be frescoed, and further painting is to be done, but sufficient progress has been made to admit of the use of the hall, and to afford an intelligent idea of what it will be when fully clothed with its further adornments.[16]

Finally, on the last morning of commencement, Thursday, June 22, 1882, the valedictory occurred in the new hall:

> When the last diploma had been borne away by the smiling recipient, Right Rev. Bishop Dwenger made a short address to the assembly in which he took occasion to congratulate the students on their peaceful triumphs, remarking that he considered the Commencement of '82 by far the most successful ever held at Notre Dame. When the Bishop had ceased speaking, the Band struck up the tender strains of "Home, Sweet Home."[17]

The building had opened, and it had served the university magnificently as the new "home, sweet home" for communal assembly at Notre Dame.

The "New" Washington Hall

Although the university demolished the first Washington Hall by early June 1882—the same month the new Exhibition Hall (within the Academy of Music) was officially dedicated during the 1882 commencement ceremonies—in a very real sense the history of the building we know today as Washington Hall began in the fall of the 1882, when the name first seems to have migrated unofficially from the remnants of the demolished 1862 clapboard structure to the new brick building that had replaced both it and the Music Hall destroyed in the Great Fire of 1879. Historians typically do not deal with the counterfactual, but if the first Washington Hall had indeed been moved and been converted into a gymnasium, as the university seriously considered doing, then the name "Washington Hall" almost certainly would have stayed with the original building. In that scenario, over time the name would very likely have fallen into disuse at the end of the life of the 1862 wooden structure, as was the case with Phelan Hall, which, when demolished in 1885, removed the name too.[18] But that is not what happened factually. The decision to raze the 1862 Senior Recreation Hall, within which was the Washington Exhibition Hall, and to build instead a completely new gymnasium freed up the name, and it took students only a summer to make the connection and to start to describe the new exhibition hall within the new Academy of Music as the "new" Washington Hall.[19]

The first reference to the "new" Washington Hall appeared in mid-September 1882, when the *Scholastic* announced, "Last Saturday evening the members of the Crescent Club held their first *sociale* in the reading-rooms, under the new Washington Hall, in the Academy of Music."[20] The word *sociale* is almost certainly meant to be "sociable," the nineteenth-century equivalent of today's "social," and the word used throughout the 1880s to describe Crescent Club events. Thus the students—if not yet the university administration—had grafted the name to the new building. The university *Bulletin* continued to describe the building as the "Music Hall" through 1896–97, after which the the name "Washington Hall" appeared officially in print.

The reading rooms mentioned in this early reference to the new Washington Hall, by the way, today contain the interior stairwells on the south side of the building which replaced the original exterior stone steps that directly accessed the second floor auditorium until 1933. These two rooms, about 13' x 20' each, were almost certainly the two reading rooms mentioned in the fall of 1882 and which served the building for the next half century. The *Scholastic* continued, "The two beautiful little rooms in the front part of the Academy of Music have been placed at the services, one of the Gradu - ating Class and the other of the Field Clubs." The new building clearly generated interest in those who would have the opportunity to use it. The *Scholastic* added that a "portion of the lower floor of the Academy of Music has been transformed into reading-rooms for the students. They have been well fitted up, wainscoted, calcimined, and made as convenient and comfortable as possible."[21] In addition to the two reading rooms, the large space directly under the auditorium became the Brownson Recreation Hall and ultimately contained billiard tables as late as the 1956 renovation, when Father Harvey put it to strict theatre use.[22]

By September 1882, then, Notre Dame had a new (but unofficial) Washington Hall that for the next 116 years (for the entirety of the twentieth century) served as the university's singular purpose-built performing arts center. Named for its predecessor, the new Washington Hall soon lost the adjective and eventually became known simply as Washington Hall. But even after the first reference to the new Washington Hall, no consistent pattern emerged with regard to the name for the new building.

Finishing the Building

Just as the Golden Dome did not yet soar above the Main Building in 1882, Washington Hall was open but unfinished. The south tower (or steeple) was not yet completed according to Edbrooke's plan, and therefore the building lacked the intended verticality needed to complement the church and Main Building. Wooden steps served the second floor entrance to the auditorium, and the simple whitewashed interior was still some years away from the creative brushes initially of Jacob Ackermann and Brother Frederick, and ultimately of Luigi Gregori and Louis Rusca. In fall 1882 construction continued apace on the campus, as it had since the Great Fire of 1879. The Local Council decided to build "a Science Hall 100 ft by 70 ft 2 Stories high" and concluded that the "gymnasium is now in complete running order."[23] Included in this continuing construction boom was the demand to complete the Main Building, with the *Scholastic* reporting by spring 1883 that work finally would begin "in earnest on the Dome."[24]

Additional interior work on Washington Hall occurred during March 1883 as the Hellenists prepared for the commencement production of *Antigone*. The first was the installation of a more decorous "ornamental railing for the gallery in the auditorium of the Hall . . . a thing of beauty and utility," perhaps replacing a temporary version. The university also ran gas lines to Washington Hall in March 1883 and thus made the original self-contained wick oil lamps obsolete:

Work has begun on laying gas-pipes to the Academy of Music, and placing gas-fixtures within the Hall. This is a move in the right direction, at least our stage managers will think so, as it will sometimes obviate the necessity of an individual (though he has been always greeted with applause) appearing before the curtain to turn down the lamps to produce dark effects.[25]

The previous May, the Local Council had "decided to receive bids for putting pipes and Gas fixtures in the Exhibition Hall," while the *Scholastic* had pushed a decision in spite of clear disagreements on technologies: "How is the new Hall to be lighted? This seems to be a point on which authorities differ. Sometimes we hear of the electric light, and again gas is spoken of. The time is short, and probably before our next issue a decision will have been reached."[26] Thus centrally controlled gas lighting replaced the individual wick lamps that had been presumably fueled by coal oil, lamp oil, or kerosene, and, in so doing, modern stage lighting techniques that require both high intensity and centralized control became possible for the first time. Washington Hall's electric lights seemed for general illumination purposes, due undoubtedly to Father Zahm's great early zeal regarding electricity, well before there seems to have been any thought of using it to light the stage.[27] What is further interesting about this report of the "lamp man" coming onto the stage to adjust the footlights is, in fact, a well-known eighteenth-century tradition that in this case carried over nearly to the end of the nineteenth century and into the age of electricity. As new balcony railing and gas lighting were being installed, the *Scholastic* reported the following progress and delays due to construction:

> The Hellenists are making preparations for the production of the "Antigone" of Sophocles. Prof. Gregori is at work designing the costumes. B. Anselm is preparing the Music. With all the accessories, it promises to outshine *Oedipus* of last year.
>
> The Stage in the Hall is receiving many improvements. It has been greatly enlarged and new scenes are being constructed. As this work must continue for some time, the entertainment intended for Easter Monday will have to be postponed.[28]

By the end of March 1883, the interior stage lighting decision had been implemented:

> Among the many improvements made in the auditorium of the Music Hall, the introduction of the gas fixtures form a very prominent feature. These, with the exception of the grand chandelier, which is to occupy the centre, have all been placed in position; they include lights throughout the auditorium, foot lights, head lights for the stage, etc. In connection with this subject, we may state that the days of "red fire" are o'er. An immense gas apparatus has been contrived, by which all the pleasing illuminating effects necessary for tableaux, etc., can be produced.[29]

The intense level of illumination gas lighting provides demands good sets (low intensity masks many sins), and the *Scholastic* reported in April that "Prof. Ackerman [*sic*] is at work on a new set of scenery for the production of 'Macbeth,'"[30] undoubtedly to accommodate the changes forced by the newly installed gas lighting. The high intensity level of gas very likely made pre-existing scenery, fine under oil-wick lamps, now appear flat and fake. Scenic artists like Professor Ackermann thus had to create new scenery that would look more "real" under the intense scrutiny of gas.

Although the university ran gas lines to Washington Hall by 1883, the building had no indoor toilet facilities until 1908, and so it made sense in May 1883 that the Local Council "decided to build a privey between the Exhibition Hall and Gymnasium for the seniors and Juniors."[31] The WC (water closet) or "privy" appears as such on the 1885 Sanborn Fire Insurance Map of the campus; it is the single building, about 7' x 14', between the gymnasium and Washington Hall (see fig. 5.2). After 1886, then, patrons of both the gymnasium and Washington Hall thus had easy access to water closets, which would also serve the new Science Hall (now LaFortune Student Center) going up just south of the new Academy of Music very close to the likely location of the original Washington Hall.[32]

Interior work in Washington Hall continued during the 1883–84 academic year, too, in a process that would transform the building from strictly utilitarian to blatantly aesthetic. The *Scholastic* noted

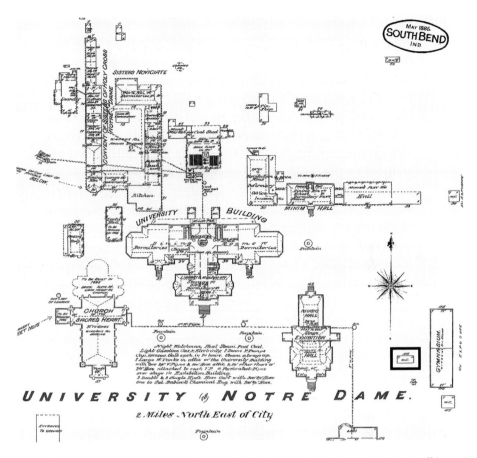

Figure 5.2. Sanborn Insurance Map, 1885. To the east of the Exhibition/Music Hall is Notre Dame's first gymnasium, a building that is about 33' x 120' x 22' high. Between the two is the 1883 water closet (7' x 14' x 7' high), a toilet facility to serve nearby buildings, including Washington Hall, which first got indoor plumbing in 1908.

that "extensive improvements are being made in Washington Hall. The wood-work has been finished, painted, and otherwise decorated."[33] So extensive was this work that the building closed for a short time in the spring of 1884 to complete the repairs, necessitating a postponement of the Philopatrians' May play.[34] The *Scholastic* further commented, "Washington Hall is being handsomely decorated by B. Frederick. All the frame work has been painted, and the fine new chandeliere is in place."[35] Brother Frederick and Jacob Ackermann painted frescoes and bronzed radiators, in addition to applying marbling and faux-wood finishes, a very popular technique at the time that made ordinary pine doors look like very expensive French walnut.[36] By fall 1884 the *Scholastic* noted "considerable improvement made in the interior of Washington Hall. The decorations of the front of the stage and the walls near by are very nice,"[37] a reference to the Ackermann drop curtain and proscenium arch decoration seen in a rare surviving picture of the stage at this time. Skilled artists and craftspersons like Professor Ackermann (scenery and paintings) and Brothers Frederick (faux French walnut doors) and Anselm (marbleized backgrounds) created a richly decorated interior appropriate to the period, one that went far beyond the original whitewashed walls. Their early work set the stage, as it were, for the international masters Gregori and Rusca to bring, once they had completed their work in the Main Building, some of that same exceptional grandeur to an already completely decorated Washington Hall. But at this early time in the building's history, Gregori's work in Washington Hall was limited to being costume designer for the Hellenists rather than painter of murals. Also in the fall of 1884, the building acquired something very practical for northern Indiana winters: "Double windows have been put up in Music Hall. The same improvement will soon be effected in the College [the Main Building], and then we may look out for a mild winter."[38] But there was no such luck; the move proved providential, and by January 1885 the recorded temperature on campus had retreated to −30° F (unofficially), one of the coldest winters on record in South Bend.

Inside the building Professor Ackermann provided a "new drop-curtain . . . admired by everyone."[39] A drop curtain flies directly in and out just upstage of the proscenium (the side away from the audience), rather than being pulled across the stage where it overlaps in the center, as with a more usual "traveler" curtain on the Washington Hall stage today. When stagehands brought Ackermann's drop curtain in and took it out, they did so only part of the way, at which point it became a valence curtain that effectively lowered the height of the proscenium to conceal from the audience the inner workings of the fly space (the area above the stage). A rare photograph (fig. 5.3) survives from the celebration of Saint Patrick's Day 1885 by the Co -

lumbians who produced an exhibition that included the drama *Robert Emmet: The Martyr of Irish Liberty*.[40] This *Robert Emmet* company photograph includes much of the Ackermann valence curtain and the Frederick wall decoration on the house right proscenium arch, a clear indication that by this time the much-admired drop curtain was in place and the interior walls had received very serious artistic attention. Although now finished, the interior detail of Washington Hall from 1885 to 1894, based on the proscenium arch in the right side of this photograph, seems devoid of any larger theme comparable to the complex later work of Gregori and Rusca in which books, music notes, and composers' names intertwine up the proscenium arch. In this 1885 photograph, Ackermann had not yet signed his new drop curtain "1885" in the house-left lower corner, but this is certainly the same teaser (first border) curtain seen in figure 5.4, the interior of Washington Hall, June 1894–June 1895, with the "new" Gregori/Rusca murals and decoration. Ackermann cleverly painted the curtain so that it was pictorially complete both raised (in the valence or teaser curtain position) and lowered (in the drop or act curtain position) to accommodate the first complexly decorated interior to Washington Hall, one that seems to have lasted for the nine years 1885–94.

Any argument over the future of electricity seems to have been over by early 1886 when the university upgraded the "electric Machine" purchased in 1882 to illuminate the new building. The *Scholastic* reported that "Mr. Wilson and his men have now completed the 'wiring' of the Main Building and St. Edward's Hall. He will fin - ish with Science hall in a few days and then begin the Academy of Music. After this, sockets and lamps will be placed in all the buildings. The large dynamo is expected daily."[41] This shows the rapid electrification of the campus buildings, from Father Zahm's seminal experiments in 1881 to de rigueur by 1886. The university had moved toward true electrification, with an inventory of electric lights by fall 1886 of 687 incandescent lights, 80 of which were in Washington Hall, along with 6 two-thousand candlepower "arc" or spotlights also likely dedicated to the theatre space, for a total of 693.[42]

The Great Fire of 1879, eternally on everyone's mind, caused the Local Council to decide "to put a Revolving fire Extinguisher in the

Figure 5.3. The cast and crews involved in *Robert Emmet: The Martyr of Irish Liberty*, Saint Patrick's Day Exhibition, March 17, 1885. A rare interior photograph of Washington Hall with the Ackermann/Frederick interior before the Gregori/Rusca modifications in 1894. Note the detail on the proscenium arch (on the right side of the photograph) and the Ackermann act curtain in the "up" or valence position and first groove legs. The five faculty seated across the front are (left to right) an unidentified brother, Father John M. Toohey, President Walsh,

Father Martin J. Regan (1883–1907 prefect of discipline), and Professor Lyons. The photograph shows the theatre had a footlight groove across the front of a curved stage. Handwritten on the back of this photograph is "The Play of Robert Emmett Mar 17.1886," but the correct date is 1885 since in 1886 the Columbians produced *Richard III* for Saint Patrick's Day, while in 1885 their play was indeed *Robert Emmet*. See *Scholastic* 18:28, March 21, 1885, 446; 19:27, March 20, 1886, 437. GNDL 13-49, UNDA.

Figure 5.4. Interior of Washington Hall, June 1894–June 1895. Gregori/Rusca completed their complex interior in June 1894, which coexisted for one year with the earlier Acker - mann "1885" drop/valence curtain and upstage scenic effects, all of which Sosman & Landis replaced in June 1895. Thus we can date this photograph to June 1894–June 1895, essentially the 1894–95 academic year, but it remains the best surviving photograph of the interior of Washington Hall before the 1956 renovation painted everything out. Notre Dame Glass Plate Negative Contact Sheets Collection (hereafter GGPP) 2/19, UNDA.

Music Hall,"[43] and by April 1887 the Local Council had also authorized "seats to be placed in the gallery [balcony] of the Exhibition Hall."[44] It is not clear what precise action occurred, since figure 5.4 clearly shows chairs in the balcony as late as 1894–95.

By March 1886 the Local Council Minutes revealed that both the exterior of Washington Hall and the interior of the Main Building still needed work, literally at the highest levels: "It was decided to finish the interior of the Dome as soon as possible also to finish the Steeple of the Music Hall."[45] The Washington Hall steeple, or tower as it was also called, reached its present height and configuration at the end of 1887 and got "proper" permanent windows in 1889. For the period 1882 through 1887, from which no photographs survive, the building must have looked something like the architect's rendering in figure 5.1, based on the surviving timbers within the tower which almost certainly formed the roof infrastructure during this five-year period.[46] By late 1887 the *Scholastic* complained, "Whoever has the contract for building the tower on Washington Hall should endeavor to complete the undertaking before winter renders it impossible. In its present condition, the tower is an unsightly object, and we can truly say of it that 'distance lends enchantment, etc.'"[47] By Christmas the work had been completed: "The scaffolding has been removed from the Washington Hall tower, and the new spire stands forth in all its beauty. . . . The tower on Washington Hall is now completed."[48] But not quite. When the tower got its specified windows in the spring of 1889, almost two years later, it would look as originally designed by Edbrooke (see figs. 5.5, 5.6, and 5.7).[49] The Local Council Minutes reported the work in May 1889, "to put the windows in the Tower of the Exhibition Hall,"[50] replacing temporary wooden shutter inserts.

The 1881 inscriptions on the east and west fronts of the tower, which survive to this day, raise interesting questions. Why was the year 1881 chosen as the date to place on a tower completed in late 1887 as part of a building dedicated in 1882 for which ground was broken in 1879, the north wing of which was occupied and in use in 1880? The Edbrooke engraving of Washington Hall further complicates this issue by showing the east front stone inscription as 1879, the year he designed the building and construction began after the

Figure 5.5. Washington Hall after the tower was completed in December 1887 (but before the installation of "proper" windows there) and with what appear to be wooden steps before the stone steps went up by July 1889. Francis P. Clark Collection (hereafter GFCL) 48/57, UNDA. Although this photograph has been airbrushed probably in an attempt to remove something in the foreground, it is very likely the earliest surviving photograph of the building after the tower was completed.

Figure 5.6. Washington Hall after July 1889: the stone steps had been installed but the tower had not received permanent windows. Note the inscription "stone" on the south tower face which has remained blank to this day. GNDL 7/47, UNDA.

ACADEMY OF MUSIC AND WASHINGTON HALL.

Figure 5.7. From *A Brief History of the University of Notre Dame du Lac, Indiana, from 1842 to 1892, Prepared for the Golden Jubilee to Be Celebrated June 11, 12 and 13, 1895* (Chicago: Werner, 1895), between 184 and 185. One of the earliest published photographs of the completed Washington Hall with "permanent" south entrance stairs, taken after 1889.

Great Fire (see fig. 5.8). This engraving also shows a south front in-scription of MUSIC HALL on two lines, while in reality that area seems always to have been left blank. Clearly, the term *Music Hall* was never the name of the entire building but seemed rather to refer to the north wing. The year 1881—the date on the tower to this day—while certainly "close" to important dates in the history of the building, seems especially unrelated to any signature events related to the struc-ture's history. Possibly the 1881 stone was cut in anticipation of an 1881 completion and dedication date, which was then delayed a year, with the stone nevertheless used years later when the tower was com-pleted in 1889? It seems unlikely the university would have forgot-ten in 1889 the 1882 dedication of the building, although it is possible those present remembered the unofficial opening as 1881 and not re-lated to the formal dedication for commencement in June 1882.

Figure 5.8. Edbrooke engraving of the new building, with the words "Music Hall" and the date "1879" on the tower, neither of which ever seem to have appeared on the building. GFCL 48/56, UNDA.

Both the north (Music Hall) and the south (Washington Hall) entrances always required a flight of stairs. At the same time in spring 1886 that the Local Council decided to finish the tower of Washington Hall, the entrance stairs also came under scrutiny. The *Scholastic* reported the decision with regard to the Main Building "to replace the temporary steps in front of the study halls by permanent staircases of iron and stone. This improvement will also be made with the entrances to St. Edward's Hall and the Academy of Music."[51] So the wooden, temporary steps were on the way out by the end of the 1885–86 academic year. There was quick confirmation from the Local

Council authorizing the placement of "Iron Stairs in front of the Se-nior & Juniors Study Hall, Minim Hall and Music Hall."[52] The *Scho-lastic* described by late summer what had been done: "The wooden steps which heretofore led to the front entrances of the study-halls and the Music Hall, have been replaced by handsome iron structures, both useful and ornamental. The canine pillars are an attractive fea-ture."[53] The reference to "canine pillars" clearly related to the north Music Hall entrance, which has retained canine newel posts to this day, and not to the south (Exhibition Hall) wooden steps erected by 1882 that would be transformed into a grand stone exterior stair-case in 1889. In spring 1889 the Local Council "decided to erect Stone Steps at the front of the Exhibition Hall,"[54] with the Financial Journal confirming completion by recording a payment on July 10, 1889, of "$445.00, Exhibition Hall Stone Steps."[55]

The first *Scholastic* of the 1886–87 academic year included a pic-ture of "Washington Hall of the College of Music" and mentioned the venue as the setting for the sixteenth annual convention of the C.T.A.U. (Catholic Total Abstinence Union of America),[56] with a de-scription that indicated a first floor devoted to "recreation & reading rooms with Juniors on the north and Seniors on the South contain-ing newspapers, periodicals, billiard tables, easy-chairs, etc." No men-tion of the band or music rehearsal spaces probably indicated that the ground-floor space at this time retained its original function as the Junior Recreation Hall, complemented by the Senior (or Brown-son) Recreation Hall to the south under the auditorium, with the second and third floors on the north wing reserved for the music pro-gram. The *Scholastic* added that the Exhibition Hall was reserved for "more formal lectures, as well as concerts and dramatic entertain-ments," and was capable of holding 1,200 persons in a setting that was "one of the largest and most attractive college halls in the coun-try."[57] The construction and expansion of the gymnasium complex east of Washington Hall rather quickly obviated the need to retain recreation spaces in the north Music Hall where the music program had great needs. Music likely took over the ground-floor space very quickly and did not leave it until 1990.

The massive building program over the years since the Great Fire of 1879 caught the nation's attention. The *New York Times* reported in 1887 that "the University of Notre Dame has a most elaborate array of substantial buildings,"[58] while local concerns remained more microcosmic. The *Scholastic* stated that "Washington Hall needs a new piano. The instrument now in the hall has become so antique and 'chestnutic' that it can scarcely tell the difference between a bar of music and a bar of soap." The *Scholastic* added that "we trust the hinges of the doors in Washington Hall will be oiled before another entertainment is held there, or at least persons should not be entering and leaving while anyone is speaking on the stage" and recommended, "If the stage curtain were lowered during the lectures in Washington Hall, the speaker's words could be better heard in the rear portion of the Hall."[59]

Exhibitions and Events 1882–1895

During the period from the 1882 dedication to the completion of the Gregori/Rusca interior in 1894, the new Washington Hall was indeed busier than ever. Exhibitions that integrated all the performing arts into a single evening since the beginnings of the university continued apace, and the new Washington Exhibition Hall both functionally and aesthetically filled the needs of an ambitious and growing institution.

In October 1882, at the festival of Saint Edward, the first official exhibition of the 1882–83 academic year, the *South Bend Times* called the building simply "the new hall" and the "large hall":

The thirty-ninth annual festival of St. Edward, the patron feast of Very Rev. Father Edward Sorin, superior general of the congregation of the Holy Cross occurred yesterday at Notre Dame, beginning on the previous evening with literary, musical, and dramatic entertainment in the new hall in honor of Very Rev. Father Sorin, the venerable founder of the university. The large hall was filled with an enthusiastic audience including the faculty and students from all the departments of the college, and a large number of visitors from this city and abroad. Father Sorin occupied the seat of honor in the center, and on either side sat the faculty, headed by the president, Rev. T. E. Walsh. The entertainment was in charge of Professor J. A. Lyons, and the programme was opened with music by the university cornet band, following which were addresses in Latin by F. A. Quinn, in Greek by W. Arnold, in German by J. S. Courtney, in French by L. Gilbert and the minim address was delivered by J. J. McGath and the address from the junior department by A. A. Zahm. The entertainment concluded with a comedy in three acts entitled "The Upstart," translated from the French by a member of the faculty expressly for this occasion. The entertainment closed about 7 o'clock with an address by Father Sorin in which he complimented the students upon the success of their efforts, and on the progress in the languages they had displayed in their addresses.[60]

By the time of the first Washington's Birthday celebration in the new Exhibition Hall, which also included the first Shakespeare play—*Julius Caesar*—in the new space, the local community heaped praise on the building, favorably comparing the evening at Notre Dame to professional commercial efforts, in what was clearly a memorable evening for the entire South Bend community:

Last evening Notre Dame was the scene of another of those literary, musical and dramatic entertainments for which the University is becoming justly famous, and an invitation to which is always more eagerly responded to than is a complimentary offer of a dress-circle seat at leading opera-house entertainments. The entertainment was given in honor of Washington's birthday, an annual event at Notre Dame. The exercises partook largely of literary and musical features, but the dramatic formed the principal part of the program. . . . The opening hour of the entertainment was announced at 5:30 o'clock, but an hour prior to that time, people began to gather in from all directions, and when the time arrived for the commencement of the exercises, the new Music Hall in which the entertainment was held was filled to its utmost capacity, gallery and auditorium, with an eager expectant audience. A great many of the city's leading business men, with their ladies were present, as were also the parents and friends of students from various parts and places. The new Music Hall, though still incomplete as far as its internal embellishments are concerned, presented a neat appearance, all profuse decoration being dispensed with. The hall was brilliantly illuminated with the electric light. The acoustic properties of the new hall are remarkable, and the ventilation and heating features are excellent. The exercises opened with a grand march by the University brass Band, which was enthusiastically applauded. Then followed a song with full chorus by the "Orpheonics," a most delightful number. W. H. Arnold's oration of the day, a grand eulogy upon the character and life of Washington, was well received. . . . Part first closed with an Overture, "Semiramis," by the University Orchestra of twelve pieces, one of the grandest numbers of the evening. By this time the audience were doubly eager and expectant, and, as the curtain rose upon the first scene of Shakspeare's matchless "Julius Caesar," the hall resounded with enthusiastic applause. . . . Faculty and audience all agree that the last exercise excelled by far any that have heretofore been held at Notre Dame. At the close of the tragedy, Mr. Lucius Hubbard, a former student and graduate of the University . . . thanked the students for their charming entertainment. Between the acts Madame Scheppers, of Chicago . . . delighted the audience with two or three operatic numbers. . . . The Fathers and Faculty in full were present at the entertainment, and also the pastors from the city churches and other clerical visitors. The new Music Hall is well fitted for theatrical representations. The stage is well arranged, and the scenes are good. The costumes employed were simply elegant and most appropriate.[61]

A serious accident on Wednesday, February 21, nearly stopped the show, however. Professor Lyons suffered a severe injury during the performance of *Julius Caesar*. The *Scholastic* reported:

A painful accident occurred early in the evening, which, if it had been generally known, would have put a speedy termination to the performance. The worthy Director, Prof. J. A. Lyons, was frightfully burned in face and hands by the explosion of a package of gunpowder which was being used to produce lightning effects.

Through the earnest efforts of the Professor, all excitement was allayed behind the scenes; and, though enduring terrible pain, he withstood all entreaties to be conveyed to the Infirmary, until he had assurances that the play would proceed without interruption. It was at first thought that serious, if not fatal, results would follow; but, with the care and attention which he is receiving, his condition is gradually improving, and, in a short time, we hope to see him once more in our midst.[62]

Lyons recovered, although his Silver Jubilee at Notre Dame had to be postponed due to his convalescence, during which time he received sympathy letters from the community's movers and shakers, including "Mr. and Mrs. Clem Studebaker," but with the hope that "though he must necessarily be confined to his room for some weeks yet, his physicians are confident that the end of the month [March] will see him ready to resume his duties."[63] By mid-March, Lyons had "so far recovered as to be able to leave his retirement, to the great delight of his pupils and many friends."[64] When Lyons returned to his teaching by the end of March, "great enthusiasm prevailed."[65] He had been out for nearly five weeks, and no sooner had he returned than the new edition of his book appeared: "Prof. Lyons will, in a few days, issue the sixth edition of the American Elocutionist. This new edition will be considerably enlarged and improved."[66] Lyons both taught elocution and directed the plays, and his textbook's sixth edition (of eight) confirmed both the centrality of elocution in the university setting in the nineteenth century and Lyons's status in the field. While the word *elocution* may now seem old-fashioned, a perusal of the Lyons textbook reveals a scientific and aesthetic approach to communication and performance useful to this day.

Plans had begun early in the fall of the 1882–83 academic year for the spring 1883 commencement, now that the new building had opened. The stunningly successful 1882 commencement-related productions, including *Oedipus Rex* in Greek, had set the highest standard. The desire naturally existed to do even more for 1883, the first commencement for which the new edifice claimed the name "Washington Hall." On a roll, the "Hellenist" Father Stoffel and Professor Gregori, the *Scholastic* reported, "are perfecting a project for the coming session which is to throw the 'Oedipus Tyrannus' completely in the shade,"[67] with plans already afoot to produce *Antigone* for the June 1883 commencement.

The celebration of the 1883 commencement began on Monday evening, June 18, 1883, in the rotunda of the Main Building with a complete program of entertainment by the Euglossians, under the direction of a recovered Professor Lyons, accompanied by the orchestra and the Orpheonics (a vocal group), a program that included orations and a scene from *Richard III.* On Tuesday evening, the Hellenists performed the Greek play in Washington Hall, the second year in a row for them to do so, in what was described as the "great feature of the Commencement exercises."[68] The *Scholastic* concluded, "The Class of '83 may well feel proud of their work. They have rivaled '82 in their drama, and though the latter have the credit of producing the first Greek play in the West, yet '83 has the distinction of publishing the first Greek libretto—a work entirely their own, the typesetting of the Greek having been done by the Professor [Stoffel] and members of the class during their free hours."[69] Brother Anselm composed the music for this production, and Luigi Gregori designed the costumes. The *South Bend Register* praised "a brilliant production, a work of untiring labor, a great credit to the university, and a delight to the large and cultured audience." The *South Bend Times* commented on the venue, saying, "The first thing noticeable, as one enters the hall, is its admirable adaptation to the purpose for which it is intended, a very exceptional feature in our public halls."[70] The *Ypsilanti Sentinel* pointed out the pedagogical value of such a production, saying, "In preparing to produce the *Antigone,* the students of Notre Dame procured the necessary Greek type and cases, and set up the matter of the text themselves. As a means of making them familiar with the language, we have no doubt this exercise was worth months of study."[71] The *Scholastic* earlier had described the printing of the 136-page libretto, with the "Greek text and the translation . . . on opposite pages, so that those who do not understand Greek can follow the play intelligently,"[72] a copy of which audience members undoubtedly had in their hands as they watched what must have been a memorable performance.

Well before commencement proper began on Wednesday eve ning, "the afternoon trains had brought crowds of new visitors, and the large hall was completely filled." The 7:30 ceremony began with music by the orchestra of the university, the oration given by an alumnus, a flute solo, the quarrel scene in the fourth act of *Julius Caesar,* and an operetta by the Orpheonics (with sixty voices and twenty-four pieces), after which the premiums were distributed, with books being given as rewards of merit. At the end, "the Band played a march, and all retired."[73]

Thursday morning at 8:30 saw the concluding (and most important) exercises of commencement held in Washington Hall: "The stage had been tastefully fitted up, and the scenes set to represent a garden picture with fountains of living water. . . . The members of the Class of '83 occupied seats upon the stage, and as the lifting of the curtain revealed them to the gaze of their fellow students, they were greeted with rounds of applause. The University Band first executed an overture, and then Mr. William H. Arnold, '83, delivered the . . . Valedictory,"[74] followed by an oration by the Right Reverend John Watterson, D.D., bishop of Columbus, who proclaimed Shakespeare a Catholic:

> Shakespeare, though often too shockingly gross and immoral for any church, yet proved he was born and brought up a Catholic. . . . In his writings, there is the clearest evidence of Catholic thought and feeling. The influence of the old faith still survived in the writing of the Elizabethan era. But the reformation at last worked out its inevitable result. . . . It remains for America to build up, stone by stone, the grand edifice of Catholic literature.[75]

President Walsh conferred awards and degrees. The entire class of 1883 could be accommodated on the stage of Washington Hall at this time, but within a decade that would no longer be the case. It is clear that 1882–83 had been a great year for the university—except for the Lyons accident—but the Hellenists and Greek plays in Greek would not return to the Washington Hall stage until 1899. The *Class Annual 1884* further regretted the dropping of the Greek play (in Greek) after just two productions (1882 and 1883) since it was "so valuable a means of education," but drama should not come at the expense of debate, which should also be cultivated.[76]

At the end of 1884, the St. Cecilians celebrated the "Twenty-seventh Annual Christmas Exercises . . . Complimentary to Rev. President

Walsh," at which the college band performed, and the old stand-by *The Recognition* was produced as it had been in previous years. The *Scholastic* glowed: "Magnificent costumes were worn in the play by the St. Cecilians, on the evening of the 17th. These, together with the splendid new scenery, added not a little to the effectiveness of the representation." The *Chicago Times* described the building as "the beautiful new Washington Hall," one of the earliest sources outside the university to give the new venue that name.[77] Two months later, the Thespians celebrated the "forty-first annual celebration of Washington's Birthday" with a program that included "Falsely Accused, a Domestic Drama in three Acts," with a cast of over twenty and with the band and orchestra providing accompaniment and entr'actes.[78]

Pre-filmic Exhibitions

Ackermann's grand drop curtain and settings would long be the norm for visual entertainment, but the period also saw early mechanical and electrical attempts that prefigured the arrival of film to Notre Dame and specifically to Washington Hall, where screenings would occur for much of the twentieth century; "scientific" demonstrations took place on the Washington Hall stage by the mid-1880s, initially satisfying the current fascination with optics by creating the illusion of "moving pictures." The *Scholastic* reported in March 1885 that Father Zahm presented "a stereopticon exhibition" with the latest technology, but this was clearly not the first time since his demonstration was "as fine a stereopticon exhibition as was ever witnessed at Notre Dame."[79] The "double magic lantern" of the stereopticon created both a 3-D effect as well as the "dissolve," the illusion of one scene or object gradually becoming another. The "Art Entertainment" that Zahm produced gave students "the opportunity of seeing some of the wonders which are revealed by the modern art of Projection,"[80] the subject of which was the "New Orleans' Exposition and World's Fair," and evidently creating the nineteenth-century equivalent of virtual reality. The *Scholastic* reported after the event, "Since the Stereoscopic exhibition last week, it is common to hear persons talk about the Exposition with as much earnestness as though they had been there, not by Father Zahm's new system, but in reality."[81] Students came to Washington Hall to experience a technology that changed their notion of reality, just as still photography had already done and as film would soon do. Also in March 1885, Professor Bailey of South Bend gave a "phenomenal astronomical lecture" in Washington Hall, using a device called a "cosmosphere," which seems to have been an early form of a planetarium projector.[82] Later that semester in May, the Scientific Association also presented an entertainment to do with "persistency of motion" in what was called a "séance," which included the demonstration of a phenakistoscope, an early motion picture device that

> had wheels over 6 feet in diameter, painted especially for the occasion by a local artist with subjects taken from photographs representing various animals, running, jumping, flying, swimming, together with the human face in the different phases of laughter: and so perfect was the result of the optical illusion that the motions of the different objects were well illustrated.[83]

It is well to remember that the illusion of movement occurs in motion pictures due to the rapid changing of fixed images just as with the pre-filmic phenakistoscope. Amidst all this science, however, the ephemeral or "live" performing arts also triumphed, especially Shakespeare.

"Let us have more of Shakspeare"

In anticipation of Shakespeare's baptismal date in April 1885, Notre Dame had prepared far beyond the usual. Father Sorin's return from Europe (his forty-third trip across the Atlantic) served as a catalyst for celebration by the Sorin Literary and Dramatic Association as the university also showcased Luigi Gregori's painterly talents. The *Scholastic* hyperbolically proclaimed:

> Signor Gregori has completed an original portrait of the immortal Shakspere, which is considered the most finished of his many beautiful productions. Taking into account the careful and minute

study which the artist brought to his work, it may be considered as truthful a representation of the great dramatist as can possibly be made. Besides consulting and measuring a death mask of Shakspere and studying the most authentic portraits, Sig. Gregori diligently weighed and compared the personal descriptions given by the best biographers, and the result, it may be said, is the best portrait of the "Bard of Avon" now existing.[84]

The *Scholastic* reported the May celebration, which included the new portrait: "The annual 'Shakespeare night' of the Euglossians was celebrated in Washington Hall, on Wednesday last [April 29], in a manner far surpassing all previous efforts. . . . The hall was well filled with a large, select and appreciative audience, comprising the *élite* of South Bend, and numerous visitors from other cities." The event began at 7 o'clock with the university orchestra under the direction of Professor Paul, followed by the "Oration of the Day," which compared Shakespeare favorably to Washington. Mr. W. E. Ramsay then "represented the great dramatist engaged in writing one of his plays" in the manner of "Gregori's ideal portrait." The South Bend St. James's Quartette did three numbers, followed by the trial scene of *The Merchant of Venice* and two scenes from *Julius Caesar.* Soprano Mrs. Antoine Maguire of Chicago performed next, followed by an oration on Shakespeare and scenes from *Richard III, Hamlet,* and *Macbeth,* concluding with a tableau composed of "Gregori's celebrated painting of Shakspeare, around which were grouped the principal characters of the plays presented, approaching with wreaths to crown the immortal Bard. It was received with great applause." Professor Howard provided closing remarks, on the invitation of President Walsh, and Professor Lyons directed the entire event (see fig. 5.9). So impressive was the event that the following week, the *Scholastic* exclaimed, "Let us have more of Shakspeare."[85]

Christmas in Washington Hall

For the 1885–86 academic year, the annual Christmas exercises occurred (as they had since 1858) for students staying on campus over the holidays, as was common in the nineteenth century:

Figure 5.9. Gregori's "ideal portrait" of Shakespeare on stage. Note the 1885 Ackermann drop curtain and first-groove legs, plus the Shakespeare "gothic" set. Gregori is front row, second from right, with Professor Lyons to his right. Although undated, this is likely very soon after the completion of the portrait in early 1885 and is perhaps a photographic record related to the April 1885

"Shakespeare at Notre Dame" event, although the actor playing Shakespeare and wreaths to crown the portrait are conspicuously missing in this photograph. The front-row dignitaries are (left to right) Father Regan, Father Toohey, President Walsh, Professor Lyons, Signor Gregori, and Professor Edwards. GNDL 19/11, UNDA.

The Juniors' Christmas Tree was formally exposed to view in Washington Hall last Wednesday night. Hardly had the curtain risen on the very pretty picture of the green tree, covered and decked with Christmas things and the mellowed light of the Chinese lanterns falling over all, when a loud tooting from behind the stage announced that His Highness, King Santa Claus, was approaching.[86]

Santa distributed candy from the tree to the juniors, followed by entertainment, including a play, attended by President Walsh and "a large audience, composed of students and many visitors from the city." The university cornet band provided "stirring numbers," and its members were "never so large and never so perfectly drilled"; this was followed by "the crowning feature. . . . 'If I were a King'—a beautiful pastoral play of four acts, written especially for the Society." The closing remarks of the president appealed "to the honor and manhood of the young men."[87] Probably because they could not get the hall any sooner, the Euglossians closed the long holiday season three weeks later with a program that included an overture by the university orchestra, selections from Shakespeare's *Richard III,* a declamation, a grand processional march arranged for two pianos, a recitation, a humorous recitation, a piano duet, another recitation, an impersonation, a comical "rustic scene" that "brought down the house," a musical prodigy at the piano, and a concluding farce entitled *Cherry Bounce.*[88]

Glee Club

The College Glee Club performed in Washington Hall in early 1888 to raise money to outfit the rugby football association,[89] and the following December demonstrated the group's wide variety and range of capabilities:

The Glee Club—It was thirty minutes past four, Thursday afternoon, when the reporter entered Washington Hall. There was great applause (when the Faculty came in). The house was full, or rather filled. All the available space in the parquet and dress circle was taken, while the balcony was crowded. It was a goodly assemblage gathered together to witness the annual performance of the University Glee Club. The entertainment was enjoyable, but we will not attempt to mention each clever act, for it would take too long to give each participant the praise due him. The singing of the quartette and of Messrs. Jewett and Smith; the witticisms of Dougherty, Melady, Kelly, Lahey, Hackett and Morton; the cornet solo by E. Howard, the "Topics of the Day" by H. Barnes; the "Meeting of the Champions," the comic drill, were all delightful features, while the club swinging was excellent. The laughable absurdity, entitled the "Somnambulistic Sanitarium" which concluded the programme, brought down the house, and everyone left the hall satisfied that they had spent a delightful evening. Credit is due to Prof. Liscomb, Mr. Dougherty and their able assistants, Messrs. Jewett, Melady and Newton, under whose direction the entertainment was gotten up. There were others who contributed to the success of the evening whose names have escaped our memory, but they all acquitted themselves creditably.

We are authorized to state that the tomahawk incident was not a part of the regular programme. The players had no designs upon any one in the audience.[90]

We can only speculate as to the nature of "the tomahawk incident," which clearly suggested unintended and involuntary audience involvement!

Father Sorin's Sacerdotal Golden Jubilee

The big event of 1888, spanning two academic years, was of course the Sacerdotal Golden Jubilee of Father Sorin, celebrating his fifty years as a priest. The "private" university celebration for students occurred in May 1888, while the public celebration involving the larger community took place the following August. Although in both instances the university transformed the entire campus, Washington Hall was little used, possibly because of the serious and sacred nature of the celebration (with no plays performed). For the spring private celebration for students, the only event in "the Exhibition Hall" was an afternoon "public reception to be tendered the venerable Gold Jubilee celebrant," which included music, elocution, and Father Sorin's speaking.[91] In August the church, Main Building, St. Edward's Hall (where the minims resided), and outdoors all served as important venues, but not Washington Hall.[92] Indeed, for the commencement exercises program in both 1888 and 1889, there was no play; in 1889, there were oratorical and musical events,[93] although Washington Hall once again became the prime venue for the Founder's Day celebration in October 1889, which coincided with the beginning of Saint Edward's College in Austin, Texas, and the centenary of the first episcopal see established in 1789 in Baltimore by Pope Pius VI. The program included an overture by the university orchestra, a vocal quartet of welcome, festal greetings from the seniors, a duet, a selection entitled "St. Edward's Day," another vocal quartet, festal greetings from the juniors, an interlude by the university orchestra, a personation — "The Anchor" by W. Ford — a quartet, festal greetings from the minims, a scene from *Richard III*, with the Duke of Gloucester and King Henry, closing remarks by the Very Reverend E. Sorin, and the grand march for retiring by the "N. D. U. Cornet Band."[94] At this same time, Gregori's portraits of Bishop Carroll and George Washington, gifts to the newly established Catholic University of America, in Washington, D.C., were also discussed. Gregori painted full-length portraits of both the father of the country, George Washington, and the father of the Catholic Church in America, Archbishop John Carroll of Baltimore. The *Scholastic* described Gregori's painting of Washington as "standing, holding in his right hand a scroll with the inscription 'Constitution of the United States, 1789.' He is in the civilian dress of continental times, and appears as if addressing the people in his official capacity as President."[95]

Debate and Elocution

Law school public debates occurred regularly throughout the early history of the new Washington Hall, and the Philodemics offered events almost as complex and varied as the exhibitions of the period. In January 1889, for example, the topic was "Should the Right of Suffrage be Restricted by Educational and Property Qualifications?" with the archbishop of Fort Wayne present and "interspersed with vocal music under the direction of Prof. Liscombe."[96] It would be unusual today, in our period of highly specialized audiences, to have "vocal music" accompany a debate.

In addition to debate, elocution continued to be of prime interest. In early February 1889, "Mr. A. A. Williams, the distinguished elocutionist . . . recited from memory the first three acts of Shakespeare's 'Julius Caesar,' portraying the various characters of the drama with the appropriate change of voice required."[97] For spring 1889 the university hired Walter C. Lyman, "one of the foremost elocutionists of the country," to teach a new elocution course, a subject pedagogically central to the university's belief that "success in the pursuit of any profession is afforded by facility, correctness and grace in the expression of thoughts and ideas."[98]

Columbian Quatercentenary

The Columbian quatercentenary made 1891–92 a very big year for the university and for Washington Hall. The *Scholastic* reported that Washington Day celebrations included the Stars and Stripes waving from every building. The entire campus geared up for these festivities, with Washington Hall serving as the communal assembly center where everyone could come and participate. Among the festivities, "the University Cornet Band, under the able leadership of the Rev. M. Mohun, played some of the most inspiring airs of our national music," a noon banquet with "turkey and cranberry sauce" was served, and at Washington Hall at 3:30 the Thespian Society provided "literary, musical, and dramatic entertainment," and the Choral Union (under Prof. Liscombe) sang "Oh, Columbia, Beloved!" after the university orchestra had opened with the overture from "Don Quixote." The oration of the day followed, by Mr. James R. Fitzgibbon (class of '92), before the production of *Julius Caesar,* with a cast of at least twenty-six (with all women's parts cut), and an interesting comment on the newly assassinated Caesar: "What made the corpse heave when Cassius's foot was planted on his gastronomic region?"[99]

Saint Patrick's Day, a traditional day of celebration and always just under a month after the Washington Day celebrations, began with mass in the church and the cornet band "in the rotunda... furnish[ing] sweet melodies for the entertainment of the dwellers in the College," followed by impressive military drills, the Sorin Hall Brigade being most noteworthy. At 3:30 "one of the largest and most select audiences of the year had gathered in the large parlors, and as soon as the doors of the exhibition hall were opened they filled every available seat in the visitors' gallery." After an overture, the grand chorus, an address, a vocal quartet, the oration of the day, and a trio, the Columbians presented *Richard III*, with a cast of at least eighteen.[100]

The quatercentenary of Columbus's bringing Catholicism to the New World was a focus at the June 1892 commencement:

> In the exercises each orator took some incident in the life of the daring navigator and amplified it; the musical part of the programme was also devoted to Columbus, and even the Right Rev. J. S. Foley, Bishop of Detroit, caught the Columbian enthusiasm, and, as orator of the day, reviewed the speeches of the graduating class and grew eloquent over the achievements of the adventurous Genoese.[101]

Hall Too Small

The three-year period from the Great Fire of April 1879 until the dedication of the new Academy of Music in June 1882 saw Notre Dame transformed physically into the campus we recognize to this day. Seven buildings went up during this intense and constant period of rebuilding, all with a consistency of architecture and materials to make the place look, for the first time, like a campus with a master plan. In terms of the Exhibition Hall, the university now had a much larger venue for communal public disclosure, one that could accommodate the entire community and its guests. Who would possibly have guessed that relentless growth would generate calls for expansion so soon, and that within a few years of its dedication the marvelous Exhibition Hall built to accommodate 1,200 could no longer meet the communal assembly needs of an ambitious and dynamic university? Directly paralleling the first Washington Hall that within a decade of its construction in 1862 had also proved to be too small, this phenomenon affirms the important lesson of theatre history of "architectural lag," the suggestion that by the time a culture builds a performance venue, the ideology behind its creation has likely changed so much that the venue is obsolete. The time that passes from recognizing the need to dedicating a structure to accommodate that need is often so long that the original need has grown or changed to the point that the new structure is almost immediately inadequate.[102]

The first indication that the new building was too small came only four years after its dedication. At the Washington's Birthday celebrations of 1886, the *Scholastic* noted, "Half-past six o'clock on Monday evening found Washington Hall—as the auditorium of the Academy of Music is called—filled to its utmost capacity with an audience composed of students, members of the faculty and a numerous throng of visitors from far and near." The program began with the "Grand Reconciliation Medley" by the university cornet band, which was followed by a twenty-minute well-prepared oration on Washington, a German waltz by the university orchestra, and Shakespeare's *Julius Caesar*, "arranged so as to permit of its rendition by males alone." Professor Ackermann's "skilful brush" provided the scenery, and the costumes arrived "expressly for the occasion from Chicago." The play had "thrilling and effective tableaux," and between the acts "excellent instrumental music was rendered by [five students], directed by Prof. Paul."[103] The *South Bend Tribune* commented, "The parts were all well committed, the prompter's services being seldom called into requisition during the progress of the play," which lets us know a prompter was a fixture of the production. The article continued its praise, citing a source who thought the play "excelled all former efforts of the Thespians," but with the important caveat that "many were unable to find standing room."[104] The auditorium was already too small for events like this not quite four years after its dedication.

This situation only got worse; three years later, regarding the June 1889 commencement, the *Scholastic* complained:

Washington Hall never contained a larger audience than the one that gathered there in the evening to listen to the interesting programme of musical, literary and dramatic exercises prepared for the occasion by the students and the alumni. The doors were opened about 7 o'clock, and long before the hour for beginning the entertainment, 7:30, every seat was taken and nearly a hundred chairs placed in the aisles and corridors occupied, while there was a row of standing spectators around the outer aisle of the main floor to the hall. The members of the orchestra were nearly crowded out of their seats by the pressure of the audience towards the stage. It was a gathering of intellect, beauty, wealth and fashion such as is seldom seen in this part of the country, the hundreds of visitors, both ladies and gentlemen, from all parts of the United States, from Mexico, the Canadian dominion and other countries, including the Faculty of the University, the alumni and students attending in a body. The audience numbered nearly 1800 souls.[105]

As early as 1890 calls also resonated to upgrade stage standards in this great space, already showing wear and tear due to being in almost constant use:

Rumors are afloat to the effect that a new and complete set of stage accoutrements has been secured for Washington Hall. This is a move in the right direction. Probably no American college can boast a theatre of such beauty and dimensions as our own. Still it cannot be denied that thus far scenic effect has not received all the attention merited. In our last play, for example, it was very uncomfortable for an audience to see local stars struggling over a dusty floor—one endeavoring to precipitate the other into the watery deep, while the audience expected the waves to flood the stage and get among their skirts at every moment. It would cost but little to supply Washington Hall with these "needful auxiliaries," and the expense incurred would be more than compensated by the advantages which our future Booths and their audiences would enjoy.[106]

At the 1891 commencement ceremonies, "visitors and students had all assembled in Washington Hall whose seating capacity of twelve hundred was taxed to the utmost."[107] And at the 1892 Columbian quatercentenary the *Scholastic* noted that "Washington Hall is a comparatively new building with a seating capacity of over 1,000; but it is getting too small to accommodate the commencement crowds." The writer went on to praise all there was to do at Notre Dame if one could not get inside the Hall: "There is, however, so much else to attract visitors at Notre Dame, that the enlargement of the handsome building will be a matter for consideration many years hence. The visitors who do not get seats in the hall pass the time in sightseeing on the campus, always at its loveliest in June."[108] Alternative options aside, Washington Hall was too small within a decade of its dedication, and if Althusser is correct that cultures reflect their ideology physically, then the decision not to enlarge or replace the building reflected the ideology of the university in the twentieth century.[109] Other larger spaces could be found for graduation, and the historical recreational function of the space would be taken over by structures constructed over time, from the first purpose-built gymnasium in 1882 and the Fieldhouse (1898–1983), to the Joyce Athletic and Convocation Center (1968). Over the years, the university added a drill hall (1943–62), followed by the geodesic-domed Stepan Center (1962). Of course the football stadium (1930) and its subsequent "doughnut" expansion (1997) provided the largest outdoor structure for audiences on campus. Music gained additional purpose-built space in 1990 with the Ricci Band Rehearsal Hall. Crowley Hall was built for mechanical engineering and went through many incarnations before the Department of Music acquired it in 1976, with the old "Huddle" or the Band Annex just east of Washington Hall serving the Department of Music before its demoliton in 1990. Plays initially provided entertainment solely in relation to a festival or celebration, and after 1882 the university would not create another purpose-built theatre until the DeBartolo Center for the Performing Arts opened in 2004. The exhibition hall model thus persisted at Notre Dame the century and a half from 1853 until 2004 and ended when the first dedi - cated theatres at Notre Dame opened in the form of the Decio Main-stage Theatre (365 seats) and the Philbin Studio Theatre (100 seats). The *Scholastic* article of 1892 assumed logically that an addition was forthcoming, something that simply never happened. The building being too small by the 1890s helps to put into perspective the growing space demands of a thriving university at a time when large assemblies were still an expected and required tradition.

As grand and as wonderful as the new Washington Hall was, especially compared with the clapboard building it replaced, it is well to remember that the new structure contained only half again more space, and the rapid growth of the university thus quickly challenged its capacity. While Notre Dame built over the years many other spaces to accommodate the programming needs originally intended for Washington Hall, the university did not open a second performing arts center until a full century after the obvious need to do so.

Patriarchs Die

Between July and November 1893, university patriarchs Sorin and Granger died, as did President Walsh. Thus by the end of the fall semester of the 1893–94 academic year, the university was not only in a state of grief, but it had been forced to transfer power to another generation of leaders.[110] The Golden Jubilee of the university, which should have been celebrated in June 1894, was postponed until June 1895, due to "the deaths of the three men who had done most to make Notre Dame what it is."[111]

The Gregori/Rusca Interior of 1894

Luigi Gregori and Louis Rusca began their redo of the interior of Washington Hall during the the renovation of 1894; their work remained essentially intact until Father Harvey's remodeling and redecoration in the summer of 1956. The only visibly surviving elements of this 1894 work are in the balcony arch ceiling, concealed above the lighting booth, and inside a "light lock" (see figs. 5.10 and 5.11), although it is likely that much of the 1894 artistry remains underneath the many layers of paint applied since the remodeling of 1956. For work on the Exhibition Hall from March 24 to July 14, 1894, the

Figure 5.10. Balcony lobby arch ceiling panel, original Rusca/Poligano 1894 painting intact, long concealed by the interior ceiling of the light booth, possibly since the construction of the projection booth around 1916, but certainly since the 1956 renovation when the Gregori/Rusca interior was painted over. The floor in this picture is on top of the ceiling of the current light booth (photograph by Greta Fisher 2006).

Figure 5.11. Area long concealed inside a "light lock" (probably since the 1956 remodeling), likely a remnant of the original Rusca/ Poligano 1894 painting, although it could possibly have survived from earlier work of Ackermann/Frederick (photograph by Ron Grisoli 2009).

Financial Journal recorded payments to Rusca, Gregori, and others for gilt cornices, mouldings, "Caps Molded," and painting, totaling nearly $1,700, or a little over 11 percent of the insured value of the entire structure, clearly a major expense.[112] In April 1894 the *Scholastic* noted in anticipation:

> When the decorations in Washington Hall are completed we shall have one of the prettiest college theatres in the country. Signor Rusca, a well-known decorator, is doing the work. He is the artist who frescoed part of the church and also the sides of the dome. His plans of the work show that Washington Hall will be indeed a thing of beauty. The coloring will be as light and gay as it is possible to have it without flashiness.
>
> In each of the four corners of the ceiling are to be emblematic figures representing Tragedy, Comedy, Music and Poetry. . . .
>
> The curtain now on the stage will be removed and a new one . . . will take its place. Some changes may also be made in the scenic appointments on the stage. The old gas foot-lights will be removed, and incandescent electric lights will replace them. No longer will our sense of smell be offended by odors of noisome gas, and the super with the torch will be forced to light his way to other scenes—his occupation's gone.
>
> After all the improvements are completed the Hall will be reopened with elaborate exercises. . . . Instead of the bare white walls we will be able to gaze on excellent portraits, grand figures and exquisite decorations.[113]

It is noteworthy that the gas lights installed in 1883 to replace the original oil lamps were obsolete by the time of the 1894 Gregori/Rusca renovation, a sign of the rapid technological change at the time, and the new electric footlights endured well into the tenure of Father Harvey, even after his 1956 remodeling. The "bare white walls" mentioned above seem incongruous with the highly decorated Ackermann/Frederick proscenium arch we know existed from the mid-1880s. Perhaps the walls in question are the expanses beyond the proscenium? No photograph seems to have survived, and it is possible that Ackermann and Frederick decorated only the area around the proscenium arch, whitewashing everything else.

The *Scholastic* described the new interior of Washington Hall that survived sixty-two years, from 1894 until the summer of 1956, as follows (see fig. 5.4):

> Of all the many improvements inaugurated by the Very Rev. President Morrissey during the scholastic year '93–'94, the artistic frescoing of Washington Hall is the most notable. There are in America theatres vast and gorgeous; but we can safely say few, if any, have an interior as chaste and beautiful as the one just now completed at Notre Dame. We were fortunate in securing the services of the famous Signor Louis Rusca, of Chicago, well known at Notre Dame for his excellent work in the dome of the University and the chapel of the Sacred Heart.
>
> The foundations of Washington Hall were laid during the administration of Very Rev. President Corby in 1880. The auditorium is octagonal in form with seats arranged after the style of an amphitheatre. In decorating the hall, the artist, while keeping in view the simplicity of architectural lines, has been able to give a pleasing and harmonious effect of neutral tints and soft colors to meet the approbation of the most fastidious critic. In tone the strong notes are walls of amber grey with panels of russet green, separated from each other by pairs of graceful pilasters of Bradilio marble with delicately gilded Corinthian capitals.
>
> The ceiling is especially beautiful in design and color. It is divided into six large panels of a light olive tint, decorated with deli - cately limned ornaments springing forth in curved lines from four round golden frames containing portraits of Shakspere, Molière, Mozart and Beethoven, painted by Gregori. From the centre of the ceiling rises a gracefully curved dome adorned with festoons of flowers and trailing vines on a background of the brightest tints seen in a morning sky. A large curved space, twelve feet wide, connecting the walls with the ceiling is embellished with skillfully executed niches, containing sitting figures of Tragedy, Comedy, Music and Poetry. These allegorical representations are of majestic proportions, graceful in pose and brilliant in color. They stand out in bold relief from landscapes softened with heavenly hues.

Immediately above the proscenium, in an elaborate frame, painted in light and shade and subdued colors, is placed a portrait of the immortal Father of our Country, holding in his hand a copy of the Declaration of Independence. On each side of Washington stand American eagles, bearing in their beaks fluttering scrolls, one of which bears the legend, "Pro Deo et Patria" [For God and Country], and the other, "E Pluribus Unum" [From Many, One]. Heroic figures of Demosthenes [house right] and Cicero [house left] in *chiaro oscuro,* clever representations of statues, stand in niches, one on each side of the stage. These, as well as the masterly portrait of Washington and the figures of the muses, are also from the atelier of our own world-renowned Gregori, who, although now in the seventy-fifth year of his age has lost none of that vigor or brilliancy so conspicuous in his earlier works. The broad frame above and at the sides of the proscenium is conventional in treatment. Highly relieved candelabra-like ornaments, with emblems of music and song in light and shade entwined with delicate garlands of flowers and variegated leaves, display the immortal names of [house right] Rossini, Balfe [house left], Haydn and Gounod, good representatives of the musicians of Italy, Ireland, Germany and France. The pedestals supporting these candelabra are inscribed with the names of Lilly [house left] and Girac [house right]—our own Father Lilly and professor Girac, masters of music in composition and execution, who devoted the best years of their lives to the developing at Notre Dame of a love and knowledge of the art divine. Distributed with rare good judgment, delicate lines of burnished gold light up the moldings and projecting bands with most pleasing effect.

The entire treatment is in the Renaissance style, a good example of the adaptability of that order to decorative work. Mr. Rusca's intelligent arranging of soft, rich tints has produced a symphony in color of exceptional beauty, its restful quiet suggesting that happy blending of tones which we find in nature. The theatrical flash usually seen in the decorations of our public halls is agreeably absent. The entire work will remain as a criterion for that which is good and correct. We congratulate Mr. Rusca, the designer of the decorations and his able assistant, Mr. Poligano, whose artistic touch did so much towards the successful execution of Mr. Rusca's plans. Professor O'Dea, Director of the Electrical Department, by his practical knowledge and indefatigable labors, has contributed in no small degree to the success of the entire scheme of decorations. Again we congratulate our Very Rev. President and Notre Dame University in possessing this gem, this perfect hall for public entertainments.[114]

Nowhere is Althusser's theory that ideology manifests itself physically more clear and obvious than in the Gregori/Rusca 1894 interior of Washington Hall. After the interior artistry had been completed, the auditorium in so many ways summed up emblematically what Washington Hall was all about, beginning with the ceiling—the heavens, if you will—from which Shakespeare, Molière, Mozart, and Beethoven looked down over all that occurred below. Along the sides of the "heavens" stood (just below the playwrights and composers) the four allegorical personifications of Tragedy, Comedy, Music, and Poetry, ready and willing to inspire and support the creation of the arts they represented. The emblematic figures served as amalgamations of four of the six categories related to the nine classical muses (see fig. 5.12), with the three muses of poetry combined into one, the two muses of music combined into one, the muses of history and astronomy ignored, and tragedy and comedy retaining their singular status. Centered directly above the proscenium, George Washington, the father of the country and namesake of the building, sat holding the Declaration of Independence, with American eagles on each side clutching banners proclaiming in Latin For God and Country and From Many, One. With Washington front and center, surrounded by the greats in the heavens, one could never forget the clear connection between God, country, and the arts. On each side of the stage below Washington, audiences always saw the two greatest classical orators, Athens's Demosthenes (383–322 B.C.), and Rome's Cicero (106–43 B.C.), standing nobly in niches between marbleized columns that supported the entire proscenium arch from which George Washington surveyed all. The fathers of classical oratory provided a foundation and support for the father of the nation. Since the days of Professors Lyons and

Figure 5.12. 1894 interior detail of fig. 5.4. The personification of Tragedy, above the audience and to the right.

Griffith in the 1860s, oratory, elocution, and debate had been central to formal education at Notre Dame, and the placing of trompe l'oeil "statues" of Cicero and Demosthenes so prominently con - firmed the central role that elocution and oratory (and debate and argumentation) had played in the history of both the university and the country.

Interwoven into the elaborate floral decoration around the pro - scenium arch were books and sheet music, along with the surnames of composers Gioachino Rossini (Italy, 1792–1868), Michael William Balfe (Ireland, 1808–70), Franz Joseph Haydn (Austria, 1732–1809), and Charles François Gounod (France, 1818–93), who represented the best of the contemporary European music world. Pedestals held the candelabra that supported the books, music scores, and com - posers' names. On these foundations were inscribed the names of the patriarchs of the music programs at Notre Dame, Father Edward

Figure 5.14. 1894 interior detail of fig. 5.4. House right proscenium arch "Girac" column supporting Rossini and Balfe. On house left "Lilly" supported Gounod and Haydn.

Figure 5.13. 1894 interior detail of fig. 5.4. Pilaster of faux Bradilio marble with trompe l'oeil statue of Demosthenes in his niche.

Lilly and Professor Maximilian Girac, who, with the help of Cicero and Demosthenes, symbolically held up the entire proscenium arch (see figs. 5.13, 5.14, 5.15).[115]

At the June 1894 graduation, the *Scholastic* recognized the redo of the interior: "When the University orchestra began Bucallossi's famous overture, 'Les Manteaux Noir,' at half-past seven, Washington Hall—the new, the glorious—was filled to overflowing. Many

Figure 5.15. 1894 interior detail of fig. 5.4. George Washington, centered in the proscenium arch above the stage. Note banners held in eagles' beaks proclaiming "Pro Deo et Patria" (For God and Country) and "E Pluribus Unum" (From Many, One). The Father of the Country appropriately holds the Declaration of Independence.

were the words of praise our visitors had for Gregori's magnificent portraits and Rusca's beautiful decorations."[116] The Gregori/Rusca interior of 1894 created "keepers of the space" to monitor all that went on there for the next six decades.

Other Changes to the Building

We cannot know with absolute certainty what changes occurred to the building in the fall of 1894, but it is clear that previously the east entrance had not been accessible. The university added wooden steps to the east entrance specifically to handle the preps from Carroll Hall (who lived in the west wing of the Main Building) whose outdoor play area or "yard" was east of Washington Hall adjacent to the northern half of the gymnasium/student play hall:

New steps leading from Carroll yard to Washington Hall have been put in place. The improvement has long been needed. In times past, the audience seated near the door were made uncomfortable by having to sit in a draught, while the students of Carroll Hall ["preps" under seventeen] filed to their seats. And the performances were delayed while six hundred people entered through one door [the west entrance]. The new entrance will, in a measure, do away with these annoyances. The students of Carroll Hall will now enter from their own side of the building.[117]

Thus additional access to the building allowed preparatory students to file into the balcony directly without having to pass through the main lobby (and make noise) while the collegiate students did the same thing through the west entrance, halving the time required to get students into the Washington Hall gallery. At the same time, the *Scholastic* called for installation of doors between the lobby and auditorium which apparently had not existed before:

A double set of doors is needed for the Music hall. This was made plain at the concert Wednesday. It is just a bit exasperating to have the attention distracted from the performance on the stage by the entrance of those who will persist in coming late for concerts. It would be an easy matter to place the present doors at the entrance of the vestibule and to put in their place a set of swinging doors heavily padded; these could also serve to keep out the cold. Music hall is so well equipped in other particulars that the neglect of this improvement is all the more evident.[118]

By the end of the 1894–95 academic year, Washington Hall had a new curtain and box set, a brass rail to delineate orchestra from auditorium to "improve the appearance of things in front of the stage,"[119] and discussion began regarding the need for additional storage space, although the singular addition to the building's exterior footprint did not happen until 1907. The *Scholastic* noted that the

Music Hall will have a new curtain for the stage at Commencement. Two well known scenic artists of Chicago are engaged upon it. They are also at work on a box scene representing an interior. This has been a much needed piece of property. A brass railing will enclose the space reserved for the orchestra. After the Jubilee exercises are over, a store house for scenery will be built. The managers will have little trouble next year in staging plays.[120]

The box set reflects a stylistic shift to realism away from wing-and-drop scenery, which had dominated the nineteenth century and was provided by early scenic artists at Notre Dame such as Jacob Ackermann. The flats needed to create box sets necessarily required additional storage space.

With advancing technology, interior photography became much more routine by 1895, as the *Scholastic* pointed out: "McDonald, the photographer, has been busily engaged in taking "flash-light pictures on the stage of Washington Hall. The musical clubs and the University Stock Company have been taken thus far."[121] Interior pictures became a new option from this time onward because of improvements in film exposure speed and flash technology, so it would no longer be necessary to photograph outside to benefit from the intensity of natural light.

The university thus replaced the Ackermann 1885 drop/valence curtain in 1895 after ten years of use and a year after Gregori and Rusca completed their interior work. It is reasonable to assume this was due to a general updating and overall professionalization that had occurred in the transformation of the interior of the building, as well as changes in staging practice. Sosman and Landis Scene Painting Studio was considered one of the best in the country at this time, and it was these artists who designed the first box set for the Washington Hall stage and generally modernized the area upstage of the proscenium arch:

> The new curtain for the stage of Washington Hall now replaces the one painted by the late Prof. Ackermann in '85. It is a real work of art. Surrounded by rich drapery whose beautiful colors blend so nicely is a representation of the ruined Athenian Acropolis. It is a faithful picture of the remains of that famous citadel. In the foreground can be seen the ruins of the Parthenon. The curtain is the work of Sosman and Landis, of Chicago, who have also furnished the stage with an elegant box scene.[122]

The clear reference to the first "box scene" on the Washington Hall stage represented a true shift in scenic technique from the wing-and-drop tradition that had been de rigueur for theatres since the Italian Renaissance. Although popularized in the English-speaking world by the mid-nineteenth century through the work of the Bancrofts and Booth, the box set clearly was not embraced universally until much later. In a very real sense, then, the building was not completed until it incorporated the work of Sosman and Landis, whose scenic work onstage undoubtedly complemented the permanent Gregori/Rusca interior in ways that the Ackermann/Frederick scenery from the 1880s could not. In the decade from 1885 to 1895, Notre Dame completely professionalized (and in the process hugely upgraded) Washington Hall, going from faculty-supported artistic work using the best local artists on campus, to importing world-class professionals to transform the space. In this important decade, there was both the will to make Washington Hall "a perfect gem" and the funding available to realize that goal. An interesting by-product of the shift to the box set from the earlier wing-and-drop system of staging was the increased demand for storage space for "flats," canvas stretched over wood frames which, when connected together, form the "walls" of box sets. Washington Hall had been designed and built with the wing-and-drop system in mind and thus had no off-stage spaces suitable for the storage of flats, a situation not remedied until the addition of 1907 when the only change in the footprint of the building occurred in its history.

The Academy of Music that Notre Dame formally dedicated in June 1882 culminated a thirty-year tradition that had begun with the creation by 1854 of the first exhibition hall in Main Building I. Although the new structure opened and was dedicated at the end of the 1881–82 academic year, not until thirteen years later was it completed, externally from the south tower in 1887 to the stone steps of the south entrance in 1889, and internally from the initial Ackermann/Frederick sets and auditorium painting in 1885, to the artistic complexity of Gregori/Rusca and Sosman/Landis in 1894 and 1895. Although both the stage and house benefited from the marvelous work of Ackermann and Frederick, Gregori and Rusca's complete redo with thematic murals and trompe l'oeil statues transformed the house just in time for the belated celebration of the Golden Jubilee, and required complementary professionalism on the stage from Sosman and Landis, who in modernizing the stage simultaneously created new and pressing needs for scenery storage. With the 1890s redo, Washington Hall had truly become a "gem" both internally and externally, with aesthetic and practical accoutrements that rivaled any such facility anywhere in the country at the time.

CHAPTER 6

GROWING PAINS, 1895–1922

The completion of the Gregori/Rusca interior of Washington Hall by 1894, followed a year later by new stage scenery by Sosman and Landis, while undoubtedly providing an exquisite backdrop for the celebration of the Golden Jubilee, also coincided with a new phase for the university. A new generation had rather quickly replaced the last of the founding patriarchs by the end of 1893, and for the first time in the university's history, those physically present at the establishment of Notre Dame were no longer around. Described by the *Chicago Daily Tribune* as "the most beautifully finished, of any college theater, in the country,"[1] Washington Hall served as one of many venues for the university's three-day celebration of its Golden Jubilee in June 1895, overlaying the graduation ceremonies in June with alumni and invited guests attending from all parts of the nation.[2] Against the larger backdrop of the Spanish-American War (1898), the assassination of William McKinley (1901), and World War I (1914–18), and under the visionary leadership of Presidents Cavanaugh and Burns, the university was transformed into the modern American university we recognize to this day. By 1922 increased enrollment numbers exceeded the physical limits of the 1882 Washington Hall, by then too small to handle even such vital communal assemblies as commencement, one of the central functions of a university "exhibition hall." Washington Hall continued to serve as the primary "town hall" for access, integration, and communal assembly, even as the rise of niche audiences made the tradition of inclusive communal exhibitions increasingly obsolete.

The national fervor related to the new Pledge of Allegiance (the genesis of which seemed to have been the Columbian quatercentenary in 1892) saw the senior class adding in 1897 to the long-established celebration of Washington's Birthday an elaborate flag presentation ceremony, thus creating a doubly patriotic exhibition that overtly melded church and state at Notre Dame well into the 1960s. The traditional exhibition related to Washington's Birthday had always been profoundly patriotic—now made even more so—not coincidentally occurring as the nation itself absorbed waves of immigrants and realized its own "manifest destiny."[3]

The choice of plays changed during this period, too, to permit men for the first time to perform important female roles and to do so convincingly (to great praise after some initial criticism), a tradition that continued into the 1920s. In addition, the huge popularity of vaudeville and burlesque at the time produced great interest in theatrical parody of the "Other" in terms of gender, ethnicity, and race, with the blackface minstrel show and its variants becoming exceedingly popular. The first overarching theatre production group began in 1895 with the University Stock Company in what ultimately proved to be a successful attempt to move beyond the various student societies— such as the Thespians and the St. Cecilia Philomatheans—ultimately to create a firmer academic connection to theatre production at Notre Dame. This was undoubtedly related to the curricular reforms of the 1920s that would restructure courses, majors, and the calendar in ways that make sense to this day.

This is also the period of Knute Rockne and the rising national interest in college football. Rockne matriculated as a student in 1910, and upon graduation in 1914 he became a faculty member. In both capacities he appeared on the Washington Hall stage, while performing his other more famous duties on the gridiron as first a football player (as a student) and then as coach (as a faculty member). Under

Rockne's leadership and with outstanding players like George Gipp, the Notre Dame football program rose to national—some would say mythic—prominence. The untimely death of Gipp in 1920 coincided with accounts of a ghost in Washington Hall, and within a few years the two unrelated events became forever fused.

Invited guests who appeared in Washington Hall during this period included such luminaries as William Jennings Bryan and Eamon de Valera; their appearances and those of many others firmly established Washington Hall as the "home of the lecture," as Stritch asserts in *My Notre Dame*,[4] and the corresponding rise of specialized, niche audiences created freestanding theatre and music events no longer part of traditional exhibitions.

In terms of structure, the singular change in Washington Hall's footprint occurred in 1907 with the addition of the set storage area in the northeast corner of the stage, while its first inside toilet was acquired the following year. Many changes took place in the orchestra pit and the interface between the stage and the audience, and technological innovations in photography permitted indoor "flash" pictures for the first time to record some of these changes; photographs have survived of Washington Hall's audiences, both appearing to be witnessing a play and watching a film (see figs. 6.1 and 6.2).

The importance of the advent of film cannot be stressed enough; it is perhaps the most significant change in the history of communal assembly at Notre Dame. Washington Hall became by 1915 the primary campus venue for screening motion pictures, reflecting an abiding and early interest in film. "Photoplays," as they were called initially, became regular and hugely popular and would be screened there at least through the mid-1960s. Moreover, before the advent of film the distance technology of the telegraph permitted by 1907 the use of Washington Hall as an assembly hall in which audiences could indirectly "witness" a football game by having a host diagram the action of the game on a large blackboard set up on the stage as reports came in to the nearby Western Union office in a string of dots and dashes. The incorporation of the mechanical/electrical miracles of the film projector and the telegraph to create Washington Hall events confirmed the country's rapid technological advances, which, ironically, ultimately rendered the nineteenth-century exhibition hall obsolete.

Figure 6.1. The first photograph of a Washington Hall theatre audience as seen from the stage. *Dome* 1912, 291.

Finally, the establishment of the university's endowment under the visionary president the Reverend James A. Burns, C.S.C., created the momentum and means to move Notre Dame into the top ranks of American universities. His goal as part of a new master plan to build a "fine arts building" recognized that the arts were central to Notre Dame's expansive future, and that the university had already outgrown its purpose-built 1882 Academy of Music. But President Burns did more than create the endowment. He closed the "Junior Department" preparatory school in 1921 and initiated the movement toward ending the grade school (where the boys were known as minims), and thus in a real sense shifted the university demographic to exclusively older, collegiate students.[5] The establishment of a coeducational summer school in 1918 of predominantly postgraduates in turn made essential the creation of a structured graduate school by 1920 and clearly added to the institution's credibility as a place of higher education. President Burns in 1920 created an associate board of lay trustees with "the responsibility of holding, investing and administering endowment funds of the University." Burns put nearly all these ducks in a row by the early 1920s for the university we know and recognize today. In his brief tenure as presi-

Figure 6.2. The first photograph of a Washington Hall film audience as seen from the point of view of the screen. *Dome* 1916, 156.

dent, Notre Dame had become fully and singularly a university, with a coeducational summer school and a graduate school able to award master's and doctoral degrees, an associate board of lay trustees to manage its endowment, and master plans for future expansion. By the early 1920s Notre Dame had become a thoroughly modern American university.[6]

The Golden Jubilee

For the three days (the "Triduum") of the Golden Jubilee commencement exercises, Tuesday through Thursday, June 11–13, 1895, Washington Hall served as a major venue, beginning with the alumni exercises on the first evening, which included the university orchestra's grand overture, the Grand Chorus of the Alumni, a mandolin sextet with guitar and autoharp, an oration, a vocal quartet, a poem, another oration by William P. Breen, closing remarks by the governor of Indiana, Isaac P. Gray, and concluding with the university orchestra's finale rendition of "America." On the second day after mass, a regatta on St. Joseph's Lake, dinner, an athletic contest, supper, and a lawn concert by the band all occurred before the graduating class held exercises in Washington Hall that included a grand overture, the Grand Jubilee Ode Chorus, a speech, an oration, a flute solo, another oration, grand concert selections by the Orpheus Mandolin Orchestra, an oration, a vocal quartet, the oration of the day by the bishop of Peoria, the Right Reverend John Lancaster Spalding, and the finale of "Hail Columbia." On the final commencement day, the closing exercises began in Washington Hall in the morning and included a vocal quartet singing "Home Sweet Home," the class poem, the valedictory, and the awarding of honors and conferring of degrees, with the university band (under the direction of Professor Preston) performing "Notre Dame Quickstep" for the finale. Commentary on the hall, designed for evening events, included the bittersweet aspect of graduation: "There is something peculiarly depressing about Washington Hall in the early morning, with the glow of the footlights gone; and to no one was this more evident than to '95 as they listened to the melody of 'Home, Sweet Home,' and realized that Notre Dame was a home to them no longer."[7] The *South Bend Daily Times*, in its news article covering the first fifty years, said of Washington Hall:

> To the left of the main building is Music Hall, containing the conservatory of music. This building includes Washington Hall, which is probably the largest and at all events the most beautifully fin-ished of any college theatre in the country. All the accessories of a well regulated theatre are here provided. Three years ago Mr. Daly's company, with Miss Rehan in the cast, gave a play in this theatre. Many distinguished orators, among whom are Henry Watterson, Daniel Dougherty, Bishops Ireland, Spalding and Keane, have been heard in this hall. The six amateurs' societies frequently present plays here with remarkable ability. There are musical societies, which add further to the diversions and instruction of the students by concerts.[8]

Against considerable odds, Notre Dame celebrated its first fifty years with Washington Hall at the center of the festivities.

Washington's Birthday and Summer School

The last Washington's Birthday celebration in the old style, by the Thespians, the university orchestra, and the Glee Club, without the focus on the American flag, occurred in 1895, and it was "one of the most splendid and successful celebrations that have been seen in Washington Hall for years." The *Scholastic* effused: "Washington's birthday is always a bright day for the Thespians. For years they have honored the name of Washington by appropriate exercises, and again and again won for themselves the glory of being the first dramatic society of Notre Dame." The *Scholastic* continued, "The Thespians surpassed themselves. Before an audience, swelled to unusual numbers by the patrons and friends of the University, they presented a programme, which, because of its difficulty, won them all the more praise." The celebration began at 4:00 P.M. with the university orchestra providing "a series of inspirational airs," followed by the Glee Club singing "Columbia, the Gem of the Ocean," an oration by a junior, the mandolin orchestra playing "A Night in Venice" with an encore, and culminating with the Thespians performing "Damon and Pythias," to high praise for the staging: "Too much praise cannot be given Mr. Joseph A. Marmon, the Stage Manager, for his excellent work behind the scenes. It has been remarked by many that the shifting of scenery has not been so effectively done for some time."[9]

The model that had existed since the 1860s changed with Washington's Birthday in 1896, due to the dedication of a new flagstaff on the campus, which itself reflected a new focus on the American flag. The *Scholastic* reported:

> The one hundred-and-sixty-third anniversary of the birth of Washington will not soon be forgotten at Notre Dame. The Alumni and the Class of '96 conspired to make it memorable. The event of the morning was the dedication of the new flag-staff, the gift of Mr. Samuel T. Murdock, '86. At ten o'clock the exercises were

begun in Washington Hall. The programme was very simple. After the singing of "America" by a grand chorus of all the students, Professor John G. Ewing, a classmate of Mr. Murdock's, presented the flag and staff to the University, and it was accepted by Father Morrissey in a few happy sentences. Another chorus, "The Star Spangled Banner," and Mr. Daniel Vincent Casey, '95, read a brief poem written for the occasion. "Columbia" followed, and the Hon. William P. Breen, '79, delivered a short but admirable address on "Washington and Our Flag." Then, the beautiful flag was raised, and with another round of cheers, the dedication was completed.[10]

The article advocated flying the flag all year—instead of reserving it for national holidays, as had apparently been the custom—in which case the wear and tear of daily use required regular replacement and that translated into the idea that the senior class should present a new flag each year to the university:

Why not a "service" flag? If one thousand square [20' x 50'] of "Old Glory" at the peak is a gallant sight on a half-dozen days of the year, surely the same spread of bunting would be an inspiration on the three hundred and sixty which are not national holidays. . . . We must needs have another flag, of course, and one paid for by a popular subscription. It would be ungrateful to raise Mr. Murdock's bit of bunting every day, for it would be whipped into streamers within a year. . . . Make the graduating class of the year its guardians; give them the honor of raising it each morning and lowering it each night; they would be proud of the distinction. . . . We cannot have too much of "Old Glory."[11]

A patriotic tradition thus began that would last into the 1960s.

At the 1896 ceremony the *Scholastic* stated that "the Stars and Stripes stretched in graceful folds across the front of the stage," the gift of "Mr. Samuel Murdock, to whom the University is indebted for the graceful flag and staff that grace the entrance to the grounds." President Morrissey said at the acceptance speech, "From this seat of learning go forth to-day the voices of hundreds of America's children proclaiming their devotion to the flag that protects them. In this Western home of Christian education have always been taught those noble principles of true liberty for which our forefathers bled."[12] The *Scholastic* pointed out that this presentation was "the first public patriotic demonstration since President Cleveland sent his now famous message to Congress, and the audience found opportunity to express their joy as much at the outcome of his *fiat* as in celebrating the birthday of our proto-president."[13] Musical and theatrical events added to the festivities.

With the plans in place by 1896, the first actual presentation of the flag to the president by the senior class in connection with Washington's Birthday celebrations occurred one year later in February 1897:

> The day was auspiciously begun in the church where at eight o'clock all the students heard Mass, which was celebrated by the Rev. M. J. Regan, C.S.C. At ten o'clock Washington Hall was crowded, when the Class of '97, in cap and gown for the first time, entered and were greeted with applause. The occasion was
>
> THE PRESENTATION OF THE FLAG
>
> to the University and to the students by the Class of '97. The University Band had played a medley of national airs, and the strains had died away when Mr. Charles M. B. Bryan, the man whom '97 chose as their representative, left his seat among his classmates and took his stand upon the stage beneath the flag he was come to present. . . . The afternoon celebration was a splendid success. Washington Hall was filled to overflowing, and the ushers, who did their work well, were kept busy. South Bend's society was there, and many of the University's friends from afar added color to the occasion. Gay flags,—the red, white and blue, and the gold and blue—hung in graceful folds from the gallery.[14]

The large flag, on display above the stage, must have dominated the room. In the true spirit of the nineteenth-century exhibition, after the orchestra played and an oration was delivered, Boucicault's enormously popular play *The Corsican Brothers* followed.[15] The new flag to replace the one that had flown the previous year became an important actor and set piece for this new addition to an old Notre Dame tradition of celebrating the birthday of the father of the country.

The sinking of the battleship *Maine* by explosion on February 15, 1898, in Havana harbor precipitated the Spanish-American War (April–August 1898) and colored the Washington's Birthday celebrations that year. The *Scholastic* reported:

> So everyone that entered Washington Hall last Tuesday morning to witness the flag-presentation exercises had just read all the "war news" in their morning papers an hour before, and as a result they listened more attentively to the many patriotic words addressed to them. . . . The Hall was tastefully decorated with the Stars and Stripes and our Gold and Blue, and across the proscenium arch hung the new flag, the gift of the Class of '98. The old flags of '96 and '97, now weather-beaten and torn, fell in graceful folds from the balcony railing.[16]

The band played "Columbia, the Gem of the Ocean," for which the audience rose to sing the chorus. Mr. Raymond G. O'Malley, president of the class of '98, presented in the name of the senior class the flag to the university (and he spoke), followed by Professor Preston and the band's thrilling rendition of "The Stars and Stripes Forever." President Morrissey then made a graceful, patriotic address and accepted the flag in the name of the university, citing "loyalty to the fundamental principles upon which rests the fabric of our glorious Constitution." Applause ensued, and the audience rose and sang "The Star-Spangled Banner." Mr. Frank Earle Hering ('98) then read an ode that was "the best poem that has ever been read by a student from the Washington Hall stage,"[17] followed by a chorus of "America" by the audience. This important flag-bearing addition to the Washington's Birthday celebration confirmed that patriotism clearly was front and center at Notre Dame, as it had been since the earliest days of the university under Father Sorin, but the event had now taken on an even more enhanced nationalistic dimension.

By 1908 the process was de rigueur but interestingly included music in another performance venue back in the Main Building. The *Scholastic* reported:

> Last Saturday, the anniversary of Washington's Birthday, was observed with the usual commemorative exercises. In the morning

the students attended Mass [in the church] in a body, and afterwards assembled in Washington Hall to listen to music, poetry, and eloquence. At the close of the exercises the University band discoursed pleasing music in the rotunda of the Main Building. Both the band and orchestra did well the part they had in the program of the day, and are a credit to their accomplished leader, Professor Peterson.[18]

In accepting the flag from the senior class, President John W. Cavanaugh spoke on the vulgarity and corruption of the day.

Washington's Birthday exercises in 1915 especially dealt with the tensions between being Catholic and being American with the Great War raging in Europe:

Although the military manoeuvres were excluded from the exercises commemorative of Washington's Birthday, yet the demonstration lost none of its accustomed solemnity and fervor. The long lines of Seniors in cap and gown were highly impressive as they marched into Washington Hall to present their flag to the University. Although this ceremony is a tradition at Notre Dame, yet it has a particular meaning at this crisis in national destiny. Again, we are Catholics, a fact which, during the present tide of bigotry and fanaticism, is worth stressing. All this was treated with fervid eloquence by Mr. Emmett Lenihan, premier orator of the class of '15, in an address presenting the flag.[19]

Lenihan emphasized the national unity the flag represented: "That flag acknowledges no hyphenated citizenship; it recognizes no German-American, no Russian-American, no English-American. It demands the unqualified allegiance of the simple American citizen."[20] Father Cavanaugh, in accepting the flag, also referred to anti-Catholic broadsheets circulating in South Bend and reaffirmed the high patriotism of Notre Dame and its men and rejected the religious fanatics.[21]

By the 1917–18 academic year, the exodus of young men to fight in World War I had reached its peak, and the 1918 Washington's Birthday exercises as a result became unique in Notre Dame history: the women of Saint Mary's College joined the men of Notre Dame for the ceremonies, as related in the 1918 *Dome*:

Aye, truly that was a day of days. Precedent, age-honored custom, the stringency of established rules, all, all shattered by the doings of a twenty-four hours. Youth and beauty of both sexes combined to honor him whose paternal hand guided the rash, impulsive colonies into firm and perpetual nationship. Not since brick was laid upon brick to evolve Washington Hall—a fitly-named scene for the function—had those walls seen or heard tell of such things. . . . "I was present when the Senior Class of the sister college made its angelic visitation"—and at the slightest evincing of incredulity—"Yes, I was. Really. I heard Miss Beatty present the service flag."[22]

Perhaps just as dislocating as women participating in the Washington's Birthday celebration in February 1918 was the creation the same year of a coeducational summer school. Mary E. Sullivan, a summer school student in that first session, pointed out, "Although Notre Dame University was founded in 1842, it opened summer courses of study on June 29, 1918, for the first time in its history. Moreover, coincident with this splendid work, the University astonished the country by opening its doors to women."[23] The opening of a coeducational summer school, while open to all women, especially served the needs of the nation's teachers in Catholic schools and colleges, many of whom were sisters in religious orders, who would flock to Notre Dame over the next forty years. Sullivan's worry that the coincident establishing of the wartime Students' Army Training Corps (SATC), "buzzing with activity" with over one thousand students on campus training to become officers, would perhaps restrict or eliminate the new summer school experiment proved unfounded.[24]

The armistice of November 11, 1918, ended both the war and the coed ceremony with regard to Washington's Birthday, however, so by February 1919 things seemed to be back to status quo ante. The *Scholastic* related the day as

a cherished tradition of the students of Notre Dame to assemble on the birthday of this Father of our Country in the hall that bears his name to pay homage to his memory and to perpetuate him as an exemplar in their minds and hearts. And it will continue to be traditional so long as patriotism is esteemed a virtue. . . . The program of the day began at nine o'clock in the morning when the members of the Senior Class in cap and gown marched into Washington Hall. The University Orchestra played the opening selection, after which the audience, led by the Glee Club, sang "The Star Spangled Banner." In words most appropriate to the occasion, George Dewey Haller, senior journalist, and president of the senior class, in the name of the class, and in keeping with the old custom, presented to the University a large American flag.[25]

With the 1921 ceremonies, the *Scholastic* related a story told by President Burns regarding Father Sorin, one repeated often by succeeding university administrators. After "the annual presentation of the Flag by the Senior Class," followed by the reading of Washington's farewell address, an oration, the class ode, and an address by the class president, President Burns talked about the patriotic tradition at Notre Dame, and he recounted the story of Father Sorin kneeling and kissing the land upon his arrival and becoming "an American that instant."[26]

In addition to Washington's Birthday celebrations in February, the newly inaugurated (and coeducational) summer session, spread over the Fourth of July holiday, created a new opportunity for the university to demonstrate its patriotism and to involve women in the festivities. In 1922 the summer session held Independence Day exercises in Washington Hall, presided over by Ellen Ryan Jolly, LL. D., who later wrote *Nuns of the Battlefield*.[27] The program included "The Star Spangled Banner" sung by the audience (with words in the program), the reading of the Declaration of Independence by a student, the song "Columbia" by the audience (with words in the program), a vocal solo, an address by the Reverend William J. Bolger, C.S.C., and the song "Notre Dame" by the audience (with words in the program).[28]

Building Changes

Washington Hall desperately needed additional storage space backstage. With plans to remedy the situation in place by 1893, the *Scholastic* wondered aloud in 1898 what had happened, describing as "lost or stolen:—The plans of the new addition to the stage in Washington

Hall."[29] But the need never lessened, and by the fall of 1907 work finally began to make the only addition to the building's footprint in its history, one that rendered Edbrooke's beautifully symmetrical design forever asymmetrical: "According to a recent action of the University council there is to be a property room extension of Washington Hall. That such an addition has come to be a necessity is a proposition which the scene shifter takes for granted."[30] By Thanksgiving, with the addition completed, there was cause for celebration:

> At last the property man who stands behind the curtain in Washington Hall is ready to welcome Thanksgiving; he is ready to celebrate at a moment's notice, if he hasn't already celebrated, for the masons and carpenters have completed their work at the northeast corner of the stage, and he has shifted his scenery into its new quarters.[31]

It is hard to imagine where his scenery had been stored before this addition, which created a new space off the stage-left wing of 14' x 18' that, while not huge, permitted scenery to be struck and stored for the first time in a convenient and designated place. A comparable space also now existed on the ground floor below stage level which initially stored band equipment but houses restrooms today (see fig. 6.3).

At about the same time, the university finally replaced the temporary wooden east steps installed in 1894 to make that entrance operational for the preparatory students: "The wooden steps used for the east entrance to Washington Hall and similar steps that have done service for the rear entrance to the Church have been removed to be replaced by concrete approaches."[32] The east entrance steps remained concrete until the 1984 renovation, when steel replaced them. The east entrance most directly accessed the stage, and it served as the de facto (but not ideal) "loading dock" for Washington Hall, in addition to providing direct student access to the balcony. Concrete was undoubtedly a better choice than wood for this heavy-use area.

No sooner had the building added valuable scene storage space and better access than it got its first indoor toilet. By March 1908 "one of the music rooms in the rear of the stage in Washington Hall has been fitted up as a wash and toilet room."[33] The 1943 university drawings of Washington Hall show a "wash and toilet room" in a space

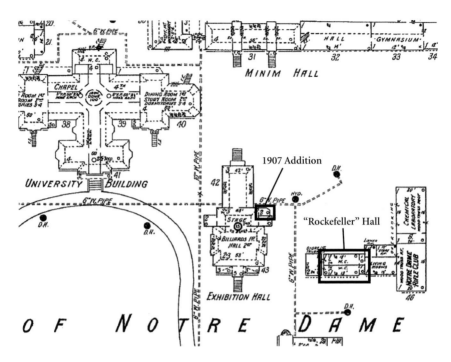

Figure 6.3. Sanborn Insurance Map 1917. Note the 1907 addition, the change in the footprint that made the building asymmetrical, and the nearby privy that served Washington Hall.

that apparently had been one of the dozen music rooms (eleven rooms are shown, plus the toilet room and a manager's room, in fig. 6.4b). (See fig. 6.4a, b, c.) The room had only toilet and lavatory functions; Washington Hall first acquired a singular shower in the 1956 renovation that created dressing rooms on the third floor. But the indoor toilet was a huge improvement, especially for the several students and building manager who lived in the building at the time. Of course, the loss of one of the music rooms to restroom facilities carried an opportunity cost. Washington Hall could eventually have proper support areas only by converting existing spaces, and that meant a gradual encroachment on vitally needed music practice rooms which over time made the second and third floors of the north wing increasingly less a part of the original Music Hall.[34]

For Seniors' Day in 1908, the stage itself showed off new scenery, perhaps as a result of finally having a proper onsite storage place, for

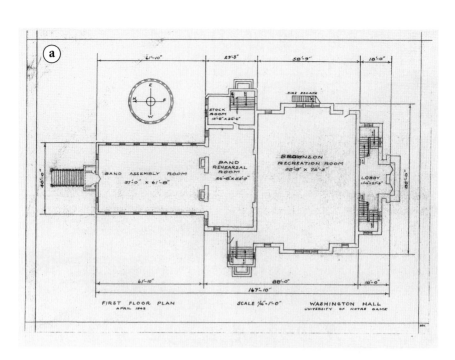

FIRST FLOOR PLAN
APRIL 1943

SCALE 1/16"=1'-0"

WASHINGTON HALL
UNIVERSITY OF NOTRE DAME

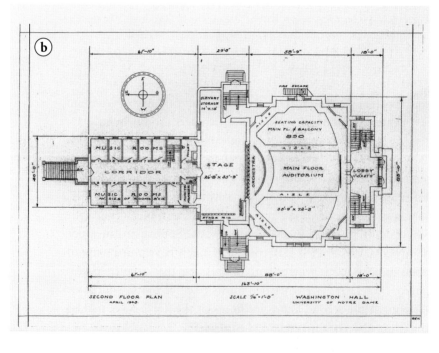

SECOND FLOOR PLAN
APRIL 1943

SCALE 1/16"=1'-0"

WASHINGTON HALL
UNIVERSITY OF NOTRE DAME

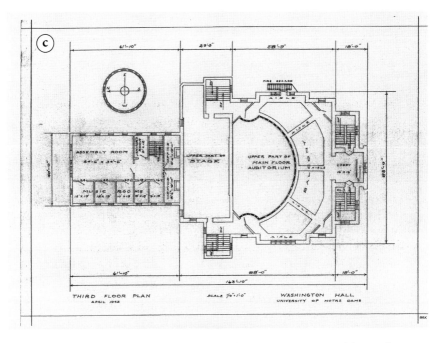

Figure 6.4a, b, c. Facilities Survey 1942–43, April 1943, Notre Dame Architectural Drawings, Plans, and Views (hereafter UNDD), UNDA. The second-floor plan shows the 1907 addition, the 14' x 18' scenery storage area with direct access to the stage, and the 1908 indoor toilet room and manager's room, each with direct access to the stage (former music rooms). The first indoor toilet in Washington Hall made it no longer necessary to leave the building to go to the privy that since 1883 had stood east of the building between Washington Hall and the Old Gymnasium (see fig. 6.3). Note the Brownson Recreation Room on the first floor and the Assembly Room on the third.

the spring production of *Twelfth Night* (see fig. 6.5). The *Scholastic* praised the "new street scene," adding, "The Easter play made use of a new scene in the stage equipment of Washington Hall. It was the work of Professor Ackerman, and is a considerable improvement on the other street scenes that have been in use."[35] But even the reality of new spaces and settings could not solve the overcrowding problems in the house:

Seniors' Day and Easter Monday are synonymous terms at the University. This year, in accordance with the well-established custom, the members of the Senior Class presented a play in Washington

The "Twelfth Night" Cast

Figure 6.5. *Twelfth Night,* with new scenery, Easter Monday, April 20, 1908. *Dome* 1908, n.p. Note the very large music stand lights, reflecting the technology of the day.

Hall in the afternoon and danced in the evening. Last year "Richelieu" was staged; this year the play was "Twelfth Night." As usual there was a large gathering in Washington Hall, so large that the capacity of the hall was taxed to the utmost.[36]

After 1915 visitors needed tickets: "In order to limit the size of the Washington Hall audiences in the future to the capacity of the theatre, it has been found necessary by the University to require tickets of admission from all visitors. Such tickets may be obtained from Rev. Joseph Burke, C.S.C."[37]

By the teens of the twentieth century, indoor photography had become possible and practical, and the *Dome* in 1912 ran a picture (see fig. 6.1), the caption of which says:

This photograph is remarkable because it is the first ever taken of an audience in Washington Hall. It shows the auditorium just as it appeared to the actors on the stage. Most of the faces, nearly all, we think, are recognizable, although of necessity, small. Father Cavanaugh is to be seen in the center, with the Faculty, who occupied the first row of seats, grouped around him. The visitors were placed as near as possible in the central part of the house, and the rest of it was filled with the students. It is regrettable that a small section on both sides is cut off, but owing to the peculiar circumstances under which the picture was taken, it was unavoidable.[38]

This picture and caption make it clear the president attended the President's Day play in Washington Hall in his honor along with the faculty, important visitors, and many students.[39] It also shows the house interior of the building, with the columns at the back of the house, as well as about sixty electric footlights in banks of three with reflectors on the stage. The balcony lobby ceiling arch clearly seen in this picture was not yet concealed by a projection booth which possibly was added as early as 1916 (see fig. 5.10).[40] In this photograph, the house lights are up (all twelve in the central chandelier) and the perfunctory stage spotlights on the balcony rail are off, since they would compromise the picture taken from the stage. Under actual performance conditions of the time, as now, the house lights would be down and the stage lights up, and actors would see very little of the house beyond the footlights.[41]

"Leading Ladies," Minstrels, and Rockne

Since the 1850s play production had been in the hands of faculty-advised student societies such as the Thespians and St. Cecilia Philomatheans, but in early 1895 things changed, with the creation of an umbrella organization to coordinate play production in what would become the precursor of the "University Theatre" Frank Kelly founded in 1926. This shift from the literary societies to a single theatre production program under various names—the Dramatic Stock Company, the University Stock Company, the Dramatic Club, and finally the Players Club—ultimately signaled the beginning of the end of the multipurpose all-encompassing "exhibition" in favor of doing plays for the sake of the plays themselves rather than as ancillary support for a larger multifaceted event. The shift was neither entirely immediate nor complete, however, with the minims, preparatory students, and collegiate classes each continuing to have unique production units until the 1920s.[42] The younger boys especially seemed keen to retain the traditional "exhibition" formula that showcased a multitude of talents in a collage of performances. In March 1895, for example, the Columbians did the play *Waiting for the Verdict* in the course of an evening that included the orchestra, Glee Club, an oration, the mandolin orchestra, a flute solo (after act 1), a violin solo (after act 2), and a finale by the orchestra, and all with apparently only a two-week rehearsal period.[43] In addition to a short rehearsal period, the rented costumes from Chicago did not arrive in time, but when the curtain rolled up at three o'clock, the costumes for the cast of thirty had been improvised with the help of Professor Edwards.[44]

The inaugural season of the new University Stock Company in 1895, however, included a one-act two-person play, *Forget-Me-Nots,* followed by *Vacation,* a comedy in two acts with a cast of eleven, including the "negro cook" Toots, the first time plays were produced with no concurrent entertainment (except for accompanying "Music by the Orchestra").[45] Play production had entered the new era of the specialized or niche audience who came to see only a play, one that is neither connected nor related to a more complex and varied exhibition. Theatre thus became a freestanding art form in its own right by 1895, and the exhibition part of the exhibition hall was fast becoming history. The next year *Richelieu* marked a high point for the University Stock Company as "the only purely *dramatic organization* at the University." Father Moloney was the director, who supervised in typical *Scholastic* hyperbole "the greatest play we have ever had,"[46] and he added something unusual on the Washington Hall stage, a female character. The *Scholastic* exulted, "It is not often that a young lady appears upon the boards of Washington Hall, but we had one with us Wednesday evening. Her name was Peter Kuntz and she was a vision of grace and loveliness. . . . His clever impersonation of Julie won the admiration of all, and De Mauprat and the King had many rivals in the audience long before the play had ended."[47] For *The Corsican Brothers* in 1897, the *Scholastic* again complimented Father Moloney, who "worked hard with the Stock Company, and has introduced new ideas and modern 'business' into local theatricals with much effect,"[48] with Peter Kuntz playing the heroine Emilie, undoubtedly an innovation for which he deserved "great praise for his interpretation."[49]

From the earliest history of Washington Hall, Father Neal Gillespie and Professor J. A. Lyons had consistently adapted existing plays and written new ones to accommodate all-male casts, with the women's parts cut completely, largely curtailed, or sometimes changed to a male character of color. Indeed, the first *Dome* in 1906 reminded the non-university reader in praising Louis Wagner's Viola in *Twelfth Night* of 1904–5 that "the feminine roles in all the plays at Notre Dame are necessarily enacted by boys," when there were female roles at all. Sometimes, the boys took on those roles in classical plays from periods when men historically played women's roles (the Greeks and Shakespeare, for example), as with the 1882 premiere in the new Washington Hall of *Oedipus Tyrannus* when the production retained the critical role of Jocasta (how could it be done otherwise?), played by W. O'Connor. But generally, even in Shakespeare where the convention for males to play female roles is certainly as strong as with the ancient Greeks, we know that faculty directors of student-acted plays at Notre Dame routinely eliminated women's parts even as late as the 1892 productions of *Julius Caesar* and *Richard III* in which no female characters appeared.[50]

A huge shift in gender depiction onstage had thus occurred by spring of 1896. Clearly just four years after the "adjusted" Shakespeare plays with only male characters, the university decided to include in its repertoire plays with important female roles and then cast males to play them convincingly, thus ending the long tradition of writing out female characters entirely. But not all young men played women as convincingly as Mr. Kuntz had as Julie and Emilie. Regarding *A Night Off,* part of the Washington's Birthday celebrations in 1898, the *Scholastic* offered the following commentary regarding three female roles: "To the 'ladies' of the company we make our very best bow. When they talked they reminded one of a contralto with a severe cold, but athletic young men can not be blamed for owning healthy bass voices. College men that attempt to portray female characters on the stage can not be criticized very severely, because perfection in this work is rare."[51] By the beginning of the twentieth century, however, the specially adapted all-male workhorse plays such as *William Tell* had given way to plays with important women's characters played by young men whose skills could gain them high praise for the convincing nature of their performances. On Saint Patrick's Day 1903, for example, the *Scholastic* praised Louis Wagner as Lady Macbeth and two years later proclaimed the "quartet of worthy young men" playing female roles in the farce, *The Balloon,* had effectively removed "a stumbling-block to our embryo histrions."[52]

The ubiquitous cross-dressing of this period, in which the male students apparently attempted fully to embody their female characters before an admiring audience, marked an important period in the history of the Washington Hall stage. The talent of such actors, when they created great female roles, seemed practically to transcend their own gender. The audience of their peers willingly suspended disbelief for the duration of the performance, resulting in happy and unselfconscious praise afterward for the cross-dressing efforts, although Robertson reminds us in *Guilty Pleasures* that "the surprise and incongruity of drag depends upon our shared recognition that the person behind the mask is really another gender."[53] Impersonation of the other sex can also be flagrantly parodic rather than utterly convincing, and both occurred on the Washington Hall stage, often within the same play.

According to the first *Dome,* however, there was nothing parodic about the 1899 production of *Oedipus Tyrannus,* a production reminiscent of the dedication production in Washington Hall in June 1882 (see fig. 6.6). The 1906 *Dome* recounts:

> On May 15, 1899, the play [*Oedipus Tyrannus*] was produced before an audience composed of Greek Scholars and friends from all over the country. The music of the choruses was composed by Prof. MacLaughlin, at that time director of the department of music. The costumes and stage settings were in perfect conformity with the Greek theatre of old, and as for the acting—each member of the cast was a star. It is only by going from what is very high to what is just a little higher still that we can say Mr. Raymond O'Malley as Oedipus and Mr. Matthew Schumacher as Jocasta were particularly superior in their parts.[54]

Figure 6.6. The May 15, 1899, production of *Oedipus Tyrannus* was performed in Greek, but with an English libretto in the program. This photograph gives a rare glimpse of the house left Cicero, as well as the wing-and-drop staging system. There are five steps from orchestra to stage both left and right but not centered. Thirty-one actors appear onstage, bearded, in Greek costumes. The Sosman & Landis permanent valence curtain had re - placed the 1885 Ackermann single curtain by this time. Note that the stage had a curved front with a row of footlights. *Scholastic* 32:32, May 20, 1899, 561; also see *Dome* 1906, n.p.

The reviewer had special praise for Washington Hall:

> Perhaps the success of dramatics at Notre Dame is in a measure due to the great privilege we enjoy in possessing our own opera house. Washington Hall is a building perfectly fitted with every means necessary to the staging of a good play. In its stage equip- ment, not a point which might carry towards a first-class perform- ance has been neglected; in its accommodations every means pos- sible has been taken to provide for the comfort and enjoyment of the audience.[55]

At the same time that cross-dressing was reaching its zenith, additional depictions of the "Other" emerged in terms of race and ethnicity, first with individual characters and eventually with the blackface minstrel show. In the tradition of Professor Stace's "Culled Pussuns" in Molière in 1870 and Professor Lyons's "first-class-looking darkey" in *The Rightful Heir* in 1881, Professor Carmody in 1898 changed a female role in *A Night Off* into that of a male African American, and thus we see race replacing gender: "In the original play the Professor's servant is a woman, Susan, but luckily in the performance last Tuesday the character was changed to that of sambo, a colored boy." The *Scholastic* praised the performance but offered advice to the players, irrespective of issues of gender and race: "When they learn that it is necessary to talk distinctly and above a conversational tone in order to fill Washington Hall, and that it is not necessary to have hands or knees moving *all* the time they are on the stage, their work will be much more acceptable."[56]

The 1898 Saint Patrick's Day celebration included among its many parts one of Notre Dame's earliest minstrel acts on the Washington Hall stage. The day began with mass at church, after which "the University Band visited main bldg and the various departments of the University, and for almost an hour the gay and the sad melodies of Ireland floated about the campus." The Columbians took over the afternoon and produced an oration and *The Celebrated Case,* with the university quartet singing the entr'acte between acts 2 and 3 (along with the mandolin orchestra of Professor Preston), followed by a finale between acts 4 and 5 described as a "Darktown Parade." There was negative commentary related to the acting and the use of the follow spotlight, but praise for Professor Carmody's work:

> Then, our college Booths should put more life into their work, and not announce a murder as if it were an every-day affair. That calcium light effect should be abolished, also—there is too much of the Bowery melo-drama element in it. The "make-ups" and costumes in Thursday's production were all that could be wished. Professor Carmody, who coached the Columbians, has the thanks of all at Notre Dame for his able work, and for the good results obtained therefrom."[57]

While a "Darktown Parade" suggests blackface performers, certainly by 1907 the complete minstrel form had fully emerged: "The Corby Hall Glee Club is preparing to put on a black-face minstrel shortly after Xmas holidays. This is something new at Notre Dame, and will be looked forward to with much interest and satisfaction."[58] At Notre Dame, interest in the minstrel show continued into the 1940s, as indeed it did nationally, especially in the medium of film.[59]

By 1910 student Cecil Birder had popularized the dual concept, creating onstage both an ideal woman and a convincing "darky." In the 1910–11 academic year, as Grace Whitney in *The Galloper,* he was "naturally endowed with the voice and personal grace required for a feminine role and did remarkably well" (see fig. 6.7).[60] That year he also played Lucy Sheridan in the senior play, *The Dictator,* and was called "our premier 'leading lady.'" By the end of the year, he was involved in the "May Day Minstrel Show" in which "Darky" Cecil Birder, apparently in blackface, performed to great acclaim. As the university moved into the twentieth century, clearly the decision was made to access a wider range of drama which included female and ethnic roles, providing acting opportunities for the white male students while also of course reinforcing racial and gender stereotypes.

With regard to the University Dramatic Club's Easter Monday senior play *The Rise of Peter McCabe,* the *Dome* in 1912 commended Cecil Birder as Mrs. McCabe, the director Father Moloney, who "by his untiring efforts, watchful eye, and beautiful earnestness, he brought forth whatever latent abilities his cast possessed," and Brother Cyprian, who did the "splendid stage scenery."[61] The *Dome* of 1912 has pictures of the "Vaudeville Show, May, 1911," in which two of the three photos show students in blackface, one also in drag, and reports that for the President's Day play, *The Redemption of Jimmie Anson,* the ladies were "attractive not only in appearance but in their acting," with Mr. Twining as Mrs. Webster, Mr. Cox as Mrs. Moore, Cecil Birder as Rose Lane.[62] By 1911–12, then, the best actors performed leading female and ethnic roles convincingly; some of them, such as Knute Rockne, also achieved fame in other areas.

While Knute Rockne is perhaps not remembered primarily for his contributions to the performing arts, his Washington Hall accomplishments as both student and faculty member are notable.[63] The

Will Some Kind Friend Write to This Lovely Maid?

I am a pretty brunette, age 38, 5-6, 150 lbs., beautiful lustrous brown eyes, soft, silky tresses of jet, full ruby lips, white skin, of velvety texture through which the rose tint gleams, fair and pure as a lily. Full 36 figure, beautifully proportioned, stylish, attractive, intelligent, educated, affectionate, jolly, vivacious, congenial, home-loving, splendid cook and housekeeper, got religion from Billy Sunday, some means. Have never loved, but "Oh my," when the right man comes along, I might think seriously. Will some lonely Romeo, older than myself, of culture and refinement, with some means and a good character, who can appreciate womanly qualities and is trying to locate his Juliet, please communicate? All letters with postage stamps enclosed will be answered.

MISS CECIL BIRDER,
Walsh Hall, Notre Dame University.

ADMIRERS OF PETER CHARLES YERNS

YOU

who have read and enjoyed his new book, *THE INCORRIGIBILITY OF THE Nth,* will be glad to know that he is to deliver a series of lectures on the subject at Notre Dame.

To appreciate Yerns' philosophy you must have the manner and voice of the author. The words are only half. Who can imitate the rising and falling of that soprano voice, like a verbal hurdle or a ride on the shoot the chutes? Some people converse in prairie articulation and inflection. Peter's inflection, however, is, as he would say, "astonishingly ubiquitous," now soaring to the skylight minor, and in the next sentence dropping to a submarine major. It is like the lowing of distant kine, and the poetic gurgle of a buzz-saw. The topic almost makes one "gush in numbers." And his words: Always there are two for one—"interesting and instructive," "obstreperous and bothersome," "unwise and indiscreet"—polysyllabic thunderbolts all.

Tickets for the Series $1.00

The Condon Bureau of Wordologists
Leo J. Condon, Prop. and Head Lecturer

Yes, Knute

Wasson's Hair Restorer is used and recommended by such prominent men at Notre Dame as James Wasson himself, Olympic athlete and discoverer of the remedy; F. X. Ackerman, popular professor and artist, and many others less well known. It is sold in large bottles by Mr. Wasson, and you will do well to lay in a large supply.

The Wasson Company, We, Us, and Myself, Inc.
Notre Dame, Indiana.

Patronize our advertisers. They need your sympathy.

Figure 6.7. Cecil Birder as Grace Whitney in *The Galloper*, Dec. 13, 1911, an example of convincing (as opposed to parodic) cross-dressing convention of the time which appeared in the *Dome* 1913, 264, in an advertisement, on the same page as Wasson's Hair Restorer, indicating that Rockne was a customer.

1913 *Dome* shows junior Knute Rockne as a member of the Notre Dame Players' Association under director Charlemagne Koehler (who had taken over from Father Moloney in 1912). There are eighteen listed members, including Koehler, with ten pictured, and Rockne played the flute in the university orchestra the same year.[64] In December 1912 Rockne played Mrs. Smith in *David Garrick,* directed by Koehler.[65] Other plays that year included the Philopatrians doing *Bob Martin, Substitute Half-Back,* with an all-male cast of seventeen presented on Washington's Birthday (directed by Brother Cyprian and written by Father Quinlan), and the senior play, *A Night Off,* performed on Easter Monday, with a cast of ten, three of whom were female characters played by males.[66]

By Rockne's senior year, the *New York Times* confirmed that his skills at left end on the football team very likely had surpassed his theatrical and orchestral talents: the forward passing of Charles E. "Gus" Dorais to Rockne dazzled (and defeated) Army.[67] Rockne and Dorais were among the earliest players successfully to realize the full potential of the forward pass and to popularize it. But impressive gridiron successes as a senior did not deter Rockne from his continued interest both as a member of the Players Club and as a flautist in the orchestra. The apparent successor to the University Stock Company, the Players Club supervised "plays, sketches and minstrels put on during the year but also in the polished delivery of our victorious debating teams and successful orators."[68]

Rockne's theatre career continued as Pearly in the senior play, *What's Next,* under the name "Kenith Rockne" on Easter Monday 1914 (See fig. 6.8). Birder played the lead role of Polly Poke, "the pert but charming country lass," confirming that he was "Notre Dame's all-time leading lady . . . the best player of feminine roles seen at Notre Dame during our time." The 1914 *Dome* continued: "Every step, every twitch of the hand, every shake of the head is girlish, and his voice makes the deception complete." As Rosalind in *As You Like it,* he "added much to his reputation as a female impersonator."[69] The skill and talent of an actor such as Birder, when he created great female roles, clearly transcended his own gender, and caused the audience of his peers willingly to suspend disbelief during the performance and happily to praise his cross-dressing efforts afterward. The

Figure 6.8. Knute Rockne, All-American flautist and actor, performing on the Washing -
ton Hall stage (lower right corner) as Pearly in *What's Next* with five other Notre Dame
"leading ladies." *Dome* 1914, 127.

utterly convincing and flagrantly ludicrous occurred simultaneously when Birder and Rockne appeared together as female characters in the same play.

At the same time that cross-dressing hits its zenith, there is clearly also a great interest in the depiction of other races and ethnic groups, most notably in the popularity of the minstrel show with the student performers in blackface. The Gold and Blue Serenaders, for example, had a minstrel show during Rockne's senior year; the picture in the 1914 *Dome* shows twenty-six performers in blackface of a cast of thirty-two (see fig. 6.9).[70] The *Scholastic* in 1915 called the second year of the minstrel show "an innovation that was better than a 16th-century tragedy."[71] Thus by the end of the academic year in 1915 the minstrel show was firmly established at Notre Dame.

After graduation in 1914, Rockne became a faculty member at Notre Dame, until his untimely death in an airplane crash on March 31, 1931. This transition, however, did little to dim his interest in the stage. During his first year on the faculty, he played two roles in the 1915 senior play, *The Girl of the Golden West*: Wockle (the Fox) and Billy's squaw.[72] No one would assert that Rockne fully embodied the feminine of Billy's squaw, and indeed having a star football player turned professor and coach depict a woman of color undoubtedly created comic recognition while emphasizing stereotypical behaviors. Emmett Lenihan, the successor to Cecil Birder, played the lead female role, directed by Professor John Drury, with Brother Cyprian the stage manager and Professor Derrick conducting the orchestra.[73] The *Scholastic* additionally suggested a drinking problem onstage: "The amount of theoretical whiskey consumed in one performance of 'The Girl of the Golden West' would easily float a dreadnaught. However, it didn't seem to have half as much effect on the players as did the teapot in 'The Rosary.'"[74] Irrespective of the true nature of stage libations, Notre Dame's new leading lady in *The Rosary*, Emmett Lenihan, played two female roles; the 1915 *Dome* included in his biography that he had "won great dramatic renown as a female impersonator."[75]

Regarding Rockne's performances on the stage of Washington Hall, Father John William Cavanaugh confirmed in his introduction to Rockne's autobiography, "Every man of his time remembers him

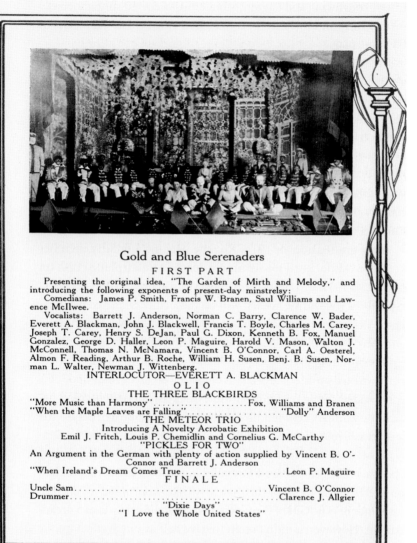

Gold and Blue Serenaders

FIRST PART

Presenting the original idea, "The Garden of Mirth and Melody," and introducing the following exponents of present-day minstrelsy:

Comedians: James P. Smith, Francis W. Branen, Saul Williams and Lawence McIlwee.

Vocalists: Barrett J. Anderson, Norman C. Barry, Clarence W. Bader, Everett A. Blackman, John J. Blackwell, Francis T. Boyle, Charles M. Carey, Joseph T. Carey, Henry S. DeJan, Paul G. Dixon, Kenneth B. Fox, Manuel Gonzalez, George D. Haller, Leon P. Maguire, Harold V. Mason, Walton J. McConnell, Thomas N. McNamara, Vincent B. O'Connor, Carl A. Oesterel, Almon F. Reading, Arthur B. Roche, William H. Susen, Benj. B. Susen, Norman L. Walter, Newman J. Wittenberg.

INTERLOCUTOR—EVERETT A. BLACKMAN

O L I O

THE THREE BLACKBIRDS

"More Music than Harmony".....................Fox, Williams and Branen
"When the Maple Leaves are Falling"....................."Dolly" Anderson

THE METEOR TRIO

Introducing A Novelty Acrobatic Exhibition
Emil J. Fritch, Louis P. Chemidlin and Cornelius G. McCarthy

"PICKLES FOR TWO"

An Argument in the German with plenty of action supplied by Vincent B. O'Connor and Barrett J. Anderson

"When Ireland's Dream Comes True.....................Leon P. Maguire

F I N A L E

Uncle Sam...Vincent B. O'Connor
Drummer...Clarence J. Allgier

"Dixie Days"
"I Love the Whole United States"

Figure 6.9. Gold And Blue Serenaders, picture with program, twenty-six in blackface. *Dome* 1914, 125.

as a sensational performer in plays requiring college boys to be not merely perfect gentlemen, but perfect ladies also. For example, he was repeatedly a scintillating success in the roles of shop-worn females or negresses or squaws or society ladies."[76] Cavanaugh believed Rockne's training on the stage helped him later as a coach, asserting that "college barnstorming later proved a providential preparation for the play-acting required to put over the coach's psychology at critical moments . . . and in getting his message across in public speeches." Cavanaugh added that Rockne also had a merit scholarship in music, which was little known: "He was also particeps criminis [partner in crime] in the orchestra, for which a modest honorarium was allowed against his college expenses," but he remembered Rockne "as a vigorous and industrious performer on the flute rather than as a virtuoso."[77]

Rockne's interest and involvement in performance on the stage of Washington Hall continued through his early years on the faculty. In March 1919, the *Scholastic* praised his abilities in the annual Knights of Columbus vaudeville:

> Coach Rockne on last Wednesday night gave another demonstration of his versatility. In a benefit performance staged for the building fund of the Knights of Columbus, he displayed a galaxy of Thespians not a bit less brilliant than his champions of the gridiron and the cinder path. The performance included only the best features of his extensive repertoire and attained the *ultima thule* in satisfaction given, if not in point of dramatic art. Any defi-ciency apparent in the presentation of the vaudeville seemed attributable to the system of scene-shifting that prevails in Washington Hall rather than to Coach Rockne's plans.[78]

The skits included characters like "Wop" Berra, "Lefty" Welch, and "ladies unusual," but it is not clear what roles Rockne played.

The connection between Knute Rockne and George Gipp makes it very difficult to mention one and not the other, although Gipp's connection to the history of Washington Hall is much less certain than Rockne's. Neither a musician nor an actor (and not much of a student), Notre Dame's first unanimous All-American, George Gipp, arrived at Notre Dame in 1917 on a baseball scholarship, but rather quickly became a football legend. His untimely death in November 1920, however, forever connected him to Washington Hall as a likely source of the now legendary ghost, a topic that warrants its own chapter in this book.

Rockne's years as a student and then as a young faculty member, when he played both female and ethnic roles on the stage of Washington Hall, underscored the times. The "ladies unusual" reference makes it clear that by Rockne's tenure the convention of males playing female roles both convincingly and ludicrously was well established. Based on the surviving pictures and his own physiognomy, Rockne likely played female roles for laughs. It is also well to remember that Washington Hall clearly supported a huge variety of events that extended far beyond "leading ladies" and white males in blackface. While these performances fascinate us today, they must be evaluated and understood in the context of the culture of the time.

As late as 1916–17, the Notre Dame Players Club had sixteen members, one of whom was Professor Lenihan, "the university's director of dramatics," who with the assistance of Brother Cyprian's "crew of stage mechanics helped heroically and furnished splendid settings" both for a December 1916 *Under Cover* (which apparently had long set changes) and a May 1917 *Twelfth Night*.[79] For the following peak war year, 1917–18, however, so many young men were fighting in France, including Lenihan, that there was no Drama Club. The Players bounced back briefly after the war, with some activity during the 1919–20 theatre year, but the 1920–21 academic year had "no theatricals," and indeed the 1921 *Dome* claimed the university had been theatre-bereft for four years: "The art of theater is in a bad way at Notre Dame. Except for one performance last year of three one-act plays . . . we haven't had a dramatic performance in four years."[80] The call went out for an experienced professional director to come on board. During this period, vaudeville in Washington Hall, sponsored by the seniors, continued, along with guest artists performing and numerous motion pictures. Well-known writer and actor Dr. Frederick Paulding, for example, made his annual visit, performing dramatic readings from *The School for Scandal* and *The Magnificent Ambersons*, while two other touring companies presented plays to less acclaim.[81] So there was a lot going on theatrically in the building during this time, even though indigenous theatre at Notre Dame, which had been a tradition since the earliest years of the university, had ebbed. The *Dome* pointed out that "lectures and concerts filled out the rest of the year."[82]

A failed attempt in 1920–21 to reorganize the Players Club led to the prescient observation in the *Scholastic* in January 1921 that perhaps the new medium of film had made theatre obsolete. "The 'Movie' vs. the Drama" first wondered if the drama would go the way of the dodo bird, mentioned William Dean Howells as the "first to see the alleged menace in the shadow stage [film]," but ultimately countered that Howells was wrong: "The drama has not been superseded by the 'movie,' and never will be, so long as printing flourishes as an art and the Americans are a reading folk." The decline of the theatre author Charles P. Mooney ascribed to dissolute behavior and irresponsibility in the profession and not to new technology, and he asserted that the spoken drama (the stage) would always excel over the "pantomimic." Mooney believed speech revealed character in ways the picture alone could not do: "The motion picture star is handicapped by the loss of the actor's greatest resource, the human voice." Subtitles simply distract and are out of synch chronologically. The drama appeals to the intellect, something the photoplay cannot do. The author recognized, however, that the photoplay "has killed off the crudely sensational drama," but that tragedy and comedy were "far beyond the reach of the film." Interestingly, Mooney never suggested that speech could come to photoplays but rather that films were likely "a passing fad, which will be discarded ere the end of another decade."[83] Film turned out not to be a passing fad and, indeed, before the 1920s ended "talkies" emerged, followed in the 1930s by the introduction of color. But neither was theatre dead; in many ways the golden age of theatre at Notre Dame was yet to emerge, although film had a huge impact on Washington Hall. The hubbub regarding the rising influence of the motion picture in relation to theatre is interesting as it relates to Washington Hall. The building had rapidly adapted to this new technology embraced by the university, so even if theatre were to go the way of the passenger pigeon, Washington Hall would have remained a center for communal assembly on the campus.

Plays shifted to the Oliver Hotel for the 1920–21 academic year, but the following year was one of revitalization, with a complete season in Washington Hall including O'Neill's *In the Zone* and a boffo production of *The Clod*. The Players Club was back up and running under the direction of Professor Daniel Sullivan ('14), and theatre had turned the corner.[84]

The "Mushin'-Picture"

In late 1908 Miss Emily Canfield gave a lecture that included "a series of stereoption pictures dealing with Venice,"[85] and thus continued the tradition established by Father Zahm in 1885 when he first demonstrated pre-filmic devices on the Washington Hall stage. By the 1914–15 academic year, Washington Hall had become the venue for screening "photoplays," an early name for motion pictures. The 1915 *Dome* recorded one of the earliest reports of film screenings in Washington Hall in an article about the student vaudeville show on December 5, 1914: "Vitagraph pictures of the Notre Dame–Carlisle game concluded the entertainment, and enabled the rooters to live over again the ecstasies of that great victory."[86] By fall 1914 Washington Hall had become a cinema house in addition to its many other functions. In early 1915 film screenings seem to have become regular. The *Scholastic* related the schedule in January:

> The moving picture shows given every Wednesday evening at seven o'clock in Washington Hall, and attended by the students of Carroll [preps, under seventeen] and St. Edward's Halls [minims, under thirteen], have been a great success. Reels are obtained every week from Chicago and only the best films are shown.[87]

The *Scholastic* praised an early historical film and in so doing illustrated the power of the new medium to teach as if it were a lecture:

> One of the most interesting numbers of the LECTURE AND ENTERTAINMENT COURSE ever witnessed at Notre Dame was given in Washington Hall on Friday morning. The life of Julius

Caesar and the various wars he was engaged in were portrayed in moving pictures which were the best we have ever seen. Fully twenty thousand people were necessary for the making of the film, and the strict adherence to the details of the Roman and Gallic street dress and fighting uniforms, made the pictures as instructive as a history lesson. We hope to have more of this kind of entertainment.[88]

In late January 1915 George Kleine's *Julius Caesar* became the first "named" film to be screened in Washington Hall.[89] The *Scholastic* disclosed, "By courtesy of the Auditorium management, the story of 'Julius Caesar' as interpreted by George Klein, was presented in Washington Hall last Friday morning. . . . Nothing could please us more than an occasional presentation of high-class motion pictures."[90] By the spring another great biopic was screened: "Through the courtesy of the Auditorium Theatre, the six-reel feature film, 'Napoleon and France,' was presented in Washington Hall Friday morning. It was a masterpiece of production and the students thoroughly enjoyed it."[91]

The 1915–16 academic year reflected an interesting tie to the past while also the huge technological changes film brought to Washington Hall. The *Bulletin* schedule in Washington Hall listed twelve concerts (September 9 through April 12), twenty-nine lectures (October 26 through April 16)—including the films *Quo Vadis* on November 9 and *The Birth of a Nation* on December 3—and four theatrical events by the University Dramatic Club (November 9 through commencement). While only two films were part of the fall semester lectures series, thirteen occupied slots for the spring (March 4 through April 29).[92] This and the year before are the only two years that films appear under the rubric "lectures," showing both the initial psychology of their genesis but also reflecting how quickly the new medium separated and self-identified.

Both *Quo Vadis* and *The Birth of a Nation* were extremely popular at Notre Dame. On *Quo Vadis*, the *Scholastic* reported:

Washington Hall has been packed to the doors upon three separate occasions during the last seven days. The "Quo Vadis" audience, the attendance upon the lecture of Doctor [James J.] Walsh, and the crowd at the student vaudeville show, testify individually and collectively to the varied interest and tastes at Notre Dame.

"Quo Vadis," shown at the University theatre Saturday morning, is a rather old picture by this time, and its once unprecedented splendors have been overshadowed by more notable accomplishments in the realm of movies. Probably, too, a large number of the students had seen the photo-drama before, but such a spectacle loses none of its impressiveness with a second exhibition. Moreover, "Quo Vadis" has the advantage of possessing a plot based on Sienkiewicz's immortal novel.[93]

The *Scholastic* announced the impending screening of *The Birth of a Nation* and then editorialized about a film that was "correct in every detail":

Through the extreme kindness of Mr. H. G. Summers of New York City, Mr. H. E. Aitken, and Mr. D. W. Griffith, the faculty was enabled to present, "The Birth of a Nation" in Washington Hall, thus saving most of the students the price of a gallery perch at the Oliver. Probably never in the history of the University were seats in the campus theatre so literally fought over as on Friday morning, December 3rd. . . .

Truly every American should see "The Birth of a Nation." It has the power of stirring one to his most patriotic depths, as was witnessed by the uncontrollable enthusiasm of the Notre Dame audience. Toward the crushed South we can feel nothing but honor for their sincerity, admiration for their struggle, and sympathy for their defeat.

As an offset to any ill-feeling that might arise against the negro race, the latter part of the picture gives us glimpses of the work that is being done in various institutions toward educating and refining the emancipated African. We should also remember in this regard that the freedom-crazed slaves were supported and incited by the diabolical white men, known as carpet-baggers, who sought to further their own interests at the expense of nationality, religion, and all that man holds dear.[94]

The *Scholastic* thanked those most responsible for making the screening possible and described an interesting local connection between art and life:

> The University wishes to thank Mr. Charles Allardt of the Orpheum in South Bend, and also Mr. Harvey Kunz of the same city for the use of rectifiers for our motion picture machines, without which it would have been impossible for us to have witnessed "The Birth of a Nation."
>
> We are grateful also to Mr. Barnes of the Oliver Opera House for his management of the whole performance and his interest in making this movie play as perfect as possible. . . .
>
> With the showing of the wonderful picture "The Birth of a Nation" at the University, an interesting fact comes to light.
>
> Frank W. Holslag, one of our students, has, among other interesting papers, an original ritual and also the secret code with an explanatory sheet of the famous Ku Klux Klan.
>
> These rare articles were given to Mr. Holslag by a close friend, Col. G. C. L. Stansel, now deceased, of Pickens County, Alabama. He was one of the organizers of that splendid society that did so much to eliminate the sufferings of the South during the dreadful days of the Reconstruction.
>
> A detailed article describing the Klan and its work and some of the trials of the southern people may be supplied by Mr. Holslag at a later date.
>
> As this information comes directly from people who were acting characters in this period, and from one who has lived with these people, and who is from those districts, it should be very interesting.[95]

While this sounds appalling to us today, the times were very different; the reaction of the *Scholastic* to Griffith's epic film paralleled much of the popular reaction around the country at that time.

After *The Birth of a Nation,* there was no turning back, and film screenings quickly became an important function of Washington Hall and adjunct to life at Notre Dame. In March 1916 the *Scholastic* reported:

It is evident from the size and enthusiasm of the crowds that the University has happened upon a popular form of entertainment in the weekly photo-play exhibitions. Wednesday afternoon's picture, Owen Wister's "The Virginian," featuring the model of virility, Dustin Farnum, was interesting and contained some good photography, but was not up to the standard set by the others that have been shown.

Another fine screen play was presented in Washington Hall, Saturday night, March 11th, in George Ade's "The County Chairman," produced by Henry Savage and the Famous Players Company. The picture entertainingly depicted the hilarity and strife connected with a rural election, a phase of life with which the Hoosier Aesop is most familiar. The cast included the jovial star, Maclyn Arbuckle, of "nobody loves a fat man fame," Willis P. Sweatnam in a familiar negro character role, and Harold Lockwood. Such diversions as these lighten the penitential burden which the Lenten season imposes, and help to pass the "per-less" nights.[96]

The 1916 *Dome* celebrated the arrival of the photoplay in the second published picture of the audience in Washington Hall from the stage perspective, except, unlike the 1912 *Dome* picture simulating the audience at a play, the 1916 picture of the house purports to show a film audience, the earliest such photograph to do so (see fig. 6.2). In the 1916 *Dome* photograph, labeled "A Typical Audience in Washington Hall," the footlights are down or off, there is a handful of musicians in the orchestra pit on the house right side, and in the upper center of the balcony there is a film reel prominently being held up by a man. I see no evidence of the projector or, indeed, any sort of projection booth at this time, although other evidence indicates that the projection booth dates from 1916. Clearly, the busy film year of 1915–16 deserved a record, and this photograph does just that. Another intriguing aspect of the 1916 *Dome* photograph of the Washington Hall house is the light source in the upper center. I originally assumed it was the twelve-lamp chandelier, the same as the one we see in clearer focus in the 1912 *Dome* photograph of a theatre production (see fig. 6.1). Could the chandelier, which we know to have been on a pulley, be moving up and/or down during the taking of the picture, which would produce the spherical blur, or is this an attempt to reproduce a sense of what it was like from the perspective of the movie screen, to see the light of the projector? The problem is that there seems to be no projector in this picture, and yet we know—from the extensive screening of movies this year, including *Quo Vadis* and *The Birth of a Nation*—that a projector was in constant use in the building. The visible rose glass and balcony lobby ceiling arch behind the light source clearly show that no permanent projection booth existed yet, but the reality is that projection likely occurred from the back of the balcony lobby, where the projection booth would soon be built. With the projector in the balcony lobby, the "throw" to the stage would have been a minimum of sixty feet. If the projector were down the central aisle of the balcony and set up at the rail, where the reel is being held up, the "throw" would have been reduced by half to thirty feet. If the projector were set up in the orchestra pit, the "throw" would have been no more than fifteen feet. Only in the balcony lobby would the projector not block the view from some seats. Before the construction of the projection booth, which elevated the projectors and also helped reduce noise in the auditorium, it is not absolutely certain where projection occurred.

As early as the fall of 1918, Notre Dame screened a film in Washington Hall produced by the Catholic Art Association of America:

"The Victim," a photo-play in nine parts, illustrating the inviolability of the seal of confession was shown in Washington Hall last Saturday evening. This is, we understand, the first production of the Catholic Art Association of America, which was recently organized to present Catholic themes and characters as they should be presented. Apart from a few scenes where the action was clearly overdrawn or needlessly prolonged, the play was commendable and the Association is to be congratulated upon the success of its initial venture.[97]

By February and March 1919, the new medium of film brought both swashbuckler Douglas Fairbanks (who "sprinted down the celluloid path into Washington Hall last Saturday night, and fought through five reels of film with ever-increasing energy") and, at this the height of the "leading ladies" period of males playing female roles on stage, one of the great female impersonators of the twentieth century, Julian Eltinge, in *The Widow's Might*:

> Although it was palpably a made-to-order medium for the display of Eltinge's charms as a female impersonator and embodied numerous far-fetched situations, it at least had the saving grace of originality and humor. The criticism so generously awarded most of the screen productions presented to the students was noticeably forgotten in the general enjoyment of this picture.[98]

During the five-year period from *Julius Caesar* in January 1915 to the end of the 1919–20 academic year, the "mushin'-picture"[99] had become commonplace, with "the newest photo-plays . . . given weekly during the winter season."[100] Film had progressed from a singular exotic "lecture" to a ubiquitous Washington Hall tradition that would continue into the 1980s.

Debate, Oratory, and Elocution

The first *Scholastic* of 1867 praised debates and lectures for their pedagogical function, and as we have seen in earlier chapters the university offered classes in oratory and elocution as early as the 1860s. The interest in debate, oratory, and elocution extended through this period and indeed throughout the twentieth century, with Washington Hall as a premier performance venue for argumentation and disputation. Issues of the day generally served as the topics for debates and oratory, such as the Law Society debates in 1895 in Washington Hall on the "gold and silver question" and "currency," and in 1898 on the constitutionality of income tax.[101] The Breen Medal Oratorical Contest became an annual high-prestige fixture in Washington Hall by 1897, and the Law Debating Society, the Philodemic Literary and Debating Association, the Philopatrians, and the St. Aloysius Literary Society all supported these activities. Oratory, the art or practice of speaking in public, and elocution, the skill of clear and expressive speech (especially of pronunciation and articulation), remain important at Notre Dame to this day, with the Arts and Letters College Seminar, a required course taken by every sophomore, focused on developing students' presentational skills. Similarly, debate at Notre Dame also has remained alive and well, incorporating both parliamentary and policy debate, thanks to the generous support of William T. and Helen Kuhn Carey and under the faculty direction of Professor Susan Ohmer.

An interesting adjunct to these oratorical and debate contests had to do with seemingly required musical accompaniment. For the oratorical contest in June 1898 judged by the Honorable Timothy E. Howard, chief justice of the supreme court of Indiana (and who received the Laetare Medal in 1898), "Professor Preston and his musicians added materially to the pleasure of the afternoon's entertainment."[102] Having "live" music (pretty much the only kind available in 1898) accompany an oratorical contest is reminiscent of the earlier elaborate exhibitions, which were quickly becoming obsolete at this time, while, at the same time it illustrates the added value of music to create mood and to elevate pleasure at public events. A week after the oratorical contest, the university held the annual elocution contest (with Father Zahm serving as one of the judges), which showcased vocal variety and impersonations of different characters, including "imitations of the Italian Guide and the Yankee Doctor."[103] By spring semester 1906 Professor Frederic Karr received approval to teach elocution classes in the Washington Hall theatre itself to prepare his students better for the reality of competing there.[104] For the December 1909 Breen Medal orations, the orchestra performed between every two speeches and during the six esteemed judges' deliberations, with the three Notre Dame professors focusing on "Thought," and the three townspersons—two lawyers and the principal of South Bend High School—focusing on "Delivery."[105] This was clearly an important event and evening in Washington Hall.

By 1921, while there was an intercollegiate university debating team, interest had ebbed: "The final tryouts for the University debating team were held in Washington Hall Tuesday before an audience altogether too small for such an important school activity."[106] Perhaps the lack of interest seen here, which was also the case for theatre at this time, reflects the growing shift to specialized, niche audiences, especially as football and film had increasingly taken over primary roles with regard to large communal assembly. Had the combination of film and football shifted communal public disclosure away from some of the traditional, venerable forms? In spite of a small crowd, debate continued that year: "The last debate of the season will happen in Washington hall, Friday, May sixth, when the Detroit University three will take up the oratorical cudgels against our glorious affirmative."[107] But this year clearly witnessed the creation of a smaller, more specialized audience, which would be the future of communal assembly. Debate would soon move from Washington Hall to smaller venues in the Law School and library which would prove completely adequate to handle the niche audiences debate now generated. Even though we do not think of the Notre Dame community decentering as early as the 1920s, in fact that is precisely what happened, as enrollment increases alone made it impossible, except in the venue of the football stadium, for everyone to attend everything. Members of the community thus began to pick and choose what they included in their more highly specialized and selective worlds. The period of Notre Dame's existence when everyone attended everything and usually did so in Washington Hall had clearly ended.

Glee Club

Notre Dame has traditionally claimed that its Glee Club has operated continuously since 1915 (although 1919 is a more accurate date because of a wartime hiatus), but evidence described in earlier chapters makes it clear that real and genuine efforts go back at least as far as the fall semester of 1874, with lots of singing groups, including "glees," described over many years, nearly all of which performed on the Washington Hall stage. The first *Dome* for 1906 contains nothing about a Glee Club but in 1907 mentions not having one for both 1905–6 and 1906–7. The 1908 *Dome* includes hall-related Glee Clubs and described Professor Peterson's efforts to organize things. The 1909 *Dome* mentions the University Glee Club performing in both Washington Hall and in South Bend, and lists thirty-two members, with Peterson in charge. The same year there is also a Brownson Glee Club (composed of senior collegiate students, as opposed to junior "prep" students). Twenty members are in the 1910 *Dome* under Glee Club with Peterson again in charge. While a university Glee Club operated probably as early as 1906 and certainly by 1909, with predecessors going back to 1874, it did not do so continuously from 1915. During World War I, most noticeably the 1917–18 academic year, there was no Glee Club at Notre Dame. In February 1919 the *Scholastic* reported, "The Notre Dame Glee Club is now to be promptly revived after its war-time interruption. An organization meeting of the university's songsters and musicians will be held in Washington Hall early next week. Everyone will welcome heartily the reappearance of the Club."[108]

Lectures, Important Guests, and Other Events

Washington Hall was always the home of the lecture and the place where important guests appeared. As crossroads of the university, students directly accessed information and celebrity in Washington Hall while at the same time integrating themselves into the larger culture. Before the world became electronically connected, it was much more critical for important persons physically to visit the campus and for audiences to fill Washington Hall physically to experience their visit, and indeed the *Scholastic* recognized early in the twentieth century the long and continuing worth of the lecture in spite of the great value of the remote communication made possible by the book: "The Lecture has come down to us as one of the earliest and most effective means of instruction, and despite the profusion of books with us, it is almost as potent a force in the educational life of to-day as it was with the academicians of old."[109] An interesting aspect of this cultural exposure, too, had to do with the concept of "famous lectures." Before mechanical and electronic recording and storage devices facilitated ubiquitous distribution, a renowned person gave the same speech repeatedly, since replays had to be recreated "live" to exist in time and space. The *Scholastic* related for example that "the Rev. F. J. Nugent, of Des Moines, Iowa, will deliver his famous lecture, 'The Lost Confessional,' in Washington Hall on Tuesday next."[110] Lectures were all uniquely ephemeral, and audiences clearly looked forward to experiencing in person the "famous lecture" they had obviously heard or read about, and the range of topics varied greatly. In the spring of 1898 Laetare medalist Eliza Allen Starr lectured in Washington Hall on the Cathedral of Santa del Fiore of Florence, while a month later the "Physical Director Beyer" conducted "an in-door athletic festival in Washington Hall . . . for the benefit of the Athletic Association. These entertainments have been famous in former years."[111]

The temperance movement had gained steam by this time, too, so it is no surprise that the Reverend James Cleary, "President of the Catholic Total Abstinence Union of America, lectured before the students and faculty" in Washington Hall. His approach was not statistical, but rather "dwelt at length upon the opportunities offered in our age and land to the college-trained young man . . . and then proceeded to show what an important part the principle of personal abstinence from liquor might be made to play in enabling young men to realize to the fullest their great opportunities."[112]

In March 1898 the Most Reverend John Ireland, archbishop of St. Paul, spoke in Washington Hall, and in spite of it being a dreary morning he made "an eloquent and elevated appeal for Catholicism and Americanism." If war comes, he asserted, this school of "religion, science and patriotism" would provide chaplains and student soldiers.[113] William J. Onahan (1836–1919), the Laetare medalist from 1890, accompanied his Grace.

The Irish connection had always been a constant at Notre Dame, but the history of Ireland by the early twentieth century made the visits of Irish guests seem especially topical and relevant. Seumas McManus (1861–1960), probably best known for *The Story of the Irish Race* (1921), visited in 1904 and "addressed the students last Wednesday in Washington Hall. His subject, 'Irish Wit and Humor,' seldom has received happier treatment. He took us for an hour or more to Mount Charles, Donegal, introducing us the while to 'Father Dan,' 'Hughey McGarrity,' 'The Postmistress' and the simple, happy peasantry and fisherfolk that dwell around Inver Bay. We also made a short stay with him at the wake, dance, and wedding, and our guide was so well informed and the excursion so enjoyable that the time seemed to pass with flying feet."[114] In early 1906 Irish language scholar Douglas Hyde (1860–1949), who founded the Gaelic League and would under the 1937 constitution become the first president of Ireland (1938–45), lectured on Irish folklore.[115] Some events had great symbolic components, too, such as the complex and formal ceremony in Washington Hall in March 1914 when the university received the sword of Irish patriot and Union Army general Thomas Francis Meagher. The 1914 *Dome* commented: "The number of automobiles lined up beside old Washington Hall that night made it look like a Chicago theatre on New Year's eve."[116] By 1919 the *Scholastic* noted the compelling interest at Notre Dame in Irish nationalism: "The green, white, and orange flag of the Irish Republic was displayed for the first time in Washington Hall during the concert last Saturday and attracted much attention," the newly formed Irish Republic parliament having declared sovereignty over all of Ireland the previous month.[117] And in mid-October 1919, the president of that new parliament, Eamon de Valera, spoke to enthusiastic students in a packed Washington Hall.[118]

Famous American politicians also spoke in Washington Hall during this period, to be sure, luminaries such as Vice President Charles Warren Fairbanks in 1906 and presidential candidate and orator Williams Jennings Bryan in 1908. The *Scholastic* reported that both uncharacteristically eschewed politics in their lectures: "Thursday evening the student body assembled in Washington Hall to listen to the Vice-President of the United States, Mr. Fairbanks. His stay was brief, but in that time he threw out many valuable ideas concerning young men and their ideals. We were a bit disappointed, however, that the renowned republican did not tell us a few things on the political order. It would have been quite apropos and appreciated."[119] Bryan seemed to have done the same thing but with more impressive presentational skills:

Yesterday, Mr. William Jennings Bryan lectured before the students in Washington Hall at ten o'clock. His subject was "Faith," a subject which he has used frequently when speaking to college men throughout the country. . . . Ignoring politics, he dealt with his subject in a manner that tended to inspire his listeners with the ambition to do noble deeds. . . . Mr. Bryan has a wonderful command over language considered primarily as a means of conveying thought as opposed to the superficial emotion which the mere elocutionist may produce, and what he said was worth the saying. . . . In discussing faith in God he uttered some very striking truths, emphasizing in particular the fact that reason can not be a basis for morality, and that men of high moral qualities need have no fear of failure.[120]

Bryan's speech was indeed a great oratorical event, a tradition that continued in Washington Hall to the Mario Cuomo speech in the fall of 1984, when great politicians came to the center of American Catholic higher education to speak to the next generation in a historic space named for the father of the country about issues of faith, morality, and justice.

Washington Hall was also always the place for keeping abreast of the religious and intellectual interests of the church. Monsignor Robert Hugh Benson (1871–1914) visited Washington Hall in April 1914 (just six months before his untimely death) and unexpectedly lectured on papal infallibility:

It had been rumored about the campus that the distinguished English visitor would make "Spiritism" the theme of his discourse, and this impression prevailed until he had appeared upon the stage. After Father Cavanaugh's felicitously phrased introduction, however, Mgr. Benson announced that he had elected to discuss the Papacy.

Father Benson's address was remarkable for the same facility of expression, cogency of reasoning, and forcefulness of phrasing, that have so characterized his novels and essays. He treated the question of Papal authority and infallibility from the viewpoint of a convert. By apt illustration, he demonstrated the necessity of some central and supreme authority. . . . Monsignor Benson made out an impregnable case for Papal jurisdiction, citing and refuting the most plausible arguments of all ages against the real supremacy of Christ's Vicar at Rome. He is a pleasing and powerful speaker, his reasoning being flawless and his presentation of fact lucid and unmistakable. He held the undivided attention of his audience throughout, sustaining interest rather by the charm of a magnetic personality and a virile argument than by rhetorical artifice or forensic sensationalism. Notre Dame is signally honored by having been included in the itinerary of this brilliant novelist, lecturer and essayist, in his visit to the United States.[121]

But there were also plenty of lectures on lighter topics, too, such as the travelogue in 1916 by "Mr. L. O. Armstrong, Special Lecturer of the Bureau of Commercial Economics, Washington, D.C. . . . on the 'Canadian Rockies' that was highly interesting and well illustrated with slides. Mr. Armstrong's voice was unusually clear, and he possessed the art of holding his audience, a happy faculty of which not every travel talker can boast."[122] And those involving science and technology were always popular, such as postwar "demonstrations of electrical phenomena, the Gyroscope and Torpedo, [which] gained the attention of the audience in a way that is seldom noticed in Washington Hall. The expressions of appreciation of the lecture were genuine."[123]

Football in Washington Hall

And as early as 1907, Washington Hall was converted during away football games into a place to experience the game under conditions as close to "live" as possible at the time. A very interesting twist on access to ephemeral events occurred in 1907 with regard to the Notre Dame–Purdue game, when "returns will be received in Washington Hall,"[124] creating a new use of the hall as a place where an audience assembled, as it did for "live" plays and lectures, to access remotely and electronically, either by telephone or telegraph, the returns of a "live" football game. This pre-radio communal way to experience a football game combined Washington Hall as its traditional place of access with a new technology that made accessible a hitherto inaccessible event: enjoying a football game in what for the era was as close to "real time" and "live" as possible.

The McKinley Assassination

Washington Hall served as the venue for the memorial for the slain William McKinley, the third of four American presidents to be assassinated during the time when a Washington Hall existed on the Notre Dame campus, but the first time for this building, the "new" Washington Hall, to be so engaged.[125] McKinley died on September 14, 1901, after having been shot a week before at the Temple of Music in Buffalo, New York. The *Scholastic* reported that President Morrissey had sent a message of condolence to Mrs. McKinley, and the faculty assembled and drew up "resolutions denouncing the crime." Further,

> following the announcement of President Roosevelt, the Reverend President laid aside Thursday as the day on which we would hold our memorial services. When we gathered in Washington Hall on this the appointed day we found the flag of mourning entwined with the stars and stripes and the gold and blue. Then we knew that we had come to pay our last respects to a great man. We knew that we had been for the past week a nation of mourners.

The memorial service began with a prayer; then Chopin's "Funeral March," performed by the band; "Lead on, O Kindly Light," sung by the student body; resolutions of the faculty, read by Dr. Austin O'Malley; and three addresses, given by Colonel William Hoynes (dean of the Law School), Professor John Ewing (history and political economy), and Joseph J. Sullivan (senior student). Hoynes said, "Like Lincoln and Garfield, he rose from the ranks of the poor and lowly, and he never forgot the ties that bound him in good will and sympathy to the plain people of the land."[126]

The 1922 *Dome* summed up the central nature of Washington Hall in the daily lives of students at Notre Dame:

> Watching Washington Hall . . . as ye editor stands on the mountain top, and trains his telescope on the Campus, his attention is especially drawn to one building where large numbers of stu-

dents gather perhaps two or three times a week. . . . Well, Washington Hall has been the epitome of a liberal education to me. It has narrowed me, it has broadened me, it has flattened me. It has cheered me when I sorrowed; it has saddened me when I rejoiced. It has been my ruination and my rejuvenation. It has been my solace and my despair. . . . Movies, music, speakers, and plays, have I seen there.[127]

During the 1921–22 academic year Washington Hall remained at the crossroads of the university and served as the doorway through which students entered both to access the world and to integrate themselves into it, the place of communal assembly, where everything important seemed to happen. Over the next decade and a half, the university would grow by leaps and bounds, adding fifteen buildings (one a year), as Washington Hall soldiered on as the single performing arts center on the Notre Dame campus.

CHAPTER 7

THE GHOST OF
WASHINGTON HALL,
1920–2004

My promise to Father Theodore M. Hesburgh, C.S.C., to write about the Ghost of Washington Hall, so inextricably connected to the history of the building, is the genesis of this chapter. No history of Washington Hall would be complete without a history of the ghost stories related to Washington Hall, the earliest published reports of which occurred during the 1920–21 academic year. Before turning to the overall historical record as related to actual or imagined ghosts that haunt the building and its environs, however, I wish first to dispel the conventional wisdom that only Washington Hall on the Notre Dame campus uniquely had ghostly encounters. Father Robert J. Austgen, C.S.C., has compiled considerable data on the many ghosts at Notre Dame that have often made their presence known in a variety of ways and at varied locations at the university.[1] Indeed, within a week of the first reported ghostly manifestation in Washington Hall in January 1921, Badin Hall had such a visitation, too, and much earlier, in 1874, Notre Dame students related a downtown South Bend "ghost story": "Our friend John went to Studebaker's shops to see the ghost, but he says Morpheus didn't give him a ghost of a chance to see." The writer added, "Our friend John don't believe in ghosts. He is not to be frightened with any stories like those which are told of the Studebaker Factory. He spent a night in the haunted room the other night and he says the only spirits which troubled him were those which he took with him."[2] Typically ghost stories relate to alcoholic excess, but for reasons not exactly clear, of all the ghost stories, the one that has survived and prospered centered on Washington Hall and has seemed singularly to have captured the imagination of the campus, probably because of its very tentative and belated connection to the death of George Gipp.

The earliest hint of something ghostly afoot landed in the *Scholastic* in early 1921: "When not communicating with hallucinations Pio Montenegro is president of the recently chartered Filipino Club of the university."[3] The hallucinatory event was described as follows:

> All the circumstances connected with certain mysterious blasts from behind were detailed by John Buckley at last Tuesday's meeting of the Notre Dame Council, Knights of Columbus, in search of sympathy or solution. Harry Stevenson whose similar nerve-racking experiences became the subject of investigation by psychopathic authorities described his sensations. Although Father Thomas Crumley could offer no satisfactory explanation for the phenomena, he presented a lucid explanation of the fascination with which many people regard the ouija board, which attraction is due to the psychological principle known as the ideomotor theory.[4]

Clearly, something was amiss by early 1921: things were going bump in the night!

In the section "Safety Valve," in the same *Scholastic* of January 15, 1921, we get the first reference to a ghost at Notre Dame but nothing related either to Washington Hall or George Gipp (who had died a month before, on December 14, 1920): "We expect that some of the excuses for absence from class will soon read 'Up all night with a ghost.'"[5] A much more complete report appeared a week later, with the single sentence, "Last week the spirits moved from Music Hall over to Badin,"[6] which confirmed that in its earliest manifestations the ghost experienced no geographical restriction to Washington Hall. On the same page in this issue, the first complete "Ghost of Washington Hall" story appeared, and we learn that while the ghost certainly could leave Washington Hall, he chose not to do so because of the cold winter weather and his lack of proper clothing. Thus marooned in Washington Hall, the ghost desperately sought solutions to geometry problems. The ghost of Washington Hall was heard but not seen in this first published report of his manifestation:

GHOST OF WASHINGTON HALL

"I'm cold," said the ghost, knocking at a door in Music Hall, "can't I come in and get warm?"

"No you can't," replied the voice from within, "and if you don't get away from this door at once, I'll report you to the Disciplinarian Department to-morrow. Ghosts are not supposed to be out after twelve o'clock. They are under the same rules as the Campus students. " [Students had 10:00 P.M. curfews.]

"You're wrong there," chimed back the ghost, "the night is the only free time I have. I'm like the athletes in this respect. If I were under campus rule what in the world advantage would I have in being a ghost? I might just as well live up over the garage with those impossible fellows."

"I tell you," repeated the voice from within, "that you can't come in here. I have the door bolted and if you dare to come through it, I have a pair of dice and I'll shoot."

"It seems unreasonable on your part," hissed the ghost, "not to let me in when you know that this corridor is freezing and that I have only my ghost clothes on. Besides I thought probably you might have the geometry problems. I have a brother ghost who has been looking for Geometry problems ever since he became a ghost. He's taking the place of a poor simp who died working on his geometry."

"I haven't the problems," returned the man inside, "I am going to copy them to-morrow from a friend of mine, and if I had them I wouldn't give them to you. You've been roaming around this hall for two weeks at the most ungodly hours and keeping us all up. Why don't you go to Corby or Sorin or somewhere else?"

"Do you think I'm going out in that snow," asked the ghost, "when the wind is blowing straight across the campus. No ghost has been given his winter clothes yet and you can't expect us to go everywhere. If I just had a pair of your heavy pajamas I would feel better but when I come to steal them you're always up. I got a pair of [student John] Buckley's but they're too big. He'll have to have an enormous ghost when he dies."

"If you don't get away from here I'll tell the president," raged the Music Haller, "and maybe he'll have the building burned or torn down and you'll be caught in the ruins."

"The president can't find me," responded the ghost. "I had his secretary running all over the campus like a dog with a can on his tail just because I whistled and pattered down the corridors. His lungs were perfect vacuums when he got back to his hall; there wasn't a breath left in him. I'll say he's one fellow I have buffa - loed. I think I could make him climb a rain pipe or a lightning rod if I chased him."

At this moment one of the professors entered the hall and the ghost vanished through the keyhole of one of the music-rooms.[7]

Later in the month, "the Player's Club . . . held a meeting Monday to investigate the alleged addition to the population in Washington Hall"; and "the Society for Psychical Research held an interesting meeting in Washington Hall Saturday evening, under the direction of John Buckley. Following the session an informal experience meeting was addressed by several of the new members."[8]

By the end of the 1920–21 academic year, the *Dome* added credence to the ghost story through repetition and embellishment of the original article, with hints at actual physical sightings, claiming that the incorporeal entity played the French horn well, terrorized the eight residents of Washington Hall, and had become the talk of campus. The author even suggested who might be the perpetrators of what had become a very convincing hoax (see fig. 7.1):

THE WASHINGTON HALL GHOST

Shortly before Christmas, the residents of Washington hall began to be bothered by night-time visits from a ghost who, though he

THE WASHINGTON HALL GHOST

Figure 7.1. The earliest surviving photograph of the Ghost of Washington Hall. *Dome* 1921, 305.

did not beat a drum, blew a French horn with much violence. At the dead of night he would wake the hall's eight intellectuals from slumber with a prodigious blast, and when they went fearfully to investigate he would be gone; he would slip pieces of paper under [student] John Buckley's door, and then take them away before John could get them; he would be on the stairs when you went up, moaning right at your shoulder, but if you turned around he would be gone; he would swish around the corner at one end of the corridor when you entered at the other; and once he scared [President Burns's secretary] Harry Stevenson almost to death. The ghost became a most-talked-about thing on the campus. Men were worked into such a state that they would jump at the slightest sound. Delegations would go to Washington Hall to sleep there, and they would come back pale and convinced. Eddie Schmidt went, and when he came back he was persuaded that "there are more things in Heaven and earth, 'Horatio' than are dreampt of in your philosophy." The ghost was the only topic of discussion at one meeting of the Knights of Columbus. Finally, the visiting investigating committees that went to Washington hall at night became so noisy that the faculty forbade them. Less and less was heard of the ghost until it was forgotten. We cannot finish the story because Carr and Manion have never told us how they did it.[9]

The first connection to George Gipp in print occurred five years later, in the 1926 *Dome,* and in so doing dramatically expanded the ghost's range from the labyrinthine student and practice rooms of the north wing of Washington Hall to the exterior (south) stone steps. Pio Montenegro ('22) once again was our man; he gained an immortal place in Notre Dame history in the 1926 *Dome* as the first person to see the Ghost of Washington Hall, as opposed to simply hearing it, and to recognize its striking resemblance to the late George Gipp:

> It was not long after the death of the immortal George Gipp that the series of inexplicable events occurred which gave rise to the tale of the Ghost of Washington Hall. Many stories of the visitations of the spirit are told; some persons closely connected with events of that time express themselves as skeptical; nevertheless, the story has been passed down from student to student during the last half-decade and has gained steadily, both in credibility and in imaginative ramifications. It is significant that the men who heard or saw the ghost believe to this day that spirit it was.
>
> On New Year's Eve, 1920, shortly after the death of George Gipp had shocked and saddened the entire campus, Harry Stevenson, who lived in Cadillac Hall[10] at the time, was visiting friends in Washington Hall. At midnight he left the room, which was on the third floor of the hall, and descended to the second floor, intending to return to his room. As he was about to descend the final flight of stairs, the notes of a bugle, masterfully played, floated through the hall, seeming to come through the corridor at the foot of the stairs. The music was accompanied by a weird howling. So startling were the sounds that Stevenson collapsed in hysterics, and was found unconscious by his friends who came in answer to his cries. Such was the first appearance of the famed Washington

Hall ghost [not an appearance at all]. Little credence was given Stevenson's story at the time, but the manifestations were encountered by other men shortly after, consisting each time of the beautifully modulated notes of a bugle, accompanied by the weird howling. Up to this time, no one had seen the ghost, nor felt it. So persistent, however, was the spirit in appearing that several students of Brownson Hall determined to ferret out the secret. Led by "Doc" Connell, these students camped in Washington Hall one night, taking turns at watching and listening. They were rewarded by hearing the usual noises, and according to their own story, by being thrown from bed by invisible hands. After the experiences of these men, no further attempts to lay the ghost were made. The manifestations continued for nearly a month.

To one man only was it given to see the Ghost of Washington Hall. At the time of the ghost's almost nightly visits to the music hall, Pio Montenegro, '22, of Brazil, lived in Science Hall [now La-Fortune Student Center], his window overlooking the entrance to Washington Hall. On several occasions, according to his account, upon glancing from his window at night, he saw a stalwart figure mounted upon a beautiful white charger galloping up the steps of the hall and through the entrance. He insisted that the figure which he had seen upon the white horse was that of George Gipp.

The last appearance of the spirit which had caused such a furor upon the campus was heard by Brother Maurilius, who lived in Washington Hall at the time. He tells of being awakened from sleep during the night by the notes of a bugle, accompanied by heavy thumps like the sound of a heavy wardrobe falling to the floor. It was three o'clock in the morning when this occurred. Brother Maurilius dressed and made the rounds of the hall, inspecting everything thoroughly, but could find no evidence of anything unusual. After this occurrence, the ghost was never again heard.

Such is the story of the ghost of Washington Hall, as gleaned from conversations with men who came in contact with it at one time or another during its periodical appearances. Many persons profess to believe that the entire affair was the product of the efforts of some practical joker, while others argue that if such were the case, the joke would long ago have come to light, along with the jokers. Such an accomplishment, say the defenders of the ghost, would have been "too good to keep." Living in the hall at the time of the ghostly visitations were John Mangan, Joseph Casasanta, Joseph Corona, Frank Kolars, John Buckley, Brother Maurilius, and others, and none of these men have been able to throw any light upon the occurrences which have been related. This much they agree upon: if the appearances of the ghost were arranged by practical jokers, one of them must have been a musician of the finest ability, for the notes of the ghostly bugle were always perfectly muted and beautifully modulated.

Whatever the truth concerning the origin of the ghostly visitations may be, the fact remains that the Ghost of Washington Hall has become the character about which many fanciful tales have been woven during time-honored "chin-fests," and the tale of the Spirit of Gipp will go down to student posterity as long as one stone of Notre Dame remains upon another.[11]

Pio Montenegro's romanticized vision, first reported in print four years after he graduated from Notre Dame, appears to be the origin of the story of the incorporeal white charger on the south steps of Washington Hall whose ghostly rider resembled George Gipp. The Montenegro story seemed completely unrelated to the talented but unseen bugle-blowing, noise-making manifestation inside the north wing of the building heard by the students living there. Thus by 1926 the clear connection had been made in print between George Gipp's untimely death and the Ghost of Washington Hall, and the two have remained forever linked in this oft-repeated bit of Notre Dame folklore. George Gipp's ties to Washington Hall (and white chargers) were loose at best. Burns outlines a series of events and activities in the weeks leading to Gipp's untimely death, none of which is related to Washington Hall, and any of which could have precipitated his infectious illness and subsequent death in the days before antibiotics.[12]

In early 1932, the *Scholastic* called the Ghost of Washington Hall "one of the famed Notre Dame traditions."[13] The article incorrectly dated the original story to December 1921 (instead of 1920) but purports to tell the real story of the "High C" trumpet note, asserting sensibly that the "finger of suspicion pointed to Joe Casasanta, who was then assistant bandmaster, and who played the trumpet." Casasanta pleaded innocent. This account says nothing about George Gipp and the white horse galloping up the south exterior stairs, but rather is the first article to implicate Casasanta as the source of the ghostly events of 1921. The *Notre Dame Alumnus* at about the same time republished the 1926 *Dome* story but added updates on some of the persons involved, including Stevenson, Montenegro, Brother Maurilius, and Casasanta.[14]

Five years later in December 1937 the *Scholastic* described the entity as the "the famous Ghost of Washington Hall" and encountered the ghost, for the first time, in the actual auditorium of the building. The writer, Donald A. Foskett, "slouched into one of the wooden seats for which the hall is famed. . . . Two minutes of deep thoughts followed, my eyes shifting from Demosthenes to Cicero, up to Washington, and back to Demosthenes. Suddenly there rolled into my ear a deep, jovial voice, 'A little early for the first show, aren't you?'" The ghost told the correspondent that, some years past, he dumped over beds and threw water and the three residents left, and no one had lived in the hall since (not at all accurate since students lived in Washington Hall until the early 1970s). The ghost added that he now attended the second showing of the movie every Saturday and has seen "practically everyone" over the years, including George Gipp and other luminaries, a clear indication the ghost is not George Gipp.[15]

The *Scholastic* predicted in 1940 that an impending vaudeville show on the Washington Hall stage would undoubtedly interfere with an ageing ghost's peace and quiet: "The traditional 'Ghost of Washington Hall' will have to take it on the lam early in December when the Knights of Columbus–sponsored vaudeville hits the ancient theatre boards again. The 'ghost' is an old man now and can't stand the hoof-pounding, jive-sending antics of Notre Dame's annual crop of enthusiastic entertainers."[16] Two years later in 1942, the ghost story returned to the pages of the *Scholastic* when author Jack Woelfle repeated the connection to George Gipp's death but also brought up new information, that of the death in 1919 of talented trumpeter Jim Minavi, a "student professor" who lived in Washington Hall when he became mortally ill. The article included a picture of Washington Hall with external stone south steps, so the mounted

Gipp story made sense. This article emphasized the audible, trumpet-tooting ghost and repeated that the only visible sighting related to George Gipp occurred in 1926.[17] By 1946 there is an actual photograph proving the Ghost had taken over not only the auditorium, but also, for the first time, the stage itself of Washington Hall: "The Horn Blows at Midnight: Ghost of Washington Hall Rides Again" included a rare photograph of the Ghost on the stage with footlights and the auditorium in the background (see fig. 7.2).[18] Never mind that the initial ghostly presence had been limited to the corridors in the north wing Music Hall where a handful of students then lived and the south (front) exterior steps, which had been removed in 1933. The 1946 article recalled the ghostly experiences of John Buckley in 1920 (rattling papers under his door), Pio E. Montenegro's ghostly rider of 1926, and the generalized trumpet blasts coming from the hall, which apparently only one resident could hear at a time. The article, signed by "Johnny Walker," clearly seems to be intended as good fun, and shrewd scholars today might question the authenticity of the photograph, which, ghostly apparition aside, remains a valuable resource regarding the footlights, stage, and house of Washington Hall in 1946. A year later around Halloween in 1947, the photograph appeared again in the *Scholastic* in "Beware—The Undead Flit About Tonight," by Joe Wilcox. Wilcox discussed ghosts (and digressed to other creatures of the night) while deciding that the Washington Hall ghost was "the stairs-walking, candle-carrying manifestation and the playful kind" whose "antics annoyed the students who used to live in Washington Hall in years past."[19] Both the *Dome* and the *Scholastic* in the late 1940s accepted the ghost as a benign resident of Washington Hall. The *Dome* speculated in 1948 that the ghost was "an obvious B-picture fan," an appropriate taste for a building famous for its screenings of such films, while the *Scholastic* went so far as to interview him and reported his endorsement of an upcoming event in Washington Hall: "We had a special interview with the ghost over in Washington Hall the other day and he confided that he expects a large turnout Monday night for the first student musical of the year. He advised that all music lovers come early and avoid the rush for this new presentation of an ancient musical drama."[20]

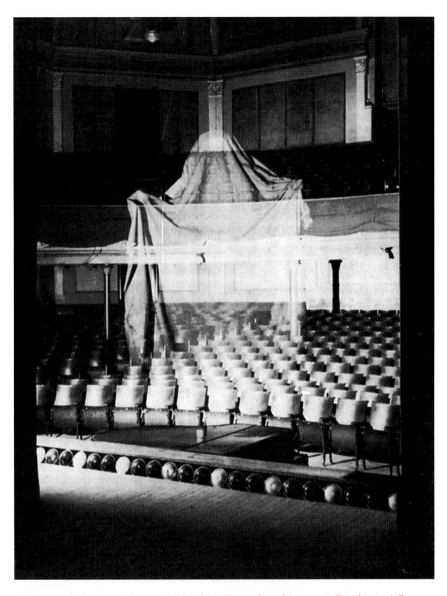

Figure 7.2. "The Horn Blows at Midnight / Ghost of Washington Hall Rides Again" includes an actual picture (caught on film!) of the Ghost on the stage with footlights and boards and an orchestra pit for a grand piano (with the auditorium in the background). *Scholastic* 87:3, April 5, 1946, 10.

By the 1950s sightings had become very personal and specific, as in the case of student Daniel Boland ('56), who, fifty years after the fact, recalled vividly what can only be described as a junk-food-eating ghost: "It was during one of those Wash Hall convocations that I first beheld The Ghost sitting on one of the upper balcony railings, his feet dangling over the edge as he quietly munched a Twinkie. But nobody believed me then, and I seriously doubt if anyone would now."[21] The ghost had come a long way from incorporeal trumpeting and bumps in the night.

We next hear about the ghost in print in 1966, when the *Scholastic* again repeated the Ghost of Washington Hall story and renewed the George Gipp connection, relating the hall directly to his death with some expansion:

> There have been many stories about the ghost in Washington Hall. One of the best is about the "Gipper." It seems that he stayed in Washington Hall with some buddies and there was no heat in the building at night. It was in that hall that he caught pneumonia which eventually led to his death. Rumor has it that the ghost in Washington Hall is that of the "Gipper."[22]

This 1966 report seemed to embody the often repeated story that George Gipp was on, under, or near Washington Hall's south exterior stone steps the night he contracted a case of pneumonia which proved to be fatal, an event that would help to explain why his ghost returned to haunt the place. While this article seemed to confirm forever the connection between George Gipp and the Ghost of Washington Hall, an *Observer* article two years later in 1968 correctly pointed out the mutability of ghostly apparitions—"the supposed fleeting spirit of George Gipp, or whatever form he now assumes"—recognizing that ghosts can assume whatever shape they choose. The *Observer* recounted that senior Joe Doyle, who resided in Washington Hall, told the story of a cousin who had had a rendezvous with the ghost two years earlier. Four students decided to investigate, and a prank turned into a genuine encounter since "something else was in there."[23]

The *Notre Dame Magazine* had two ghost-related stories in 1974, the first about Joe Sinnott ('76) who lived in the hall and discussed the apparition that might be one of several different persons, including George Gipp, "a construction worker who . . . fell to his death while working in the fly loft in the late 1800's," or a musician who died onstage. This appears to be the earliest published account of the construction worker story (who ultimately becomes a steeplejack). In the second story, the writer claimed clearly tongue in cheek that the ghost is a former student who strayed onto the Saint Mary's College campus.[24] A year later, the *Scholastic* approached the ghost story singularly from the perspective of George Gipp, repeating the claim that he contracted an ultimately fatal case of pneumonia because of spending the night on the steps of Washington Hall. An interview with the ghost followed in which the ghost revealed he was a quarterback at Notre Dame and not George Gipp at all. The ghost of George Gipp had gone elsewhere for more peace and quiet, it seemed.[25]

J. P. Morrissey's *Scholastic* article in May 1977 entitled "Evicting the Ghost of Washington Hall" dealt with the desperate need to renovate the building and the plans afoot to do so and, in spite of the title, has nothing to do with incorporeal apparitions. Just nine months later, however, his "Exorcising the Ghosts of Washington Hall," part of a development appeal in *Notre Dame Magazine,* reminded the alumni that "according to legend, the place is haunted" and repeated the George Gipp story and transformed the construction worker specifically into a steeplejack.[26]

In fall 1977 the *South Bend Tribune* article by Charles Davis "Phantom at Notre Dame: Ghost of Washington Hall" provided detailed information about the first 1920–21 encounter and some serious explanation of events. The instruments in storage appeared to "play" remotely, even without mouthpieces in place. At the end of the article, Davis confessed that he perpetrated the hoax by accessing the instruments through a hole in the back of the instrument storage cupboard adjacent to his room. He connected an enema bag hose to a mouthpiece, slipped the hose through the hole and into the cupboard and blew, thus creating the incorporeal sound attributed to the ghost. By the time lights came on and a human examination of the cupboard took place, Davis had removed the hose, so it appeared that the horns had made noise even without mouthpieces. Could Davis's explanation, however, have produced the perfect high C note claimed by original auditors?[27] Nevertheless, it is almost certain that Charlie Davis ('21), whose grandniece, Jinny Porcari Keough ('78), recounted that he "told his 'Ghost of Washington Hall' story at family gatherings," was indeed directly involved in the creation of the initial hoax in 1920–21.[28]

A three-part series in the *Observer* in the spring of 1979 stands as perhaps the most definitive report on the Ghost of Washington Hall. Claiming to be based on an earlier interview with Clarence "Pat" Manion ("among the last surviving eyewitnesses to the episode"), author Phil Hicks attempted to make less opaque some of the more cryptic comments in the initial *Scholastic* and *Dome* reports. The author correctly cited the original story as being half a century old, but quickly added a new twist:

> Perhaps the most conventional explanation for the "ghost" has been the "Gipper's Ghost" version which connects the spirit with All-American George Gipp, who in 1920 supposedly slept on the hall's steps the night before contracting his fatal illness. Other unexplained spirits have been attributed either to Brother Cajetan, whose unmelodious peck horn playing was said to haunt the Hall, or to a steeplejack who in 1886 fell from a lofty Hall construction perch to his death.[29]

We have previously heard nothing about Brother Cajetan, and the steeplejack story is very recent; while the former got little traction, the latter has persisted to this day. I have found nothing about a workman's death in 1886 related to any building on campus, and, indeed, during the lengthy reconstruction period after the Great Fire of 1879, the *Scholastic* bragged that not a single death occurred. Falls and injuries happened, to be sure, and ironically one slater who managed to survive building Washington Hall later died in a fall at a Chicago construction site. Dorothy Corson also found nothing about a steeplejack's death in her extensive unpublished manuscript "Untimely Deaths on N. D. & S. M. C. Campuses 1840s–1990s," in which she exhaustively chronicles accidental deaths. According to Corson, workers died in 1925 (gymnasium), 1930 (law library), and 1938 (Rockne Memorial), but she found nothing from the 1880s to support the steeplejack story.[30] We know from the *Scholastic* that a non-fatal accident occurred during the construction of the new Washington Hall, however, in June 1881: "One of the masons engaged on the addition to the Academy of Music fell while at work on the walls, Saturday last, and broke his leg. Rev. Dr. Neyron set the broken limb."[31] This accident may be the genesis of the later steeplejack story, or it may also have been created completely without foundation. Although the construction worker/steeplejack connection to the Ghost has been published repeatedly since 1974, it remains unconfirmed.

The second part of the *Observer* series in 1979 emphasized the ghost story becoming public as a result of Father Crumley speaking about ghosts of Ireland to the Knights of Columbus. The Reverend Thomas Aloysius Crumley, C.S.C., a professor of philosophy at Notre Dame from 1898 to 1934, must have spoken at the Knights of Columbus around December 1920, about the time the stories started to appear in the *Scholastic*. Night vigils in the band room of Washington Hall occurred in attempts to encounter the ghost, in spite of a 10:00 P.M. curfew. A couple of beds were set up there. A young John Joseph Cavanaugh (later priest and university president) is implicated.[32]

The third part of Phil Hicks's story relates how President Burns's secretary, Harry Stevenson, got involved and heard the incorporeal horn, and how Brother Maurilius, who "ran the pie store around the corner" remained skeptical. Part 3 related everything to the horn-blowing episodes and gave no information about George Gipp, the white charger, or any physical appearances. The author surmised that students created the hoax to get Brother Maurilius on board and then proceeded to explain how they did it: first they dropped a dead weight to wake him as Joe Casasanta blew the horn. Brother Maurilius became a convert and suspected demonic involvement that he reported to the provincial, Father O'Donnell, who promptly had an "unofficial" exorcism done, after which the horn never blew again. The story is off one year in dating the series of events from "November of 1919 until April or May the next year," but it confirms again the auditory nature of the event: "I never *saw* anything; I just *heard*." The interviewed person reported a presence but "never attributed it to the Devil or the spirit of George Gipp or that steeplejack or any of those things."[33]

Four years later, the *Observer* in 1983 gave a bit of history of the building, reported the 1920 genesis of the story, and added both the appearance of a ghost "in a bowler hat" and footsteps on the roof. Toni Rutherford interviewed Father David Garrick (then rector of Keenan Hall) about his encounter with the ghost. Father Garrick reported that, when a student in the 1960s, he saw a ten-foot-tall ghost in the north end third-floor area of the building. He admitted it may have been "a trick of the imagination" but claimed to believe in the ghost. He then went on to explain the nature of "theatre ghosts," that is, those who love theatre and watching productions: "When an actor goes on stage, he becomes the character he portrays . . . this released energy builds up and becomes the typical theater ghost." The article repeated the fallen steeplejack and George Gipp explanations and also suggested a new one, that of a student "who fell while working on lighting equipment."[34]

Even the *South Bend Tribune* article that dealt with the changes in the theatre program brought about by my joining the Notre Dame faculty in 1984 mentioned the Ghost of Washington Hall, as though the building and the ghost were inseparable. The article claimed that "ghost reports always have been part of the Washington Hall story," and that legends have blamed the ghost on George Gipp, the steeplejack, and a "1921 tuba-tooting ghost." In the article, both Tom Barkes and I reported working all summer of 1985 in the building "without hearing any strange noises," but Barkes related the recent visit of a "ghost photographer" who very seriously "snapped pictures with infrared film" and who was "dead serious."[35] The *Dome* in 1986 included a one-page spread entitled "Ghostbustin" and listed four theories. In addition to the two very well known ones connected to the construction worker and George Gipp, the *Dome* added ones about a student in the 1950s falling to his death and another connected to Father Zahm's brother—which typically did not make the other articles.[36]

Regis Coccia reported in the *South Bend Tribune* in 1990 that Barkes believed the ghostly noises were very likely expanding and contracting pipes, but even Barkes admitted he had seen odd things, and Coccia tied the story once again to George Gipp. In the summer of 1997 the *Scholastic* traced ghosts to the unconfirmable 1886 death of the steeplejack, but quoted Barkes as "saying that all the noise is probably attributable to echoes and pipes." A Gipp-oriented Halloween-related story appeared in the *Scholastic* in 1998. Christina Ries, while serving as an administrative assistant for the Department of Film, Television, and Theatre, confirmed that, just after Christmas break in January 2003, an unexplained (and slow) door closing in the hallway outside the costume shop occurred, adding to the notion that those who work in the building, over time, inevitably had stories to tell. The *South Bend Tribune* interviewed me in 2005 for historical particulars related to the initial 1920–21 events.[37]

Today it seems clear that what very likely began as a college prank to frighten a superstitious rector over the winter of 1920–21 became a self-perpetuating campus legend through both constant repetition and creative embellishment, especially the quickly realized connection of the first sighting to the untimely death of football legend George Gipp. For those enamored of ghost stories, it is easy to think that a building like Washington Hall where so much communal assembly had occurred might retain the "spirit" or "essence" or some extranatural wisp of those events, which then manifested incorporeally in and around that space. This chapter attempts neither to prove to believers nor disprove to skeptics the existence of a ghost in Washington Hall, but rather to report what others have seen, heard, and thought over the past eighty-five years. Readers will have to make up their own minds.

CHAPTER 8

MORE THAN THE HOME OF
THE LECTURE, 1922–1956

By the time the Ghost had taken up permanent residence in Washington Hall, the University of Notre Dame was bursting at the seams; 1921–22 was the last academic year spring commencement exercises could be singularly and routinely focused in Washington Hall, a portent for a future when Washington Hall decreasingly was able to meet the communal assembly needs of the university. Indoor venues such as the Fieldhouse (1898), Cushing Engineering Auditorium (1932), and finally the Navy Drill Hall (1943) largely took over functions for which Washington Hall had been originally designed.

While Washington Hall could no longer handle commencement Sunday itself, it could still accommodate many events associated with the weekend. In 1923 the Friday night "Informal Senior Night" showcased the senior quartet, comic speeches, songs, and musical performances on piano, violin, clarinet, banjo, and drums, and concluded with a parade of wooden soldiers by the university orchestra. On Saturday events from morning until night included the university orchestra performing the grand march from Verdi's *Aida* and a selection from Wiegand's *Robin Hood*, a welcome address by the president of the senior class, an address by President Walsh, a speech entitled

"The Heritage of Notre Dame," a senior ode, and a valedictory, before ending with Luigini's *Ballet Egyptien* by the university orchestra. The late evening featured the entertainment of professional opera singers and musicians from Chicago.[1] The *Dome* for 1923 remarked directly on the historical shift: "Past Commencements have been held in the crowded limits of Washington Hall; the scene of the one of 1923 will be the University Quadrangle."[2] While a lot continued to occur in Washington Hall, the shift of the actual Sunday commencement to the spaciousness of all outdoors was a watershed event for Washington Hall.

Because its capacity could never increase in relation to the rapidly growing university it was designed to support, Washington Hall during this period became the venue of smaller niche audiences; then as now, not everyone might want to hear opera singers on Saturday night even if there were a venue large enough to accommodate all.[3] In spite of the growth of niche audiences, Washington Hall retained a great emotional appeal as the first or default venue of choice, from plays to Glee Club concerts, from first-year orientation to intercollegiate oratory and debates.

The most obvious change to the structure of Washington Hall during this period was the removal of the south exterior stairs (see fig. 8.1). In 1933 interior staircases replaced the exterior south stairs that had previously allowed direct access to the second-floor lobby and auditorium. These new interior south staircases occupied what had been two ground-floor rooms, which most recently housed Bill's Barber Shop and the Western Union Office, businesses forced to relocate as a result of this modification.

The *Scholastic* reported as early as September 1932 that Bill's Barber Shop in Washington Hall was no more:

> In mentioning changes on the campus the fact that Bill has removed his barber shop from the basement of Washington Hall to the Badin Hall sub must not be overlooked.
>
> Five chairs of the latest style, modernistic mirrors, and the last minute barber furnishings have been installed in the new shop. A shoe shine parlor is operated in connection with the establishment. The hours are from 7:30 a.m. to 8 p.m.[4]

Figure 8.1. Washington Hall's exterior south entrance stairs, removed and replaced by interior staircases in 1933, necessitated the relocation of Bill's Barber Shop and the Western Union Office, which had previously occupied the ground-floor rooms that became interior staircases. This is one of the last photos of Washington Hall's exterior south steps, from *Scholastic* 66:7, Nov. 4, 1932, 2.

Figure 8.2. Students on the south entrance stairs to Washington Hall in the early 1930s. Note the Western Union sign on the southwest corner of the building where the office was; Bill's Barber Shop occupied the southeast corner. Both offices were taken over by interior staircases with the conversion. Bagby Negatives (hereafter GBBY) 45 G/307, UNDA.

The telegraph office had been moved, too, during that fall semester (see fig. 8.2). The *Notre Dame Alumnus* reported:

SHOPS SHIFTED

The campus barber shop, under the guidance of William Roach, genial Bill the Barber, has moved to the basement of Badin Hall, where all the luxuries of the tonsorial palaces are installed, including a shoe-shine stand. Adjacent to him is the campus clothing store, conducted by Leon Livingston.

The campus Western Union office has been moved from Washington Hall to the former site of the clothing store, next to the late Rockefeller Hall.

And the old steps of Washington Hall will soon be no more.

The entrance will be moved to the ground floors adjoining the Brownson "rec" hall, and inside stairways are designed to prevent the pre-opening crush of students that used to rock the stones of the old steps and corrugate the skins of those unfortunate enough to be on the railings.[5]

The loss of these two important offices overnight made Washington Hall less of a multipurpose student center than it had historically been. The band and orchestra (and entire music program) continued to use and occupy the north wing, and the Brownson Recreation Room under the auditorium of Washington Hall continued to resonate with the resounding crack of billiard balls. The interior staircases provided the auditorium with protected interior stairs at long last—no small advantage in northern Indiana's harsh climate—but at the loss of two valuable ground-floor rooms (see fig. 8.3).

This is also certainly the period when the building, with or without exterior south steps, came into its own as what Stritch called "the home of the lecture."[6] J. D. Porterfield eloquently reminisced in the *Scholastic* on the significance of those who had walked up the now-replaced south exterior stairs for lectures and events: Knute Rockne ("student, teacher, and beloved coach"); Professor M. J. McCue (engineering dean); G. K. Chesterton; Hilaire Belloc; Dr. James J. Walsh (Laetare medalist); Joseph Scott (Laetare medalist); Frank Ward O'Malley ("newspaper man"); Etienne Gilson (French lecturer); S. P. Grace (Bell Labs); W. B. Yeats; Eamon de Valera; Dr. F. Payne (cytologist); Col. William Hoynes (law dean); Dr. H. H. Newman (zoologist); George Gipp; the Four Horsemen; a score of All-Americans; the Abbey Players; the Paulist Choir; and the Welsh Singers.[7] Porterfield's list dealt with his student generation, but it nevertheless confirms how truly Washington Hall served as the crossroads of the university at this time, and how the people who were greeted there and who spoke there were as central to the ideology of the university as the plays, concerts, and annual ceremonies.

Porterfield's reminiscences from his own student years regarding the many great personages who walked up the exterior south stairs to lecture in Washington Hall remind us how impossible it is

Figure 8.3. Washington Hall after the removal of the south exterior stairs in 1933. Note the diagonal slate pattern on the tower roof, an aspect of the original Edbrooke design. Notre Dame University Photographer (hereafter GPHR) 45-0062, UNDA.

in this limited space to deal with the many thousands who spoke on the Washington Hall stage from 1922 to 1956. But a limited sampling of some of the truly exceptional persons from the period might include G. K. Chesterton, W. B. Yeats, Guglielmo Marconi, Eugenio Cardinal Pacelli, the Reverend Monsignor Fulton J. Sheen, and Lt. Thomas A. Dooley.

Thomas Stritch saw the Chesterton lectures in 1930–31 as "a historical watershed in the history of Notre Dame and especially the history of Washington Hall."[8] M. Clay Adams ('32) recalled the Chesterton lecture as follows:

> An interesting memory was when G. K. Chesterton, the pre-eminent British author, philosopher and wit, was invited to give a series of lectures. Students had to pay for the lecture series which were, of course, held in Washington Hall. Mr. Chesterton was a portly and very impressive looking man, with a large mustache, flowing white hair and a strong, professorial British accent. As he walked onto the stage for his first lecture, he greeted the students in a deep, sonorous voice, using the precise French pronunciation of Notre Dame, "Gentlemen of NOTR' DAHM." Almost in one loud voice, the entire student body shouted back at him, "NOTRE DAIM!" Chesterton smiled and took the admonition in good humor and apologized humbly. From then on he and the student body were on the same wavelength throughout the lecture series. He was enchanting and spell-binding.[9]

After his death at sixty-two in 1936, the *New York Times* said Chesterton was "for more than a generation the most exuberant personality in English literature."[10]

W. B. Yeats lectured in 1933 on the Irish Renaissance, and the *Scholastic* reported, "Himself a non-Catholic, Mr. Yeats speaks of an indigenously Catholic country with an admirable broadmindedness, but with some decidedly set views which must not always mesh perfectly with the more developed Irish Catholic mind."[11]

Marconi arrived the fall of 1933 for a lecture and to receive an honorary degree, all in Washington Hall. The *New York Times* noted: "Guglielmo Marconi, inventor of wireless and a Senator of Italy, received the honorary degree of Doctor of Laws today at Notre Dame University in a special convocation. . . . The only previous recipient of an honorary degree from Notre Dame at a special convocation was Gilbert K. Chesterton, the English essayist, in 1930. Degrees are usually awarded at the June graduation exercises."[12] At the special convocation, Washington Hall was packed. According to the *Scholastic,* "More than 900 students and faculty members assembled to honor the distinguished senator." Father Miltner (standing in for an infirmary-bound President O'Donnell) praised Marconi "whose experiments . . . have brilliantly demonstrated once more the Catholic principle of the essential unity of science and religion." But Marconi was not prescient in all things. Regarding television, the *Scholastic* reported that Marconi proclaimed, "Television is not quite ready for the world" and added, "In defense of his own invention, Senator Marconi stated that the spoken word will always be more important than the picture. For this reason, he said, television has not been received as enthusiastically as was the radio."[13] This parallels the notion at the time that sound would ruin movies, and that silent movies were actually preferred to the newfangled invention of "talking movies," which would prove transitory.

Inarguably a high point for lectures on the Washington Hall stage occurred in the fall of 1936 when "Eugenio Cardinal Pacelli, first papal secretary of state ever to visit this country, was awarded the honorary degree of Doctor of Letters by the University Sunday afternoon, Oct. 25, at a special convocation in Washington Hall."[14] Less than three years later, of course, Pacelli became Pope Pius XII. The *New York Times* noted the hall "was decorated in gold and blue,"[15] and the *Scholastic* added that the cardinal granted a holiday not only to Notre Dame but also to Saint Mary's, to great approbation.[16]

A month later, the very popular Reverend Monsignor Fulton J. Sheen concluded a lecture series on Communism. The *Dome* described Sheen as "Catholicism's most eloquent apostle in its drive against Communism." The *Scholastic* marveled, "It is a rare sight to see Washington Hall packed to capacity four nights in a row," which the *Dome* affirmed, saying, "The largest crowds of the year gathered to hear the lectures."[17]

Almost twenty years later, Dr. Tom Dooley, Navy physician and humanitarian, spoke in Washington Hall. The *Scholastic* said, "Lt

Thomas A Dooley, Medical Corps, U.S. Naval Reserve, will speak in Washington Hall on Friday, April 13. Dooley will recount his experiences with the Navy's 'Passage to Freedom,' in which 750,000 refugees were transferred from North to South Viet Nam. A reception will follow in the Student Center. Admission is free."[18]

But all who spoke were not cardinals and world-class dignitaries with household names. There were many other activities in Washington Hall besides lectures, of course. After pointing out the use of Washington Hall by the theatre and the debate programs, the 1933 *Dome* especially noted the enduring relationship between music and Washington Hall:

> The Band, the Glee Club, the Symphony Orchestra, the University Theater Orchestra, the Jugglers, and the Linnets offer fields for the musically minded. The Band plays at all athletic contests, and takes several trips each year. The Glee Club gives concerts and also makes a tour annually. The Symphony Orchestra presents recitals in Washington Hall. The University Theater Orchestra provides a musical program during the intermissions in the plays. The Jugglers play popular orchestral music, and the Linnets enact operettas.[19]

Evenings in Washington Hall included everything from a magic show to a lecture on the opening of King Tut's tomb, and even precocious marionettes performing *Robin Hood*. In 1940 the *Scholastic* effused:

> Washington Hall Has Magic and Mummy . . . Everything from an Egyptian mummy case to a collection of rare handcuffs accompanied the illusionist, Lockman, when he made his appearance here last Monday evening. Card and rope tricks "with the kind assistance of a few gentlemen of the audience," amused and amazed our local prestidigitation fans. . . . Mr. Lockman . . . devoted half of his program in demonstrating the art of manacled escape. . . . Mr. George Samuel Kendall, noted traveler, lecturer and Egyptologist, lectured on "The Wonders of the Ancient World." With the aid of projected photographs, Mr. Kendall offered a representation of archaeology's crowning efforts of the past 100 years. . . . The startling discovery and opening of King Tut Aunk Amen's

tomb occupied the major portion of Mr. Kendall's informative discourse. The splendor of the burial chamber, with its gold coffin and triple shrines of gold and blue more than met the expectations of Dr. Howard Carter and Lord Carnarvon, discoverers of the tomb. . . . The late Dr. Carter, who presented his secrets to Mr. Kendall, expressed that realization when he reported: "When I entered the ante-chamber and beheld the most marvelous sight in modern history, I wept."[20]

When the famed Tony Sarg Marionettes performed *Robin Hood* on the Washington Hall stage in 1940, the *Scholastic* discussed with fascination the complexity of marionettes' shooting arrows with such skill as to split an arrow with an arrow, even revealing the "Deep Bark Secret." In addition, the troupe's *The Man on the Flying Trapeze,* an obviously complex skill set for marionettes because of an apparent overabundance of strings, was another jaw-dropping demonstration of Sarg's genius which generated additional commentary.[21]

It is well to remember that the 1930s were arguably the last decade, however, before mechanical and electronic innovations irrevocably and permanently altered the human communication paradigm. Film, radio, and phonographs permitted remote access to culture and integration into it over both time and distance. The new communication models met many of the needs historically satisfied solely through ephemeral communal assembly. Radio lectures started at Notre Dame in 1932, for example, perhaps the earliest form of what we today call "distance learning," at a time when the *Scholastic* also ran advertisements for a radio—a student special for $12.95, "complete with tubes," which translates into about $200 in 2009 dollars, the cost of an electronic device such as an iPod touch.[22]

The University Theatre

The academic reorganization of the university by 1923 spearheaded the creation of the University Theatre by Professor Francis Kelly, an organization that served as the model for the production arm of a modern academic unit. In addition, the creation of a school of fine arts (within the College of Arts and Letters) and an academic major in speech and drama provided by the end of the 1920s parallel structures to those we find in the contemporary university today. The Speech and Drama Department both offered an academic major in speech with electives in drama, and produced plays on campus through the University Dramatic Club.[23] The 1923–24 *Bulletin* included Shakespeare and drama courses in English and four theatre courses under the rubric public speaking and lists expressive movement (a precursor to acting), stage art, impersonation, and modern stagecraft.[24] Although plays had been done regularly by students at Notre Dame with faculty direction since 1845, and the various theatre groups—the Thespians, the St. Cecilia Philomatheans, and others—supported very active theatre seasons, academic courses related to a major seem to have their genesis in the general curriculum modification in 1923 which put in place a major system we would recognize today. The *Bulletin* also reminds us that the Department of Music remained headquartered in Washington Hall where it managed twenty practice rooms, each with a piano, an indication of their continued full occupation of the north wing.[25] With the Brownson Recreation Hall below the auditorium, the theatre program necessarily must have rehearsed plays and built sets elsewhere when not on the stage itself. A stagecraft course offered in spring 1927 met "in the Little Theatre in the basement of Walsh Hall" and thus confirmed the location of one off-site venue; by the 1930s we know that the Law Auditorium was used for evening rehearsals.[26]

The 1925 *Dome* lamented the lack of theatre in Washington Hall, although the venue was in constant use for musical events, debate, lectures, film, and classes as it retained its supportive recreational function. The 1925–26 academic year saw a major revitalization for theatre under Frank Kelly; it was a time to create new traditions, such as women playing female roles, as the university theatre program took over production responsibilities from former student groups (the Thespians and the Philomatheans). Under Frank Kelly, theatre rose like a phoenix.

Francis "Frank" William Kelly, professor of speech and drama from 1924 to 1951, founded the University Theatre in 1926, although formal play production courses had been offered earlier. The structures and traditions he created and supported from the mid-1920s have continued to this day at Notre Dame. Kelly did not work alone, however; his collaboration with both the talented English professor and playwriting instructor Charles Phillips and a supportive administration sparked the creation and showcasing of new drama. The *Alumnus* pointed out their achievements in 1932:

> Modern drama at Notre Dame took a tremendous step ahead in 1924–25 with the advent of two of its guiding geniuses during the years that have followed—Prof. Charles Phillips and Prof. Frank Kelly. Between them they have made of the University Theatre (and the co-operation of the Rev. J. Hugh O'Donnell, C.S.C., '16, cannot be omitted here) one of the most effective workshops of the drama in modern college history.[27]

Kelly and Phillips followed in the great tradition of Gillespie and Lyons from the 1860s. The University Theatre coordinated "all theatre activities on campus, including The Player's Club, The Monogram Club, and student productions," and answered not to a dean or academic unit but rather to a committee similar to what we would call today Student Affairs.[28] The premiere season program for 1926–27 described the University Theatre as

> an amalgamation of all the activities of the University of Notre Dame which are devoted to the dramatic and allied arts. By its organization, all campus work along these lines is coördinated, and Notre Dame's tradition of high class dramatic endeavor is advanced. The University Theatre operates as a clearing house for student playwriting, production, directing, scene design, costuming, as well as for musical composition (vocal and instrumental), orchestration, and stage presentation. With its active Production Unit covering not only stage direction, playwriting, composition, etc., but business management as well, the University Theatre purposes to be practical as well as artistic. . . .
>
> The program for the 1926–27 season of the University Theatre includes, in addition to the premiere of this date ("The Fool of God" and "Lord Byron"), three other large productions—a com-

plete musical comedy in Mid-Winter, a Post-Lenten presentation of three original one-act plays written by students of Mr. Phillips' Playwriting Class (English 31), and in June an elaborate historical pageant picturing the story of Notre Dame.

The present premiere offers for the first time in the stage annals of Notre Dame a program originating entirely on the campus. The two plays are written, respectively, by a member of the faculty and by two students of the Department of Music. The direction, music, and mounting are wholly the production of the students under the supervision of Prof. Frank W. Kelly and Prof. John J. Becker. This premiere, then, illustrates the special creative purpose of the University Theatre.[29]

While Professor Frank W. Kelly served as director of the University Theatre, Professors John J. Becker and Joseph J. Casasanta, both in the Department of Music, were members of the committee that ultimately controlled the organization, and thus Music had great input into and influence over this new organization.[30]

Women Onstage

Kelly's creation of the University Theatre coincided with a new casting policy: in the first production of the University Theatre, Doris McKowen played Mary in *Lord Byron,* and in subsequent University Theatre productions, women played female roles.[31] By the University Theatre's third season (1928–29), Notre Dame produced Shakespeare's *Julius Caesar* for the first time on the Washington Hall stage with the roles of Portia and Calpurnia played by women.[32] By *The Taming of the Shrew* in December 1929, faculty wives played the two female roles, and in the program there is a statement of appreciation to them and their husbands for their kindness "in assisting in the production of the play."[33] This ideological shift encouraged townswomen and students at Saint Mary's College to get involved in theatre at Notre Dame, thus ending the tradition firmly established in the 1890s of males playing female roles, which itself replaced the custom in the first half century of the university's history of producing only plays with all-male roles. This new model continued until the mid-1930s; as late as March 1935, Albert L. Doyle directed *Turn to the Right* with five women playing female roles (and a rare confirmation that rehearsals occurred in the Law Auditorium).[34]

The 1934–35 academic year was the last, however, in which women played female roles as a retrogressive period intruded on the new custom. By fall 1935 the newly inaugurated president John F. O'Hara stated that he "would like to see the return of male impersonations of female characters"[35] and thus ushered in a new casting policy for the University Theatre that lasted for a generation of undergraduate students. By March 1936 the same Albert L. Doyle, who a year earlier had cast women, directed *The Comedy of Errors* with all men and stated that he hoped "the innovation of students to play feminine leads will prove successful enough to warrant the continuance of the practice on the campus."[36] For three full academic years from 1935 to 1938 men played female roles. It was not until Thomas E. Mills directed *Room Service* in the fall of 1938 that women once again took the Washington Hall stage. Thus first-year students entering in the fall of 1934 saw women on the stage that year but not again during their time at Notre Dame; students entering in the fall of 1935 did not see women onstage until their senior year.

After a student generation of no women onstage, the *Scholastic* described the casting "innovation" in *Room Service* in the fall of 1938 as nothing less than an invasion: "Washington Hall is a strange place these nights. For the first time in many moons, young women have invaded our hallowed sanctuaries and are working hand-in-hand with these 'Irish' actors of ours for the greater glory."[37] The *South Bend Tribune* stated the obvious and went on to theorize: "Feminine voices will ring throughout Washington hall in a legitimate student play at Notre Dame. Having virtually exhausted the supply of good plays with completely masculine casts, the university will henceforth bring in young women to take part in student productions."[38] The *Scholastic* expressed trepidation regarding audience reaction: "You can always tell what mood the house is in after the first few minutes of the show. Tonight is different though. The prime worry isn't how the show'll be received. It's about the girls. This is the first time in years that girls have played a Notre Dame show."[39] The initial worries dissolved under "thunderous applause" and a curtain call (unusual at the time).[40] With *Room Service,* Father O'Hara's experiment with the past ended, and women henceforth typically played women's roles. Occasionally after this time, a male played a female in what I have called earlier a convincingly theatrical role and for a conceptual or artistic reason, such as in the April 1940 production of *She Stoops to Conquer,* directed by Father Matthew Coyle, in which a male student played Mrs. Hardcastle.[41] But the tradition after *Room Service* was women as women; when afterward males played females on the Washington Hall stage it would usually be as the flagrantly parodic in which there was no attempt to conceal the actor's true gender.

"Minstrel Chuckles"

Although the issue of women playing female roles seemed firmly settled by the end of the 1930s, it would take another decade for the minstrel show to fade into Washington Hall history. From its origins by 1870, the tradition of blackface thus continued as part of the "theatrical sphere"[42] into the 1940s. In March 1923 the Monogram Club presented the Monogram Minstrels in Washington Hall with the program including an interlocutor, end men, and a multitude of "numbers" ranging from sports poses to a xylophone solo. While clearly the evening had a traditional minstrel portion, it was in actuality much more of a variety show with many acts.[43] Throughout the 1920s and 1930s, members produced these variety shows in Washington Hall involving minstrels and the staging of "Vodville," "Absurdities," and "High-Jinks." The 1923 *Dome* included a photograph showing four Monogram Minstrels onstage in blackface with a caption that says the interlocutor and his four end men had fifty-five "colored breth'ren." In 1924 the *Dome* referred to the program as "The Absurdities of 1924 . . . A Notre Dame Institution Mortifying the Notre Dame Man," directed by Joseph Casasanta ('23) in his first year on the faculty. A male student played Sophie, the female victim in a melodrama with a villain in one of the skits, while another scene incorporated a traditional minstrel act called "Blackface

Chatter" with Bones and End Men. The *Dome* compared the minstrel episode favorably to popular radio and film singer and comedian Eddie Cantor.[44]

By 1934 a new singing group, the Linnets, proved "Music's the Thing" through the minstrel format.[45] The 1934 *Dome* reported:

> The demonstration was divided into two parts. The first argument took the form of an old-time Southern minstrel, chorus of thirty, six end men and the interlocutor, performing their antics and chanting Southern melodies on the lawn of a Virginia mansion. A musical travelogue consisting of tunes associated with Notre Dame, then west to the Indian Reservations, Hawaii, India, Germany, France, England and thence to the United States again clinched the argument. This breezy journey was executed within the self-styled night club, "Not-A-Dame Inn." . . .
>
> The minstrel ensemble, with its end men, Mammy songs, interlocutor and southern ballads, was favorably received by even the extreme campus critics.[46]

As late as 1934, the *Scholastic* had only the highest praise for the minstrel show, but change was in the air. The Eva Jessye Choir performed in Washington Hall in November 1938 with the *Scholastic* describing the performance as "examples of the finest Negro folk literature covering the entire field of Negro composition for choral presentation." It reviewed the performance the following week very positively, describing it as a "smash hit" that "received a warm response from the large crowd," and described them to the audience as "one of the original groups from the colored opera 'Porgy and Bess.' "[47] With both the vaudeville format and its associated minstrel show getting a bit long in the tooth, there was an active attempt at revival in 1939–40:

> Years ago, when Notre Dame was just beginning to grow, students and faculty used to throng into Washington Hall on the night of the student vaudeville show. Father John Talbert Smith, president of the actor's Guild during the early years of this century, suggested student vaudeville during one of his lectures here. The Knights of Columbus fostered the idea and awarded cash prizes

for the cleverest acts. These vaudevilles were a combination of an opera, a three-ringed circus, and a good musical comedy. Students danced, sang, imitated, and on one occasion a campus club produced a minstrel show. Walter O'Keefe and Charley Butterworth, topnotchers in today's entertainment world, were among the winners in the past.[48]

It is not at all clear to what extent the blackface minstrel format was central to student variety shows on the Washington Hall stage. The fall 1939 Knights of Columbus vaudeville show "A Smash Hit Revival" apparently had no minstrel or blackface acts in spite of a photograph from the 1938 *Dome* that suggests otherwise.[49] The 1940 version included blackface performers, but they lost to a hillbilly act.[50] By the 1940s the Monogram Club members stopped the minstrel acts altogether and shifted to parodic drag routines that typically included ethnic, veiled women dancing awkwardly if not suggestively. The *Scholastic* related that the "famed 'beef trust' will again perform its intricate dances, and such twinkle-toed individuals as 'Moose' Piepul, Tad Harvey, Tom Gallagher, Joe DeFranco, Benny Sheridan, Jim Brutz, and other football players will test the construction of the Washington Hall stage."[51] The sexist Monogram Absurdities thus replaced the racist Monogram Minstrels rather directly.

While it is easy today to be harshly critical of attempts to resurrect the minstrel show in the 1940s, it is well to remember the times and the overall insensitivity in the dominant white majority culture at the time. Irving Berlin's *Holiday Inn* (1942), starring Bing Crosby and Fred Astaire, had a minstrel number in which Crosby and Marjorie Reynolds, the entire band, white waiters, waitresses, and cigarette girls performed in blackface for the Lincoln's birthday celebration. Indeed, Reynolds's character, Linda Mason, complained that putting on blackface would make her look "ugly." The only African American actors in the movie are the cook, Mamie, and her two children (who at least all have speaking roles). By Berlin's *White Christmas* in 1954 there is no longer anyone in blackface, but the film incredibly retains a minstrel number: Bing Crosby and Danny Kaye play tambo and bones to Rosemary Clooney's interlocutor. They also wear red gloves instead of white. The only African American in this film, however, is the incorporeal arm of the club-car bartender who is preparing drinks, and he is mute. Closer to home at Notre Dame, the band's half-time show for the Iowa game as late as fall 1957 included a "'Minstrel Show,' featuring songs of the minstrel show days in the South," including "Swanee," "Rock-a-Bye Your Baby to a Dixie Melody," and "Waiting for the *Robert E. Lee*,"[52] undoubtedly paying homage to American music history but incorporating a format considered inappropriate today.

Although the Knights of Columbus annual "contest" returned "after being a wartime casualty,"[53] by 1947 vaudeville shows with their seemingly ubiquitous minstrel components had outlived their own American history. The *Scholastic* article title said it all: "K. C.'s Shaggy Performers Apply Finishing Touches to Vaudeville's Corroding Corpse."[54] This format was over as the Washington Hall stage welcomed groups like the Fisk Jubilee Singers, and the first black students matriculated at Notre Dame.[55]

Before and After the War

The fortunes of University Theatre had declined by the mid-1930s, but they perked up during the war years and were revitalized completely by the early 1950s. The *Scholastic* reported in fall 1936 that the chronic physical limits of Washington Hall were not the problem but rather student lethargy:

> Into what special form of lethargy has the University Theater fallen? For some unknown reason it never has been found necessary to enlarge the facilities at Washington Hall to accommodate the throng of ambitious actors, but at least in the past there was some activity and we did see some good productions. This year things seem to have hit a definite impasse. No word of secret rehearsals has leaked out, and certainly no public plans have been announced.
>
> Once more the cause lies in the student ranks. No one else is to blame if a strictly student activity is allowed to die a slow death. Faculty direction will be immediately forthcoming at the first sign of student interest.

The student theater is one of the oldest of extracurricular activities, it is one of the richest in tradition, and one of the most valuable in the training it gives. It seems a shame that so little can be done on our campus to utilize the skill we must possess, to work under the fine direction that is available, and to foster an activity that once ranked at the top in any list of activities.

Student publications from various other schools outline ambitious plans, review many student productions, reveal a general campus enthusiasm for theatricals. Wayne University in Detroit, smaller than Notre Dame and with students scattered over an entire city manage to produce a play a month.

The University Theater group will undoubtedly issue a call for candidates in the near future—a good response would go a long way toward reviving campus dramatics.[56]

A year later, the *Dome* recorded the turnaround, stating that the "reorganized Dramatic club has this year won for itself new campus prestige. Under the direction of Mr. Thomas E. Mills, this group won instant acclaim with its professional presentation of 'Journey's End.'"[57] By December 1941 the University Theatre did Shakespeare's *The Merry Wives of Windsor,* a production that began rehearsals before Pearl Harbor but opened afterward (see fig. 8.4).[58]

Cecil Birder replaced Shakespeare with Gilbert and Sullivan during the war years. Birder graduated from Notre Dame in 1912 and had acted on the Washington Hall stage as a "prep" as early as 1909–10; he went on to be Notre Dame's leading lady in the early teens. Professor and head of the Department of Speech by 1940, he created a group called the Notre Dame/Saint Mary's Savoyards which operated under the University Theatre.[59] The Savoyards' Gilbert and Sullivan operettas received high praise as alternatives to Shakespeare, but after four consecutive years audiences grew tired and wanted to see the return of the Bard, regular musicals, and student-written plays. Both *A Tailor-Made Man* and *Let's Get Going* departed from the recent tradition of Shakespeare and Gilbert and Sullivan, with hugely popu-lar performances in spring 1943. *A Tailor-Made Man* had been a big hit on Broadway in 1917 which Father Coyle revived, and *Let's Get Going* proved to be the first student-written musical in twenty-five

The
Merry Wives of Windsor
by
WILLIAM SHAKESPEARE

UNIVERSITY OF NOTRE DAME
December 15 and 16
1941

Figure 8.4. Program frontispiece, *The Merry Wives of Windsor* (Dec. 15, 16, 1941), with William M. Hickey as Falstaff with dagger and tankard. William Farmer private collection.

years (the *Scholastic* claimed), an obvious parody of student and faculty life at Notre Dame, one of many plays on that topic that would be produced in the 1940s and early 1950s, thus filling out the 1942–43 year.[60] The author of *Let's Get Going*, the talented Edward Cashman, returned to Notre Dame after the war to continue his musical comedy writing.[61]

In the war years, there were also variety shows written and produced by the resident cadets in the V-12 Navy College Training Program, most notably in January 1944 when a new fortnightly revue premiered: "'Nights and Daze' Rocks Washington Hall; V-12 Premiere is Huge Success."[62] Two weeks later, the *Scholastic* effused:

> The venerable old face of George Washington, mellowed through nearly fifty years of existence to a dusty palish yellow, glowed the bright crimson of a stop light for over an hour Tuesday night as the *hottest* variety show in ancient Washington Hall's history smouldered over the wooden planks of her stage. The V-12 unit's bi-weekly production of "Nights and Daze" reached new heights in the roughness of its humor, as the jammed-packed auditorium nearly burst at the raucously bellowed reception the show was accorded.[63]

These events in Washington Hall mirrored what was going on at the university, with its accelerated academic years but with many men coming for a short time, getting commissioned, and going off to war. The war would finally end, and when it did, the university started to get back to the way it had been before Pearl Harbor, but with the inevitable changes made manifest in all American culture by the war years of the 1940s.

Although "ancient, sagging" Washington Hall had paled and showed its age, the structure nevertheless returned to the center of communal assembly after the war with an almost nonstop procession in 1946–47 of plays, concerts by the Glee Club and symphony orchestra, music recitals, Knights of Columbus vaudeville, the Savoyards doing Gilbert and Sullivan, Washington's Birthday celebrations, and lectures by distinguished guests. But perhaps most exciting was the postwar return of student Edward Cashman with "many of the same men who brought the sensational 'Let's Get Going' to the campus in 1943" to produce his much anticipated second musical, *Meet the Missus*. The musical had a cast of fifty-five "Notre Dame students and girls from South Bend and Vetsville," a twenty-one-piece orchestra conducted by Cashman himself, with "five striking sets" and a revolving stage, a first in the history of Washington Hall.[64] Cashman continued his musical comedy efforts a year later with *It Ain't Hay* in May 1948.[65]

It is well to remember that even after the war, the University Theatre had an extracurricular—that is, nonacademic—function that included essentially all the performing arts under its wing. (It would not be until the mid-1950s that Father Arthur Harvey more narrowly defined the role of the University Theatre as a cocurricular complement to an academic program in theatre that produced plays only.) The *Scholastic* confirmed the postwar configuration that had existed since the beginning in 1926. Newly appointed director William J. Elsen had the task

> to bring the best of student productions to the boards of Washington Hall. . . . The University Theater, a subsidiary of the Department of Student Welfare, comes under the direct supervision of the Committee on Student Entertainment, composed of the Rev. Joseph A. Kehoe, C.S.C., chairman; Mr. Daniel S. Pedtke, Glee Club Director; Mr. H. Lee Hope, Director of the Band; the Rev. Louis Thornton, C.S.C., representing the Notre Dame Concert and Lecture Series; and William J. Elsen [the director of the University Theatre].[66]

For the next three years, there was no student-written musical in Washington Hall, but Elsen revived the tradition in 1950–51. The plays that year were *The Man Who Came to Dinner* in the fall, *Harvey* in February, and the student musical *Mr. and Mrs. Broadway,* by Bill Carey and Dick Marshall, in April (with Goethe's *Faust* scheduled the second week of May but postponed until fall 1951). In the *Scholastic* at the time, Walt Collins praised "the success of the rejuvenated University Theatre during the past year," and called for even more attention to the performing arts by recommending the creation of a drama society "to handle the stage presentations."[67] This was also a period of growth, experimentation, and revitalization, in spite of the building's ageing, fading interior and largely nineteenth-century accoutrements. By fall 1951 William Elsen, with the addition of John Tumpane, was ready to carry the theatrical creativity of the earlier student-written plays one step further with the creation of an experimental theatre to "fill a long-standing need for creative, dramatic activity and an outlet for such activity," with the goal "to do occasional plays with definitely limited audience appeal and one-act plays of original meaning."[68] Nothing could confirm more the growing interest and recognition of niche audiences than this new experimental theatre, while at the same time, the emphasis on original work continued the mission of Frank Kelly at the creation of the University Theatre in 1926.

The postponed production of *Faust* inaugurated the 1951–52 season with Joe Huebner in the cast,[69] directed by Leonard Sommer, who "broke stage" by using all of the Washington Hall auditorium for entrances, exits, and scenes: "Not all scenes will be designated by the closing of the front curtain."[70] This creative directing style was the future, of course, a precursor to the environmental theatre movement of the 1960s where lines between actor and audience and stage and house were no longer traditionally drawn, while at the same time prefiguring the later innovative work of Professor Reginald Bain.[71] The *Scholastic* stated with enthusiasm with regard to *Faust,* "The University of Notre Dame Theater, under the direction of Mr. William Elsen, has grown immeasurably in stature during these past four years. This presentation stands as strong evidence of the progress that has been made."[72]

At the same time the University Theatre was going great guns, the access of others to Washington Hall clearly limited the extent to which the University Theatre could grow. The Saturday films in Washington Hall, along with events such as the visit of the Catholic Players as a feature of the concert and lecture series, emphasized the inability of two objects to occupy the same space at the same time.[73] For the next production, there were no weekend performances at all because of these continuing conflicts, with the Catholic Players performing Shakespeare and Molière on the same Washington Hall stage the University Players used to open *Old Heidelberg* just four days later.[74] The review of this disappointing production noted the lack of access to the stage.[75] By spring 1952 it was possible to cancel the Saturday afternoon film screening in Washington Hall "to allow for the dress rehearsal of the Student Musical which opens on Sunday evening," but the two evening screenings still took place.[76]

The new musical in the spring of 1952 was *Stay Tuned for Addle-man,* with book and lyrics by Charlie Shubert and Jack Hynes and music by Jerry Costello.

The *Scholastic* ran a three-page article on the play including eight photos, one showing the flat-front stage of Washington Hall and another the rehearsal room (likely the assembly room on the third floor of the north wing). A month later the show received praise as "a rousing success . . . with the invaluable aid from Prof. John Tumpane."[77] The *Notre Dame Alumnus* recognized the appointment of John Tumpane as director of the University Theatre and Michael Casey as assistant director and quoted Tumpane as saying, "In time we are hopeful that our University Theater will become not only a theatrical center for this area, but that it also will be a school for actors, writers, and directors, inculcated with the finest traditions of the theater and Notre Dame."[78]

With the Reverend J. J. Walsh at Marquette, Tumpane wrote *Vile Bodies* for March 1953 (from the Evelyn Waugh novel), an American premiere production with "masterful" settings by Michael Casey and a cast of fifty-six.[79] Two months later, the University Players produced *Brute Farce,* the last student-written musical to be performed under the auspices of the University Theatre (stage managed by Donald Rathgeb).[80] Thus spring 1953 was the third year in a row for a student musical, with *Mr. and Mrs. Broadway* in 1951 and *Stay Tuned for Addleman* in 1952. There was no student musical in spring 1954 (the proposal was vetoed for a variety of reasons including script issues). In 1955 Father Arthur Harvey, never a lover of student shows and who by that time had taken over the program, solicited original scripts but found them lacking and relied on established Broadway hits; the period of student musicals was over.

The early December 1953 production of *Kiss Me Kate* on the Washington Hall stage had no more than a month of rehearsals. Gene Gorski had the male lead in this production, his first appearance in a

University Theatre production, in which first-year student Reg Bain worked backstage. Gorski later described Washington Hall at this time as "the center of artistic life."[81] Other productions that year included *Three Men on a Horse* (a last-minute substitute for *Mister Roberts,* which had strong administrative opposition), *The Lady's Not for Burning* (in which freshman Phil Donahue first appeared on the Washington Hall stage), three one-act plays, and "the state-wide Invitational One-Act Play Festival."[82] Tumpane also produced a "festival of the arts" to showcase the dedication of the new O'Shaughnessy Hall and its gallery of art, where he envisioned his new "experimental theatre" performing. Events included a performance by the Fine Arts Quartet (a professional group from Northwestern with regular appearances on ABC), a film series, and the University Theatre "readers theatre" production of *Hedda Gabler.* The year ended with *Where's Charley* for graduation as a replacement for the student musical directed by Marion Leszczynski. It is clear that the period immediately before the official arrival of Father Arthur S. Harvey, C.S.C., was a very intense, active, and vital time for Notre Dame theatre and Washington Hall. In a very real sense, too, Father Harvey arrived before he arrived, having been passionately interested in both Notre Dame and Notre Dame theatre since the mid-1940s. But during the academic year 1953–54, the scuttlebutt was that a new director of theatre was already in the wings. Reg Bain recalled:

> Father Harvey was a *presence.* I first became aware of that *presence* over half a century ago at a rehearsal in Washington Hall when I was a freshman. I noticed a black clad man observing our work from the shadows of the back row of the theatre and asked a friend, "Who is that?" "That's the man who is going to take over the theatre next year," he said.[83]

Nuns' Summer Theatre

In the summer of 1954—the last before Father Harvey took over Notre Dame's theatre program—the tradition of the Summer School Nuns Play continued. No better example of the niche audience exists than one composed only of members of religious orders who

Figure 8.5. Nuns at summer commencement on the Washington Hall stage, Aug. 3, 1937, UDIS 25/10, UNDA.

attended the summer plays at Notre Dame that were performed by nuns attending summer school. The creation of a coeducational summer school in 1918 had made Notre Dame by the 1950s a veritable mecca for teaching nuns across the country who wanted (and needed) to gain additional certifications and to get advanced degrees. Half the summer school students were nuns. The earliest picture of nuns getting diplomas at summer commencement on the Washington Hall stage survives from 1937 when 60 percent of the advanced degrees awarded (a total of thirty) went to nuns (see fig. 8.5). The number of nuns graduating in 1937 reflects a demographic that would have a direct impact on Washington Hall over the next two decades.

By summer 1940, fifteen nuns served as seamstresses in the costume shop in Cushing Hall of Engineering for *Twelfth Night*, with the inauguration of the Summer Drama Project, the first indication of their involvement with theatre but certainly not their last.[84] By the 1950s the nuns had long left the costume shop to produce and act in original plays and musicals on the Washington Hall stage, performing them in their habits as they were required to do (rather than in theatrical costumes) before audiences composed exclusively of members of religious orders. When they wanted to present a play to the public, they did so by double casting the show with laypersons who could then perform publicly before other laypersons. Oftentimes their plays related directly to national conferences, such as the National Congress of Religious of the United States in 1952 and the Tenth Biennial National Convention of the Catholic Theatre Conference in 1955, both of which complemented and provided synergy to the nuns' endeavors on the stage along with extensive use of Washington Hall as the primary performance venue.

For the summer of 1953, Michael Casey, assistant director of the University Theatre, seems to have been the catalyst for the nuns' theatre with his new play, *A Soul in Fine Array,* his first creative effort at Notre Dame, which he both wrote and directed while he also directed the nuns in a summer readers theatre production of *Hedda Gabler. Newsweek* inquired for more information about this play about a nun who dies of an incurable disease, including a request for pictures of this unique production for religious audiences only, staged July 23–24, 1953, in Washington Hall (see fig. 8.6).[85]

In summer 1954 the tradition of the summer school nuns' play continued, with the first effort on the campus from Saint Mary's professor Natalie E. White, who both wrote and directed *Seven Nuns at Las Vegas,* a double-cast show with laypersons performing before a lay audience for one of the three performances. The religious cast used eight nuns from eight different orders, a C.S.C. brother, and five lay actors (in nonreligious roles) for the two performances reserved for "religious only" audiences, July 25–26, 1954. The press release explained, "Actually, the play is double-cast. Two performances will be presented by an all-nun cast for priests, Brothers and Sisters enrolled in summer school. A third performance will be given a cast of local actresses for the public."[86] The *South Bend Tribune* further recounted:

Figure 8.6. Nuns' Summer School Theatre, July 23–24, 1953, GDIS 35/07, UNDA. The back of the photograph reads "Curtain call for 'A Soul in Fine Array,' written and directed by Michael Casey. The nuns all teach speech and dramatics in high schools throughout the country." Photograph by M. Bruce Harlan.

The summer theater season in the South Bend–Mishawaka area rolls into high gear this week with the production of an original play by a local author at the University of Notre Dame.... The only public performance of the play will be given at 8:30 o'clock tonight in Washington Hall with a cast of local actresses directed by Miss White. Performances limited to the religion order members attending the university this summer, with nuns taking over the religious roles, will be given this afternoon and Monday night.[87]

Saint Mary's College Superior Sister Mary Agnes described the play as "completely delightful in every sense and will long be remembered for its charm. It was particularly timely, since the Community is opening a house in Las Vegas in September."[88] The Notre Dame *Alumnus* reported the play as follows:

The Notre Dame Department of Speech, in cooperation with Miss Natalie E. White, Summer Theatre Director at ND and an Instructor in Drama, Speech, and Playwriting at St. Mary's College, presented a farcical play written by Miss White.

The play, *Seven Nuns at Las Vegas,* concerns seven Sisters who find themselves and their convent miraculously transplanted from Indiana to the desert near the Nevada resort city. While there the nuns turn the thoughts of vacationists and natives from entertainment to religious contemplation. The farce reaches its finale when the nuns are returned, again miraculously to Indiana.

Three performances of the comedy were given on July 25–26. Two performances [July 25 matinee and July 26 evening] were presented by an all-nun cast for priests, Brothers, and Sisters enrolled at the Summer Session. A third showing [July 25 evening] was given for the public by a cast of local actresses.

Miss White was formerly associated with the Pasadena Playhouse and has a doctorate in Drama from Yale University.[89]

For the summer of 1955, White penned the nonmusical *The Billion Dollar Saint,* with June performances connected to both Alumni Association activities and the Catholic Theatre Conference, which included a wide variety of plays and theatre workshops all over campus, radiating from a very actively used Washington Hall. Fred Syburg directed this layperson production with Reginald Bain in the title role. (Also that summer the nuns rehearsed *Domitille,* written by the cloistered Sister Mary Francis, P. C., who would also go on to write *La Madre* for summer 1957.) With Washington Hall the primary venue, events for the four-day conference included *The Billion Dollar Saint,* acting and directing demonstrations, play competitions involving *Parade at the Devil's Bridge, Romance of the Willow Pattern,* and *Blithe Spirit,* and productions of *Hotel Universe, The Lady's Not for Burning,* and *The Crucible.* Additional high school plays included *Room Service* (act 1), *Pierre Patelin, The Princess Marries a Page,* and *Everyman,* as well as a dance drama demonstration. The conference concluded with a candlelight procession and benediction at the Grotto following a banquet, and the high school students did second performances of their plays before attending a student mixer in the Drill Hall.[90]

In summer 1956, White presented the farce with music *The Complaining Angel,* but in the engineering building and not Washington Hall, due to remodeling going on there, and it was this production that *Life* chronicled in photographs.[91] The Notre Dame *Alumnus* had the following praise:

> PLAY STARRING 8 NUNS
> WINS NATIONAL PRAISE
>
> Eight nuns attending the 1956 University of Notre Dame summer session stole the show and drew favorable national reviews for their leading roles in "The Complaining Angel," a musical farce staged on the campus. Author-director of the rollicking play was Natalie E. White, whose preceding play, "Seven Nuns at Las Vegas," was premiered at Notre Dame in 1954.
>
> "The Complaining Angel" featured a nuns' ballet and eleven songs, through which were interwoven the trials of a guardian angel, exhausted by a series of tough assignments, who thinks she has a soft touch when re-assigned as a nun.[92]

In summer 1957, the nuns did *La Madre,* by Sister Mary Francis, P. C., with the venue not stated; by the summer of 1960, with 1,373 nuns taking courses at Notre Dame (nearly half of the 2,877 summer-school students), graduation had shifted from Washington Hall to the Drill Hall.[93] The nuns' summer theatre was a vital part of the history of Washington Hall, one that pulled together sacred and secular aspects of life in a way unique to Notre Dame.

Father Art Harvey

Father Arthur S. Harvey, C.S.C., took over in the summer of 1954 as acting director of the University Theatre, with Professor John Tumpane going on leave for a year but never returning. Harvey, a trained accountant and "no newcomer to theatre," had for the past dozen years been "associated with the Little Theatre movement, and was one of the founders of the famed Blackfriar's Guild while continuing special studies at Catholic University."[94] In spite of the clear success and great promise of John Tumpane and Michael Casey, the administration brought in Father Harvey to set the future course of Washington Hall at Notre Dame. With Tumpane on leave, Father Harvey took over a thriving University Theatre in the fall of 1954 and molded it into his own vision so seamlessly that within a decade the myth existed that he created the University Theatre.

If not the father of the University Theatre, Father Harvey did indeed serve as a keystone figure. Father Art, as he was affectionately called by his colleagues, functioned not only as director of theatre during this time, but also as the manager of Washington Hall and arbiter of much that went on there: the future of Washington Hall was in his hands. His worthy goal always was to create a great academic theatre program at Notre Dame, modeled after his beloved Father Hardtke's pioneering work at Catholic University, and he did this by recreating the great Broadway and West End plays he personally witnessed in his annual travels. As manager of Washington Hall he also asserted complete control over all theatre at Notre Dame, the consequence of which was to end student-written musicals, dormitory-produced "shows," and other ancillary theatrical attempts not directly connected to his vision of what University Theatre should be.

Father Harvey's first year brought together the team that would work together for a generation, a collaboration that would connect the theatre program in Washington Hall directly to the twenty-first century. His first directorial effort on the Washington Hall stage in the fall of 1954 was *Detective Story,* a play with an abortion theme. Frederic Syburg designed lights and setting, and sophomore students Reginald Bain and Philip J. Donahue acted, along with graduate student Eugene Gorski and local stage veteran Hildegarde Vargyas, with faculty member Edward L. Doyle assisting.[95] After the cancellation of *Mister Roberts* the previous year, it was reassuring to students that Father Harvey would tackle (and be able to produce) a play that dealt with such a difficult and controversial topic.

By spring semester 1956, Phil Donahue had the lead in *The Caine Mutiny Court Martial,* and the following fall played Biff in *Death of a Salesman,* with Reg Bain as Bernard and Georgia Ann Weber (who later became Mrs. Bain) as Miss Forsythe. With regard to Biff, the *South Bend Tribune* said presciently, "Donahue handled the emotional role effectively and convincingly."[96] Father Harvey dropped the graduation student musical in favor of Broadway's *Seventeen,* following Tumpane's lead in his last year, both cases likely casualties of the lack of a producible student-written script. Father Art would never direct a student-written musical, however, and *Seventeen* was the first in a series of hugely successful Broadway musicals he and his colleagues staged in Washington Hall over the next decade and a half.

Father Harvey's second year coincided with the dedication of university-owned, campus-located WNDU-TV in the fall of 1955, although students had done internships at WSBT-TV by 1953. The dedication program first proclaimed that "while Notre Dame's graduates can be numbered in the thousands, WNDU-TV will make the University's resources for education, information and entertainment available to millions," and then described Professor Green's 1899 transmission of the first wireless message in this country from Sacred Heart to Saint Mary's College[97] and the awarding of Marconi's honorary degree on October 14, 1933. The program honored Brigadier General David Sarnoff, chairman of the Radio Corporation of America (RCA), as it proudly continued, "WNDU-TV is destined to serve as a center for training Notre Dame men in the communications arts." Father Hesburgh hoped for "a deeper sense of how television can be used as a force for the betterment of Mankind in our day," adding that "a university can no more ignore television today than universities of the past could have ignored the discovery of printing."[98] WNDU-TV signaled the importance of television as a powerful medium of remote communal assembly, one that brings access and integration right into the living rooms of its viewers. In all of the dedication festivities (and perhaps fittingly) not one event occurred in Washington Hall. O'Shaughnessy Hall, the Morris Inn, the Gymnasium (with singer Eddie Fisher), the Drill Hall, the Notre Dame–Indiana football game on Saturday in the stadium, and the new studios themselves in a purpose-built 60' x 40' building with 24' ceilings—all were venues used in the dedication. The station went on air July 15, 1955, and served 155,000 television families in the larger population of 661,000. Two nights of WNDU-TV broadcasts reached as many persons as a year of sold-out houses in Washington Hall.[99]

In spring 1956 Father Harvey directed *Finian's Rainbow* to great acclaim, with the *Scholastic* praising the production as "hit-crammed, dance sparked, laugh-studded, thought-provoking."[100] But even as the shift to Broadway musicals over student-written ones had been made, the physical world was changing. Along with Notre Dame investing hugely in its own television station, Saint Mary's College was building a new performing arts center across the highway. At the same time, the university's own appraisal determined that the nineteenth-century exhibition hall known as Washington Hall had "inadequate plumbing facilities" and "old style electrical equipment," and would need "complete redecorating."[101] A theatre with no audience restrooms could not compete in this new world, so it was clear that Father Harvey had his work cut out for him; he would have to remodel Washington Hall if he could not replace it outright.

Film and New Media

The 1920s at Notre Dame were the decade of Rockne, of course, which firmly established and perpetuated Notre Dame as a football powerhouse, winning national championships in 1924, 1929, and 1930 (repeated in the 1940s under Frank Leahy). The rapidly growing American fascination with football shifted communal assembly from indoor exhibitions and events in Washington Hall where no more than a thousand could participate, to outdoor gridiron competitions in venues that could hold tens of thousands. This transformation, already begun in the teens during Rockne's student days, increased due to the huge celebrity of players like George Gipp. Rockne's continued success as a coach after Gipp's untimely death in 1920 created an American myth so great that Hollywood made two films about it, *The Spirit of Notre Dame* (1931) and *Knute Rockne All American* (1940), with the actor who played Gipp in the latter returning to Notre Dame as president of the United States in 1981 to deliver the commencement address, and in 1988 for the dedication of the twenty-two-cent stamp commemorating Rockne's one hundredth birthday.[102] In fall 1953 John Gueguen recognized the integrative value of seeing these very special films in Washington Hall at his new-student orientation:

> Just got back from Washington Hall, the auditorium . . . where I received my first big dose of that hard to describe stuff they call the Notre Dame spirit. First Johnny Lujak made a nice sort of speech (he ended up by saying the team is so crippled up they'll never win a game) and then we saw 2 movies: The Spirit of Notre Dame, and Knute Rockne, All American. Both were wonderful and it felt like the whole audience was one instead of many different persons from all over the country when the show was over.[103]

Perhaps like many of the young men in the audience, Gueguen seemed to have missed another purpose of the orientation meeting, which according to the *Scholastic* was "to make it a point to attend Mass and receive Communion every morning."[104] Be that as it may, generations of new students saw both films in Washington Hall as part of their orientation, instilling in them the spirit of Notre Dame.

Washington Hall thus continued as the university's primary venue for film screenings throughout the period 1922–56; indeed, before the opening of Cushing Engineering Auditorium in 1932, it was the only public film venue, although Cushing would ultimately prove the better space for screenings. The Edbrooke design of the Washington Hall auditorium was always less than ideal in terms of audience sight lines. The seats with obstructed views (by the pillars supporting the balcony) were always notoriously unpopular, but those on the far right and left could be just as problematic. Indeed, an actor standing center stage can move only thirteen feet upstage (away from the audience) before losing audience members on the far right and left of the house. This structural reality made a large portion of the stage itself invisible to many seated in the house. The severe angles created for audience members seated to the far right and left generated complaints for generations. The angles for film screenings were especially bad:

> The University's venerable theatre, Washington Hall, dates from the '80s. It was originally built for stage shows only, so when you

go broke and have to take in "The Shiek" of a Saturday at a free movie, sit in the middle. Otherwise, everybody on the screen will look like the thin man. The theatre has a reputation for being haunted, but the subterranean rumble you will hear is probably only the pool balls in Brownson recreation room, which is under the theatre.[105]

Sound with film came to Washington Hall by the fall of 1926. The *Scholastic* reported that "Fr. Carey has announced that 'talking movies' will be exhibited in Washington Hall next Monday evening," and a week later, that "talking movies" had indeed been "exhibited in Washington Hall," apparently a documentary on the history of the telephone along with "a comic." The article went on to explain the Vitaphone technology that required precise calibration of a "large composition disc resembling a phonograph record" and the actual film.[106] Permanent sound equipment came in 1930:

SOUND EQUIPMENT IN

WASHINGTON HALL

The installation of Motiograph sound equipment is now in progress in Washington Hall. It is expected that the work will be completed for the week-end of October 4, the date of the opening of the football season. Mr. William Richardson is in charge of the work. The regular concert and entertainment series will also be continued as in past years.[107]

The projection staff included three men, two students, and a genial technician named Hank. At this time, students still physically cranked the sound cinema projector, and sound emanated either from the film itself or from records or rolls carefully coordinated with the projected film.[108]

In fall 1931 Universal's *The Spirit of Notre Dame* had its world premiere in South Bend, made all the more poignant by Rockne's untimely death in a plane crash the previous March, with the film becoming something of a memorial to him.[109] The film, however, was not a great success. Nine years later in 1940, the premiere of *Knute Rockne, All American* at South Bend's four cinema houses and in Washington Hall mesmerized the nation and confirmed a legend in a way the previous film had not done. Kate Smith broadcast her radio program from the auditorium of John Adams High School in South Bend as part of the "Rockne Week festivities," where she was accompanied by the Notre Dame Glee Club singing "God Bless America" while the Notre Dame Band performed live on her show "from the campus studios in the Engineering Building."[110] One of the young actors in the film planned to stay in town to broadcast the football game between Notre Dame and the College of the Pacific: "Ronald Reagan, who plays the part of George Gipp in the Rockne film will broadcast at least a quarter of the game. Reagan is a former NBC sports announcer, and broadcast a world series before he was claimed by Hollywood."[111]

While it was a no-brainer to decide to screen such films as *Knute Rockne, All American* in Washington Hall, for other choices the system of selection needed regularly to be explained as students manifested complaints with less than gentlemanly behavior. Father George Holderith, the rector of Howard Hall in charge of selection at this time, pointed out that all movies had been prescreened, and that he both read reviews and solicited student input. He then visited the distributors' offices in Chicago and booked films, with Notre Dame getting the lower, nontheatrical rate.[112] Other avenues existed to bring films to campus: the French Club screened René Clair's *Le Million* in Washington Hall as early as March 1934 "for the instruction and entertainment of the members of the University," thus establishing the art-film precedent at Notre Dame very early.[113]

Whether because of the selection, free admission, or simply the youthfulness of the all-male audiences, behavior at film screenings in Washington Hall seemed to have been a perpetual problem. By the 1933–34 academic year things had gotten so bad there was concern the building might collapse:

> Saturday night . . . the audiences at both shows rocked the building with their rhythmic, tramping accompaniment to the music of the program. . . . Washington hall is a substantial building, but it was never intended to withstand concerted attack. Army units are known to break step when marching over bridges in order to relieve the strain on the structures. Campus movie addicts might observe the moral and discontinue their stamping of feet lest some

evening they find themselves draped over the billiard tables in Brownson "Rec" with an unimpeded view above them clear to the roof of Washington hall.[114]

During World War II, Father Eugene Burke contracted for the movies shown in Washington Hall, with students' complaints of out-of-date films.[115] The *Scholastic* surmised that the delays had to do with South Bend: "The reason why the movies in Washington Hall are so outmoded is that the South Bend theatre operators prevailed upon the film industry to withhold the new pictures until they have been exhibited in South Bend movie houses three times. The agreement dates back to the early nineteen hundreds."[116] In fact the contract included Chicago, which increased delays sometimes to three months.

While probably related neither to film selection nor to audience behavior, it is important to note the death of Brother Canute in Washington Hall during a film screening at about this time. The *Notre Dame Alumnus* reported in April 1946:

> Death came suddenly to Brother Canute. He was in Washington hall at the movie Saturday afternoon. God called him quietly during the course of the show. When the lights were turned on after the performance, it was discovered what had happened.
>
> The news of the tragedy travelled rapidly. Three laymen, old friends of Brother, hurried to the hall to see if they could help. They knelt in prayer while the rosary was recited. Their first remark to the religious on watch was Brother Canute was an institution at Notre Dame. When old grads hear of his death, they will voice the same opinion. Brother came to Holy Cross in 1891. He was here for 55 years.[117]

Brother Canute's death seemed not to stop bad student behavior and complaints. The *Scholastic* in 1947 printed an "Ultimatum at Washington Hall" letter to the editor lamenting the behavior of students at films in Washington Hall and thanking Father Kehoe for delivering an ultimatum, apparently during a screening. The response was that the jeering and catcalls were justified because of the choice of "a Z-picture, that was made when Mary Pickford and Clara Bow were still tots . . . so old that the titles include the notice: 'With the Revolutionary New Sound.'"[118]

By 1951 Washington Hall continued to screen readily available films as the Engineering Auditorium took over the role of "art film" house, screening "foreign" films sponsored through the English and the Modern Languages Departments.[119] Students could easily attend both since the screening days seemed not to conflict. The *Scholastic* considered the Washington Hall series of films the "Best in Entertainment" which "Lures Mobs Weekly":

> Both weekend and holiday eve, year after year, the huge and ever-growing crowds have stormed the doors of venerable old Washington Hall to witness this spectacle—to laugh at it, scoff at it, applaud it, heckle it, but above all to be entertained by that time-honored form of free amusement known to all as the Saturday night movies.
>
> Since the first presentation, back in the days before the sound-track when records were used, the movies today in Washington Hall attract an average of 1300 students—three showings a day.
>
> The films are obtained on a regular rental basis from the stocks offered to the area by the leading film producers. The reason for no "first runs" is that the films are from secondary stocks of shows that have already been presented by the commercial movie houses throughout the district.
>
> Selections from the available shows are made by Brother Rob - ert, curator of Washington Hall, with the approval primarily of the Office of Student Affairs. The individual films are selected from available stock on their artistic merit and entertainment value, at the same time complying with the demands of good taste and propriety.[120]

Washington Hall was an important venue for audio recordings and radio during this period just as it was for film. By 1940 the north wing housed the audio collection students could access, as well as the equipment needed for them to listen to their own recordings.[121] In addition, Washington Hall apparently contained radio studios by the 1940s. The *Scholastic* announced in 1945 that the "Notre Dame

Radio Club is Presenting Three Weekly Shows on Local Stations," and encouraged "all those who wish to gain a little experience in the techniques of radio to report at the Washington Hall studios for an audition."[122] Alas, auditions seem not to have gone well for everyone, because the next month, as radio programs were originating from the Washington Hall studios, the *Scholastic* asserted that the Radio Club was a poorly administered clique that welcomed no new blood and "needs a shot in the arm."[123]

Washington Hall had been the default venue for film screenings at Notre Dame since 1915, but it was not until the 1950s that the serious academic study of film and telecommunications began with the pioneering work of Ed Fischer and Jerome Fallon.[124] The Department of Speech offered "Radio & Television Production Procedures" taught by Fallon as early as 1953, with the name shifting to "Telecommunication Arts" by 1956. The first film course to make the official *Bulletin* was Fischer's "The Screen Arts" in 1961–62, but he very likely much earlier "introduced film studies at Notre Dame" both in terms of an academic course and hands-on film production, with the first student-made film in 1953, *Shake Down the Thunder*.[125] Thus the new media competed with theatre even before Father Harvey directed his first musical on the Washington Hall stage. The handwriting was on the wall by the early 1950s regarding the future. The electronic and mechanical miracles associated with the new media increasingly and unrelentingly rendered the nineteenth-century exhibition hall obsolete.

1955–1956 Visitors

In spite of the building's decrepitude, infrastructural inadequacies, and desperate need for renovation, Washington Hall supported a remarkable season in the 1955–56 academic year. The 1956 *Dome* described the venue as

> Washington Hall, seventy-five years old,
> The theatre, concert hall, lecture room of Notre Dame,
> A quaint reminder of all things beautiful,
> In a tradition two thousand years old.[126]

This tradition that year included, in addition to the regular university music concerts and drama productions, events running the gamut from Father Hesburgh's opening lecture, "Courtship and Marriage" (in his fourth year as president), to Zelma Watson George and her Negro spirituals, the Juilliard String Quartet, and Clarence Cramer's Opera Festival. The final concert presentation of the year in a venue about to be radically modernized showcased two of the greatest avant-garde artists of the twentieth century, Merce Cunningham and John Cage. On the Washington Hall stage on May 18, 1956, surrounded by the fading 1894 Gregori/Rusca murals and trompe l'oeil statues, the innovative Merce Cunningham Dancers premiered *Galaxy, Lavish Escapade,* and *Suite for Five (in Time and Space).*[127]

CHAPTER 9

MODERNIZATION,
1956–1984

When I teach a tragedy such as *Oedipus Rex* or *Hamlet* to a class of undergraduates, I always point out the complex nature of prosperity and adversity. While Oedipus personally ends the play in adversity, the city of Thebes experiences a new prosperity with the curse lifted. Hamlet personally ends the play in the ultimate adversity of death and likely eternal damnation of his soul, while the nation of Denmark prospers with the accession of Fortinbras. Just as the good or ill fortune of the state versus the individual can work in diametric opposition, so can a building and its tenants. This chapter begins with the extraordinary accomplishments of Father Arthur Harvey who ran the theatre program at Notre Dame out of Washington Hall from 1954 until 1969. But Washington Hall was built as an exhibition hall and not as a single-function theatre, so it could be argued that the first half of this period, while perhaps more prosperous for theatre than some other periods, in a very real sense moved the building away from its roots as it acquired and supported specialized, niche audiences and shouldered less and less of its burden for communal access and integration. To be sure, the big issue was obsolescence—the building was simply too small—but new venues such as O'Laughlin auditorium in the Moreau Center for the

Arts at Saint Mary's College (1955), and the auditorium in the new Memorial Library (1963) at Notre Dame provided spaces that competed mightily with the grande dame of performing arts centers, Washington Hall. In addition, one could argue that Father Harvey's 1956 remodeling and redecoration that transformed Washington Hall from its origins as a nineteenth-century exhibition hall into a twentieth-century theatre ultimately decreased its perception as the crossroads of the university: a more active and professionally oriented theatre program required larger chunks of Washington Hall's time and space, the consequence of which was that other groups had less. Washington Hall nevertheless remained a vital and important communal venue through the 1950s. As alumnus Daniel Boland ('56) remembered, "In my day, so long ago, Wash Hall was all we had for movies, legitimate theater presentations, speeches, convocations, once-a-year talks by the President, on and on."[1] Another issue of the day had to do with the incongruous situation that, at the very time Harvey, Syburg, and Bain created superb university theatre at Notre Dame, theatre as an art form experienced a decline as film and television overtook them in cultural importance. Additionally, if indeed the Harvey years (1954–69) ushered in a golden age for theatre at Notre Dame, the cooperative program with Saint Mary's College soon shifted theatre's critical mass across the highway to that beautiful campus's impressive Moreau Center for the Arts, and Washington Hall fell into disrepair to the point that by the early 1980s the building was closed for nonelective repairs and a renovation.

As we have seen in previous chapters, Washington Hall had been for decades too small for the needs of a growing national university, and thus other venues had replaced many of its functions; even musical events with a long-standing tradition in Washington Hall, such as Glee Club concerts, had been forced by the mid-1950s to add additional performances if they wished to continue performing there (and would eventually leave the building entirely for larger venues). Because Washington Hall could not get larger as the university grew—indeed, each renovation reduced rather than increased its seating capacity because of changing space, comfort, and safety requirements—the venerable structure's value as a communal assembly hall diminished as the twentieth century progressed. The

1956–84 period began with a modernization and ended with a required renovation of that modernization, the former setting the stage for the Harvey golden years and the latter allowing the building one final burst of artistic revitalization as it completed the last two decades of its journey as the sole performing arts center on the campus of the University of Notre Dame, the subject of the final chapter of this book.

"Remodeled and Redecorated"

If not handwriting then certainly gray paint was on the wall by the end of the summer of 1956 when the university remodeled and redecorated Washington Hall and, in so doing, transformed a multipurpose "exhibition hall" into a modern theatre for Father Harvey's third season (1956–57). The *Notre Dame Alumnus* reported on his extensive plans in progress for Washington Hall:

> Notre Dame's venerable Washington Hall, scene of thousands of concerts, plays, lectures and historic convocations since its dedication in 1882, is being completely remodeled and redecorated this summer. Scheduled for completion by September, the project includes new seats, carpeting, stage curtains, radiant heating, a cinemascope screen and public address system.
>
> According to Rev. Arthur Harvey, C.S.C., director of the University Theatre, virtually all of Washington Hall's facilities will be new or greatly improved even though no major structural changes will be made in the 75-year-old building. Workmen already are busy from backstage to the lobby and scaffolding rises from the orchestra floor to the ceiling.
>
> The seating capacity of Washington Hall when remodeled will be 848, only slightly less than at present. New automatic uplift chairs with light oak arms and upholstered in red mohair will be installed in the orchestra and balcony. The aisles and side areas of the theater proper are to be carpeted in charcoal grey while variegated black and white rubber tile has been chosen for the flooring beneath the seats.

The ceiling of the campus theater will be painted persian grey and the walls and woodwork will be crystal grey. The proscenium arch is to be framed in two tones of grey with gilt. A brilliant gold velour front curtain with matching valence has been ordered for the stage. The gold motif will be carried out in grand drapes covering the windows.

Father Harvey said that all lighting fixtures in the building are to be replaced. New down lights will provide illumination from the ceiling and recessed lighting will be installed under the balcony. A super carousel lightolier, suspended from the center of the ceiling, will be the only decorative lighting fixture in the theater.

Always known for its favorable acoustics for dramatic and musical events, Washington Hall's acoustics will be improved further with the installation of fibre glass material in the rear walls as well as by a new public address system recessed in the walls.

For the first time, three dimensional movies will be shown there with the installation of a cinemascope screen and the necessary additional projection and sound equipment. The remodeled building will have radiant heating and a new ventilating system throughout. Backstage, a new silver ripple traveler curtain, a new dimmer unit for the recently installed light board and new nylon rope rigging will add to the attractiveness of theatrical productions and to the efficiency of stage crews.

Washington Hall's lobby and mezzanine, too, will be completely redecorated. They will be painted in sandal-wood and coral, but the natural oak of the grand staircase will be preserved. The masks of tragedy and comedy, traditional symbols of the theater, will be inlaid in the center of the lobby's tile floor.[2]

Father Harvey had transformed Washington Hall into a theatre building, literally painting over Gregori's emblematic homage to music, oratory, and American history which filled the space, in what Tom Barkes has called "a declaration of ownership."[3] This renovation said loudly and clearly that the space was no longer an exhibition hall but was now the theatre for the theatre program (see fig. 9.1).

Nowhere is Althusser's theory that ideology manifests itself physically in culture more clear and obvious than in both the Gregori/

Figure 9.1. Scaffolding in place for the summer 1956 remodeling and redecorating, taken from the stage looking into the house. Photograph by M. Bruce Harlan, GPHR 45-2867, UNDA.

Rusca 1894 interior of Washington Hall and in its subsequent paint-over in the Harvey remodeling sixty-two years later. When that interior was painted out in the summer of 1956, a huge shift occurred ideologically. The Gregori keepers and guardians of Washington Hall were no more. They were no longer Notre Dame's role models, inspiration, and sentinels of the arts. The father of the country with Declaration of Independence in hand, now ignominiously covered under a coat of gray paint, no longer watched over the audiences in Washington Hall with his supporting cast of Shakespeare, Molière, Mozart, and Beethoven, along with emblematic representations of Tragedy, Comedy, Music, and Poetry. No longer did Demosthenes and Cicero, classical fathers of oratory and declamation, support the proscenium arch standing on the foundational names of Lilly and Girac, progenitors of the music programs at Notre Dame. No longer did the names of European composers Rossini, Balfe, Haydn, and Gounod emerge artistically from among intertwined music notation and pastoral leaves framing the proscenium arch.

The 1956 remodeling also undoubtedly made economic sense in the modern age when respect for the past had ebbed. It is difficult to remember now just how little interest the modern period had in the past except to reject it, with concepts like "urban renewal" demolishing 1890s row houses in American cities in favor of highways and steel-and-glass buildings. The demand in the 1950s to modernize everything at the expense of the past was high and pervasive. Our world today has absorbed modernity while still paying respect to the past—even embracing it—but the world of the 1950s was an "out with the old, in with the new" period in which gray paint covered over and "cleaned up" the earlier century's craftsmanship and "old-fashioned" artistic expression. And besides, who alive in 1956 remembered anything about Lilly and Girac? Which students could readily distinguish the accomplishments of Demosthenes from those of Cicero? Who had ever heard of the Irish composer Balfe? Even George Washington himself had receded into early American history. What the remodeling and redecorating of 1956 did not do was to add fly and wing space to the building or adjust the "nonstandard" size of the proscenium arch opening, expensive structural changes Father Harvey desired but never attained throughout his career.

In a *Scholastic* interview five months before the paint-over of the theatre, Fred Syburg stated that a lot of very practical work had already been done backstage: "The University Theater has expanded and modernized . . . the offices of the theater staff, the carpenter shop, the paint room, the costume room, dressing rooms, makeup rooms and the lounge." There was a new switchboard for lighting so that any dimmer could control any circuit to increase stage lighting flexibility and options. There was a new ticketing system (at a time when most music events did not require tickets), and most significantly, spaces behind the stage that "once provided practice shelter for aspiring musicians, are equipped as dressing rooms."[4] Music practice rooms that had existed in Washington Hall since 1880 had now morphed into theatre spaces, and so the practice rooms had to go elsewhere, such as the nearby Band Annex Building, the original

Huddle. On the third floor of the north wing (the Music Hall), for example, two large dressing rooms replaced former music rooms, one with the building's first and only shower. On the second floor, both Syburg and Harvey acquired offices in spaces that historically had been music rooms. And, although not mentioned anywhere, the building's first restroom facilities for the audience were installed on the ground floor by taking over some of the space of the Brownson Recreation Hall under the auditorium, with access behind the staircases (these spaces are offices today of the building manager and technical director).

In the same summer of 1956 that saw Washington Hall remodeled and redecorated, Saint Mary's College completed the Moreau Center for the Arts. With seating for about 1,300 in O'Laughlin Auditorium and a little over 300 in the Little Theatre, the Moreau Center represented a glorious commitment to the arts made manifest through architecture. Nevertheless, it ultimately stunted the performing arts at Notre Dame. O'Laughlin, with its seating capacity, was precisely the sort of space Notre Dame needed but did not build, in part, no doubt, because Saint Mary's had just done so. Instead of quickly following up with its own performing arts center at that time to accommodate the realities and needs of a major university in the second half of the twentieth century, Notre Dame came to see the marvelous building across the highway as a substitute space rather than as a catalyst for competition, so much so that by the early 1980s Notre Dame theatre faculty had offices in Moreau and worked primarily in that venue. When Saint Mary's opened O'Laughlin Auditorium, the University of Notre Dame had 5,684 students and a faculty of 457. No indoor facility on the Notre Dame campus at that time could accommodate all the students and faculty, with the possible exception of the Navy Drill Hall, a sports facility that doubled as an assembly and performing arts venue when needed. In spite of this troubling demographic reality, Washington Hall remained the only theatre on campus, and it therefore continued to be in high demand as a center for communal assembly.

The same year he asserted ownership over a cosmetically very different Washington Hall (and his third year on the job), Father Harvey allowed to go uncorrected the notion that the University Theatre began with him, ignoring the fact that Frank Kelly had founded the University Theatre nearly thirty years before as part of a long tradition dating back to 1845 of faculty-directed, student-acted, cocurricular theatrical productions. Whether he did so consciously or not, Father Harvey's redoing Washington Hall over the summer of 1956 and his accepting others describing the University Theatre as his recent creation ushered in a new era at Notre Dame. His contributions over the next dozen years were significant, but it was no secret that since Father Harvey saw Washington Hall as the only theatre on campus, he worked throughout his career to limit nontheatrical access to the building. His efforts proved only partially successful, of course, because the demands on the building from every quarter remained high throughout the twentieth century and only began to be relieved with the opening of the DeBartolo Center for the Performing Arts in 2004.

Father Harvey's actions seemed very territorial in his reformatting strictly as a theatre space a multi-use performing arts venue that had been built also to accommodate music, oratory, debate, lectures, and dance. At the same time, the unchallenged claims of University Theatre genesis produced a very real sense that a new theatre age had dawned, and the refurbished Washington Hall was the home of this new effort even if at the expense of other disciplines and interests. There is a genuine opportunity cost involved: when one event occurred on the Washington Hall stage, another could not, and Father Harvey understood that. If the university decided to support theatre in the mid-1950s, to permit Father Harvey to reproduce at Notre Dame the gold standard Father Hardtke had achieved at Catholic University, then sacrifices by others would have to be made. All units suffered from Notre Dame's lack of performing arts venues, a situation that undoubtedly contributed to the overall perception that the arts were not central to Notre Dame's mission.

Because Father Harvey required rehearsals onstage whenever possible, Washington Hall became unavailable to others for long periods. To be sure, Father Harvey brought back a much more rigorous rehearsal schedule as the norm, something Frank Kelly had created in the 1920s but which had been inconsistently applied over the years. Throughout this period, however, the Department of Music required

Washington Hall for its many regularly occurring events, lectures and classes continued to be given there, and important guests visiting the campus nearly always tried to make a Washington Hall appearance, although increasingly the much larger and more flexible Drill Hall had become the venue of choice for traditional communal assembly, with Washington Hall more and more attracting niche audiences to more narrowly circumscribed events.

Thomas Stritch correctly determined that Father Harvey brought stability to the drama program.[5] Father Harvey's vision went far beyond mere stability, however; he wanted to create a cocurricular drama program of the highest standard, and to do that he had to change the university's thinking about the only theatre on campus—Washington Hall. Father Art went about his work not simply to revitalize theatre but rather to claim it as his own and to claim Washington Hall as the exclusive home of the theatre program on campus. Father Art's vision ultimately and permanently shifted the 1882 Academy of Music into the center of theatre on campus. Within three years of taking over, Father Art had claimed ownership of the building as a theatre and had transformed the space.

As the previous chapter demonstrates, however, clearly things had not been awful in the years right before Father Harvey took over the program. Nearly all administrators arrive thinking they will bring "rebirth" and "renaissance" to the unit they lead, and that often becomes the talk that becomes the myth that becomes the fact. The truth is that in every era there is good work being done (and sometimes not so good), and all administrators stand on the shoulders of those who have gone before them.

Father Harvey's goal as a director was reproductive rather than conceptual.[6] Acting editions of plays often provide specific information about the premiere professional production, including detailed stage directions and ground plans for the sets, costume plots, property lists, and sound requirements. Directors tend to toss out nearly all of this and come to a play with their own unique perspective or "concept" which may use bits and pieces from productions they have seen but would rarely attempt to reproduce movement-for-movement and action-for-action from any previous production. Father Harvey instead came at the process with the goal of bringing to the audiences the closest he could get to a reproduction of the original he had seen on Broadway or in London's West End. Students of the 1950s and 1960s had generally not traveled as extensively as they have now—they had not seen shows on Broadway, for example—and one great service the theatre program could provide was a production as it had originally been done. We often see this tradition continuing today as regional and bus-and-truck touring companies claim that their casts, settings, and budgets reproduce in every way the original Broadway production.[7] An inveterate audience member himself, Father Harvey traveled over breaks and summers to see plays in New York City, Stratford (Ontario), and London's West End.

Father Harvey's attempts to reproduce what he had seen professionally nearly always produced success. As a director, he had an incredible memory and could therefore recall exactly how each moment played out to duplicate it on the Washington Hall stage. With Father Harvey there was never any question about innovative creative input from the lighting, scenery, and costume designers: their task was to get the show as close to the original as possible. When audiences attended a Father Harvey production, they were witnessing a reasonable facsimile of the professional original. He used the term "pin-point blocking" to describe his method of manipulating actors on stage with absolute precision and consistency. Nothing was left to chance in his productions, and the discipline he required of his casts undoubtedly helped to make his shows very solid.[8]

What Father Harvey did not have, however, were the professional actors and the huge budget, so his shows by definition could not come up to the level of Broadway, but he nevertheless did whatever he could to get around these problems. While recognizing and nurturing student talent, he also relied on professional guest artists and experienced townspeople to strengthen the overall acting pool for his shows. And although he could never overcome the deficiencies of the architectural limitations of Washington Hall, he could either choose essentially one-set shows (such as *Death of a Salesman*) or go the wing-and-drop route, with the many sets needed for musicals simply painted in two dimensions on flats or drop curtains that could be rapidly and easily moved about the stage (such as *My Fair Lady*).

Father Harvey's constant complaint about the nonstandard size of the Washington Hall proscenium opening in no small way reflected his frustration at never being able on that stage to reproduce precisely what he had seen professionally on Broadway. Washington Hall required him to compromise, but his audiences nearly always saw meticulously crafted reproductions of what he had seen in the great theatres of the world, and that was a huge cultural and artistic advantage for the community at a time of much greater geographic insularity and much less elective travel.

Father Harvey's demand for "professionalism" necessarily required much longer periods of occupancy of the theatre. In theatre, there is a "move-in" or "load-in" day on which the company in rehearsal gets inviolate possession of the theatre in which it will soon perform. For traveling shows of one-night duration, the company frequently "loads in" on the day of the performance, when the crews set up, and the actors—at best—have a quick run-through on the stage to get their bearings and check lighting and sound levels. Father Harvey brought to the program the concept of serious build and rehearsal periods.[9] Each group using the building required a move in (or load in), rehearsal without an audience, performance before an audience, and strike (or removal). If a theatre group rehearsed nightly on the Washington Hall stage in preparation for a play, the opportunity cost of those rehearsals was that for those days the stage could not be used for another function, during which time the building was considered "dark" to the public. In addition, if the theatre group once moved in could get pre-empted or "bumped"—that is, moved off the stage to allow a lecture for one evening—then the loss of that rehearsal onstage greatly jeopardized the integrity of the production. A one-night "bump" out of seven, after all, translated to a 14 percent loss of rehearsal time for that move-in period. As the university added more and more functions to Washington Hall to fulfill its multipurpose assembly hall mission, it unwittingly found itself in the awkward position of robbing Peter to pay Paul. Indeed, to make matters worse, even the one-night lecturer is not always happy to have to talk in front of a set for a play. If the curtain is simply closed, as could occur in the days when sets tended to be built completely upstage of the proscenium arch (that is, behind the curtain), it limits the speaker's space to the forestage or apron area, when the ideal place to speak is stage center. Thus, no one wins in this situation; everyone ends up compromising. When the university decided in the early 1950s to bring in Father Harvey to create on the Washington Hall stage the highest quality undergraduate theatre productions possible, of necessity Father Harvey required a great deal of exclusive time on that stage. In so doing, the university came into direct conflict with its own other competing goals: as Washington Hall became a much better theatre in the 1950s, it became a much less useful exhibition hall for all other nontheatre users.

An interesting confluence of production circumstances and needs made Father Harvey early in his tenure a de facto proponent of coeducation at Notre Dame. Father Ted Hesburgh later called the 1972 move to coeducation "one of the best things we ever did," while at the same time recognizing how impossible it would have been to achieve in the 1950s.[10] But because of the audience demand and student interest in large-cast "Broadway" musicals and Father Harvey's exceptional ability to direct them, coeducation occurred regularly through University Theatre productions on the Washington Hall stage. The tradition of women playing female roles established by Frank Kelly coupled with Father Harvey's affection for musicals made Washington Hall by the 1950s into a second home for Saint Mary's College women and thus a unique island of coeducation. Barbara Benford Trafficanda (Saint Mary's College '59) recalled the exceptional situation as "a wonderful *natural* co-ed atmosphere not available . . . on our campuses."[11] Father Harvey's first musical produced in the redecorated and remodeled Washington Hall in May 1957, *Good News,* reflected the reality of the situation: the company photograph captured a forty-five-person cast composed of twenty-one women and twenty-four men (see fig. 9.2).

As important as how many can attend an event is how many events can occur in a given period of time in a venue. Complicating the multipurpose origins of Washington Hall were the changing tastes in theatre production. Even well into the Harvey years, it remained customary to start a play by opening the curtain to reveal the first scene with no design element of the play extending downstage (toward the audience) beyond the edge of the proscenium arch that

Figure 9.2. *Good News,* the first musical in the remodeled Washington Hall, May 1957. Note Phil Donahue (first row, fifth from left). In this cast of forty-five, twenty-one are women, or 47 percent, seventeen years before Notre Dame became coeducational. Jerry Dodge (first row, third from left) created the role of Barnaby in the original Broadway production of *Hello, Dolly!* in 1964. Courtesy of Barbara Benford Trafficanda (middle row, eighth from left). Photograph by M. Bruce Harlan, GPHR 45-3089, UNDA.

frames the stage space. The curtain closed for scene changes, during which time stagehands came out from the wings on both sides of the stage and moved out the old setting and brought in the new, as silently and as quickly as possible, but never in the sight of the audience. The curtain then reopened to reveal the new setting as the play continued. By the mid-1960s this custom, rooted in the nineteenth century, had changed; the innovative director and theatre professor Reginald Bain was especially noted for creative directorial concepts that ignored "fourth-wall realism," jettisoned the curtain entirely, and used the auditorium for entrances, exits, and playing space. This new staging model had the unintended effect of reducing multipurpose use of the venue because it was no longer possible simply to "close the curtain" and have another event—such as a lecture—in front of it. Requests to use Washington Hall after a production had "moved in," always an inconvenience, could no longer be accommodated at all. Closing the curtain to permit a lecture to occur in front of a concealed set no longer had meaning. Thus at the same time its myriad clients continued to make their reasonable demands on Washington Hall, the theatre program singularly demanded more—almost exclusive—access to that space, and it was clear that nontheatre users did not understand (or did not care) about the process described above. By the 1963–64 academic year, the student editor of *The Voice* called on Washington Hall to open "its doors to new ideas of *usage* and an easier method of *availability*." A few months later the student editor targeted Father Harvey's methods as the source of the lack of access to Washington Hall, lamenting that "the 'tight' control of Washington Hall was examined in hope of opening it up for a wider range of activities."[12] It had become crystal clear that two objects could not occupy the same space at the same time, and innovations in staging practices by creative directors like Fred Syburg and Reg Bain essentially made Washington Hall less and less available to the other groups for which it had been originally designed. It is little wonder that by the end of the period covered in this chapter that theatre had left Washington Hall entirely for the more accessible venues of the Moreau Center at Saint Mary's College.

"Broadway" Musicals

Father Harvey committed the university to the staging of popular musicals, in sharp contrast to the past when student-written musicals were all the rage. After *Seventeen* and *Finian's Rainbow* (the two years before the remodeling), the University Theatre produced in the redecorated Washington Hall *Good News* in 1957, followed by *Oklahoma, The Boy Friend, The Most Happy Fella, Babes in Arms, South Pacific* (Father Hesburgh's personal favorite), *The Fantasticks, My Fair Lady* (Father Harvey's critical triumph), *The Threepenny Opera,* and in the spring of 1966 *The Medium.*[13] Beginning in 1966–67, the first year of the cooperative program with Saint Mary's College, the venue shifted from Washington Hall to O'Laughlin Auditorium with *How to Succeed in Business Without Really Trying* (the only time Father Harvey directed in O'Laughlin), followed by *Guys and Dolls* (Bain directed) and *Camelot* (Bain directed, with Father Harvey on leave). In 1969–70, with Father Harvey no longer running the University Theatre, there was no musical, but Reg Bain directed *Oliver* in spring 1971 and Roger Kenvin *Showboat* in 1972. Washington Hall re-emerged as the default venue for the summer program in 1972 due to funding issues at Saint Mary's, with productions of *The Skin of Our Teeth, Summer - tree,* and *The House of Blue Leaves.* Bain recalled that "Washington Hall was not air-conditioned and it was brutal. But the shows were fairly successful and we survived. . . . Fred's production of *Blue Leaves* was truly brilliant, and one of the best things he ever did."[14]

Father Harvey not only renovated the space, but he also worked to elevate the study of drama and theatre. The *Dome* in 1957 described the way in which he reorganized and brought innovation to the University Theatre with goals to "provide an outlet for people interested in drama for the sake of drama or for an extra-curricular activity . . . a workshop for freshmen and sophomores with class instruction and stage experience . . . [and to] offer a major sequence of drama classes in the Department of Speech, allowing for a concentration in drama."[15] Although Notre Dame had offered courses related to theatre probably going back to the 1860s, Father Harvey's remodeling of Washington Hall provided a physical home for the academic theatre department he had been asked to head.[16]

The first year in the remodeled and redecorated Washington Hall began with Arthur Miller's Pulitzer Prize–winning play *Death of a Salesman,* just seven years from Broadway. With a cast that included Phil Donahue and Reg Bain, this production was a great triumph for serious theatre at Notre Dame and was quickly followed by *Macbeth,* directed by Fred Syburg, the first Shakespeare play in the newly renovated space, and the musical *Good News.* This was perceived as a new era in "the new Washington Hall," a term not heard since the fall of 1882.[17]

As the tenth anniversary of Father Harvey's shepherding the University Theatre approached, Fred Syburg said, "The University Theatre was organized under its present director, Rev. Arthur S. Harvey, C.S.C., in 1953. At that time Father Harvey put into effect a plan that he had prepared in the course of a year's consultation and study before he was named to head the Theatre. This plan viewed the Theatre both as a training ground for students interested in the theatre arts and as a medium of cultural education for the University and the community." Syburg also mentioned the interest in other media, reporting that a film of *Hamlet* had been made with the prospect that "future plans include more television presentations and further experimental productions."[18] *Hamlet* fulfilled Father Harvey's dream; he had seen John Barrymore play the role thirty years before in 1932.[19] In his time as director of the University Theatre, Father Harvey directed only two Shakespeare plays, *Hamlet* and *King Lear,* in both cases with the lead roles played by student actors who would go on to distinguished professional careers, Richard Kavanaugh and David Clennon.[20] The other two Shakespeare plays produced during this time were *Macbeth* and *Othello,* both directed by Syburg, although Catholic University's National Players had regularly brought Shakespeare to the Washington Hall stage since their first visit to Notre Dame in 1950. Father Harvey, who clearly understood the value of film and television, taped *King Lear* at WNDU studios "for future viewing." He even enlisted the aid of Terrence Spencer of Catholic University to edit and redirect "the play for television" as he had done two years earlier for *Hamlet.*[21]

In the fall of the 1963–64 academic year, of course, the United States endured the fourth assassination of an American president, John F. Kennedy. Beginning on Friday, November 22, 1963, and for the next nine days a paralyzed nation stayed glued to its televisions during a Thanksgiving holiday that seemed to hold little to be thankful for. Father Hesburgh went immediately to Hyannis Port to be with the Kennedy family and then on to Washington for the funeral. Washington Hall, setting for "solemn and impressive" memorial services for Garfield in 1881 and McKinley in 1901, was for President Kennedy as dark and silent as it had been for Lincoln in 1865.[22] The end of this academic year saw Father Harvey at his peak with the production of inarguably "the best of his musicals," the "lavish" *My Fair Lady* (see fig. 9.3).[23]

Figure 9.3. "Get Me to the Church on Time" scene from *My Fair Lady,* May 1964, one of Father Art's many great triumphs on the Washington Hall stage, with Robert Oberkoetter as Alfred P. Doolittle (center) and a cast of fifty-eight. Photograph by M. Bruce Harlan, Arthur Harvey Papers (hereafter GHRV) 04-17, UNDA.

The Cooperative Program

The first academic year of the cooperative program with Saint Mary's College, 1966–67, brought opportunities to the theatre program, challenges to Father Harvey, and an obvious shift away from Washington Hall as the sole performing arts venue. As head of the cooperative program the first two years, Father Harvey said,

> On the occasion of the opening production of our merged theatres at St. Mary's and Notre Dame, and in the name of the theatre faculty and members of our "theatre family," we are most grateful to the students, the faculty, and the administrations of St. Mary's and Notre Dame for their kind co-operation in making this merger a reality. We are most grateful, too, to all of our loyal subscribers and benefactors, and to our audiences in the past who have given us encouragement in our work and who, by their thoughtful

criticism, have helped us toward the goal of a significant contribution in theatre.[24]

For the first season, *The Potting Shed* and *The Playboy of the Western World* were performed in Washington Hall (with the annual visit of the National Players of Catholic University touring with *The Merchant of Venice* and *The Birds*), but *The Tempest, The Playboy of the Western World, The Madwoman of Chaillot,* and *How to Succeed in Business without Really Trying* took place in O'Laughlin, and Washington Hall's role as the primary venue for the University Theatre had ended.

Father Harvey wanted a centered world of great Broadway and West End plays and musicals reproduced on the stage of his beloved Washington Hall through a University Theatre that operated with rules and discipline with one person in charge. Change was in the air, not the least of which related to the post–Vatican II world in which Father Harvey found himself, a new world that called for a new commitment on the part of the clergy to collegiality and collaboration with the laity. It was after all "the sixties." Father Harvey undoubtedly wanted to keep theatre at Notre Dame, and the cooperative program must have been a disappointment to him.[25] It would soon be time for him to move on to the Main Building and permit others to navigate this brave new world, something Professor Reg Bain would do with great creativity, industry, and insight.

Although Washington Hall as the center of theatre at Notre Dame had ended, especially with regard to musicals, Bain scheduled his fall production of Ionesco's *Rhinoceros* there during the tumultuous year 1968–69, a production in which he asked the impossible of his Notre Dame students—to rehearse rather than to attend a football game—an apt illustration of the degree to which the world on campus had become decentered. Bain recounted:

> For a variety of reasons . . . we got a late start and I was short of rehearsal time. The Saturday before the scheduled opening was a football game day. In those days, the campus literally closed down during football games. Everything was closed even more so than today (including the library). I asked the cast if they would consider the possibility of forgoing the game and having a run-through. There was some reluctance. It was rather rare in those days to ask

anyone to miss a football game. However, eventually all agreed and we had the rehearsal. I mention it because for many of the students in the cast, it became a kind of symbol of that "Washington Hall as creative oasis" idea. Indeed, the band took off just as we were starting the run with students chanting, etc. (Pretty much as today.) And here was this group of theatre students in 1968 (the year is important) doing this rather strange play (I did the show with all the characters as white-faced clowns) about the "evils" of conformity (social, political, cultural, etc.). One of the cast members came up to me as the band took off with the crowd following and said something like, "Look, the 'rhino' syndrome!"[26]

This seminal production of *Rhinoceros* also added another function to venerable Washington Hall. The camaraderie of the show created in the cast and crews the need for something sacred, and student cast member (and seminarian) Don Dilg organized a mass in the third-floor lounge after a performance. There were other sacred times in secular Washington Hall, too. When long-time custodian Harry Priebe died in 1975, Bain and Syburg scheduled a memorial mass for him on the stage. Bain always saw the Eucharist as a "natural way" to celebrate "the bonding that takes place through the work of the theatre."[27]

Festivals

Of the many conferences and festivals associated with Washington Hall, one of the most important and enduring is the Sophomore Literary Festival, which began in 1968 but was inspired by its immediate predecessor, the Faulkner Symposium, and operated into the 1990s. William O'Rourke says in his foreword to Linda DeCicco's book on the festival, "Each year students at Notre Dame get to see accomplished writers alive and writing, celebrating the literature of the here and now."[28] Within a year, this author-specific festival had broadened its scope, so that for March–April 1968, the new Sophomore Literary Festival "turned into a mammoth event . . . a week long, and what might be called the cultural highlight at Notre Dame for 1968."[29] Both Granville Hicks, chief editor of the *Saturday Review*, who gave the keynote address, and Ralph Ellison, author of *Invisible Man,* spoke in Washington Hall, as did other literary luminaries such as Norman Mailer and Joseph Heller, although the festival also used additional campus venues such as the library auditorium, Stepan Center, and the Center for Continuing Education.[30] Then doctoral student James McKenzie recalled especially the role Washington Hall played as a mass communication venue when he and others received the incredibly sad news of the assassination of Martin Luther King, Jr.:

> In those technologically simpler days, most of us learned of Dr. King's assassination from the lips of Joseph Heller, who walked onto the stage of a packed Washington Hall to begin his reading, only to tell us the unspeakable news from Memphis. After saying he had initially thought about canceling his reading, he had decided instead to read the Snowden death scene from his classic *Catch-22.* I especially remember his mentioning that Snowden's refrain about cold came to him from Lear on the heath. It was a powerful, unforgettable reading.[31]

Perhaps the most surprising conference held at Notre Dame, however, was the February 1969 "Pornography (and Censorship) Conference," which "opened with a reading by Allen Ginsberg which packed Washington Hall." As one might expect, the conference was largely censored out of existence, with a great deal of physical opposition from the St. Joseph County sheriff's office: "The Citizens for Decent Literature brought a complaint. The cops brought a warrant and mace," and the *New York Times* headline proclaimed:

A FILM IS SEIZED
AT NOTRE DAME U.
POLICE AND STUDENTS CLASH
OVER PORNOGRAPHIC MOVIE.[32]

James Roberts ('71) recalled that "Washington Hall was the venue for ribald poetry readings by Al Goldstein of *Screw Magazine,* and a musical play that included a chorus line of high-kicking women dressed in full religious nuns' habits singing 'Morning Horniness.'"[33] The sixties were the sixties, and even the venerable Washington Hall at Notre Dame could not escape them. Allen Ginsberg returned to Notre Dame for the 1979 literary festival and read his work in Washington Hall just as he had done at the 1969 Pornography and Censorship Conference, but the other guests by that time—David Mamet, William Gaddis, Larry McMurtry, John Frederick Nims, Hilda Morley, Ishmael Reed, and Robert S. Fitzgerald—spoke in the spacious and comfortable library auditorium.[34] Similarly, for the 1980 Sophomore Literary Festival only one of the nine authors, David Hare, presented in Washington Hall; the others used the library auditorium, with receptions afterward in the library lounge. Washington Hall simply could not accommodate Sophomore Literary Festival needs and demands.[35] The center of the campus had shifted; the traditional crossroads of the university, now much less traveled, had been bypassed.

The *Scholastic* related in 1971 the history of the Contemporary Arts Festival, an annual event that took place mostly in Washington Hall. Student Chris Murphy began the weeklong Festival of the Arts in 1966 with a local grant, out of which grew the Contemporary Arts Festival, which continued for the next five years.[36] Tom Henehan remarked in his 1968 *Scholastic* editorial that he viewed "such facilities as Washington Hall" as the focal point for "a renaissance of student literary and cinematic efforts," although he was highly critical of his peers' preference for the Sophomore Literary Festival:

> The Festival of Contemporary Arts held last week was one of the finest events ever held at Notre Dame. After last year's conglomeration of stodgy dance and opera and early American film, the program this year was notably vital and contemporary to the point of improvisation. Besides the fine professional work of poets, filmmakers, and dancers, audiences were treated to the best of student work in drama and music. The spontaneity and creative experimentation evident in the festival added a new dimension to the cultural life of the University, one which must become an everyday aspect of Notre Dame. We must develop a living arts scene so that "The Contemporary Arts" no longer have to occasion a special event, so that creative work by students and other young people will no longer be seen as one of several brief springtime cultural extravaganzas.

Unfortunately, Notre Dame chose to ignore this festival. . . . Washington Hall is packed with adoring fans who gawk at Joseph Heller and listen as he reads a few of the better (and more familiar) passages of his classic novel, but the same auditorium is half empty for Twyla Tharp's Dance Company, the outstanding group in the New York avant-garde, as they premiere a new number.[37]

Part of the problem with the troupe had to do with the choice of venue: "Had the program been presented in a gymnasium, as was requested, the audience would have had a better sense of vertical composition, instead of watching from above or below."[38]

The *Scholastic* went on to reflect the upheaval of the times and negative criticism towards standard, traditional theatre fare:

> The dramatic arts are in a state of upheaval at Notre Dame; the staff of the speech and drama department will undergo a major turnover before the fall, when a new director will be installed. The recent success of the Guerrilla Theater ["Gorilla" in other sources] has greatly intensified student interest in performance and has created opportunities for writing and directing small-scale experimental works.
>
> Since its inception five years ago, IPP [Impersonal Pronoun Productions] has provided the best theater in the area . . . providing a more exciting program than the ND-SMC Theater's cautious productions of standard material.[39]

But even if the new theatre proved first rate, its niche audiences in this newly decentered world were small.

Lectures characteristic of the late 1960s included luminaries such as LeRoi Jones (Amiri Baraka), who said in the spring of 1969 that "the black man is in no existential dilemma; he is simply oppressed."[40] In the fall of the same year, Senator Charles Goodell came to talk about Vietnam:

> The appearance of Sen. Charles Goodell in Washington Hall this afternoon cannot help but add fuel to the Vietnam Moratorium drive on campus. Goodell, a supposedly conservative Republican

appointed by Nelson Rockefeller to fill the seat of the late Robert Kennedy in the Senate, has crawled further on a limb than anyone in his party, and further too than most Democrats, by calling for a complete withdrawal of all United States forces from Vietnam by December 1, 1970.[41]

Washington Hall's old walls could certainly handle controversy.

Disrepair

As the years passed following the Harvey remodeling of 1956, with the building in constant use, by the 1970s many groups viewed Washington Hall as decrepit and in a state of disrepair. A fire in the lighting system shut down the theatre after the December 1974 production of *Fellows*; before reopening in earnest, the building required a major renovation after years of deferred maintenance. Reg Bain recalls, "The original problem was simply the lighting system but that led to larger discussions about total renovation."[42] J. P. Morrissey wrote in the *Scholastic* with hope for the building in the spring of 1977:

> Like the proverbial poor relation, Washington Hall stands in its place; tall, proud, shabby. Its grey-yellow walls are a constant reminder to its more fortunate kinsmen of their neglect. It is almost embarrassing.
>
> Fortunately for all of the Notre Dame community, this neglect is recognized and something is being done about it. Washington Hall, that 89-year old white elephant, is going to be renovated. . . . The price tag on the deal [is] slightly over $2,500,000. . . .
>
> The administration is apparently concerned about the lack of usable theater space on the Notre Dame campus. . . . The only feasible alternative seemed to be a renovation of Washington.[43]

To be completed by 1979–80, the plan called for gutting the building and starting over inside, and included a proper "black box" space to accommodate the movement in educational theatre toward experimentation and increased audience interaction. Morrissey wrote a follow-up article for *Notre Dame Magazine* in which he said the renovation included a black-box lab theatre in the basement and would be completed by 1981, although the funding had not yet been secured.[44] Theresa Rebeck confirmed in the *Scholastic* in the spring of 1979, "For years, Washington Hall has existed in a shocking state of disrepair." The Fieldhouse, with its dirt floor, was also a mess. She believed the university's inadequate, out-dated, and ill-maintained venues shortchanged Arts and Letters' communal assembly programs.[45]

The theatre program had pretty much relocated to Saint Mary's College before Mitchell Lifton arrived to chair the department; with no theatre in Washington Hall by 1975–76, physically and proximally no part of Notre Dame/Saint Mary's theatre was on the Notre Dame campus. In Lifton's second year, 1979–80, and in spite of the continuing deterioration of the building, which had not been renovated in spite of plans to do so, Bain nevertheless directed *Hamlet* on the Washington Hall stage (with guest artist Lance Davis), the first time in several years the theatre program had used the space for a mainstage show. For the October 1979 production, the program noted, "Lance Davis, an alumnus of the department, is a professional actor. This season marks the re-opening of Washington Hall, one of the oldest existing academic theatres in the country. This fine theatre has not been used as a prime production facility for the past five years. Substantive work recently done on the building enables us to use it once again."[46] Reg Bain more accurately recalled that "*Hamlet* did re-open the theatre but the balcony was kept closed because we were told it was not yet safe. Tickets were only sold in the orchestra area."[47]

In spite of Syburg's directing *The Inspector General* in 1981–82 to commemorate the one hundredth anniversary of the dedication of Washington Hall, this was a low point for this venerable building both in its specific role as the singular theatre on campus and in terms of its traditional functions for music, lectures, and classes. It was clear to all that a major renovation was desperately needed, and indeed, by the early 1980s, under new leadership and with a new mission for Washington Hall, the university transformed the building into the structure that served as the catalyst for the revitalization of theatre on the Notre Dame campus.

Film

Recalling the fondest memories of his years as an undergraduate at Notre Dame (1959–63), Father "Monk" Malloy has spoken and written of Washington Hall and Brother Robert, also known as "Brother Movie." Brother Robert maintained order at screenings with a cane that he used to signal to the projectionist to stop the film, at which point he would reprimand the audience of young men for "wisecracks, hisses, and catcalls" before threatening to cancel the film entirely, which he apparently rarely, if ever, did.[48] Among his many duties during his long life, Brother Robert was curator and manager of Washington Hall, 1943–53 (at which time he became porter in Corby Hall until 1965, before retiring to Holy Cross House), although it is clear from Father Malloy's recollection that Brother Movie's commitment to proper audience decorum in Washington Hall continued long past his official duties there. In 1961 the *Scholastic* confirmed the need for improved deportment by publishing the following set of rules from Father Carey, the vice president for student affairs:

WASHINGTON HALL

Your attention is called to the following points pertaining to conduct at events in Washington Hall:

1) By order of the State Fire Marshal, all aisles must be cleared and all patrons seated. Smoking is prohibited at all times in all parts of the theater.

2) No one is to reserve, or save, seats of another at movies.

3) Audible comments, or demonstrations of any sort—other than normal laughter—show a lack of refinement, and are offensive to other patrons. Such unbecoming conduct will be dealt with severely by the Student Council and the disciplinary department of the University.

4) Coats and ties are required for all events other than movies.[49]

Rules and laws are reactive rather than proactive; everything proscribed above had already happened repeatedly going back even before the advent of film. As early as 1895, the *Scholastic* had taken the collegiate students to task for "ungentlemanly conduct";[50] later, as film debuted, it complained of students in the audience who "mani - fest themselves by boisterous clapping on the occurrence of any unexpected incident, by stamping their feet, by semi-witty attempts to imitate the entertainers, and by a raucous applause when a student escorts a young lady to a seat."[51]

When English professor Don Costello arrived, he encouraged and popularized the serious and pervasive interest in film at Notre Dame through his early work with the film society dubbed Cinema 61. Although Costello focused his efforts on screenings and discussion rather than on formal academic course work, his early mentoring of stellar students like Dudley Andrew (now an endowed professor of film and comparative literature at Yale University) make it easy to describe him as the father of film studies at Notre Dame, without in any way taking away from Ed Fischer's earlier pioneering efforts. Professor William Krier, who has taught film courses at Notre Dame over the past thirty years, asserted that Costello "opened up film to a vast number of students in that first decade."[52] When Costello arrived in 1960–61, the free Saturday afternoon Washington Hall films were all popular but dated films designed strictly to entertain. Costello believed the bad films fostered bad behavior and set about to correct things, and he and student John Ohala therefore organized the Notre Dame Student-Faculty Film Society in 1962, which was wildly successful over the next decade. They bought film-making equipment (with revenues from screenings) and turned it over to students in communication arts who made films for academic credit, and since that time film studies has been an incredibly popular and dynamic option at Notre Dame.[53] But because many of the "artsy" films the society wished to screen were available only in 16 mm at the time, Washington Hall could not accommodate them, and so a lot of serious film screening had to be conducted elsewhere, especially in the engineering auditorium. Costello helped to solve the problem of deteriorating conditions in Washington Hall, however, by accepting the assignment of choosing the 35 mm films for that setting, but options were limited because those films also had to be in current distribution. The *Scholastic* later reported on the new system for film selection:

The past paternalistic policies of the University spawned the traditional Saturday Night Movie at Washington Hall. Designed to eliminate the roaming of students through South Bend streets, the series created a problem of its own. The evolution of the series into a "Saturday Evening Horror Show" was largely due to the usual poor-quality films shown and the august need of Notre Dame's moviegoers to "blow off steam." Three years ago the first problem was solved when the University asked Dr. Costello, Chairman of the Student-Faculty Film Society, to choose the pictures for Washington Hall. The result was the presentation of many first-rate motion pictures at no cost to students, faculty members and their families.[54]

The reduced number of better films—quality over quantity— seemed to have transformed audience behavior in Washington Hall:

Something is gone from the Notre Dame scene. As noted last week, the Washington Hall of the past is no more. Gone are the days which found crowds gathering at 5:45 for the 6:45 show. The pushing, shoving mob scene as the doors opened ten minutes before show time has disappeared with the class of '64 and no longer is a Sister or SMC'er taking her life in her hands when she attends one of the performances there. In fact, to some extent she is no longer risking embarrassment because of the loud remarks of campus wits. Washington Hall is definitely a changed place.

At last Saturday night's 6:30 showing of "Black Orpheus," for example, a neat line waited for tickets and then half-filled the theater. Notes on the movie were provided and only a vague "atmo-sphere" of the "old" Washington Hall was discernible. Noise from the audience was present, and it varied from occasional booing of the villain to shouts when the subtitles failed to appear, but the boisterous catcalls were gone, even though some students still expressed doubt that Washington Hall was the place for dates.

In any event the new Washington Hall is undoubtedly a change for the better; it may just take a little while to adjust to the improvement.[55]

No longer a general audience of barely postadolescent males with nothing else to do on a Saturday night, this niche audience attending *Black Orpheus* respectfully occupied rather than raucously filled Washington Hall to see this specific film. With the rise of niche audiences, Washington Hall experienced a decline in its more universal communal functions.

When hired in 1978–79 by Notre Dame, Mitchell Lifton, the first film person to chair the Cooperative Department of Speech and Drama, soon created a new department of Communication and Theatre that officially recognized the burgeoning academic interest in film studies. He also focused on the long overdue renovation that would be needed to make Washington Hall the home of the new department.[56] In his first year, Lifton promised changes, and he clearly hoped to transform the building into primarily a film venue. By February 1979 he had added Monday night movies in Washington Hall with "thirteen major foreign films," which the *Scholastic* praised:

> Recently, a touch of class returned to Notre Dame. A new film series is upon us: Monday Night Movies at Washington Hall. . . . Not long ago, Notre Dame regularly screened some of the finest films available. One of its film series had received national acclaim. These were gradually dropped, however, when the Student Union gained full control of film programming. . . . This semester, the Administration granted the Speech and Drama Department the right to screen films in Washington Hall . . . the first step towards a large-scale improvement of the film situation at Notre Dame.[57]

Lifton thus created "a serious and comprehensive film program" at Notre Dame. He believed that motion pictures, what he called "the principal communicative vessel of the twentieth century," could not be ignored in the academy.[58] In the absence of a purpose-built film building, this new program and focus put huge additional pressure on Washington Hall. If a serious academic film program must also emanate from this venerable space, where would all the other events occur that historically had taken place there? The opportunity costs of the new focus were very high, and the university by the early 1980s had truly hit the wall with regard to Washington Hall. Lifton articulated a more precise identity for the department, one that centered on a future in film and television rather than on the past in theatre, and besides, theatre had proper venues at Saint Mary's College accessible through the cooperative program. He hoped the new department of Communication and Theatre he created in 1980–81, now cooperative with Saint Mary's College only with regard to theatre, would break down "the 19th-century notion of the disciplinary cubbyhole."[59] To achieve these worthy goals, he would need to shepherd through a major renovation of Notre Dame's nineteenth-century exhibition hall, one even more extensive than the Harvey efforts of 1956.

CHAPTER 10

RENOVATION AND REVITALIZATION, 1984–2004

In 1984 the Joyce Athletic and Convocation Center, with over eleven thousand seats, could not accommodate all Notre Dame students and faculty, much less townspeople and guests. As it had grown the university had not created large indoor venues that could continue to provide communal access and integration at a single sitting, as had been the case when the 1882 Washington Hall was planned and built. The solution was the creation of niche audiences—subsets of the larger whole—with Washington Hall itself becoming a venue much patronized by these groups.[1]

This is the period of very serious need for a new performing arts center or a purpose-built facility for the academic units. Not withstanding its history, charm, and past service to Notre Dame, nothing about Washington Hall proved adequate to the needs of a major American university in the 1980s. Then why did it take twenty more years to open a new performing arts center? With the benefit of hindsight, it is clear now that Notre Dame would ultimately have a new state-of-the-art performing arts center, but in 1984 we could neither see nor predict the future. Numerous plans had been advanced over the years, nearly all of which involved in some way redoing

Washington Hall and letting the theatre program continue to share the building with the Department of Music. The problem in 1984, as now, was that the demands for theatrical rehearsal and performance venues at a university were just huge, and to have turned Washington Hall exclusively into a theatre facility, while meeting some of the needs particular to that unit, would have greatly limited access for others, from the Department of Music, which had occupied the building a full two years before the theatre program, to those who continued to see the space as "the place of lectures." Venerable Washington Hall could not be all things to all persons.

The academic and pedagogical programmatic needs of Notre Dame with regard to the performing arts had simply outstripped the university's physical resources, and decisions had not yet been made that would give the performing arts the kind of purpose-built spaces necessary for growth and prosperity. Although the academic units expressed their needs vocally (and constantly), it was entirely possible that professors' careers would begin and end in Washington Hall well into the twenty-first century as they had done for the entirety of the twentieth. Despite plans for various performing arts centers from the 1920s through the 1940s and beyond, more pressing priorities postponed serious consideration for a new performing arts center until the generous DeBartolo bequest of 1986 catalyzed the process that would still take another eighteen years to come to fruition as the Marie P. DeBartolo Center for the Performing Arts.

Most might agree that the university delayed much too long complementing Washington Hall with newer and more up-to-date facilities. Certainly the impressive Moreau Center for the Arts across the highway at Saint Mary's College, coupled with a twenty-four-year cooperative program in theatre, made a new building on the Notre Dame campus from the mid-1950s to the mid-1970s perhaps seem redundant as more immediate needs were met, especially if the planned merger of the two campuses had in fact occurred as originally envisioned.

Home Again of the Lecture . . .

In September 1984 New York governor and likely presidential candidate Mario Cuomo continued the great oratorical tradition going

Figure 10.1. New York Governor Mario Cuomo speaking in Washington Hall in the best tradition of nineteenth-century oratory on a stiflingly hot evening before the building was air-conditioned, Sept. 13, 1984; his speech was entitled "Religious Belief and Public Morality: A Catholic Governor's Perspective." Photograph by M. Bruce Harlan, GPHR 35-9184, UNDA.

back even before William Jennings Bryan in 1908 of prominent politicians speaking in Washington Hall on issues important to them and to the country (see fig. 10.1). The *New York Times* reported that "Mr. Cuomo spoke at the invitation of the department of theology, which asked him to lecture on the role his Catholic faith plays in governing," adding that Cuomo "shares with many politicians who are also Catholic a view that abortion is wrong but that they should not seek to overturn the current legal situation in which the choice of whether to have an abortion is left to individual women in most cases." His position put him at odds with church leaders who wanted "laws against abortion." Washington Hall's limited capacity could not hold all interested in the speech: "His [Cuomo's] appearance drew great interest on the Notre Dame campus. Many students were turned away and had to watch the address on closed circuit television. . . . Several dozen antiabortion demonstrators picketed outside Washington Hall, where he appeared."[2]

Speaking at the invitation of Father Richard P. McBrien, the chair of the Department of Theology, who had also invited the controversial Father Hans Küng three years earlier,[3] Governor Cuomo addressed what he called the "hard questions," those related to the idea that "the Catholic public official lives the political truth most Catholics through most of American history have accepted and insisted on: the truth that to assure our freedom we must allow others the same freedom, even if occasionally it produces conduct by them which we would hold to be sinful." He went on to assert, "I protect my right to be a Catholic by preserving your right to believe as a Jew, a Protestant or non-believer, or as anything else you choose." He added, "We know that the price of seeking to force our beliefs on others is that they might some day force theirs on us." Proposing that "abortion has a unique significance but not a preemptive significance," he explained:

> Apart from the question of the efficacy of using legal weapons to make people stop having abortions, we know our Christian responsibility doesn't end with any one law or amendment. That it doesn't end with abortion. Because it involves life and death, abortion will always be a central concern of Catholics. But so will nuclear weapons. And hunger and homelessness and joblessness, all the forces diminishing human life and threatening to destroy it.

He went on to say,

> Approval or rejection of legal restrictions on abortion should not be the exclusive litmus test of Catholic loyalty. We should understand that whether abortion is outlawed or not, our work has barely begun: the work of creating a society where the right to life doesn't end at the moment of birth; where an infant isn't helped into a world that doesn't care if it's fed properly, housed decently, educated adequately; where the blind or retarded child isn't condemned to exist rather than empowered to live.

He pointed out the change in perception of Catholics by the 1980s:

The Catholic Church has come of age in America. The ghetto walls are gone, our religion no longer a badge of irredeemable foreignness. This new-found status is both an opportunity and a temptation. If we choose, we can give in to the temptation to become more and more assimilated into a larger, blander culture, abandoning the practice of the specific values that made us different, worshipping whatever gods the marketplace has to sell while we seek to rationalize our own laxity by urging the political system to legislate on others a morality we no longer practice ourselves.

And he reminded his audience to remember their roots:

Or we can remember where we come from, the journey of two millennia, clinging to our personal faith, to its insistence on constancy and service and on hope. We can live and practice the morality Christ gave us, maintaining His truth in this world, struggling to embody His love, practicing it especially where that love is most needed, among the poor and the weak and the dispossessed. Not just by trying to make laws for others to live by, but by living the laws already written for us by God, in our hearts and in our minds.

He urged his audience to "be fully Catholic; proudly, totally at ease with ourselves, a people in the world, transforming it, a light to this nation. Appealing to the best in our people not the worst. Persuading not coercing. Leading people to truth by love. And still, all the while, respecting and enjoying our unique pluralistic democracy. And we can do it even as politicians."[4] Unlike William Jennings Bryan, who eschewed politics when he talked about "faith" in his 1908 appearance in Washington Hall, Mario Cuomo embraced both politics and religion, both church and state, but the seventy-six years between their speeches saw very little change with regard to venue and format. Both came to the crossroads of American Catholic higher education to speak in a historic space named after the father of the country about the combined and unconflicted duties of good Catholics who are also good Americans.

The Renovation of 1984

In the fall of 1984, as Mario Cuomo spoke to a packed house, the rebirth of the building was at hand as a thorough renovation neared completion largely unseen from the auditorium itself.

The guiding principle behind the 1984 renovation of Washington Hall presupposed that the theatre program would remain cooperative with Saint Mary's College and would therefore stay exclusively on that campus, with the film and television units moving into Washington Hall from their woefully inadequate spaces in the "Loft" of O'Shaughnessy Hall (essentially a converted attic). Washington Hall's auditorium was to serve as a cinema house and the stage as a production facility. The professor and department chair who oversaw the 1984 renovation, Mitchell Lifton, a talented and dynamic film/television professional, provided input into the renovation of Washington Hall which included a permanent upstage cyclorama wall, which would make it possible to use the stage of Washington Hall as a soundstage for film and television production (as well as providing much-needed access from the third floor of the north wing to the backstage areas). With the renovated light/projection booth and a new retractable film screen, the stage of Washington Hall was to become the department's film/television production facility, with the auditorium providing a much-improved venue for film screenings. With theatre staying on the Saint Mary's campus, Washington Hall logically would become the place where the film/television program would thrive and prosper, film having been a part of the building's history since at least 1915.

But these were not the plans the university carried out; by the time the renovation of 1984 had commenced the administration had decided instead to revitalize the theatre program at Notre Dame.

The renovations of 1984 fulfilled the prophecy of the Harvey 1956 renovation by turning the building more than ever into a space more exclusively equipped to support the performing arts, with the Department of Communication and Theatre gaining unshared access to two important spaces, the laboratory theatre and the scene shop. The newly created "black-box" laboratory theatre (37.5' x 37.5') on the completely renovated third floor of the north wing occupied space where the green room, dressing rooms, and several offices had been since the 1956 remodeling. Both the green room and dressing rooms (each with a shower and makeup areas) moved to the second floor of the north wing where previously half a dozen offices had existed that had been created from even more numerous music practice rooms original to the building. The scene shop continued to be directly under the Washington Hall auditorium, the old Brownson Recreation Hall area, but the public restrooms were moved toward the center of the building near the new elevator. The 1956 restroom spaces became windowed offices for the yet-to-be-hired building manager and newly on-board designer and technical director, Willard Neuert, who worked his magic and quickly transformed a trashed space filled with debris into an orderly scene shop, equipped with tools and the appropriate area in which to work in spite of its low ceiling and limited access to the stage above. At the same time, of course, the focus was split because the 1984–85 season would be largely produced in venues on the campus of Saint Mary's College, not only because of the cooperative nature of the theatre program at that time, but also because Washington Hall had been closed for renovations and was just now reopening. Only one play of the 1984–85 Notre Dame/Saint Mary's season occurred in Washington Hall: Sophocles' *Electra,* directed by Reg Bain, in the early spring of 1985 as a shakedown to test the building's functionality.[5]

Music, of course, retained the ground level of the north wing after the 1984 renovation, with at least two faculty offices for the band director, Luther Snavely, and the jazz band director, Father George Wiskirchen, C.S.C. ('51). The band and orchestras also had additional gerrymandered spaces below the stage.

Thus the 1984 renovation modernized restroom facilities for the audience, created proper theatre dressing rooms for both sexes, added an elevator for the first time in the building's history for audience access to the mainstage auditorium and balcony, carved a black box theatre out of the third-floor Music Hall north wing rows of small offices and practice rooms, and moved the green room down to the second floor adjacent to the new theatre dressing rooms. It also created dedicated offices for both the building manager and technical director where the original public restrooms had been, and eliminated a warren of rooms on the ground floor under the auditorium seating for a minimally adequate (if low-ceilinged) scene shop. Additionally, the renovation gave the north wing for the first time an internal stairway to all three floors. Further, a hall along the back wall of the stage, while reducing mainstage stage depth by four feet, provided for the first time direct third-floor north wing access to the auditorium, as well as, even more importantly, backstage access to stage right and left wing spaces without a person's having physically to go outside the building, as performers and crew members had been forced to do for a century! All these important changes brought this nineteenth-century building up to adequate (if minimal) standards for the performing arts in the late twentieth century.

The new Laboratory ("black box") Theatre on the third floor (north end) proved perhaps the most valuable facility improvement to the theatre program in spite of the intrusive vertical columns. Ideally suited to classes and smaller "experimental" projects, the Laboratory Theatre nurtured student directing projects such as the challenging play *Bent* (1988), hosted innovative faculty work with Kevin Dreyer's new translation of Triana's *Night of the Assassins* (1991), and supported new student drama through the creation of the New Playwrights Workshop (1998). The only two theatres on the Notre Dame campus between 1984 and 2004 were in Washington Hall.

Classes No More

Despite the renovation of 1984 the tradition of scheduling classes and examinations in Washington Hall that began in 1906 continued; not until the fall of 1992 with the opening of the DeBartolo Classroom Building did classes formally end there. The spring semester of the 1991–92 academic year, for example, saw the last general chemistry classes starting early each morning. The instructor at that time was Maurice Schwartz, assisted by Karen Morris, who remembered the following:

> Since our classes began at 8:00 am, I frequently had to be in the building by 7:30. I loved the peace and quiet . . . and sometimes was startled by students entering early for class. . . . One day, I lectured for two sections and had to compete with the pigeons!

They had gotten into the tower and were flying around inside. One had landed on the stage and as I tried to "shoo" it off, it just kept strutting away from me (reminded me of a diva trying to "one up" the hack performer on stage)! Students were laughing so hard that I just dismissed them for the day (can't compete with that sort of talent). It was nearly the end of class anyway, and I didn't want the bird to create a mess on the stage—or on me![6]

This was the last semester Washington Hall burned its candle so completely at both ends, with fifteen-hour days, beginning in the early morning with 450-student sections of chemistry, and ending with rehearsals and full-house performances of plays in the evening such as *Our Town* and *King Lear*.

By spring 1992 the university stopped using the theatre auditorium for departmental examinations (in spite of some strong faculty objections), although the interest in the space for exams and classes remained high for years. The Department of Communication and Theatre felt it had a firm commitment from the administration once the DeBartolo Classroom Building opened never again to schedule examinations or classes in Washington Hall, which was clearly no longer a satisfactory place for exams to be held or classes to be taught, if indeed it ever had been. The new seating had no desk arms attached, and the house lighting was so low as to make it difficult to take notes or to use solar hand-held calculators popular at the time. Plus, the normal wear-and-tear of classes trashed the building constantly and unmercifully.[7] One of the many functions of the multipurpose exhibition hall had ended—helped in no small degree by the opening in 1992 of the DeBartolo Classroom Building. By the early 1990s, then, Washington Hall auditorium was no longer a classroom facility, and arts events could be produced without the quotidian distraction of classes and examinations also being scheduled there.

The Band Has Left the Building

Units of the Department of Music had continued to occupy the ground floor of the original Music Hall north wing and the space under the stage of Washington Hall after the 1984–85 renovation, as they had always done. When the new Ricci Band Rehearsal Hall opened in 1990, however, Music left Washington Hall, where it had resided continually since 1880, for 110 years, with the result that the theatre program within the department of Communication and Theatre became the single academic residential tenant even though the various musical ensembles would continue to perform on the Washington Hall stage. Before the theatre program could occupy the spaces vacated by Music, however, providence intervened. As the band was preparing to move out and into the new band building on the eastern periphery of campus, the St. Michael's Laundry (founded in 1934) burned to the ground the night of November 16, 1989. Until a new laundry could be built, the administration decided to convert the ground floor of the north wing of Washington Hall not into the planned theatre rehearsal room but instead into a "temporary" self-serve laundry. Until the dedication of the new St. Michael's Laundry building north of campus in 1992, washers and dryers commandeered much of the space previously occupied by the band.

More tweaking of Washington Hall followed as the theatre program finally took over former music spaces. The band offices in Washington Hall under the stage, with some modification, became areas for costume construction and storage, with an office for talented costume designer Richard E. Donnelly. There was also room for property storage, a couple of faculty offices, and a small design classroom in what could be called the 1992 post-band changes. The band practice space became known as Room 110, a rehearsal hall, which, in spite of the many structural support columns throughout it which hold up the north wing of the building (and also appear on the third floor in the Laboratory Theatre), was of adequate size for rehearsing mainstage productions before move-in to the auditorium proper.

With the band relocated to the eastern edge of campus, the administration razed the Band Annex in 1990, the original location of the Huddle and the last remaining bit of the informally named "Rockefeller Hall," a collection of buildings and additions dating from the late nineteenth century which had originally housed the privies serving both Washington Hall and Notre Dame's first gymnasium. With the replacement of the Band Annex by a courtyard, a century of tradition of having ancillary buildings just east of Washington Hall ended, although the expanded and adjacent LaFortune Student Center (originally Science Hall) long before had assumed all of Rockefeller Hall's functions.

Revitalization

The visionary leadership of Arts and Letters Dean Michael Loux and University Provost Timothy O'Meara created a different reality for the 1984 renovation when they decided that theatre as an academic program mattered and must be a part of the modern Notre Dame. They jettisoned the idea of converting Washington Hall into a sound-stage and cinema house to accommodate the fledgling film studies program (with all theatre located at Saint Mary's College through the cooperative program), and instead embraced and supported the re-emergence of an active theatre program at Notre Dame.[8] Since the academic mission of the College of Arts and Letters was to bring great theatre back to the Notre Dame campus, the Department of Communication and Theatre necessarily had a priority at Washington Hall and was able over the ensuing two decades to mount noteworthy seasons. At the same time, the Jazz Band and Glee Club, opera, and other performing groups connected to the Department of Music continued to use Washington Hall regularly to further their academic goals and artistic interests.

The increased excitement over theatre returning to the Notre Dame campus created new problems because of the time and space issues, as a conscious shift to Washington Hall as the theatre building on campus occurred, even though myriad other events continued to require that venue for purely practical reasons.

The renovation of 1984 spearheaded an ensuing revitalization of the theatre program centered in Washington Hall. Tom Barkes brought professional management to Washington Hall when he arrived in the summer of 1985, and as a result the building operated equitably and at peak capacity for nearly two decades. Notre Dame hired Barkes, with a newly minted M.A. in arts administration from the University of Michigan, to serve as building manager during the academic year and to use "slow" summers to plan and to market the

Department of Communication and Theatre mainstage theatre season for the following year. The renovation of 1984 had neither upgraded the heating system from the Harvey 1956 remodeling nor added air-conditioning, so summer use of the building would likely continue to be minimal.[9] The send-off in Washington Hall in May 1987 for the Strategic Moment, a major fund-raising initiative, required at least a temporary measure for cooling the auditorium, but wisdom prevailed at that time, and the entire building was centrally air-conditioned. Technology serves as a powerful force of change in the performing arts (as it does indeed in all society); overnight, as a result of the installation of central air-conditioning, Washington Hall became a comfortable and much sought-after summer venue. With this important infrastructure change, Barkes's audience-free summers ended abruptly as the down times long associated with hot weather ended. With Barkes on board, the university established a complex system for access to the building that would ensure consistency and a sense of fairness. Coincidentally a native of nearby Mishawaka, Indiana, Barkes brought to Washington Hall not only a knowledge of the community outside Notre Dame's door, but also, as a former professional dancer, he completely understood the problems of the artist in performance. During summer 1985, he put into place procedures for managing the building properly as he served in the secondary but hugely important role of season subscription manager and publicity director for the Department of Communication and Theatre, which would be over the next nineteen years a major tenant and user of the building. With renovated theatre spaces now available in Washington Hall, Notre Dame's academic theatre program could once again begin to realize its full potential on the Notre Dame campus.

Barkes created a system that for the next two decades would rarely see a "dark" night in Washington Hall; it was common for the building to have 90 percent use during this time, with only one in ten days having no one using the auditorium. Barkes repeatedly sold 60 percent of the season before the first day of classes, with 13 percent of the first-year class being season subscribers. Barkes's dogged, aggressive, and hugely successful marketing techniques and skills on behalf of Communication and Theatre made palpable the revitalization of theatre, while at the same time maximizing other groups' use of and access to Washington Hall at a time of ever-increasing demand.

With support from the Provost's Office, Barkes ushered in a period of defined control of the building, a somewhat thankless task, whereby no groups got to use the building as much as they might have wished, but nearly everyone with genuine needs had an opportunity to use it, a policy that maximized occupancy of the campus's only purpose-built theatre.

Shakespeare and Productions

The success of Communication and Theatre's production of *The Tempest* (with guest artist Robert Stormont as Prospero) in the 1985–86 academic year reinforced Dean Michael J. Loux's decision to reaffirm a long tradition at Notre Dame in the academic theatre program of producing Shakespeare regularly. Notre Dame had produced Shakespeare since 1847, and indeed in 1901 the *Scholastic* had asserted that Shakespeare formed "part of the daily study of the higher classes in English. Besides exercises on analysis, criticism, plot, and characterization, at least two of his plays are done annually on the stage by some of the dramatic societies connected with the University."[10] Since the creation of the cooperative program in 1966–67, however, Shakespeare had been done mostly at O'Laughlin Auditorium on the Saint Mary's campus (with the exception of some visiting troupes). When Reg Bain directed *Hamlet* on the Washington Hall stage in 1979–80 (with guest artist and alumnus Lance Davis in the title role), it was the first time since Father Harvey's *King Lear* in 1964–65 that Shakespeare had been performed by the Notre Dame theatre program in Washington Hall. With *The Tempest* in March 1986 the long and revered tradition re-emerged and became once again common and regular; indeed, the department offered in quick succession productions in Washington Hall of *Macbeth* and *Twelfth Night* all to support the artistic and pedagogical goal of giving theatre students the opportunity to produce Shakespeare regularly during their college years.

The popularity of *Twelfth Night* in November 1988 perhaps best signified that the revitalization of theatre had occurred and with it the return of Shakespeare to campus. In "Fast-paced Shakespeare Packs Washington Hall," Carla Johnson in the *South Bend Tribune* says it all: "The romantic comedy played to a full house Thursday night at Washington Hall and is destined to play to full houses for the remainder of its short run."[11] The *Observer* opined that the production "should be commended not only for the performances, but for [the director's] innovative theme."[12] Senior Tony Lawton, who played Sir Toby Belch, would return to Notre Dame as a professional to direct *Oedipus Rex* in 2001 and to star in *Galileo* in 2002.

The National Players (long associated with Catholic University) toured with *The Taming of the Shrew* in fall 1990, followed by the department's doing its own productions of *King Lear* in April 1992 and *Julius Caesar* a year later, with the organization that would become Actors from the London Stage (AFTLS) bringing *Hamlet* to the Washington Hall stage in November 1993. Student Lab Theatre productions of *Macbeth* in spring 1994 and *Othello* in spring 1996 occurred, along with Actors from the London Stage returning with *Macbeth* in winter 1996. The Shakespeare effort culminated in "The Year of the Bard" for 1997–98, which included: Siiri Scott's beautifully directed *Rosencrantz & Gildenstern Are Dead*; student Mark Seamon's directing *The Compleat Works of William Shakespeare (Abridged)*; AFTLS returning with *A Midsummer Night's Dream*; and ending with Reg Bain's brilliant *As You Like It*. In 2000 the premiere production of Summer Shakespeare at Notre Dame's *The Taming of the Shrew* in Washington Hall, and AFTLS transferring its American base to Notre Dame, followed in 2004 by the hiring of Peter Holland as the McMeel Family Chair in Shakespeare Studies, ultimately fulfilled and completed the revitalization begun with *The Tempest* in 1986 and reflected a devotion and commitment extending back to the first production of Shakespeare on the Notre Dame campus in 1847.

The 1997–98 academic year was more than the Year of the Bard, however, and to get a sense of the quantity and quality of activity that Washington Hall supported in the late 1990s when the occupancy rate was consistently very high, it is well to peruse the schedule (based on Barkes's calendar for the year) and note the following activity beginning in August:

> Honor Code Orientation; Gender Issues Orientation; Alcohol Awareness Orientation; Communication & Theatre (COTH) meeting, auditions, & first read-through; Umesh Garg Indian Association performance; COTH rehearsals; Notre Dame Opera audi-

tions; performances of *Rosencrantz & Guildenstern Are Dead*; Pas-querilla East Musical Company (PEMCO) rehearsals and performances of *Joseph and the Amazing Technicolor Dreamcoat*; mid-semester break (dark); a music performance; Black Images rehearsal; Glee Club rehearsal and concerts; Black Images performance; an Athletic Department speaker; COTH rehearsal; Notre Dame Orchestra rehearsals and performance; Student Activities present Mark Nizer Serious Comedy; COTH rehearsals and performances of *The Compleat Works of William Shakespeare (Abridged)*; Thanksgiving break (dark); Asian Allure rehearsals and performances; Voices of Faith Gospel Concert; Shenanigans rehearsal and performance; Notre Dame Chorale's *Messiah* rehearsal and performances; Study Days, exams, and Christmas break (all dark).

Second semester began in January:

COTH meeting and auditions; St. Ed's Players rehearsals and performances of *Rhinoceros*; International Students Organization rehearsals and Talent Show; AFTLS technical rehearsal, "one-handers" and performances of *A Midsummer Night's Dream*; Student Players rehearsals and performances; Sophomore Literary Festival; the Notre Dame Jazz Band in conjunction with Junior Parents Weekend; PEMCO rehearsal and performances; Troop ND and the Notre Dame Orchestra rehearsals and performances; spring break (dark); Troop ND; Glee Club rehearsals and performance; an Elvis impersonator; Asian American Play; Notre Dame Opera Workshop rehearsals and performances; Shenanigans rehearsal and performance; COTH rehearsals and performances of *As You Like It*; *Soundtrack to Life* rehearsal; Notre Dame Orchestra rehearsals and performance; *Soundtrack to Life* performance; finals week (dark); Volunteer send-off rehearsal; a meeting; graduation rehearsal and graduation weekend.

During this period, Tom Barkes also brought to campus many outstanding groups to complement and supplement the work of the department and to enrich cultural life at the university. Especially noteworthy were: the National Theatre of the Deaf; the San Quentin

Players production of *Krapp's Last Tape,* with Rick Cluchey and directed by Samuel Beckett; the always innovative and avant-garde Theater Grottesco; National Players (reinstating a connection with Catholic University going back to 1950); A Center of Theatre Education and Research (ACTER), which in 2000 became Actors from the London Stage (AFTLS); the Juilliard School Drama Division; and Dynamo Theatre. With additional support from Provost Tim O'Meara, Barkes brought to Washington Hall Qi Shu Fang's Peking Opera Troupe of Shanghai and Preservation Hall Jazz.

Having been retired from the department for nearly twenty years, Father Art Harvey returned for two encore directorial assignments: *Death of a Salesman* in October 1987, with guest artist and alumnus Daniel Daily as Willy Loman (see fig. 10.2), and four years later *The Crucible,* thus spanning forty-six years of work on the Washington Hall stage, from his first directorial effort in 1945, *Shadow and Substance.*

Fred Syburg's seminal production of *Amadeus,* with a cast of twenty-six, occurred in March 1988, which Tom Stritch accurately remembered as "a brilliant success."[13] Perhaps more than any other play of the period, *Amadeus* palpably affirmed the revitalization of the theatre program at Notre Dame, from Richard E. Donnelly's stunning costumes to Will Neuert's remarkable set and lights and the hugely talented company. The show ran to sell-out audiences in Washington Hall for all five performances. This was the ticket to have in March 1988, and there were even rumors of scalping.

This is the period that saw the end of the cooperative theatre program with Saint Mary's College. In May 1990 it was announced that Notre Dame and Saint Mary's would separate their seasons, resulting in completely independent theatre programs, so the 1990–91 year was the first after twenty-four years not to be connected to Saint Mary's College, coincidentally also the year of Fred Syburg's retirement. In the program of his final production (in which student Siiri Scott played the lead) in April 1991, as chair I wrote:

Congratulations to Fred Syburg
This production has special significance for both the cast and the department. At the end of this academic year, Professor Frederic

Figure 10.2. Cast of Arthur Miller's *Death of a Salesman,* Oct. 1987, directed by Father Arthur S. Harvey. Seated first row, from left: Jim Nelis, Nick Simon, Kevin Kennedy, Daniel Daily, Matt Nash, Siiri Scott, Jack Blakey. Standing second row, from left: Kassie Misiewicz, Diane Tracy, P. J. Gibbons, Nancy O'Connor, Laurie Shea, unknown, Rachel Durkin, unknown, Father Art Harvey (seated), unknown, Mark Costanzi, Michael Murphy, Willard Neuert, Robin Dvorak, Ted Manier, Marty Tracey. GHRV 04-43, UNDA.

Syburg will retire after thirty-seven years of teaching and service. *The Good Woman of Setzuan* will be Professor Syburg's final directing assignment as an active member of the Department of Communication and Theatre.

It has been my great privilege to work with Fred over the past seven years. He is an excellent teacher, a superb director and a consummate gentleman. Most importantly, students and their needs have always come first with Fred. I will especially miss his quiet strength and astute counsel.[14]

The department celebrated Syburg's retirement with a dinner on the Washington Hall stage. It seemed the best and, indeed, only place for the event.

Although he retired in 1991, Fred Syburg returned five years later not as a director but rather as an actor playing the key role of God in *Christ's Passion*. Thirty-eight actors (thirteen of whom were first-year students) created fifty-two characters in 102 costumes on the stage on which were depicted heaven, hell, and earth, and it remains one of the largest productions of the period in Washington Hall. In retirement, Syburg returned a second time to direct a rousing *Tartuffe* in fall 2003.

Reg Bain directed his last production, *The Love of the Nightingale,* in April 2000 before beginning a year's sabbatical as a prelude to formal retirement, forty-seven years after his initial backstage work as a first-year student working on the December 1953 production of *Kiss Me Kate*. Director of Theatre Richard E. Donnelly announced Bain's retirement in the program, effective a year later:

> For 47 years, Dr. Reginald Bain has been an active member of the Notre Dame Community. He has directed and acted in more departmental productions than anyone in the history of Notre Dame Theatre. The show you are seeing this evening is the last play Dr. Bain will direct for the Department of Film, Television, and Theatre before he achieves Emeritus status. After a year of sabbatical leave next season, Dr. Bain will retire from the University in the spring of 2001.
>
> The thousands of students and faculty who have worked with Dr. Bain have grown to respect his spirit and admire his artistic vision. Since his first directing project in 1966–67, *The Madwoman of Chaillot,* through his current production of *The Love of the Nightingale,* students have had the opportunity to work with one of the finest directors at any university. They have laughed and cried with him, onstage and offstage. He has had an impact on the career choices of a vast number of students.
>
> It is with the utmost respect for Dr. Reginald Bain that I ask you to celebrate with the cast and crew of *The Love of the Night - ingale,* as well as the faculty and students of the Department of Film, Television, and Theatre, this final directing project of Dr. Bain.

Reg is a treasured colleague. On behalf of the Notre Dame students, faculty, and theatre audiences, I thank him for allowing us to be a part of his theatrical world.[15]

As with Syburg, the department hosted a retirement dinner for Bain on the Washington Hall stage. It was indeed the end of an era; Syburg's and Bain's direct involvement with Washington Hall totaled seventy-eight years.

The fall 2001 production of *Antigone* in some ways paralleled the December 1941 production of *The Merry Wives of Windsor*, for which rehearsals began before Pearl Harbor but with performances afterward. The casting of *Antigone* occurred at the beginning of September along with the first read-through, and rehearsals commenced on the first of October for a late November opening. Thus all the production decisions had been made before 9/11, and yet the entire production took place after that date, and this with regard to a Greek tragedy that deals with war and utter destruction. The company met after 9/11 to discuss our forever altered world and whether or not the show would (or should) go on, and if so, how? The directorial concept changed, as did the setting, both more appropriately to deal with the searing reality of the times, and the rehearsal process began in October with the company feeling great uncertainty about the future.

Also planned well before 9/11 was the multidisciplinary "Galileo and the Church Conference" scheduled for April 2002. Spurred by the interest from former provost and inveterate arts supporter Timothy O'Meara and philosophy professor and Galileo expert Ernan McMullin, the conference was a high point in the history of the Washington Hall stage with the staging of Bertolt Brecht's *The Life of Galileo*, guest-directed by Holger Teschke from the Berliner Ensemble with guest artist Tony Lawton ('89) in the title role (see fig. 10.3). This stunningly successful production, tied in as it was to an academic conference, set the stage quite literally for continued cross-disciplinary university-wide efforts in subsequent years that would generate exciting and innovative productions of *Arcadia* (2005) and *Doctor Faustus* (2008), both in the DeBartolo Performing Arts Center.

By the 2003–4 academic year, the DeBartolo Center for the Performing Arts on the southern periphery of campus was poised to

Figure 10.3. Bertolt Brecht's *The Life of Galileo* directed by Holger Teschke (standing), with guest artist Tony Lawton ('89) as Galileo (seated on left), and with Katy Kertez as Virginia, April 2002, as part of the larger "Galileo and the Church Conference." *Scholastic* 143:11, April 11, 2002, 32.

accept the migration of the theatre program from Washington Hall. The final departmental production in Washington Hall was *Arms and the Man,* directed by Ann-Marie Stewart, in the spring of 2004, thus marking the end of an era for Washington Hall which began nearly a century and a quarter before in the spring of 1882. At the conclusion of *Arms and the Man,* Ken Cole and his able students struck the set and prepared for the July 2004 move—lock, stock, and barrel—into the new facility. The Department of Film, Television, and Theatre moved out of the building on schedule, and for the first time since the spring of 1880 Notre Dame faculty members no longer had offices in Washington Hall. Washington Hall after 2004 came directly under the management of the director of performing arts and the Office of Student Activities, and thus a huge chapter in the history of the performing arts at Notre Dame ended.

Monk's Vision

President Edward "Monk" Malloy's visionary decision to proceed with a new performing arts center ultimately transformed the university and the larger community. Having been a student at Notre Dame himself in the early 1960s and having dedicated his life and career to Notre Dame, Father Malloy realized that a great modern university needed specialized, purpose-built venues for the performing arts and that Notre Dame was deficient in this area. Washington Hall—grand as it was at its dedication in 1882—was always an exhibition hall, a place trying to be all things to all persons, a place intended to bring together the whole community to learn, to commemorate, to transform, and to entertain. No such multipurpose space can ever also be an ideal theatre, a perfect concert hall, or an excellent cinema house. Washington Hall's stage was too small for dance, the orchestra pit was too small for musicals, the sight lines worked best for one person talking onstage rather than for a stage filled with actors. The huge windows on the east and west sides of the house, despite massive curtains and masking paint, made matinee and summer evening performances a director's nightmare. Father Hesburgh was undoubtedly right when he said that the university did not build a larger performing arts center sooner simply because of other even more pressing priorities, but the need had existed for decades. Over the years, the gymnasium, the Fieldhouse, the Drill Hall, Stepan Center, the Joyce Center, Crowley Hall, the Band Annex, the Band Building, and other such venues took pressure off Washington Hall but never addressed the underlying issue, that the university had functionally outgrown Washington Hall within ten years of its dedication in 1882.

At the same time, by the late 1980s the DeBartolo bequest, which included an earmark for a performing arts center on the south anchor of a new quadrangle, generated excitement and anticipation that Notre Dame would finally build a second performing arts center. The administration shelved the plans developed over 1988–92 for a variety of reasons, but the need only grew, and with great perseverance new plans were generated and approved, and construction began, with completion in summer 2004 for the inaugural 2004–5 season. In addition to its five main performance venues and its own staff of nearly two dozen, the state-of-the-art Marie P. DeBartolo Center for the Performing Arts houses the Department of Film, Television, and Theatre and those Department of Music faculty members associated with the organ (sacred music), the Glee Club, and the orchestra/chorale.

The Future of "this gem, this perfect hall for public entertainments"

In fall 1894, just as Washington Hall was at last completed, the *Scholastic* certainly got it right when describing the building as "this gem, this perfect hall for public entertainments,"[16] but the building has also been an industrial diamond where much of the very hard work has occurred. The question remains unanswered as to whether the University of Notre Dame will restore its gem—a true jewel in its crown—to late nineteenth-century luster. As the university embraces the twenty-first century, the need for venues for "public entertainments" continues unabated, even as audiences have become both more specialized and dispersed. With the opening of the DeBartolo Center for the Performing Arts in 2004, the focal point for the performing arts moved to the south perimeter of the campus, where the massive new building with its five communal venues (quickly dubbed DPAC by students) dramatically reinforced the ideology reflected in Father Sorin's decision first to build a freestanding exhibition hall in 1862, and then to combine music hall and exhibition hall functions into one structure in 1882 to create the university's first performing arts center. With Notre Dame's second performing arts center up and running, Washington Hall can focus on becoming once again the gem the *Scholastic* described in 1894, with the venerable structure now a very special place for very special events.

The new DeBartolo Performing Arts Center gives Notre Dame the opportunity for the first time in living memory to restore Washington Hall to its nineteenth-century glory, to bring back the 1894 Gregori murals depicting Washington, Shakespeare, Molière, Beethoven, and Mozart; the personifications of Tragedy, Comedy, Music, and Poetry; and the trompe l'oeil statues of Demosthenes and Cicero on each side of the proscenium arch that included the names of early music professors Lilly and Girac, and composers Rossini, Balfe, Haydn, and Gounod, all overseen by George Washington. Complementary to the successful restoration of the Main Building, Washington Hall could become once again the nineteenth-century structure it originally was, albeit with all the contemporary appurtenances needed to make it functional today, such as air-conditioning, access for the disabled, and adequate restroom facilities. A restored Washington Hall would provide a grand living venue for communal assembly for all sorts of groups at Notre Dame where the university might wish to emphasize its mission and history at the center of the campus. A restored Washington Hall, with the Gregori/Rusca interior walls once again accessible in all their splendor, supported by a fully functional backstage and infrastructure, would continue nobly for another century or more to provide cultural access and integration at the very crossroads of the university.

An 1845 Reference to a Theatrical Performance at Notre Dame

For the Catholic Herald.
Bertrand, Aug. 7th, 1845.
Mr. Editor—I attended the public distribution of premiums to the students of the University of Notre Dame du Lac, which took place on the first of this month, and being the first thing of the kind which ever took place in this section of the country, the numbers who attended the novel scene were large and respectable. About 9 o'clock in the morning, the entire vicinity of the University was crowded with all kinds of traveling vehicle; while the different apartments of the University and its vicinity, were scrutinized and examined according to each one's taste. The different apartments of the University were closely examined by many strangers who had never before visited the institution; all expressing themselves highly pleased with every thing they saw, especially the clean, airy, and spacious dormitories of the pupils; others ranged along the shores of the adjacent lakes, while the Catholic portion, especially the ladies, might be seen clustering round the chapel on the island dedicated to Our Lady of the Lake, and entering it as it were by stealth, (for its doors are not open to the public) to offer a hasty but earnest prayer for the conversion of sinners, of which the good Father Marrivault was sure to remind them. But the greatest rush was to the saloon occupied by the splendid museum—lately purchased by the institution from Dr. Cavalli of Detroit, who had been collecting it at a great expense for many years. It is a splendid collection of beasts, birds, fishes, reptiles, antiquities, &c. &c., from the various parts of the globe, and the rapid changes undergone by the features of many an unsophisticated child of the west, while scanning the big black bear, the gaudy and magnificent bird of paradise,

---

The Catholic Herald (Philadelphia), Thursday, Aug. 28, 1845, 275–76.

the austere and imperative tribe of eagles, until he arrived at the inexplicable Chinese curiosities, exhibited the admiration and interest they felt in reviewing the valuable collection. All were deeply engaged, and apparently forgetting what had brought them to the lake, when the warlike sounds of the big drum of the South Bend band was heard booming through the woods. Shortly after the band came into view, drawn by four horses, and accompanied by a number of ladies and gentlemen; on their arrival, the music saloon was thrown open, and was soon crowded to a complete jam: how many remained outside I cannot tell, as I made sure to be among the "ins." As soon as all the apartment could contain were admitted, the students commenced a play, which for the space of an hour, kept the audience in a roar of laughter; after which the great work of the day—the distribution of premiums commenced. This pleasing task was performed by the Rev. Mr. Shaw of Vincennes, who appeared several times to be much interested whilst bestowing the coveted prize, and placing the crown of distinction on the brow of the delighted and victorious. During the distribution many incidents occurred which drew forth the warm applause of the entire audience; out of many I will relate one— among the number who received the greatest number of crowns and premiums, was a little fellow named Haquin, about 12 years of age, from your good city of Philadelphia. His great success enlisted the entire audience in his behalf, even the Rev. Mr. Shaw could not conceal his admiration of the young and promising pupil. The boy's dress, though comfortable, still denoted that he was not among the favored children of fortune. Feeling a more than ordinary interest in the little fellow, I ascertained after all was over, that he is an orphan boy, and was brought to the University of Notre Dame du Lac from St. John's Orphan Asylum, Philadelphia. But here he stood, equal, aye, superior to the cherished sons of the rich and wealthy, carrying away the marks of honor and distinction, which would occupy such conspicuous places, if acquired by his wealthy competitors; but he, poor fellow, has no place for them but a small wooden box, where they will be unseen and uncared for, by all save himself. But they will not be useless, far from it: they will cheer and encourage him to greater efforts, and remind him of the unceasing care and more than parental kindness which God provided him with in the place of his natural parents. I select this from many similar examples at this institution, as being calculated to give us a better idea than the most general description of the things noiselessly and silently being done at the U.N.D. du Lac.

I am, Mr. Editor, yours truly,
M. R. K.

Figure 1.1. The triumvirate of three major "original" buildings, the Main Building or "Golden Dome" (1879), the Basilica of the Sacred Heart (begun 1871), and Washington Hall (begun 1879), which form the central core of the University of Notre Dame to this day. Aerial view of Main Quad—Color, Oct. 1994, Notre Dame Copy Negatives Collection (here - after GNEG) 09A/41, UNDA.   3

Figure 1.2. Close-up of Washington Hall, from fig. 1.1. The poster above the entrance to Washington Hall advertises the Department of Communication and Theatre's *Waiting for Godot,* directed by the Reverend David Garrick, C.S.C., and produced Oct. 12–16, 1994. Aerial view of Main Quad—Color, Oct. 1994, GNEG 09A/41, UNDA.   4

Figure 2.1. Main Building I—Engraving, 1843, GNEG 11A/01, UNDA. This building very likely contained the "music saloon" described at the 1845 commencement.   15

Figure 2.2. Main Building I—Engraving as part of ND advertisement, GNEG 11A/003, UNDA. This must be around 1854 because of the additional east and west wings and a new façade. The 66' x 40' east wing (on the right) contained the university's first "exhibition hall" occupying the second and third floors with a recreation hall underneath on the first (or ground) floor. This east wing configuration of the Main Building served the needs of the university until the 1862 opening of the freestanding 100' x 50' Senior Recreation Hall, which contained an exhibition hall that would be named Washington Hall in 1864.   21

Figure 2.3. Panorama of Notre Dame Campus—Engraving, c. 1856, GNEG 09A/05, UNDA. This engraving shows clearly the new east and west wings on Main I in context with the entire university, including the lower freestanding structure northeast of the Main Building (to the right) which was likely the building that included a "music room," three classrooms, and one piano-equipped practice room on its first floor. The second floor contained four dormitory rooms and one more music practice room.   22

Figure 2.4. Cast outside Washington Hall at a first (ground) floor entrance, probably on the "short" or west side of the building. Father Lemonnier in the center front row dates the photograph to his two years as president, 1872–74, in what may be the earliest photograph of Washington Hall. The ornamental caps over the windows probably date to 1862. The reverse of this photograph says "III-40 1874 Exhibition Hall in Background, front row (left to right) A. Stace, J. A. Lyons, A. Lemonnier, unidentified [Marcellinus], and J. Edwards." Thomas J. Schlereth Photographs (hereafter GTJS) 6/9, UNDA.   27

Figure 3.1. *A Guide to the University of Notre Dame, and the Academy of St. Mary of the Immaculate Conception, Near South Bend, Indiana* (Philadelphia: J. B. Chandler, 1865), frontispiece, GNEG 09A/03-04, UNDA. Note the north-south disposition of building 3 (the Washington Exhibition Hall). The artist's exaggerated perspective appears to place the Manual Labor School parallel to and southwest of Washington Hall, when in reality it was much farther south. This engraving reflects the 1862–65 period because it precedes the building of the Music Hall in 1865 and the subsequent removal of Washington Hall south and ninety degrees into an east-west disposition to make the two buildings parallel.   32–33

Figure 3.2. Enlargement of fig. 3.1, frontispiece, GNEG 09A/03-04, UNDA, of the central campus, with the Washington Exhibition Hall building 3. Note the elongated window bays on the west front, perhaps to reflect the two-story height of the interior auditorium.   34

Figure 3.3. Blowup of Charles Shober lithograph 1865, shows the original north-south configuration of Washington Hall (before the complementary Music Hall was built) with Washington Hall (number 3) complementing the church just as it does today. This lithograph is a rare topographical map from a very narrow period in Notre Dame's history, after the Exhibition Hall was built in 1862, but before both the Music Hall went up by the end of 1865 and the Exhibition Hall was moved ninety degrees in 1866 from a north-south configuration to an east-west one, the position it would stay in until it was demolished in 1882. To achieve the point of view of the *Guide* engraving in figs. 3.1 and 3.2, the observer would be directly south of Saint Mary's Lake looking northeast toward the center of campus. Notre Dame Printed and Reference Material Dropfiles (hereafter PNDP) 10-Aa-05, UNDA.   35

Figure 3.4. *A Guide to the University of Notre Dame, and the Academy of St. Mary of the Immaculate Conception, Near South Bend, Indiana.* (Philadelphia: J. B. Chandler, 1865), 27, engraving of Washington Hall in its original north-south configuration. Note seven bays on long west front and ground floor entrance with portico in the middle of the building.   36

Figure 3.5. *Dome* 1920, 145, showing exterior stairs on the first Washington Hall leading to the second (auditorium) level, probably on the "long" side of the building. Date and play are unknown, but Father Colovin in the center front row dates the photograph to his years as president, 1874–77. The elevated entrance to Washington Hall was added in 1871, probably on the north side with exterior stairs accessing the second floor. This is the best surviving picture of the exterior entrance to the first Washington Hall. Note the platform at the top of the stairs above the portico, almost certainly to access the auditorium directly.   38

Figure 3.6. The first Washington Hall, c. 1866, on the lower right side with the new Main Building II and parallel Music Hall to the north. Note the long curved-top upper-floor windows. This configuration would last until the Great Fire of 1879. Notre Dame Life Photograph Collection (hereafter GNDL) 06-16-02, UNDA.   45

Figure 4.1. A single stereopticon frame of the burned university soon after the Great Fire in April 1879. The gabled building on the right is the burned-out masonry Music Hall (Junior Recreation Hall), built in 1865. GNEG 11A/15, UNDA.   73

Figure 4.2. A close-up of fig. 4.1 showing the destroyed Music Hall. GNEG 11A/15, UNDA.   74

Figure 4.3. An engraving of the burned-out campus of Notre Dame, c. 1879, which shows how the prevailing wind from the southwest destroyed the Music Hall but skipped Washington Hall (lower right), out of range of both the direct firestorm and its radiant heat. "Donations from France for Rebuilding Main Bldg 1880 (Reconstruction de l'Université catholique de Notre-Dame du Lac)," UNDR 3/06, UNDA.   75

Figure 4.4. Willoughby J. Edbrooke (1843–96), architect of the new Main Building (the Golden Dome), Academy of Music (Washington Hall), Science Hall (LaFortune), and Sorin Hall (the first freestanding dormitory). Edbrooke also served as architect for the U.S. Treasury in Washington, D.C., and the state capitol in Atlanta. Notre Dame Portraits Collection (hereafter GPOR) 4/8, UNDA.   77

Figure 4.5. Architect Christopher K. Dennis's rendering of Washington Hall, winter 1880–81, with the north Music Hall wing completed and occupied by the Music Department, but with the south Exhibition Hall wing constructed above grade to the "water table" and roofed over to create a large, indoor, dirt-floor recreation area.   89

Figure 5.1. Architect Christopher K. Dennis's rendering of the exterior of Washington Hall c. 1885 from the southwest, with the "temporary" tower (replaced in 1887) and wooden stairs (replaced by stone in 1889).   100

Figure 5.2. Sanborn Insurance Map, 1885. To the east of the Exhibition/Music Hall is Notre Dame's first gymnasium, a building that is about 33' x 120' x 22' high. Between the two is the 1883 water closet (7' x 14' x 7' high), a toilet facility to serve nearby buildings, including Washington Hall, which first got indoor plumbing in 1908.   111

Figure 5.3. The cast and crews involved in *Robert Emmet: The Martyr of Irish Liberty,* Saint Patrick's Day Exhibition, March 17, 1885. A rare interior photograph of Washington Hall with the Ackermann/Frederick interior before the Gregori/Rusca modifications in 1894. Note the detail on the proscenium arch (on the right side of the photograph) and the Ackermann act curtain in the "up" or valence position and first groove legs. The five faculty seated across the front are (left to right) an unidentified brother, Father John M. Toohey, President Walsh, Father Martin J. Regan (1883–1907 prefect of discipline), and Professor Lyons. The photograph shows the theatre had a footlight groove across the front of a curved stage. Handwritten on the back of this photograph is "The Play of Robert Emmett Mar 17.1886," but the correct date is 1885 since in 1886 the Columbians produced *Richard III* for Saint Patrick's Day, while in 1885 their play was indeed *Robert Emmet.* See *Scholastic* 18:28, March 21, 1885, 446; 19:27, March 20, 1886, 437. GNDL 13-49, UNDA. 114–115

Figure 5.4. Interior of Washington Hall, June 1894–June 1895. Gregori/Rusca completed their complex interior in June 1894, which coexisted for one year with the earlier Ackermann "1885" drop/valence curtain and upstage scenic effects, all of which Sosman & Landis replaced in June 1895. Thus we can date this photograph to June 1894–June 1895, essentially the 1894–95 academic year, but it remains the best surviving photograph of the interior of Washington Hall before the 1956 renovation painted everything out. Notre Dame Glass Plate Negative Contact Sheets Collection (hereafter GGPP) 2/19, UNDA.   116

Figure 5.5. Washington Hall after the tower was completed in December 1887 (but before the installation of "proper" windows there) and with what appear to be wooden steps before the stone steps went up by July 1889. Francis P. Clark Collection (hereafter GFCL) 48/57, UNDA. While the "1881" on the west face of the tower cannot be easily read, the south front inscription space is blank, as it is today. Although this photograph has been airbrushed probably in an attempt to remove something in the foreground, it is very likely the earliest surviving photograph of the building after the tower was completed.   118

Figure 5.6. Washington Hall after July 1889: the stone steps had been installed but the tower had not received permanent windows. Note the inscription "stone" on the south tower face which has remained blank to this day. GNDL 7/47, UNDA.   119

Figure 5.7. From *A Brief History of the University of Notre Dame du Lac, Indiana, from 1842 to 1892, Prepared for the Golden Jubilee to Be Celebrated June 11, 12 and 13, 1895* (Chicago: Werner, 1895), between 184 and 185. One of the earliest published photographs of the completed Washington Hall with "permanent" south entrance stairs, taken after 1889.   120

Figure 5.8. Edbrooke engraving of the new building, with the words "Music Hall" and the date "1879" on the tower, neither of which ever seem to have appeared on the building. GFCL 48/56, UNDA.   121

Figure 5.9. Gregori's "ideal portrait" of Shakespeare on stage. Note the 1885 Ackermann drop curtain and first-groove legs, plus the Shakespeare "gothic" set. Gregori is front row, second from right, with Professor Lyons to his right. Although undated, this is likely very soon after the completion of the portrait in early 1885 and is perhaps a photographic record related to the April 1885 "Shakespeare at Notre Dame" event, although the actor playing Shakespeare and wreaths to crown the portrait are conspicuously missing in this photograph. The front-row dignitaries are (left to right) Father Regan, Father Toohey, President Walsh, Professor Lyons, Signor Gregori, and Professor Edwards. GNDL 19/11, UNDA.   132–133

Figure 5.10. Balcony lobby arch ceiling panel, original Rusca/Poligano 1894 painting intact, long concealed by the interior ceiling of the light booth, possibly since the construction of the projection booth around 1916, but certainly since the 1956 renovation when the Gregori/Rusca interior was painted over. The floor in this picture is on top of the ceiling of the current light booth (photograph by Greta Fisher 2006).   143

Figure 5.11. Area long concealed inside a "light lock" probably since the 1956 remodeling, likely a remnant of the original Rusca/Poligano 1894 painting, although it could possibly have survived from earlier work of Ackermann/Frederick (photograph by Ron Grisoli 2009).   143

Figure 5.12. 1894 interior detail of fig. 5.4. The personification of Tragedy, above the audience and to the right.   148

Figure 5.13. 1894 interior detail of fig. 5.4. Pilaster of faux Bradilio marble with trompe l'oeil statue of Demosthenes in his niche.   149

Figure 5.14. 1894 interior detail of fig. 5.4. House right proscenium arch "Girac" column supporting Rossini and Balfe. On house left "Lilly" supported Gounod and Haydn.   149

Figure 5.15. 1894 interior detail of fig. 5.4. George Washington, centered in the proscenium arch above the stage. Note banners held in eagles' beaks proclaiming "Pro Deo et Patria" (For God and Country) and "E Pluribus Unum" (From Many, One). The Father of the Country appropriately holds the Declaration of Independence.   150

Figure 6.1. The first photograph of a Washington Hall theatre audience as seen from the stage. *Dome* 1912, 291.   158

Figure 6.2. The first photograph of a Washington Hall film audience as seen from the point of view of the screen. *Dome* 1916, 156.   159

Figure 6.3. Sanborn Insurance Map 1917. Note the 1907 addition, the change in the footprint that made the building asymmetrical, and the nearby privy that served Washington Hall. 169

Figure 6.4a, b, c. Facilities Survey 1942–43, April 1943, Notre Dame Architectural Drawings, Plans, and Views (hereafter UNDD), UNDA. The second-floor plan shows the 1907 addition, the 14' x 18' scenery storage area with direct access to the stage, and the 1908 indoor toilet room and manager's room, each with direct access to the stage (former music rooms). The first indoor toilet in Washington Hall made it no longer necessary to leave the building to go to the privy that since 1883 had stood east of the building between Washington Hall and the Old Gymnasium (see fig. 6.3). Note the Brownson Recreation Room on the first floor and the Assembly Room on the third. 170–171

Figure 6.5. *Twelfth Night,* with new scenery, Easter Monday, April 20, 1908. *Dome* 1908, n.p. Note the very large music stand lights, reflecting the technology of the day. 172

Figure 6.6. The May 15, 1899, production of *Oedipus Tyrannus* was performed in Greek, but with an English libretto in the program. This photograph gives a rare glimpse of the house left Cicero, as well as the wing-and-drop staging system. There are five steps from orchestra to stage both left and right but not centered. Thirty-one actors appear onstage, bearded, in Greek costumes. The Sosman & Landis permanent valence curtain had replaced the 1885 Ackermann single curtain by this time. Note that the stage had a curved front with a row of footlights. *Scholastic* 32:32, May 20, 1899, 561; also see *Dome* 1906, n.p. 177

Figure 6.7. Cecil Birder as Grace Whitney in *The Galloper,* Dec. 13, 1911, an example of convincing (as opposed to parodic) cross-dressing convention of the time which appeared in the *Dome* 1913, 264, in an advertisement, on the same page as Wasson's Hair Restorer, indicating that Rockne was a customer. 180

Figure 6.8. Knute Rockne, All-American flautist and actor, performing on the Washington Hall stage (lower right corner) as Pearly in *What's Next* with five other Notre Dame "leading ladies." *Dome* 1914, 127. 182

Figure 6.9. Gold And Blue Serenaders, picture with program, twenty-six in blackface. *Dome* 1914, 125. 184

Figure 7.1. The earliest surviving photograph of the Ghost of Washington Hall. *Dome* 1921, 305.   209

Figure 7.2. "The Horn Blows at Midnight / Ghost of Washington Hall Rides Again" includes an actual picture (caught on film!) of the Ghost on the stage with footlights and boards and an orchestra pit for a grand piano (with the auditorium in the background). *Scholastic* 87:3, April 5, 1946, 10.   215

Figure 8.1. Washington Hall's exterior south entrance stairs, removed and replaced by interior staircases in 1933, necessitated the relocation of Bill's Barber Shop and the Western Union Office, which had previously occupied the ground-floor rooms that became interior staircases. This is one of the last photos of Washington Hall's exterior south steps, from *Scholastic* 66:7, Nov. 4, 1932, 2.   225

Figure 8.2. Students on the south entrance stairs to Washington Hall in the early 1930s. Note the Western Union sign on the southwest corner of the building where the office was; Bill's Barber Shop occupied the southeast corner. Both offices were taken over by interior staircases with the conversion. Bagby Negatives (hereafter GBBY) 45 G/307, UNDA.   226

Figure 8.3. Washington Hall after the removal of the south exterior stairs in 1933. Note the diagonal slate pattern on the tower roof, an aspect of the original Edbrooke design. Notre Dame University Photographer (hereafter GPHR) 45-0062, UNDA.   228

Figure 8.4. Program frontispiece, *The Merry Wives of Windsor* (Dec. 15, 16, 1941), with William M. Hickey as Falstaff with dagger and tankard. William Farmer private collection.   242

Figure 8.5. Nuns at summer commencement on the Washington Hall stage, Aug. 3, 1937, UDIS 25/10, UNDA.   248

Figure 8.6. Nuns' Summer School Theatre, July 23–24, 1953, GDIS 35/07, UNDA. The back of the photograph reads "Curtain call for 'A Soul in Fine Array,' written and directed by Michael Casey. The nuns all teach speech and dramatics in high schools throughout the country." Photograph by M. Bruce Harlan.   250

Figure 9.1. Scaffolding in place for the summer 1956 remodeling and redecorating, taken from the stage looking into the house. Photograph by M. Bruce Harlan, GPHR 45-2867, UNDA.   267

Figure 9.2. *Good News,* the first musical in the remodeled Washington Hall, May 1957. Note Phil Donahue (first row, fifth from left). In this cast of forty-five, twenty-one are women, or 47 percent, seventeen years before Notre Dame became coeducational. Jerry Dodge (first row, third from left) created the role of Barnaby in the original Broadway production of *Hello, Dolly!* in 1964. Courtesy of Barbara Benford Trafficanda (middle row, eighth from left). Photograph by M. Bruce Harlan, GPHR 45-3089, UNDA.   275

Figure 9.3. "Get Me to the Church on Time" scene from *My Fair Lady,* May 1964, one of Father Art's many great triumphs on the Washington Hall stage, with Robert Oberkoetter as Alfred P. Doolittle (center) and a cast of fifty-eight. Photograph by M. Bruce Harlan, Arthur Harvey Papers (hereafter GHRV) 04-17, UNDA.   279

Figure 10.1. New York Governor Mario Cuomo speaking in Washington Hall in the best tradition of nineteenth-century oratory on a stiflingly hot evening before the building was air-conditioned, Sept. 13, 1984; his speech was entitled "Religious Belief and Public Morality: A Catholic Governor's Perspective." Photograph by M. Bruce Harlan, GPHR 35-9184, UNDA.   295

Figure 10.2. Cast of Arthur Miller's *Death of a Salesman,* Oct. 1987, directed by Father Arthur S. Harvey. Seated first row, from left: Jim Nelis, Nick Simon, Kevin Kennedy, Daniel Daily, Matt Nash, Siiri Scott, Jack Blakey. Standing second row, from left: Kassie Misiewicz, Diane Tracy, P. J. Gibbons, Nancy O'Connor, Laurie Shea, unknown, Rachel Durkin, unknown, Father Art Harvey (seated), unknown, Mark Costanzi, Michael Murphy, Willard Neuert, Robin Dvorak, Ted Manier, Marty Tracey. GHRV 04-43, UNDA.   309

Figure 10.3. Bertolt Brecht's *The Life of Galileo* directed by Holger Teschke (standing), with guest artist Tony Lawton ('89) as Galileo (seated on left), and with Katy Kertez as Virginia, April 2002, as part of the larger "Galileo and the Church Conference." *Scholastic* 143:11, April 11, 2002, 32.   312

Chapter 1. The True Ghosts of Washington Hall

1. The Reverend Theodore M. Hesburgh, C.S.C., interview with the author, Oct. 3, 2003.

2. Louis Althusser, "Ideology and Ideological State Apparatuses," in *Lenin and Philosophy and Other Essays* (New York: Monthly Review Press, 1971).

3. Robert Tittler, *Architecture and Power: The Town Hall and the English Urban Community c. 1500–1640* (Oxford: Clarendon Press, 1991), 131.

4. See W. H. Auden, "The Poet & the City," in *The Dyer's Hand and Other Essays* (New York: Random House, 1962), 72–89. Auden asserts that revelatory personal deeds occur in the private sphere in the modern world, with the public sphere the place we make our living but do not disclose. In the postmodern world since Auden wrote, we have seen a return to the revelatory public sphere in reality television shows, on-camera wedding proposals, and YouTube's premise of "Broadcast Yourself."

5. See Robert T. Burns, *Being Catholic, Being American: The Notre Dame Story, 1842–1934* and *Being Catholic, Being American: The Notre Dame Story, 1934–1952,* 2 vols. (Notre Dame, Ind.: University of Notre Dame Press, 1999, 2000).

6. If not before, the election of John F. Kennedy in 1960 settled forever the issue of being American and being Catholic.

7. I wish neither to ignore nor to disparage African drumming, Native American smoke signals, and European signal fires (beacons), all of which were ancient forms of distance communication (if perhaps more limited in terms of content and speed than electric telegraphy).

8. Since Morse had invented the telegraph on May 24, 1844, remote transmission of information was newly possible at this time, but not until Bell invented the telephone in 1876 could music be remotely

accessed. Edison's phonograph in 1877 was the first step toward making "stored" music a reality. Of course, striking clocks (fourteenth century), music boxes (eighteenth century), and player pianos (nineteenth century) all prefigured the eventual electrical revolution.

9. See Jim Collins, *Uncommon Cultures: Popular Culture and Post-Modernism* (New York: Routledge, 1989).

10. See the *OED*. We retain the dynamic quality of the word today when referring to someone who displays outrageous behavior in public.

11. This parallels the growth in the nation. The 1880 census recorded the U.S. population at just over 50 million. By 1920 it had more than doubled to just over 106 million. In 2000 the population had more than doubled again to nearly 250 million. A renovation of the Joyce Center in 2009 reduced the seating of its largest venue from 11,418 to 9,800.

Chapter 2. Before the First Washington Hall, 1842–1864

1. See the appendix for the complete article. By the mid-nineteenth century, the word *saloon* could mean a drinking bar, but a more usual meaning from the mid-eighteenth century was "a large apartment or hall, esp. in a hotel or other place of public resort, adapted for assemblies, entertainments, exhibitions, etc." (*OED*). M. R. K.'s reference to the South Bend band arriving by horse-drawn wagon suggests that Notre Dame did not yet have its own functioning band in 1845.

2. In addition to premiums—rewards or prizes for excellence (still given at 4-H county fairs in Indiana)—students were awarded a first and second accessit (honorable mention from *proxime accessit*, that is, "he came nearest"). Commencement ceremonies occurred possibly as early as 1843 and certainly by 1844, and Lyons's *Silver Jubilee* describes Alexander Coquillard as the first student at Notre Dame (34, 93). Notre Dame awarded its first earned degrees in 1849 to Cornelius Henry Gillespie and Richard A. Shortis, both of whom became Holy Cross priests. Father Shortis (1815–87) taught at Notre Dame from 1854 to 1860. Father Gilles pie (1831–74) had a distinguished career at Notre Dame from his graduation until his death. Father Neal Gillespie's sister, of course, was Mother Mary Angela Gillespie, C.S.C., the founder of Saint Mary's Academy (later College) in 1844. Their mother and stepfather, Mary and William Phelan, were early patrons and donors.

3. Local Council of the Trades, 1845–46 (June 27, 1846), 1970/15, 37, Indiana Province Archives Center (hereafter cited as IPAC).

4. Council of Professors, II (July 1, 1846), 1970/02, 9, IPAC. Father François (Francis) Cointet, C.S.C., was born in 1816 in France and ordained a diocesan priest in LeMans in 1839. He arrived in spring 1843 for the Notre Dame mission and began his Holy Cross novitiate that fall, professing Sept. 5, 1846, during which time he was director of studies at Notre Dame. He worked in New Orleans 1849–51 where he died of cholera in 1854. Initially buried in the crypt at Notre Dame, his body was transferred to the Log Chapel in 1987. See Edward Sorin, C.S.C., *The Chronicles of Notre Dame du Lac,* trans. John M. Toohey, C.S.C., ed. James T. Connelly, C.S.C. (Notre Dame, Ind.: University of Notre Dame Press, 1992), 130–31.

5. Archives of the Minor Chapter, 1847–1854 (June 28, 1847), 1970/15, n.p., IPAC. Lyons (*The Silver Jubilee of the University of Notre Dame, June 23rd, 1869* [Chicago: E. B. Myers, 1869], 37–38) credited as founders of the performing arts programs Brother Basil (band and philharmonic societies), Father Shaw (literary societies, which created the traditions of the Thespian and Dramatic societies), and Professor Girac (college choir). The purchasing power of $55 in 1847 equals almost $1,500 in 2008. See Lawrence H. Officer and Samuel H. Williamson, "Purchasing Power of Money in The United States from 1774 to 2008." Measuring Worth, 2009. URL http://www.measuringworth.com/ppowerUS/ (accessed June 10, 2010).

6. Summer Shakespeare returned to Notre Dame in 1940 with the inauguration of the Summer Drama Project's production of *Twelfth Night,* under the direction of Robert W. Speaight, for which fifteen nuns attending summer school worked in the costume shop in Cushing Hall of Engineering as seamstresses for the show. The performance venue was outdoors for this production (on the south side of the Commerce Building, now Hurley Hall) and not in Washington Hall. In 2000 Summer Shakespeare at Notre Dame premiered in Washington Hall with *The Taming of the Shrew*; in 2004 *Romeo and Juliet* was the last Summer Shakespeare production in Washington Hall before moving to the Decio Mainstage Theatre in the DeBartolo Center for the Performing Arts in 2005 for *Henry V.*

7. Brother Gatian's "Journal Kept by the Secretary to Serve in the Composition of the Chronicle" (hereafter cited as Brother Gatian's "Journal"), Feb. 8, 1847–Jan. 10, 1849, 1970/02, 11, IPAC. This confirms that the Notre Dame Band was in place by July 4, 1847. In complete contrast, low morale caused by rampant disease plagued the later August commencement. Gatian reported, "The plays were poorly executed. Not over a hundred strangers were present" (14).

8. Brother Gatian (Urbain Monsimer), 1826–60, came to the United States from France in 1841 with Father Sorin. When he used the word *shed* in English, indeed he may have meant *appentis*—the connotation of *shed* in English—but he could just as easily have meant *hangar* (outbuilding) or *atelier* (workshop), both of which relate to larger and more substantial structures.

9. Archives of the Minor Chapter, 1847–1854 (Nov. 2, 1847), 1970/15, n.p., IPAC. Also in Local Council Minutes [Transcriptions] (March 1846–Aug. 27, 1857), 1970/15, 28, IPAC.

10. And while the band needed both rehearsal and performance spaces on campus, it is well to remember that the peripatetic cornet band performed off-campus, too, at such venues as the home of Alexis Coquillard on June 30, 1849. See *South Bend Register,* June 28, 1849, f. 2, col. 4. Coquillard (1795–1855) is traditionally viewed as the founder of the city of South Bend.

11. "The new church, instead of being built upon the hill at a distance from the college, will form a lateral wing of the same college, this being more advantageous to the community and to the University, since one or two large rooms may be placed easily reserved under that church." See Archives of the Minor Chapter, 1847–1854 (Dec. 4, 1847), n.p., IPAC. Also in Local Council Minutes [Transcriptions] (March 1846–Aug. 27, 1857), 29.

12. Lyons, *Silver Jubilee,* 32. Notre Dame was a largely self-sustaining community well into the twentieth century. Not only did the university farm the land surrounding the academic buildings on its property two miles north of South Bend, but it also owned considerable acreage in the northeast quadrant of St. Joseph County which supplied the growing needs of an ever-expanding campus. Father Alexis Granger, C.S.C. (1817–93), was in charge of the St. Joseph Farm early on, with the nearby unincorporated community of Granger coincidentally bearing his name (Timothy Edward Howard's *A History of St. Joseph County Indiana* [Chicago: Lewis, 1907] attributes the name of the town founded in 1883 by Thomas J. Foster to the Grange movement of the late ninteenth century; see 1:310–11). The Holy Cross Brothers operated the St. Joseph Farm through the 1970s, and the property was sold in 2008.

13. Archives of the Minor Chapter, 1847–1854 (May 22, 1848), n.p., IPAC. According to Father Sorin, construction on the barn began during the summer of 1845. The structure was 80' x 40' with a full basement and an 8' ceiling "which can winter 200 sheep and in which all the potatoes and other roots that the farm produces and that need to be pro-

tected from freezing may be stored away." Sorin predicted it would last twenty-five or thirty years; in a later hand a note in the margin states that the "old barn was pulled down in 1896." Sorin indicated that the Dec. 17, 1856, fire consumed the horse stable "and all that belonged to it," a different structure from the sheep and hay barn described above. See Sorin, *Chronicles,* 51, 190–91.

14. Barns can make very good theatres and continue to serve as "found" spaces for theatre companies. The Barn Theatre in Augusta, Michigan, occupied an abandoned dairy barn in 1949 and has continued for over half a century as Michigan's oldest professional Equity summer stock theatre company. There is also Round Barn Theatre in Amish Acres near Nappanee, Indiana.

15. Brother Gatian's "Journal," July 5, 1848, 23–24, IPAC.

16. Archives of the Minor Chapter, 1847–1854 (Dec. 18, 1848), n.p., IPAC.

17. Arthur J. Hope, C.S.C. *Notre Dame: One Hundred Years,* rev. ed. (Notre Dame, Ind.: University of Notre Dame Press, 1948), 79.

18. Sorin, *Chronicles,* 88–89.

19. Archives of the Minor Chapter, 1847–1854 (June 17, 1850), n.p., IPAC.

20. Neal H. Gillespie's letter to his mother [Mrs. Phelan], Feb. 21, 1852, Thomas Ewing Family Papers (hereafter cited as CEWI) 3/01, University of Notre Dame Archives (hereafter cited as UNDA). The Forty Hours devotion is "a form of prayer before the Blessed Sacrament as it is solemnly exposed during an uninterrupted period of forty hours" (*The HarperCollins Encyclopedia of Catholicism,* ed. Richard P. McBrien [New York: HarperCollins, 1995], 536). Although frequently connected to Holy Saturday, in this case the penitential event preceded Ash Wednesday (Feb. 25 in 1852). David-Augustin de Brueys wrote the farce *L'Avocat Patelin* (*The Wheedling Lawyer*) in 1706, based on an anonymous fifteenth-century French farce. While Joseph J. Ellis may be correct that Washington's Birthday had become a national holiday by 1790 (*His Excellency: George Washington* [New York: Knopf, 2004], 194), Washington's papers suggest that efforts had begun as early as 1778. Washington was born on Feb. 11, 1732, under the Julian (Old Style) calendar, but with the adoption of the Gregorian (New Style) in 1752, his birthday became Feb. 22. See Donald Jackson and Dorothy Twohig, eds., *The Diaries of George Washington,* vol. 6, *January 1790–December 1799* (Charlottesville: University Press of Virginia, 1979), 282, and Donald Jackson, ed., *The Diaries of George Washington,* vol. 1, *1748–1765* (Charlottesville: University Press

of Virginia, 1976), 6. Also see "The Papers of George Washington" at http://gwpapers.virginia.edu/project/faq/index.html (accessed Aug. 15, 2008). Max Girac was professor of Latin, Greek, French, and Music from 1850 to 1869. George Woodworth, the "captain" of St. Joseph Company's disastrous trek in 1850 to the California goldfields funded by the university, had two sons at Notre Dame during this period. See Marvin R. O'Connell, *Edward Sorin* (Notre Dame, Ind.: University of Notre Dame Press, 2001), 253–62, 340.

21. Description & Inventory of Notre Dame Buildings 1854/10, Notre Dame Miscellaneous University Records (hereafter cited as UNDR) 4/9, UNDA.

22. Minutes of the Local Council, May 12, 1856, 5r, IPAC.

23. Minutes of the Local Council, Jan. 19, 1857, 8v, IPAC.

24. Minutes of the Local Council, Nov. 30, 1857, 28, IPAC. In this case, a wood shed is clearly a large free-standing structure.

25. Financial Journal #5, June 14, 1862, Early Notre Dame Student, Class, and Financial Record Books (hereafter cited as ULDG), 245, UNDA.

26. Minutes of the Local Council, June 3, 1861, 57r, IPAC.

27. Minutes of the Local Council, June 30, 1862, 67r, IPAC.

28. See *Catalogue* (June 26, 1861), for Dramatic Society information and the *Scholastic* 5:42, June 29, 1872, 3.

29. Minutes of the Local Council, May 12, 1862, 66r, IPAC. This word *shed* here clearly means a substantial building, since we know the outcome of this project is a 100' x 50' three-story structure.

30. Minutes of the Local Council, May 19, 1862, 66r, IPAC. The terms *junior* and *senior* are confusing, of course, because of today's meanings. At this time, students aged seventeen and over typically composed the senior or collegiate division (also called Brownson Hall or College); those thirteen through sixteen were in the junior or preparatory division (also called Carroll Hall or College); and grade school pupils below age thirteen formed the minim department (St. Edward's Hall). Strict age segregation occurred and extended to recreational facilities. Adding to the complication is that by the 1880s, a student retained minim status until he turned fourteen, and there would eventually be junior and senior years for college students as exist today. See *Scholastic* 15:2, Sept. 17, 1881, 27. The word *minim* is short for minimus, a designation for the youngest pupils common to boarding schools.

31. Minutes of the Local Council, May 26, 1862, 66r; June 16, 1862, 66v; June 23, 1862, 66v, IPAC. This likely refers to James O'Brien, who was professor of rhetoric and elocution. Brother Peter (Felix Whaller), 1823–85, is buried at Notre Dame; Brother Isidore (Patrick Crowley),

1828–98, is buried in Holy Cross College in New Orleans. Brother Maximus (Eugene Petit), 1821–96, was born in France and is buried in Assumption Cemetery near St. Edward's University in Austin, Texas; Brother Gabriel (Bernard Smyth or Smith), 1833–94, was born in Ireland and is buried in the C.S.C. Community Cemetery at Notre Dame.

32. Minutes of the Local Council, June 30, 1862, 67r, IPAC.

33. Financial Journal #5, June 14, 1862–Aug. 26, 1862, 245, 255, 265, 294, ULDG, UNDA. Bills would always be paid after goods arrived or work occurred, and thus reflect earlier activity. The nails and bricks paid for in July and August of 1862 were very likely delivered and used earlier.

34. *Scholastic* 5:42, June 29, 1872, 3.

35. Sorin letter to Mrs. Phelan, July 24, 1862, CEWI, 1/03, UNDA.

36. "Thomey" is almost certainly Thomas W. Ewing, Mrs. Phelan's grandson, who came to Notre Dame in 1861 at age ten and stayed until 1869.

37. Sorin letter to Mrs. Phelan, Aug. 4, 1862, CEW1 1/03, UNDA. Mary Madeline Miers Gillespie Phelan (1804–87) and her second husband, William, of Lancaster, Ohio, were early patrons and donors. It is no exaggeration to assert that their major donation in 1855 saved the university; O'Connell states that the contribution "can hardly be over-emphasized" (348). Two of Mrs. Phelan's children from her first marriage were the Reverend Cornelius (Neal) Gillespie, C.S.C. (1831–74), an 1849 graduate; and Mother Mary Angela Gillespie (1824–87), who would become the first director of the Academy at Bertrand which would become Saint Mary's College. From her marriage in 1821 to John Purcell Gilles-pie, she had three children. The third Gillespie child, Maria Rebecca (1828–92), married the Honorable Philemon Beecher Ewing (1820–96), who was the first child of Senator Thomas Ewing (1789–1871) and Maria Wills Boyle (1801–64), whose uncle was Philemon Beecher (1776–1839). Senator Ewing had informally adopted William Tecumseh Sherman at the age of nine, and Sherman married Ellen Boyle Ewing in 1850. Mr. Gillespie died in 1836, and his widow married William Phelan (1793–1856) of Lancaster, Ohio, in 1841 (Sharon Sumpter, e-mail to author, Aug. 4, 2006). Also see *Guide to the Microfilm Edition of the Thomas Ewing, Sr., Papers* (Notre Dame, Ind.: University of Notre Dame Archives Publications, 1967); Thomas T. McAvoy and Lawrence J. Bradley, *Guide to the Micro-film Edition of the William Tecumseh Sherman Family Papers (1808–1891)* (Notre Dame, Ind.: University of Notre Dame Archives Publications, 1967); and *Scholastic* 16:9, Nov. 4, 1882, 137–38.

38. Financial Ledger #5, Jan. 8, 1863, 376–77, ULDG, UNDA.

39. Minutes of the Local Council, Sept. 29, 1862, 70r, IPAC.

40. Minutes of the Local Council, Oct. 6, 1862, 70v, IPAC. In 1862 $200 had the purchasing power of almost $4,500 in 2008, about the cost of a professional billiard table today (www.measuringworth.com).

41. Minutes of the Local Council, Dec. 22, 1862, 74v, IPAC.

42. Minutes of the Local Council, Jan. 24, 1863, 76r–v, IPAC.

43. Minutes of the Local Council, Feb. 9, 1863, 78v, IPAC. Five hundred dollars in 1863 had the purchasing power of nearly $9,000 in 2008 (www.measuringworth.com). Notre Dame provided professors in the 1860s room and board in addition to their salaries.

44. Financial Ledger #5, 157, 866, ULDG, UNDA. From January through June of 1861, for example, the university spent more on musical instruments ($504.08) than on chemistry equipment ($369.48).

45. Minutes of the Local Council, June 1, 1863, 81r, IPAC.

46. Minutes of the Local Council, June 22, 1863, 81v, IPAC. George O'Brian was principal of the Deaf and Dumb Department and professor of Latin and English, 1862–66; M. Campion was professor of Latin and Greek, 1864–67.

47. See Thomas J. Schlereth, *The University of Notre Dame: A Portrait of Its History and Campus* (Notre Dame, Ind.: University of Notre Dame Press, 1976), 101, and *Scholastic* 5:42, June 29, 1872, 3.

48. Financial Journal #5, Dec. 9, 1863, 543, ULDG, UNDA. The total cost was $211.97 paid to A. S. Baker. Like any construction project, this could be considered a cost overrun of nearly 17 percent above the $1,200 established cost of the building.

49. *New York Tablet* 7:41, March 12, 1864, 10–11. Brother Basil also directed the orchestra for the June 1864 Exhibition Day (see Minutes of the Local Council, May 23, 1864, 91r, IPAC). The Province Archives confirm that Brother Basil (John Magus) was born in Freihung, Bavaria, in 1828 and professed his vows in 1853. He served as professor of music and organist from 1854 until his death in 1909, and was the person authorized to purchase new pianos to replace those burned in the Great Fire of 1879 (Jacqueline Dougherty, e-mail to author, Oct. 20, 2004). M. La Chassaigne was professor of drawing and painting. Howard was professor of mathematics and astronomy, and served as secretary of the faculty.

50. *New York Tablet* 7:41, March 12, 1864, 10–11.

Chapter 3. The First Washington Hall, 1864–1879

1. *A Guide to the University of Notre Dame, and the Academy of St. Mary of the Immaculate Conception, Near South Bend, Indiana.* (Philadelphia: J. B. Chandler, 1865), frontispiece. Also see *Twenty-First Annual*

Catalogue of the Officers and Students of the University of Notre Dame, Indiana, for the Academic Year, 1864–65 (Notre Dame, Ind.: Printed at the Office of the "Ave Maria," 1865), frontispiece, the first catalogue in which this engraving appears.

2. *Guide*, 26–28.

3. Sorin letter to Mrs. Phelan, March 1, 1864, CEWI 1/03–06, UNDA. Sorin wrote in his own hand on the blank side of "To the Patrons of the University of Notre Dame," a very early example of a "form" document that could be easily personalized. *A Brief History of the University of Notre Dame du Lac* confirms that Washington Hall also "was adorned with the benevolent portrait of the Father of his country" (88).

4. See *Scholastic* 12:4, Sept. 28, 1878, 54–56. For productions of *The Enchanted Hostelry* or *The Seven Travellers* in 1869, 1873, and 1878, there was no fly space to create the descent of Mysticus.

5. Minutes of the Local Council, March 21, 1864, 88r–v, IPAC.

6. Minutes of the Local Council, May 16, 1864, 90v, IPAC.

7. *Scholastic* 5:42, June 29, 1872, 3. *Henry IV* was the first Shakespeare play produced at Notre Dame (in conjunction with the 1847 commencement).

8. Minutes of the Local Council, Nov. 14, 1864, 99r–v, IPAC.

9. Sorin letter to Mrs. Phelan, Oct. 20, 1864, CEWI 1/4, UNDA.

10. Minutes of the Local Council, Sept. 27, 1864, 97v, IPAC.

11. Howard, *History of St. Joseph County* (2:638); Randy McGuire (e-mail to author, March 22, 2006); Joan Zurhellen (e-mail to author, May 19, 2006).

12. Minutes of the Local Council, Sept. 18, 1864, 96v, IPAC.

13. Financial Journal #5, Nov. 4, 1864–Aug. 11, 1866, 711–1081, ULDG, UNDA.

14. Minutes of the Local Council, Nov. 14, 1864, 99r–v; Nov. 21, 1864, 100r, IPAC.

15. See Financial Journal #5, Jan. 28, 1865, and Oct. 6, 1865, 757, 924, ULDG, UNDA.

16. Minutes of the Local Council, Aug. 30, 1865, 8, IPAC. Knute Rockne also received a merit scholarship in music when he was a student at Notre Dame. See *The Autobiography of Knute K. Rockne,* ed. Bonnie Skiles Rockne, intro. John Cavanaugh, C.S.C. (Indianapolis: Bobbs-Merrill, 1930), 44.

17. Minutes of the Local Council, Feb. 20, 1865, 104v, IPAC. The superior general administers the worldwide Congregation of Holy Cross, while the (father) provincial heads a province within the Congregation of Holy Cross. The (father) superior supervises an institution or ministry

within a province. Jacqueline Dougherty at the Provincial Archives stated, "The Superior General would be like a president, a Provincial like a governor of a state and a Superior like a mayor of a city in a state" (e-mail to author, Jan. 12, 2007).

18. Having purchased a new grand piano for Washington Hall in 1986, the university constructed a secure "box" stage left in the wings both to house and protect it when not in use.

19. Minutes of the Local Council, April 17, 1865, f 107r, IPAC.

20. Local Council Minute Book, May 22, 1865, 1; May 29, 1865, 1; June 19, 1865, 3, IPAC. Fifty cents in 1865 equals almost seven dollars in 2009.

21. *Twenty-First Annual Catalogue*, 60.

22. Wilson D. Miscamble, ed., *Go Forth and Do Good: Memorable Notre Dame Commencement Addresses* (Notre Dame, Ind.: University of Notre Dame Press, 2003), 47.

23. Ellie Ewing letter to General Sherman, July 8, 1865, CEW1 1/4, UNDA. Sherman's lifelong nickname was "Cump," which his niece spells "Comp" in her letter. See McAvoy and Bradley, *Guide to the Microfilm Edition*, 7.

24. Local Council Minute Book, Sept. 11, 1865, 9, IPAC.

25. Financial Journal #5, Dec. 9, 1865, 962: "$515.67, 20 workmen, one up to 10 days at $3.50, including 9477 ft. Lumber @ 25.00 to P. Huff for $236.92," ULDG, UNDA.

26. Local Council Minute Book, Sept. 11, 1865, 9, IPAC.

27. Local Council Minute Book, Sept. 11, 1865, 9, Sept. 18, 1865, 9–10, IPAC. Brother Adolphus (Patrick Walsh, born in Waterford, Ireland, between 1819 and 1829, but most likely in 1827, and died in Watertown, Wis., in 1888) was the director of working brothers in 1864 and became the assistant prefect of the senior department in 1866.

28. Calculations of the loss in the fire of 1879, Notre Dame Miscellaneous University Records (hereafter referred to as UNDR) 4/11, UNDA.

29. Local Council Minute Book, Oct. 2, 1865, 10, IPAC.

30. Local Council Minute Book, Nov. 30, 1865, 15, IPAC.

31. Local Council Minute Book, Feb. 12, 19, 1866, 22, IPAC.

32. Local Council Minute Book, Feb. 26, 1866, 23, IPAC.

33. Local Council Minute Book, April 9, 1866, 27, IPAC.

34. Local Council Minute Book, Jan. 7, 1867, 45, IPAC. Brother Anthony (Henry Reissacher), born in Germany in 1817, professed vows in 1853, and died in 1874 at Notre Dame and is buried there. From the 1850s he was director of apprentices and sacristan; by 1864 he was a blacksmith

and director of the blacksmith shop. Brother Isidore (Patrick) Crowley, born in Ireland in 1828, was a novitiate in 1866, professed vows in 1868, and from the 1880s until his death in 1898 served at Holy Cross College in New Orleans where he is buried.

35. Local Council Minute Book, Oct. 9, 1866, 39, IPAC.

36. Local Council Minute Book, Oct. 1, 1866, 38, IPAC.

37. See the National Climatic Data Center (U.S. Department of Commerce) at http://www.ncdc.noaa.gov/oa/climate/online/ccd/snowfall.html for additional information (accessed Aug. 17, 2008).

38. Local Council Minute Book, Sept. 10, 17, 24, 1866, 36–37, IPAC.

39. Local Council Minute Book, March 2, 1868, 69; May 25, 1868, 72, IPAC.

40. *Scholastic* 1:2, Sept. 14, 1867, 6. The *Scholastic* began life as *The Scholastic Year* (1 & 2) and thereafter was known as the *Notre Dame Scholastic, The Scholastic,* and *Scholastic.* Throughout the body of this book, I call it the *Scholastic,* and in notes it appears as simply *Scholastic.*

41. *Scholastic* 1:3, Sept. 21, 1867, 6.

42. Local Council Minute Book, Sept. 23, 1867, 63, IPAC.

43. *Scholastic* 1:5, Oct. 5, 1867, 7. The *OED* defines *grainer* from the 1830s as "one who paints in imitation of the grain of wood or the markings of marble." It is clear from this description that the white panels were roughened or "frosted" to accept a frieze coat, a thin layer of plaster on which murals could be painted.

44. *Scholastic* 1:17, Dec. 28, 1867, 3–4.

45. *Scholastic* 1:24, Feb. 15, 1868, 2–3.

46. *Scholastic* 1:24, Feb. 15, 1868, 3. Allen A. Griffith was professor of elocution at Notre Dame 1866–69 and wrote *Lessons in Elocution with Numerous Selections, Analyzed for Practice,* 2nd ed. (Chicago: Adams, Blackmer, and Lyon, 1865), and *A Drill Book for Practice of the Principles of Vocal Physiology, and Acquiring the Art of Elocution and Oratory* (Chicago: Adams, Blackmer, and Lyon, 1868). Elocution classes at this time seem to have been scheduled early in the second semester. These classes supported the elocution and oratory area from which the present-day Department of Film, Television, and Theatre claims its provenance.

47. *Scholastic* 1:26, Feb. 29, 1868, 1–3.

48. *Scholastic* 1:41, June 12, 1868, 6–8; 1:43, June 27, 1868, 2. C. A. B. Von Weller was professor of painting and drawing, 1867–71.

49. *Scholastic* 2:7, Oct. 17, 1868, 53–56. Also see Joseph A. Lyons, *The Silver Jubilee of the University of Notre Dame, June 23rd, 1869* (Chicago: E. B. Myers, 1869), 201–5.

50. Lyons, *Silver Jubilee,* 206, 210.

51. Ibid., 210–13.

52. Ibid., 225–28, 230.

53. Ibid., 65–66.

54. *Scholastic* 2:7, Oct. 17, 1868, 54.

55. *Scholastic* 2:13, Nov. 28, 1868, 102; 2:15, Dec. 19, 1868, 117; 2:18, Jan. 9, 1869, 142–43.

56. *Scholastic* 2:18, Jan. 9, 1869, 142–43.

57. Washington Day celebration program, 1869, William Farmer private collection.

58. Father Augustus Lemonnier died at the age of thirty-five on Oct. 29, 1874, just a month after his approval of this constitution, having served only two years as president of the university. Born in France on April 8, 1839, he entered the Congregation of Holy Cross in 1860, came to America in 1861 (where he joined his uncle, Father Sorin, at Notre Dame), and was ordained a priest on Nov. 4, 1863. His obituary in the *Scholastic* 8:6, Oct. 31, 1874, 56, praised his many talents, including writing "several very fine dramatic productions," and pointed out that he "was always noted for the encouragement he gave to the Fine Arts at Notre Dame. An amateur in painting, he did all in his power to promote a love for art among the students of the College. It was through his efforts that the monthly musical entertainments were established at the University, and to him are the different musical, literary and dramatic societies indebted for much of their success." Today we most often associate Father Lemonnier with the founding of the library; indeed, the Lemonnier Circulating Library was so named almost immediately upon his death.

59. *Philomathean Constitution* (1858), 6–7, St. Cecilia Philomathean Society (hereafter referred to as UCPS), UNDA. Cornelius "Neal" H. Gillespie was active in theatre and music for a quarter of a century, from the early days of the university until his death two weeks after Father Lemonnier's on Nov. 12, 1874, at the age of forty-three. He founded both the Thespian Society and the St. Aloysius Philodemic Society and first directed the St. Cecilia Philomathean Association. Also highly literarily inclined, he both created and served as the first manager of the *Scholastic* as well as being instrumental in the establishment of the Ave Maria Press. On his death, the Chorus became the Gillespie Choral Union, a recognition also of his abiding musical interests. Joseph A. Lyons was professor of Latin and elocution from 1858 to 1888. With the untimely deaths of both Lemonnier and Gillespie, Lyons ably took on added responsibilities both for "exhibitions" (beyond his previous involvement

with the Philomatheans) and as publisher of the *Scholastic* for the next generation. See *Scholastic* 8:9, Nov. 21, 1874, 105–6.

60. *Philomathean Constitution* (1858), 6–7, UCPS, UNDA.

61. *Philomathean Constitution* (1858), 11 [printed], 9 [handwritten edited version], UCPS, UNDA.

62. "Draft for Prospectus for Notre Dame. August 15, 1868," Edward Sorin, C.S.C., Collection 1868, 1970/01, 65–66, IPAC.

63. *Philomathean Constitution* (1858), 14–15, UCPS, UNDA.

64. Lyons, *Silver Jubilee*, 246; *Scholastic* 1:5, Oct. 5, 1867, 3. Originally the organization was called "The St. Aloysius Literary and Historical Society." Saint Aloysius Gonzaga (1568–91) is the patron saint of Catholic youth.

65. *Scholastic* 6:36, May 17, 1873, 285–86. Father Michael B. Brown was professor of Latin and Greek, 1862–74; he founded the St. Edward's Society and served as prefect of studies under Father Lemonnier.

66. Lyons, *Silver Jubilee*, 248.

67. *Scholastic* 4:20, June 3, 1871, 6.

68. *Scholastic* 4:19, May 27, 1871, 6.

69. Ibid., 7.

70. Local Council Minute Book, April 28, 1871, 109, IPAC.

71. Local Council Minute Book, Feb. 21, 1873, 135, IPAC.

72. *Scholastic* 6:25, March 1, 1873, 194–95.

73. *Scholastic* 8:11, Dec. 5, 1874, 138.

74. *Scholastic* 8:39, June 23, 1875, 584. The university blessed the cornerstone of the new Sacred Heart Church on May 31, 1871, but four years later the church was not yet totally completed, although the nave was apparently serviceable. See *Scholastic* 4:20, June 3, 1871, 5–7.

75. Lyons, *Silver Jubilee*, 251.

76. *Scholastic* 3:16, April 16, 1870, 126.

77. *Scholastic* 3:17, April 30, 1870, 135.

78. *Scholastic* 6:27, March 15, 1873, 212. The earliest use of the word *minstrel* appeared in 1873 but in reference to Italian singing minstrels in the European rather than the American blackface tradition. The term *minstrel* has a long and distinguished history in English, of course, and only became related to race in a pejorative way in the nineteenth century. As early as 1450 in Bristol, England, for example, we know that guild payments to minstrels occurred. See my *Records of Early English Drama: Bristol* (Toronto: University of Toronto Press, 1997), 7, 153. The *OED* cites the first use of *minstrel* in relation to blackface performers nearly four centuries later in 1843. Oscar G. Brockett and Franklin Hildy confirm

that "the Minstrel Show was given its distinctive form" by 1846 with large companies by the 1870s and declining to "a mere curiosity" by 1919 (*History of the Theatre,* 9th ed. [Boston: Allyn & Bacon, 2003], 336–37). The format continued at Notre Dame with amateur blackface minstrel shows produced from the late nineteenth century until the 1940s, and Hollywood films paid homage to the "curiosity" in such films as *White Christmas* as late as the 1950s.

79. *Scholastic* 4:20, June 3, 1871, 7.

80. Ibid.

81. Local Council Minute Book, Jan. 10, 1873, 132, IPAC.

82. *Scholastic* 8:22, Feb. 20, 1875, 315.

83. *Scholastic* 8:13, Dec. 19, 1874, 169.

84. *Scholastic* 8:11, Dec. 5, 1874, 138–39.

85. *Scholastic* 8:19, Jan. 30, 1875, 268.

86. *Scholastic* 8:22, Feb. 20, 1875, 315.

87. *Scholastic* 8:23, Feb. 27, 1875, 329–30.

88. *Scholastic* 8:26, March 20, 1875, 377. Thomas F. O'Mahony was professor of natural sciences 1872–75.

89. *Scholastic* 8:38, June 12, 1875, 569–70.

90. Pope Pius IX, Giovanni Maria Mastai-Ferretti (May 13, 1792–Feb. 7, 1878) was made archbishop of Spoleto in 1827 and was elected pope in 1846. During his papacy of thirty-two years (he died the year after his Golden Jubilee), the dogmas of the Immaculate Conception (1854) and papal infallibility (the First Vatican Council, 1869–70) were declared. Pio Nono was beatified in 2000.

91. The *South Bend Herald* asserted this was the first time Father Haid's play had been produced "in the west" (*Major John Andre* prompt-book, William Farmer private collection). At the annual summer exercises eight years later, in 1885, the St. Cecilia Philomathean Society presented *The Execution of Major John Andre,* a historical drama in five acts, with a cast of characters identical to that of this 1877 production of *Major John Andre.* It is almost certainly the same play, although it has not been determined to what degree Haid used as a basis for his work William Dunlap's 1798 *André,* which is often credited with being the first American tragedy with an American subject. John André, a British officer and coconspirator of Benedict Arnold, was convicted of spying and hanged at the age of thirty on Oct. 2, 1780.

92. *South Bend Herald* clippings in the *Major John Andre* prompt-book. William Farmer private collection.

93. South Bend *Daily Tribune,* June 4, 1877, William Farmer private collection. The "Whiskey Ring" was a scandal exposed by 1875 which in-

volved the theft of federal taxes on liquor by corrupt but powerful Republican politicians.

94. Handwritten in *Major John Andre* promptbook. William Farmer private collection.

95. *Scholastic* 3:17, April 30, 1870, 126.

96. I am reminded of my arrival at Notre Dame in the summer of 1984, when I had a powerful computer on my desk that connected to nothing else but an adjacent printer. Useful for spreadsheets and word processing, it would take another decade before e-mail and the Internet seamlessly connected my desktop device to the larger world, and it is difficult now to remember "how we did things" before the introduction of this incredible technology. The same was true for telegraphy, telephonics, wireless radio transmission, film, and television, all transformative communication technologies.

97. *Scholastic* 7:13, Nov. 22, 1873, 100; 8:4, Oct. 17, 1874, 28; 8:22, Feb. 20, 1875, 315. James L. Ruddiman was instructor in telegraphy 1874–75.

98. Telegraph day books, Western Union Office, n.p., Nov.–Dec. 1875, ULDG 16/1 and 16/2, UNDA.

99. *Scholastic* 11:32, April 16, 1878, 506.

100. Alexander Graham Bell (1847–1922) invented the telephone in March 1876.

101. *Scholastic* 12:3, Sept. 21, 1878, 47.

102. *Scholastic* 12:5, Oct. 5, 1878, 78–79. *The Hidden Gem,* by Cardinal Wiseman, was previously produced at Notre Dame in June 1859 and again in the winter of 1863.

103. *Scholastic* 12:7, Oct. 19, 1878, 109.

104. Ibid.

105. *Scholastic* 11:3, Sept. 15, 1877, 42: "Washington Hall, is, we understand, to be lighted with gasoline. It will be a good thing to get rid of the lamps." This probably indicates a shift from wick to mantle lighting, which produces much higher intensity, with kerosene the likely fuel.

106. See Brockett and Hildy, *History of the Theatre,* 366.

Chapter 4. Rebuilding After the Great Fire, 1879–1882

1. *New York Times,* April 24, 1879, 5.

2. *Scholastic* 13:1, Aug. 23, 1879, 11. The university apparently purchased the first replacement piano in October for $150 from "Miss Tong,"

according to Financial Ledger #7, Oct. 11, 1879, 1064, ULDG, UNDA. Lucius G. Tong was professor of bookkeeping and commercial law from 1863 to 1882. Max Girac, as noted in chapter 2, was professor of Latin, Greek, French, and music from 1850 to 1869.

3. Local Council Minute Book, May 14, 1879, 93, IPAC.

4. For Sorin's March 20, 1879, letter to Corby, see Marvin R. O'Connell, *Edward Sorin* (Notre Dame, Ind.: University of Notre Dame Press, 2001), 649. The pencil-written "calculation" of April 30, 1879, included hundreds of feet of "steam pipe" with regard to the destroyed Music Hall, but of course the Great Fire of 1879 originated in the Main Building. See calculations of the loss in the fire of 1879, UNDR 4/11, UNDA.

5. *Scholastic* 12:34, April 26, 1879, 534.

6. *Scholastic* 12:35, May 10, 1879, 545.

7. Ibid., 546.

8. *Scholastic* 13:6, Oct. 11, 1879, 90.

9. *McGee's Illustrated Weekly,* Saturday, May 17, 1879, 402. Advertisements in *McGee's* indicated optimistically that Notre Dame would reopen the first Tuesday in September at "Terms Greatly Reduced."

10. *Scholastic* 12:38, May 31, 1879, 594.

11. *Scholastic* 12:41, June 21, 1879, 641.

12. *Scholastic* 12:44, July 12, 1879, 690. The combined footprint of the 1862 Washington Hall and the 1865 Music Hall was 9,000 square feet, while the total footprint of this proposed structure was 10,000 square feet, an 11 percent increase in space. The actual building that went up, however, had a footprint of about 13,600 square feet, with about 10,000 square feet devoted to the Exhibition Hall alone and an additional 3,600 square feet assigned to the Music Hall, a rather significant 40 percent increase over the total of the two pre-1879 venues.

13. The junior play room is today's ground-floor rehearsal hall (Room 110) but was for much of the building's history and until 1990 the band rehearsal hall. The senior play room today contains the scene and costume shops, a few offices, and storage spaces but was until the 1950s the Brownson (Senior) Recreation Room, containing billiards tables and a piano.

14. *Scholastic* 13:23, Feb. 14, 1880, 361.

15. *Scholastic* 13:28, March 20, 1880, 440.

16. *Scholastic* 13:1, Aug. 23, 1879, 10. The new building would flank the Main Building as a counterpart (*pendant*) to the church. Arthur J. Stace was professor of bookkeeping, mathematics, surveying, and civil engineering from 1862 until his death in 1890.

17. Local Council Minute Book, Sept. 27, 1879, 104, IPAC.

18. Provincial Council Minutes 1870–1880, Oct. 1, 1879, f25v, IPAC. It is difficult to determine the actual cost of building the 1862 Washington Exhibition Hall and the 1866 Music Hall, but the combined figures range from $2,220 to $5,000 (figures that are further problematic because the purchasing power of the dollar declined greatly from 1862 to 1866 due to deflation). Nevertheless, the new building represented an upgrade with $15,000 committed to it initially. In reality, by the time the new Academy of Music opened officially in 1882, the construction costs appear to be right at $30,000, so clearly cost overruns were a fact of life in the nineteenth century just as they are today.

19. *Scholastic* 13:4, Sept. 27, 1879, 59.

20. Ibid.

21. *Scholastic* 12:43, July 5, 1879, 672–73.

22. *Scholastic* 13:6, Oct. 11, 1879, 91.

23. *Scholastic* 13:7, Oct. 18, 1879, 104.

24. Ibid., 105.

25. *Scholastic* 13:8, Oct. 25, 1879, 122. The white bricks (now called Notre Dame yellow) were the face bricks, that is, the ones visible on the exterior of buildings, and were originally made from the marl from the area that is devoid of iron oxide, which gives bricks a red color when fired. The Financial Ledger #7, Oct. 25, 1879, 1071, ULDG, UNDA, recorded the expense for brick at $1,695, while a week later (1073), it was only $166.97, one tenth as much and clearly showing the drop-off in supply.

26. *Scholastic* 13:20, Jan. 23, 1880, 312.

27. *Scholastic* 13:12, Nov. 22, 1879, 186.

28. Local Council Minute Book, Nov. 28, 1879, 110, IPAC.

29. *Scholastic* 13:13, Nov. 29, 1879, 201–2.

30. *Scholastic* 13:16, Dec. 22, 1879, 250.

31. *Scholastic* 13:14, Dec. 6, 1879, 213.

32. Ibid., 214–15; 13:16, Dec. 22, 1879, 247.

33. *Scholastic* 13:22, Feb. 7, 1880, 342.

34. *Scholastic* 13:25, Feb. 28, 1880, 391–92.

35. *Scholastic* 13:27, March 13, 1880, 425–26, 439; 13:28, March 20, 1880, 439–40. James Farnham Edwards (1850–1911) came to Notre Dame as a minim at the age of nine and never left. He became a professor of history and taught at Notre Dame from 1872 to 1910. His early interest in preservation and conservation made him "first among the prominent people who have worked to shape the Archives and its collections," and prefigured the seminal librarianship of Father Paul Foik, C.S.C., and

Father Thomas T. McAvoy, C.S.C. See http://archives.nd.edu/about/
history.htm (accessed June 4, 2010).

36. *Scholastic* 13:35, May 8, 1880, 553.

37. *Scholastic* 13:36, May 15, 1880, 568.

38. *Scholastic* 13:42, June 26, 1880, 660.

39. *Class Annual 1884*, 9–11.

40. Local Council Minute Book, Aug. 5, 1880, 129, IPAC.

41. Local Council Minute Book, Sept. 17, 1880, 132, IPAC.

42. Local Council Minute Book, Oct. 8, 1880, 134, IPAC. In 1880s
construction parlance, the term *water table* referred to a horizontal exterior finish board that covered the seam between the foundation and the
building wall and which was topped by a two-inch drip cap, or in masonry construction "a projecting base course, beveled at the top for weathering." See Frank D. Graham and Thomas J. Emery, *Audel's Carpenters
and Builders Guide #2* (New York: Theo. Audel, 1923), 774, 777; and
Henry H. Saylor, *Dictionary of Architecture* (New York: Science Editions,
1963), 184. Today *water table* more typically refers to the distance below
grade to the upper surface of residual groundwater (nine to twenty-two
feet at Notre Dame).

43. Local Council Minute Book, Feb. 18, 1881, 145, IPAC.

44. *Scholastic* 14:38, June 11, 1881, 611.

45. Ibid., 612. The Reverend Louis Neyron, M.D., was professor of
anatomy, physiology, and hygiene from 1863 until 1887.

46. A "Jim Crow" play popular at the time. Actor Thomas Dartmouth
Rice (1808–60), billed as an "Ethiopian delineator," was not the first white
actor to appear in blackface but rather popularized this performance tradition that profoundly influenced generations of American entertainers
(see *ANB*).

47. *Scholastic* 14:39, June 18, 1881, 625, 630.

48. Local Council Minute Book, June 24, 1881, 155, IPAC.

49. *Scholastic* 14:40, July 2, 1881, 633–35. The rotunda is about 35' x
35', the same size as the university parlor, which was also a popular venue
for communal assembly in the new Main Building.

50. *Scholastic* 15:13, Dec. 3, 1881, 190–91.

51. *Scholastic* 15:1, Aug. 27, 1881, 10.

52. *Scholastic* 15:2, Sept. 17, 1881, 27. Financial Journal #8, Sept. 30,
1881, 175, ULDG, UNDA, includes payments to complete work on the
exhibition hall at $3,176 to the carpentry shop, and $604.16 to the blacksmith for slate and tin work.

53. *Scholastic* 15:4, Oct. 1, 1881, 50.

54. Ibid., 54. Garfield was buried in Lakeview Cemetery, Cleveland, Ohio.

55. *Scholastic* 15:6, Oct. 15, 1881, 80. Professor Griffith organized the Euglossians in 1868 for the sole purpose of studying elocution, "which enables a reader or speaker to convey clearly, forcibly and agreeably the meaning of what he reads or speaks" (*Scholastic* 15:7, Oct. 22, 1881, 97).

56. *Scholastic* 15:6, Oct. 15, 1881, 80.

57. Ibid., 80–81.

58. In the United States, Thomas Edison is credited with inventing the incandescent bulb in 1879. The Reverend John Augustine Zahm, C.S.C., 1851–1921, a true pioneer in the application of electric lighting as well as an early proponent of academic research, was professor of physical sciences, 1872–1906, and served as provincial, 1898–1906. Father Zahm's younger brother was no less distinguished as a scientist: Albert Francis Zahm (1862–1954), the father of American aerodynamics (and probably no less important to the field than the Wrights) was professor of mechanical engineering, 1883–92.

59. *Scholastic* 15:12, Nov. 26, 1881, 174.

60. *Scholastic* 15:9, Nov. 5, 1881, 126.

61. Alex Comparet letter to the Reverend Edward Sorin, Dec. 28, 1881, UNDR 20/12, UNDA. The Tabor Opera House in Denver opened in 1881 and survived until 1964. Thirty-two dollars in 1881 equals almost seven hundred dollars in 2009. See measuringworth.com (accessed July 27, 2009).

62. Jacob Ackermann taught in the Fine Arts Department from the 1850s until 1890. Brother Frederick (Edmund Kräling), 1850–1917, entered Holy Cross in 1875.

63. *Scholastic* 15:16, Dec, 24, 1881, 238.

64. *Scholastic* 15:20, Jan. 28, 1882, 300.

65. Local Council Minute Book, Feb. 24, 1882, 174, IPAC.

66. *Scholastic* 15:25, March 4, 1882, 380. The "20th ult[imo]" means the twentieth of the previous month, that is, Feb. 20, 1882. M. Lachassaigne was professor of drawing, 1862–64. Carl A. B. Von Weller, F. R. A., was professor of drawing and painting in the 1860s and provided artistry for plays.

67. *Scholastic* 15:26, March 11, 1882, 398.

68. *Scholastic* 15:29, April 1, 1882, 448; 15:31, April 15, 1882, 476–77; 15:33, April 29, 1882, 511.

69. *Scholastic* 15:33, April 29, 1882, 511: "All the members of the Faculty are expected to be present without further invitation." It was the "most brilliant affair of the kind ever given at Notre Dame" (527).

70. *Scholastic* 15:33, April 29, 1882, 512. Reprint from *South Bend Tribune*. Shakespeare would first be done in the new venue in the fall of 1882. For enrollment numbers, see *Annual Catalogue* 38 (1881–82), 5–10.

71. Local Council Minute Book, May 12, 1882, 179, IPAC.

72. *Scholastic* 15:38, June 3, 1882, 592.

73. *Scholastic* 15:37, May 27, 1882, 575.

74. *Scholastic* 15:38, June 3, 1882, 591. The demolition revealed an ancillary business in the old building: "Some interesting discoveries were made during the demolition of Washington Hall. The report that large sums of money were brought to light under the corner occupied by the pie-store is, however, unfounded. Change is handled a little too carefully in that region to permit any such results."

Chapter 5. The "New" Washington Hall, 1882–1895

1. Local Council Minute Book, Sept. 15, 1882, 185–86, IPAC, states that insurance for the new Music Hall had been renewed for $15,000, the Main Building and its contents for $80,000, the church for $20,000, for a total for the university (including St. Joseph Farm at $7,000) at $155,200. Financial Ledger #8, ULDG, 40–41, UNDA, confirms by the time of the dedication in June 1882, however, the university had spent about $30,000 on the structure.

2. *Scholastic* 15:40, June 17, 1882, 620, 622. Colonel Donn Piatt (1819–91) apparently inadvertently and precipitously freed the slaves in Maryland early in the Civil War and later became a well-known journalist who wrote about the great men he had known, including Abraham Lincoln.

3. The oratorical contest for the graduates and Euglossians took place in the rotunda of the Main Building on Monday, June 19, 1882.

4. *Scholastic* 15:41, July 1, 1882, 642–43.

5. *Scholastic* 15:39, June 10, 1882, 604. The Reverend Nicholas Stoffel, C.S.C., was professor of Greek from 1874 until his death in 1902. Luigi Gregori (1819–96) was professor of painting, 1873–78 and 1880–91. He returned in 1894 to complete the interior of Washington Hall (painted over in 1956) and is best known today for the interior frescoes and the Columbian murals in the Main Building.

6. *Scholastic* 15:38, June 3, 1882, 591.

7. *Scholastic* 15:40, June 17, 1882, 623.

8. *Scholastic* 15:40, June 17, 1882, 624. The "college portico" likely refers to the primary entrance to the Main Building.

9. *South Bend Times* 17:25, June 23, 1882, also known as *The Weekly Times*. With 700 downstairs and 500 in the gallery (balcony), the new hall seated 1,200. Total seating in 2009 is 571.

10. *South Bend Times* 17:25, June 23, 1882. Mr. Nobels is almost certainly Brother Anselm (Léopold Nobels, born c. 1835), who was professor of vocal music from 1882 until 1896, after which he apparently settled in Canada. He professed July 22, 1883, at the age of forty-eight.

11. Financial Journal #8, June 30, 1882, ULDG, 285, UNDA: $3,100 Exhibition Hall to carpenter costs; 287, $556.00 "Bill of Chairs from The Robert Mitchell Furniture Co. Cin. O."; July 1, 1882, 288, $50.00 "Fr[eigh]t on Chairs."

12. *Scholastic* 15:41, July 1, 1882, 938 [misprint for 638]. It is interesting to note that electricity was not yet perceived as a 24/7 technology.

13. *Scholastic* 15:41, July, 1, 1882, 639. The obituary of Gregory Vigeant, Sr., "Chicago Pioneer Architect" (1853–1918), appeared in the *Chicago Tribune*, May 19, 1918, 15.

14. *Scholastic* 15:41, July 1, 1882, 639.

15. Reprinted in ibid., 641.

16. Reprinted in ibid., 641–42. The gallery (or balcony) could accommodate the entire student body of four hundred in 1882.

17. Ibid., 643.

18. The Phelan name vanished from the campus when the first science building, Phelan Hall (about 23' x 50' x 40' high), was demolished in 1885, replaced by the new Science Hall (now LaFortune Student Center), just south of the 1882 Academy of Music. Phelan Hall was also used for lectures, a function that would shift to the new Washington Hall after 1882. The Phelans, whose benefaction saved the university in 1855 and whose donation directly solicited by Father Sorin paid for the construction of the first Washington Hall in 1862, have since 1885 had no nominal representation on the Notre Dame campus, and the same could very well have also happened to the father of the country.

19. *Scholastic* 16:2, Sept. 16, 1882, 28, reported that "work on the new Gymnasium is progressing rapidly. When completed it will be a fine building. Its dimensions will be 145 ft. long, 45 ft. wide, and 25 ft. in height. We understand there will be an annex in which will be found the confectionery store and barber shop." Since the new gymnasium (constructed size was 33' x 120' x 22' high) ultimately was smaller than the first Washington Hall (which was 50' x 150'), it must have made economic sense to start anew rather than to try to move and to remodel the existing structure. We know the first Washington Hall had a sloped auditorium

floor—ideal for audience sight lines to the stage but impossible for a gym floor—which would have required expensive structural changes. It is not known whether any materials from the demolished Washington Hall were recycled for use in the new gymnasium or other buildings.

20. *Scholastic* 16:2, Sept. 16, 1882, 28. The name "Washington Hall" on the south entrance of the building today appeared in 1989 at building manager Tom Barkes's request so patrons from town could more easily find the building (e-mail to author, July 15, 2004).

21. Ibid., 27–28. Calcimine (also kalsomine), originally a trade name, became a generic term for a kind of white (or tinted) wash for walls.

22. Names of spaces can be confusing, as noted earlier. In the 1880s Brownson Hall was also the name of the dormitory for the senior division or department (boys seventeen and older) located in the east wing of the Main Building, just as Carroll Hall was the dormitory for the junior division or department (boys thirteen or fourteen up to sixteen, or "preps") in the west wing. "Brownson Hall" and "Senior Department" were thus synonyms at this time. Brownson Hall Recreation Room on the lower level of Washington Hall beneath the auditorium thus functioned as the Senior Recreation Hall. This is all the more confusing because of current notions of "juniors" and "seniors" as third- and fourth-year college students and Notre Dame's having a freestanding Brownson Hall just north of the Main Building. Orestes August Brownson (1803–76), editor, educator, and philosopher, converted to Catholicism in 1844, and, according to *ANB*, "devoted the rest of his life to creating a vision of a Catholic America." Hope effuses that Brownson was "America's greatest Catholic philosopher of the nineteenth century" (*Notre Dame*, 248), while John McGreevy, in *Catholicism and American Freedom: A History* (New York: Norton, 2003), praises Brownson as "the most influential American Catholic intellectual of the nineteenth century" (44). Brownson's body lies in the crypt of the Basilica of the Sacred Heart at Notre Dame.

23. Local Council Minute Book, Nov. 10, 1882, 190, IPAC; *Scholastic* 16:13, Dec. 2, 1882, 203.

24. *Scholastic* 16:28, March 24, 1883, 443. The *South Bend Tribune*, reprinted in *Scholastic* 17:49, Dec. 8, 1882, 1, described the plans for the summit to be topped off with "a statue of the blessed Virgin, 16 feet in height, all gilt and at night wholly bathed in light from a dozen of electric stars, starting from its feet, and forming an elliptic cincture, 25 feet wide, and reaching a point 15 feet above the head of the statue. Will not this be a sight?"

25. *Scholastic* 16:26, March 10, 1883, 411. It is noteworthy that the new Academy of Music had electricity for "occasional" ancillary lighting before it had natural gas lights.

26. Local Council Minute Book, May 19, 1882, 179, IPAC; *Scholastic* 15:37, May 27, 1882, 575.

27. Gas lighting with its great benefits of control and intensity had dominated stage lighting in theatres in the United States since the 1850s. We creatures of the electric age forget (or never knew) that gas lighting significantly advanced stage lighting precisely because of the greatly increased levels of intensity, which permitted the extensive use of filtered (colored) light, with the added bonus of centralized control from a single location concealed from the audience. Indeed, strong debate occurred regarding the superiority of gas over electricity, with Sir Henry Irving (1838–1905) eschewing electricity throughout his stellar career. See Brockett and Hildy, *History of the Theatre,* 338–39, 365–66.

28. *Scholastic* 16:27, March 17, 1883, 426.

29. *Scholastic* 16:29, March 31, 1883, 459.

30. *Scholastic* 16:30, April 7, 1883, 475.

31. Local Council Minute Book, May 11, 1883, 199, IPAC.

32. Local Council Minute Book, July 13, 1883, 203, IPAC.

33. *Scholastic* 17:33, April 26, 1884, 523.

34. *Scholastic* 17:34, May 3, 1884, 540.

35. *Scholastic* 17:36, May 17, 1884, 570.

36. *Scholastic* 18:19, Jan. 17, 1885, 304. Financial Journal #8, ULDG, UNDA, recorded the following payments: Dec. 31, 1884, $250.00 "Exhibition Hall to J. Ackerman" (669); Jan. 31, 1885, $500, for Exhibition Hall and $500 for "Dome" (679); and June 30, 1885, $150.00, Exhibition Hall to J. Ackermann, for "work on scenes" (734). Peter Lysy has advised me that we would not expect to find payroll accounts for Brothers Frederick and Anselm, C.S.C. members of the religious order, as we do for lay professors. "Brother Frederick and his men" gilded the new dome for the first time in the fall of 1886, and indeed today's restored Main Building contains many faux-wood-grained doors inspired by his early craftsmanship. See *Scholastic* 20:3, Sept. 18, 1886, 52.

37. *Scholastic* 18:8, Oct. 25, 1884, 124.

38. Ibid.

39. *Scholastic* 18:15, Dec. 13, 1884, 237.

40. *Scholastic* 18:28, March 21, 1885, 445, 449. A heroic rebel figure in Irish history, Robert Emmet (1778–1803) was convicted of high treason

by the British government and hanged. The German virtuoso The-odor Hoch (1842–1906), a flamboyant and popular cornet soloist of the time, brought down the house with his entr'acte performance with the cornet.

41. *Scholastic* 19:19, Jan. 23, 1886, 309.

42. *Scholastic* 20:11, Nov. 13, 1886, 181. Science Hall with its ninety incandescent lights was on the same "Circuit No. 2" as Washington Hall. The Main Building and the rest of the university were on "Circuit No. 1" with thirty-nine lights alone dedicated to the dome.

43. Local Council Minute Book, Sept. 24, 1886, 60, IPAC.

44. Local Council Minute Book, April 15, 1887, 71–72, IPAC.

45. Local Council Minute Book, March 5, 1886, 49; April 2, 1886, 51, IPAC.

46. With Tom Barkes and Greta Fisher, former managers of Washington Hall, I viewed the interior of the tower in August 2006. Having ascended the very steep stairs to the light booth high in the balcony lobby, we climbed a vertical ladder to access the area above the light booth ceiling where two original panels of the lobby arch decorated by Rusca/Poligano (1894) survived the 1956 remodeling (see fig. 5.10). We then accessed yet another ladder to get above the balcony lobby ceiling, where we were genuinely "in the attic." In this area it was possible to observe in the tower interior a roof infrastructure at an even higher level, which almost certainly contains the timber infrastructure of the original temporary tower roof (from 1882 to the end of 1887 when the tower was completed). Architect Chris Dennis recreated this vertical journey in fall 2008 with building manager Ron Grisoli and building technical director Kathleen Lane as he prepared a conjectural drawing of the building both before the completion of the tower and when the south Washington Hall entrance stairs were wooden (see fig. 5.1).

47. *Scholastic* 21:12, Nov. 26, 1887, 189.

48. *Scholastic* 21:14, Dec. 24, 1887, 236–37.

49. Financial Journal #9, ULDG, UNDA, includes the following payments from Sept. 30, 1887, through Dec. 31, 1887: $200 masons work on tower (31); $170 carpenters work on Tower (32); $408 blacksmiths work on Tower (33); $200 slating tower (64); $120 for Tower plus $130 labor & material to Blacksmith shop (tin and hardware) (65).

50. Local Council Minute Book, May 10, 1889, 120, IPAC.

51. *Scholastic* 19:33, May 1, 1886, 532.

52. Local Council Minute Book, May 13, 1886, 53, IPAC.

53. *Scholastic* 20:1, Aug. 14, 1886, 23.

54. Local Council Minute Book, April 12, 1889, 118, IPAC.

55. Financial Journal #9, 256, ULDG, UNDA.

56. *Scholastic* 20:1, Aug. 14, 1886, 5, 17. The C.T.A.U. dates to 1871 but was based on the work in the 1850s of Father Theobald Mathew, described by the *Catholic Encyclopedia* as "the apostle of temperance." The temperance movement achieved ultimate success, of course, with the ratification of the Eighteenth Amendment in 1919 (repealed by the Twenty-first Amendment in 1933).

57. *Scholastic* 20:1, Aug. 14, 1886, 13. As originally constructed, the ground-level recreation spaces in Washington Hall were internally accessible neither to each other nor to upper floors.

58. *New York Times,* May 29, 1887, 12.

59. *Scholastic* 21:25, March 10, 1888, 397; 21:30, April 14, 1888, 476.

60. *South Bend Times* 17:42, Oct. 20, 1882; also see *Scholastic* 16:6, Oct. 14, 1882, 88–92.

61. *South Bend Register,* Feb. 22, 1883, reprinted in *Scholastic* 16:24, Feb. 24, 1883, 381. This February 1883 production of *Julius Caesar* was the first Shakespeare play done in the new hall.

62. *Scholastic* 16:24, Feb. 24, 1883, 378.

63. *Scholastic* 16:25, March 3, 1883, 394. Clement Studebaker (1831–1901), a blacksmith and wagon builder, opened H. & C. Studebaker in South Bend with his brother Henry in 1852. With another brother, John, the company became "the largest horse-drawn vehicle manufacturer in the world," according to *ANB.*

64. *Scholastic* 16:27, March 17, 1883, 426.

65. *Scholastic* 16:29, March 31, 1883, 458.

66. Scholastic 16:30, April 7, 1883, 475. The popular textbook's full title was *The American Elocutionist and Dramatic Reader for the Use of Colleges, Academies, and Schools,* 3rd ed., rev. (Philadelphia: J. H. Butler, 1874).

67. *Scholastic* 16:1, Aug. 5, 1882, 11–12.

68. *Scholastic* 16:41, June 21, 1883, 645–46.

69. Ibid., 646–47.

70. Reprinted in the *Scholastic* 16:42, June 30, 1883, 670–71.

71. Reprinted in the *Scholastic* 16:41, June 21, 1883, 651. Sophocles' *Antigone* has been produced only one other time on the Washington Hall stage, Nov. 28 to Dec. 2, 2001.

72. *Scholastic* 16:39, June 9, 1883, 616.

73. *Scholastic* 16:42, June 30, 1883, 657.

74. Ibid., 658–59.

75. Ibid., 661–62. Shakespeare's religious affiliation became a subject of intense speculation in the second half of the nineteenth century. The *ODNB* credits writer and literary scholar Richard Simpson (1820–76) as "one of the first to advance the theory that Shakespeare was a Roman Catholic," the topic picked up here by the bishop of Columbus.

76. *Class Annual 1884*, 28.

77. *Chicago Times*, Dec. 18, 1884, reprinted in *Scholastic* 18:16, Dec. 20, 1884, 251, 256, 257. President Walsh's patron saint was Saint Thomas (Dec. 21).

78. *Scholastic* 18:25, Feb. 28, 1885, 396–97. *Waiting for the Verdict* is an alternate title of *Falsely Accused*.

79. *Scholastic* 18:28, March 21, 1885, 444.

80. Ibid.

81. *Scholastic* 18:27, March 14, 1885, 433; 18:29, March 28, 1885, 464–65. The World's Fair of 1884, also known as the World Cotton Centennial, was held in New Orleans from Dec. 16, 1884, to June 2, 1885, the site of which is Audubon Park today.

82. *Scholastic* 18:29, March 28, 1885, 465–66.

83. *Scholastic* 18:38, May 30, 1885, 604–5. The word *séance* at this time could mean any sort of meeting or discussion without today's spiritualistic connotation. The phenakistoscope, according to the *OED*, consisted "of a disc or drum with figures representing a moving object in successive positions arranged radially on it, to be viewed in such a way (e.g., through a fixed slit) that the persistence of the successive visual images produces the impression of actual motion when the disc or drum is rapidly rotated."

84. *Scholastic* 18:24, Feb. 21, 1885, 386. Also see *Scholastic* 18:32, April 25, 1885, 530. Shakespeare was baptized on April 26, 1564, probably within five days of his (unknown) birth date as was customary at the time. By the eighteenth century, April 23 had been popularly accepted as his date of birth, not coincidentally connecting him eternally to Saint George, England's patron saint.

85. *Scholastic* 18:34, May 2, 1885, 540–41, 546; 18:35, May 9, 1885, 560.

86. *Scholastic* 19:16, Jan. 2, 1886, 261.

87. Ibid., 261–62.

88. *Scholastic* 19:19, Jan. 23, 1886, 304.

89. *Scholastic* 21:20, Feb. 4, 1888, 316.

90. *Scholastic* 22:15, Dec. 1, 1888, 253.

91. *Scholastic* 21:36, May 26, 1888, 575–76, 596; 21:37, June 2, 1888, 593.

92. *Scholastic* 22:1, Aug. 25, 1888, 1–15. Also see *A Brief History of the University of Notre Dame du Lac, Indiana, from 1842 to 1892* (Chicago: Werner, 1895), 207–18; and Hope, *Notre Dame,* 235–39.

93. *Scholastic* 21:40, June 20, 1888, 648.

94. *Scholastic* 23:6, Oct. 12, 1889, 93.

95. Ibid. The *Encyclopedia of Catholicism* describes Archbishop John Carroll (1736–1815) as "the first Catholic bishop in the United States" (231); he headed the first episcopal see established in 1789 in Baltimore by Pope Pius VI (1717–99; served as pope from 1775). Catholic University has no record of ever having received the portrait of Washington, although the one of Carroll remains in its possession.

96. *Scholastic* 22:21, Jan. 26, 1889, 349. Frederick J. Liscombe taught vocal music 1888–93 and seems also to have directed some of the plays during this time, too. Racial suffrage came in 1870 with the Fifteenth Amendment; women's suffrage came fifty years later in 1920 with the Nineteenth Amendment.

97. *Scholastic* 22:22, Feb. 2, 1889, 369.

98. Ibid. Walter C. Lyman was professor of elocution 1888–90.

99. *Scholastic* 25:25, Feb. 27, 1892, 426–30.

100. *Scholastic* 25:28, March 19, 1892, 474, 480. Colley Cibber (1671–1757) was an early British theatre actor-manager and adapter of Shakespeare and Molière whose version of *Richard III* became the standard acting text for well over a century and indeed was used here.

101. *Scholastic* 25:42, June 25, 1892, 713.

102. Mark C. Pilkinton, "Lessons of Theatre History" (lecture, University of Notre Dame, Notre Dame, Ind., Aug. 31, 2010).

103. *Scholastic* 19:24, Feb. 27, 1886, 385–87.

104. Reprinted in ibid., 389–90.

105. *Scholastic* 22:43, June 29, 1889, 702–3.

106. *Scholastic* 23:27, March 15, 1890, 433.

107. *Scholastic* 24:41, June 27, 1891, 653. Washington Hall in 2008 had a total seating capacity of 571, with 363 seats on the main floor and 208 in the balcony. It is hard to imagine the space containing three times that number.

108. *Scholastic* 25:42, June 20, 1892, 714.

109. See Louis Althusser, "Ideology and Ideological State Apparatuses," in *Lenin and Philosophy and Other Essays* (New York: Monthly Review Press, 1971).

110. Father Thomas E. Walsh, C.S.C. (1853–93), with Morrissey succeeding him as president; Father Alexis Granger, C.S.C. (1817–93);

and Father Edward Sorin, C.S.C. (1814–93). See "The Story of Notre Dame" at http://archives.nd.edu/episodes/sorin/sorin-e.htm (accessed Aug. 15, 2008).

111. *Scholastic* 27:39, June 30, 1894, 684.

112. Financial Journal #9, 864, 871, 882, 884, 886, 889, 891, 896, 897, 903, ULDG, UNDA.

113. *Scholastic* 27:31, April 28, 1894, 540. The "well-known decorator" Rusca is almost certainly the person the *Biographical Dictionary of Kansas Artists (Active Before 1945)* describes as follows: "Rusca, Louis. *fl. 1880s, Kansas City.* Fresco artist. Worked with Jerome Fedeli & Co., located at 1036 Main in Kansas City and in 1886 advertised as 'Fresco artists, residences, theatres, churches, offices, banks, banners, restoration of oil paintings. All work done in the most artistic style'" (185).

114. *Scholastic* 27:39, June 30, 1894, 683–84. Michael O'Dea was professor of telegraphy and typewriting (which became applied electricity) from 1884 to 1895.

115. Father Edward Lilly, C.S.C., was professor of music from 1863 until his untimely death at age thirty-four on December 30, 1879. See *Scholastic* 13:17, Jan. 3, 1880, 263. Girac and Lilly were the only two Notre Dame professors whose names formed part of the 1894 interior decoration.

116. *Scholastic* 27:39, June 30, 1894, 685.

117. *Scholastic* 28:9, Nov. 3, 1894, 143. I am especially indebted to Peter Lysy in Notre Dame Archives for helping me figure out precisely which entrance to the building likely correlated to the Carroll Hall yard (e-mail to author, April 13, 2010).

118. *Scholastic* 28:25, March 16, 1895, 402.

119. Ibid., 401.

120. *Scholastic* 28:33, May 18, 1895, 541.

121. *Scholastic* 28:35, June 1, 1895, 573. George Eastman invented paper roll film in 1884 and introduced the Kodak camera in 1888, with the mass-produced "Brownie" appearing by 1900. McDonald Studio, founded in 1861, continues in business in South Bend in 2010 as the oldest photography studio in the area.

122. *Scholastic* 28:36, June 8, 1895, 599–600. There are two Professors Ackermann who designed for theatre at Notre Dame: Jacob Ackermann created the 1885 act curtain and may have worked at Notre Dame as far back as the 1850s; and Francis Xavier Ackermann, who taught mechanical drawing from 1890 to 1938. Regarding Sosman and Landis, Crabtree and Beudert point out, in *Scenic Art for the Theatre: History,*

Tools, and Techniques (St. Louis: Butterworth-Heinemann/Focal Press, 1998), 272, that "Chicago was a railroad hub and became the center of the scenic industry outside New York City," and that firms like Sosman and Landis "employed twelve to twenty full-time scenic artists." Among those was Thomas Gibbs Moses (1856–1934), who would become a nationally renowned set designer.

Chapter 6. Growing Pains, 1895–1922

1. *Chicago Daily Tribune,* May 19, 1895, 33.

2. Based on the year Indiana granted the university a charter (1844) and not the year of founding (1842), the Golden Jubilee had been planned for 1894, but the deaths and ensuing mourning periods of President Thomas E. Walsh and patriarchs Father Alexis Granger and Father Edward Sorin between July and November 1893 postponed the Golden Jubilee until 1895.

3. John Louis O'Sullivan (1813–95) may have been one of the first to describe the concept of manifest destiny in "The Great Nation of Futurity," *The United States Magazine, and Democratic Review* 6:23, Nov. 6, 1839, 426–30.

4. Thomas Stritch, *My Notre Dame: Memories and Reflections of Sixty Years* (Notre Dame, Ind.: University of Notre Dame Press, 1991), 123.

5. *Dome* 1921, 253. See "Romantic Carroll Hall Is Gone."

6. While praising the vision of President Burns during his rather brief tenure as president (1919–22), I do not wish to ignore or minimize the significant accomplishments of his immediate predecessor, the Reverend President John William Cavanaugh, C.S.C. (1905–19), during whose time much of the groundwork was laid for Burns's dramatic achievements.

7. *Scholastic* 28:36, June 8, 1895, 600; 28:37, July 6, 1895, 653, with the sermons and speeches published in their entirety, 601–41, and a detailed narrative of events on 643–64. Bishop Spalding had been instrumental in the founding of Catholic University of America in 1877.

8. *South Bend Daily Times,* June 11, 1895, 2.

9. *Scholastic* 28:23, March 2, 1895, 368–72. Marmon was a student 1891–97; Father James J. French, C.S.C., supervised the Thespians at this time and served on the faculty from 1887 to 1912.

10. *Scholastic* 29:21, Feb. 22, 1896, 338. The Reverend Andrew Morrissey, C.S.C. (1860–1921), was president of Notre Dame 1893–1905.

William P. Breen (1859–1930) as a student played Metellus (Cimber) in the Washington's Birthday production of *Julius Caesar* in 1877, the year he received his degree (the '79 in the article is a misprint). He later became a major benefactor to the university, endowing both the Breen Medal in Oratory (first recorded as such in 1897) and a chair in the Law School. Today Breen-Phillips dormitory (1939) survives, named in honor of his brother-in-law, Frank B. Phillips ('80), and him. See Patrick J. Carroll, C.S.C., *William P. Breen: In Memoriam* (Notre Dame, Ind.: University of Notre Dame du Lac, 1931).

11. *Scholastic* 29:21, Feb. 22, 1896, 338.

12. *Scholastic* 29:22, Feb. 29, 1896, 354–55. The Pledge of Allegiance, written by Francis Bellamy in 1892, quickly became popular in schools, where henceforth a flag was displayed. Emendations over the years added to Bellamy's original fifteen-second pledge, culminating in the addition in 1954 of the two words "under God" (inspired initially by the Knights of Columbus) to produce the pledge recited today. Along with the Columbian Exposition of 1892 came a renewed interest in flying the flag, and the "flag ceremony" added to the Washington's Birthday celebration undoubtedly reflected this shift toward public emblematic nationalism at a time of massive immigration.

13. Ibid. See p. 357 for the complete program.

14. *Scholastic* 30:21, Feb. 27, 1897, 343. The Reverend Martin Joseph Regan, C.S.C., served as prefect of discipline from 1884 until 1907.

15. At midcentury, English actor Charles Kean (1811–68) had become famous for playing the dual roles of the twin brothers in this play adapted for the stage from the Alexandre Dumas *père* novel that premiered in London in 1852. The Corsican trap, a theatrical device that made a character appear to rise from below and glide the full width of the stage, is named after the play that demanded the device. (See Brockett and Hildy, *History of the Theatre*, 359, 360, and 364.) While it is clear that production values were high, we do not know whether Father Moloney installed a genuine Corsican trap in the floor of the Washington Hall stage.

16. *Scholastic* 31:21, Feb. 26, 1898, 370.

17. Ibid., 371–72.

18. *Scholastic* 41:22, Feb. 29, 1908, 364.

19. *Scholastic* 48:21, Feb. 27, 1915, 346.

20. Ibid., 347.

21. Ibid., 348.

22. *Dome* 1918, 232.

23. *Scholastic* 52:7, Nov. 23, 1918, 103. Graduate study had previously been available to women during the regular year; Sister Mary Frances Jerome and Sister Mary Lucretia each received master's degrees in June 1917. See First Women to Graduate/Receive Degrees, PNDP 06-Wo-1, UNDA.

24. The old Lemonnier Library in the Main Building became a barracks during 1918–19, housing 120 men, and Old Carroll Gym in "Rockefeller Hall" (or Row) east of Washington Hall received a large wooden addition (50' x 125') to serve as a mess hall. See *Scholastic* 52:1, Oct. 12, 1918, 9, 10. Notre Dame largely escaped the influenza epidemic.

25. *Scholastic* 52:17, Feb. 22, 1919, 277–80.

26. *Scholastic* 54:18, Feb. 26, 1921: "With Washington in His Hall," 306–7. The Washington's Birthday flag tradition continued through the 1961–62 academic year.

27. Ellen Ryan Jolly, *Nuns of the Battlefield* (Providence, R. I.: Providence Visitor Press, 1927), deals with the significant contribution sisters of religious orders made during the American Civil War.

28. Program, [Tuesday] July 4, 1922, William Farmer private collection. There is an American flag colophon inside the program, followed by a list, "Sisters of Holy Cross Who Served as Nurses in the Civil War [from Mother M. Angela (Eliza Gillespie) to Sister M. De Chantal (Barbara Knoll)—65]." Additionally, "Notre Dame Post No. 569, G.A.R." has a list of twenty-one deceased members from the Civil War, including the Reverend William Corby (chaplain, 88th N.Y. Infantry), to the fifty-five "Notre Dame Men Who Died in Service, 1917–1918." Father William Augustine Bolger, C.S.C., (1875–1951) was professor of economics and politics from 1911 to 1945; the middle initial in the program is very likely a misprint.

29. *Scholastic* 31:21, Feb. 26, 1898, 375.

30. *Scholastic* 41:6, Oct. 19, 1907, 95.

31. *Scholastic* 41:10, Nov. 16, 1907, 159.

32. *Scholastic* 41:4, Oct. 5, 1907, 64.

33. *Scholastic* 41:23, March 7, 1908, 383.

34. This appropriation of space continues. When the DeBartolo Classroom Building opened in 1992 with seventy-four classrooms, the net gain campus-wide was considerably less than seventy-four due to classrooms elsewhere immediately being converted to other uses in anticipation of the new classroom building.

35. *Scholastic* 41:26, March 28, 1908, 431; 41:29, May 2, 1908, 495–96. Rather than the Jacob Ackermann who painted the 1885 valence curtain,

this is almost certainly Francis Xavier Ackermann, who taught from 1890 to 1938 and whose overlapping dates with this event make him the likely scenic artist.

36. *Scholastic* 41:28, April 25, 1908, 475.

37. *Scholastic* 49:12, Nov. 27, 1915, 190. Father Burke (1876–1940) was professor of sociology and history (and later Christian doctrine) from 1909 to 1924. In 1915 he was prefect of discipline.

38. *Dome* 1912, 291.

39. President Cavanaugh's patron saint was Saint John the Apostle, whose feast day is December 27, but the President's Day programs confirm that the university moved up this event (December 6–13 between 1905 and 1913, for example) to be able to celebrate before students left campus for the Christmas holidays (President's Day 1880s–1910s, Notre Dame Printed and Reference Materials Dropfiles [hereafter referred to as PNDP], 70-PR-01, UNDA). This event is not to be confused with today's Presidents' Day in February; Notre Dame Archivist Peter Lysy has also pointed out that "President's Day did not celebrate the Notre Dame president's birthday but rather the feast day of his saint" (e-mail to author, July 15, 2009).

40. "The Washington Hall Renovations, Preliminary Report," Cole Engineers/Architects/Planners, South Bend, 1981, posits a 1916 construction date for the projection booth. William Farmer private collection.

41. The convention of lowering house lights during performances is fairly recent, however, having been popularized by the 1870s in London by Henry Irving (1838–1905) and at Bayreuth by Richard Wagner (1813–83) as a result of innovations related to gas lighting.

42. While we associate the Columbians with the minims (boys under thirteen) and the Philopatrians with the preparatory students (boys thirteen to seventeen), things get confusing during this period because there were both the Philopatrians of St. Edward's Hall (minims) and the Philopatrians of Carroll Hall ("preps").

43. *Scholastic* 28:25, March 16, 1895, 403.

44. *Scholastic* 28:26, March 23, 1895, 416.

45. *Scholastic* 28:35, June 1, 1895, 573.

46. *Scholastic* 29:35, June 6, 1896, 578; 29:36, June 13, 1896, 598. Father William Alan Moloney, C.S.C. (1869–1935), had a long and distinguished career at Notre Dame from 1895 through 1934.

47. *Scholastic* 29:36, June 13, 1896, 595; also see 596.

48. *Scholastic* 30:21, Feb. 27, 1897, 343.

49. Ibid., 344.

50. The five nineteenth-century productions in Washington Hall of Shakespeare's *Julius Caesar* (from 1877 to 1892), for example, had no women characters. Carmody's effort in February 1900 put Portia and Calpurnia back into the play, played by Orrin A. White and Louis E. Best, but it would be Frank Kelly's production in March 1929 in which women— Pauline Jellison and Irma Collmer—played the roles for the first time on the Washington Hall stage. Professional touring companies operated differently, however, so that when Augustin Daly's Company of Comedians performed *The Prayer* and *A Woman's Won't* in June 1891, for example, Ada Rehan received high praise (see program for Augustin Daly's Company of Comedians, June 15, 1891, PNDP 76-No-01, UNDA, and *Scholastic* 24:40, June 20, 1891, 636–37). Daly (1838–99), who received the Laetare Medal in 1894, was a playwright and actor who managed a highly regarded company and New York theatre, and Rehan (1859–1916) was his talented leading actress.

51. *Scholastic* 31:21, Feb. 26, 1898, 372–73. Augustin Daly's farcical comedy *A Night Off* premiered in New York at Daly's Theatre on March 4, 1885, to great acclaim. See *New York Times,* March 5, 1885, 4.

52. *Scholastic* 36:25, March 21, 1903, 408; 38:24, March 25, 1905, 392 (with a cast picture on 391). Touring professional companies continued to present mixed gender plays, as with the Nov. 21, 1905, production of the Daniel Sully Company's *Our Pastor* with five women.

53. Pamela Robertson, *Guilty Pleasures: Feminist Camp from Mae West to Madonna* (Durham, N.C.: Duke University Press, 1996), 11.

54. *Dome* 1906, n.p.

55. Ibid., n.p. South Bend had at least three opera houses at this time: Good's Opera House, Price's Theatre, and Oliver Opera House. This is a period when even small towns such as Gosport, Indiana, had their very own opera houses.

56. *Scholastic* 31:21, Feb. 26, 1898, 372–73. Also see *Scholastic* 14:35, May 21, 1881, 562–63. Although probably derived from a Sudanese word for "uncle," the word *sambo* had apparently already become a pejorative term for African Americans by 1898, a year before Helen Bannerman's book *Little Black Sambo* (set in India where she lived for thirty years) first appeared in England. By the 1930s illustrated variants of the story emphasized negative racial stereotypes related to African Americans, culminating in the egregiously offensive and insensitive Castle Films 1935 cartoon.

57. *Scholastic* 31:24, March 19, 1898, 420–21. The calcium source was a piece of quicklime (calcium oxide), hence the alternative name of

"limelight," an early stage lighting instrument that provided intense and focused illumination. First used theatrically at Covent Garden in London in 1837, the limelight was widely used by the 1860s.

58. *Scholastic* 41:10, Nov. 16, 1907, 159. Brockett and Hildy (*History of the Theatre*, 336–37) point out that "the Minstrel Show reached the peak of its popularity between 1850 and 1870. After 1870, companies began to increase in size, some including more than one hundred performers. The popularity of the form declined, nevertheless, and by 1896 only ten companies remained. By 1919 there were only three, and soon the Minstrel Show was a mere curiosity." Structurally, the minstrel show "was divided into two parts. In the first, the performers were arranged in a semicircle, the tambourine player at one end and the 'pair of bones' player at the other. These 'end' men came to be called Tambo and Bones. The 'middle' man, or Interlocutor, served as master of ceremonies and exchanged jokes with the end men between musical numbers. The second part, or 'olio,' consisted of specialty acts and songs." Also see Samuel A. Hay, *African American Theatre: A Historical and Critical Analysis* (New York: Cambridge University Press, 1994) and Carl F. Wittke, *Tambo and Bones: A History of the American Minstrel Stage* (Durham, N.C.: Duke University Press, 1930). Fredric Jameson ("Reification and Utopia in Mass Culture," *Social Text* 1 [Winter 1979]: 130–48) asserts that popular culture forms (including blackface performances) create simultaneously revolutionary and reactionary desires. Also see Phillip B. Zarrilli, et al., *Theatre Histories: An Introduction* (New York: Routledge, 2006), 319–24.

59. The *ANB* entry for Thomas "Daddy" Rice (1808–60), who created the character of Jim Crow by 1831, emphasizes the century-long impact of the minstrel show on perceptions of race: "Minstrel shows ('Ethiopian operas') began featuring white actors in blackface; later, African-American actors in similarly exaggerated makeup appeared in comparable entertainments. Minstrel shows and blackface were enthusiastically received throughout the United States and predominated as a favored popular entertainment for one hundred years, firmly establishing racial stereotypes of African Americans that were not shattered until the middle of the twentieth century. Audiences unfamiliar with blacks or those threatened by racial difference found enjoyment, and perhaps security, in Rice's outrageous characterization." Film picked up the minstrel stage tradition and continued it notably with Al Jolson's "Mammy" in *The Jazz Singer* (1927), in which he performed the song in blackface with white gloves. Mickey Rooney and Judy Garland appeared in blackface in *Babes on Broadway* in 1941, and a year later Bing Crosby appeared with Marjorie Reynolds in

blackface in *Holiday Inn* in the number "Abraham." Crosby, Danny Kaye, Vera Ellen, and Rosemary Clooney performed a "Minstrel Number" (but in whiteface with red gloves) in *White Christmas* in 1954. Spike Lee's *Bamboozled* (2000) brilliantly assesses the minstrel convention and the representation of African Americans on stage.

60. Richard Harding Davis's play is incorrectly recorded as both *The Treasure* and *The War Correspondent* in the 1911 *Dome* (n.p.) and in *Scholastic* 44:13, Dec. 17, 1910, 211.

61. *Dome* 1912, 156, 158. Father Moloney's name is consistently spelled *Maloney* in this source. Brother Cyprian (James O'Hara), C.S.C., (1857–1935), taught at Notre Dame from 1895 to 1931, first in the preparatory school and later as professor of accounting. He also served as director of backstage operations in Washington Hall and chairman of the executive committee of the Philopatrians.

62. *Dome* 1912, 154–55. President's Day refers to the university president's saint's day and should not be confused with today's holiday related to U.S. presidents.

63. Knute Kenneth Rockne was born March 4, 1888, in Voss, Norway, but was raised in Chicago. The *Encyclopedia Britannica* entry credits Rockne as the "football coach who built the University of Notre Dame, Indiana, into a major power in U.S. college football. The success of his teams and his humorous, colourful personality captured the public's imagination during the 1920s, the 'golden age' of American sports."

64. *Dome* 1913, 131, 137.

65. Ibid., 235–37.

66. Ibid., 264. An advertisement for hair restorer in the 1913 *Dome* refers to Rockne—"Yes, Knute"—and makes clear that he was already both popular and losing his hair, although in all fairness he had entered college as a mature student in his twenties. See fig. 6.7.

67. College football made the forward pass legal in 1906 but with restrictions that made it very risky because of the loss of possession if the pass was incomplete. In his autobiography, Rockne credits a very courageous Coach Eddie Cochems at St. Louis University with calling the first forward pass in football on Sept. 5, 1906, despite this risk. Further rule modifications in 1910 and 1912 made passing a more practical option by the time Rockne was a college player. Carlisle's 27–6 upset of Army in 1912, with Native American Jim Thorpe pitted against cadet Dwight Eisenhower, prefigured the Dorais/Rockne success at Notre Dame by one year. Interestingly, in "Thorpe's Indians Crush West Point," Thorpe's punt return and speed running got far more notice than forward passing,

which garnered this singular comment: "The Indians got away four passes that were very cleverly executed, and these gained considerable ground. The cadets tried the forward pass a few times and it failed every time" (*New York Times,* Nov. 10, 1912, S1). It is also well to remember that in Rockne's senior year it was fellow actor and All-Western/All-American football player Raymond Eichenlaub to whom Coach Jesse C. Harper paid tribute on the Washington Hall stage during the student vaudeville show, calling him "one of the greatest football players that ever crossed a gridiron" (*Scholastic* 67:27, May 9, 1914, 648).

68. *Dome* 1914, 97, 122.

69. Ibid., 122, 124, 126–27. Both Birder and Rockne also ran track at Notre Dame as students. While Rockne was not in the cast of *As You Like It,* he probably played in the orchestra that provided eight musical numbers for the evening, two of which were done during the course of the play.

70. Ibid., 125. This seems to be the peak period of insensitivity related to "racist hilarity," with a full-page graphic in the *Dome* using the words *nigger* and *nig,* and a blackface cartoon character (185). It was not until the 1940s that an African American, Edward B. Williams ('47), attended and graduated from Notre Dame.

71. *Scholastic* 48:19, Feb. 13, 1915, 315. Also see *Dome* 1915, 208.

72. *Dome* 1915, 213. Charles Soldani, an Osage from Oklahoma and sole Native American student at Notre Dame in 1914 and 1915, was typecast as "Billy Jack Rabbit, an Indian," in this production. Soldani recalled the irony years later in an interview in Notre Dame *Alumnus* (29:6, Nov.–Dec. 1951) that "a Norwegian from Chicago played his squaw in the play" (4). Soldani went on to have an active twenty-year career in Hollywood movies. David Belasco wrote and produced the melodrama *The Girl of the Golden West* in 1905 and novelized it in 1911. Puccini chose it as the basis for an opera, *La Fanciulla del West,* which premiered in 1910, and motion picture versions include those in 1914 (Cecil B. De-Mille), 1923 (Edwin Carewe), 1930, and 1938 (starring Jeanette Mac-Donald and Nelson Eddy).

73. *Scholastic* 48:29, May 1, 1915, 482–83. John Drury was professor of elocution 1914–15. Emmett George Lenihan (Ph.B., '15) was professor of elocution 1915–17. The Ph.B. (Bachelor of Philosophy) was one of many undergraduate degrees offered at this time.

74. Ibid., 484. *The Rosary* was staged on President's Day 1915, Professor John Drury's first show in which he played Father Kelly.

75. *Dome* 1915, 63. Professor Lenihan was "eminently successful" as a director. See *Scholastic* 49:10, Nov. 13, 1915, 156; 49:14, Dec. 11, 1915, 231.

76. *The Autobiography of Knute K. Rockne,* ed. Bonnie Skiles Rockne, intro. John Cavanaugh, C.S.C. (Indianapolis: Bobbs-Merrill, 1930), 43.

77. Ibid., 43–44.

78. *Scholastic* 52:18, March 1, 1919, 299. The term *ultima thule,* the most mysterious or extreme place, can also mean an unattainable goal, as in this context. Thule, to the Romans, was the most northerly and farthest-off island. The word survives today in the name of the U.S. Armed Forces' northern-most installation in Greenland.

79. *Dome* 1917, 160.

80. *Dome* 1921, 180.

81. Frederick Paulding (1859–1937) was a popular actor, playwright, and drama lecturer who "for his contributions to the drama . . . received the degree of Doctor of Letters from Holy Cross College" (*New York Times,* Sept. 8, 1937, 23). The *Washington Post* called him an "old time Shakespearean actor, playwright and English lecturer" who was "a great nephew of Washington Irving" (Sept. 8, 1937, 10).

82. *Dome* 1921, 181.

83. *Scholastic* 54:12, Jan. 15, 1921, 222–23.

84. *Scholastic* 54:14, Jan. 29, 1921, 241; *Dome* 1922, 207–10.

85. *Scholastic* 41:22, Feb. 29, 1908, 366.

86. *Dome* 1915, 207.

87. *Scholastic* 48:17, Jan. 30, 1915, 286.

88. Ibid.

89. At least four filmed versions of Shakespeare's *Julius Caesar* had been produced by early 1915, three in the United States and one in Great Britain, the first apparently in 1908. The *New York Times* reported the following on Nov. 1, 1914: "George Kleine, producer of the photodrama 'Quo Vadis,' announces 'Julius Caesar' as his next big, spectacular photo drama. 'Julius Caesar' was made in the house of Cines, who also gave 'Quo Vadis' to the motion photo stage. It is claimed that 20,000 people found employment in the making of this photo drama and 25,000 costumes were used. A miniature City of Rome was built six square blocks in size. Antony Novelli, who was so successful as Vinitius in 'Quo Vadis,' and as Antony in 'Antony and Cleopatra,' has the role of Caesar. Mr. Kleine will give the first presentation of this photo drama at the Candler Theatre on Thursday at 10:30 A.M. making it a special performance for the press and the motion-picture exhibitors of Greater New York" (X9).

90. *Scholastic* 48:17 [misprint; should be 18], Feb. 6, 1915, 299.

91. *Scholastic* 48:30, May 8, 1915, 500.

92. *Bulletin* 11:4, 1915–16, 33–36.

93. *Scholastic* 49:10, Nov. 13, 1915, 157.

94. *Scholastic* 49:14, Dec. 11, 1915, 230.

95. Ibid., 231. A rectifier converts alternating current into direct current and is used commonly in electronic devices, all of which require direct current.

96. *Scholastic* 49:25, March 18, 1916, 406. Macklyn Arbuckle (1866–1931) was a cousin of Roscoe "Fatty" Arbuckle (1887–1933). Fasting was common during Lent at this time, so the reference may be to supperless nights on the evenings before receiving Holy Communion.

97. *Scholastic* 52:8, Nov. 30, 1918, 123.

98. *Scholastic* 52:17, Feb. 22, 1919, 284; *Scholastic* 52:19, March 8, 1919, 315.

99. As described by Father Aloysius Crumley, C.S.C., professor of philosophy, psychology, and English from 1898 to 1934, in the *Dome* 1921, 181.

100. *Bulletin,* 1919–20, 40.

101. *Scholastic* 28:21, Feb. 16, 1895, 338; 28:33, May 18, 1895, 537; 31:28, April 23, 1898, 490. The United States had adopted the silver standard by 1785 and added gold for a de facto bimetallic standard by 1873, with the gold standard legally established in 1900 and lasting until 1971. The Sixteenth Amendment to the Constitution allowing Congress to levy a federal income tax was ratified in 1913, four years after its 1909 passage by Congress, but the issue of federal income taxation had long been a point of discussion and debate, especially since the 1895 Supreme Court ruling denying Congress the right to tax income in *Pollock v. Farmers' Loan & Trust Co.*

102. *Scholastic* 31:34, June 4, 1898, 588.

103. *Scholastic* 31:35, June 11, 1898, 605.

104. *Scholastic* 39:21, March 10, 1906, 360; 39:30, May 19, 1906, 509. Frederic Karr was professor of elocution and oratory from 1904 to 1906.

105. The Breen Medal orations, Saturday, Dec. 4, 1909, 7:30 P.M. Program, William Farmer private collection.

106. *Scholastic* 54:15, Feb. 5, 1921, 262.

107. *Scholastic* 54:23, April 23, 1921, 430.

108. *Scholastic* 52:14, Feb. 1, 1919, 225.

109. *Scholastic* 35:1, Aug. 1, 1901, 15.

110. *Scholastic* 28:23, March 2, 1895, 366.

111. *Scholastic* 31:29, April 30, 1898, 506; 31:30, May 7, 1898, 522. Catholic art historian Starr (1824–1901) was the first woman to receive the Laetare Medal (1865). Paul Beyer was instructor of gymnastics from 1893 to 1899.

112. *Scholastic* 31:19, Feb. 12, 1898, 342.

113. *Scholastic* 31:23, March 12, 1898, 402. President McKinley asked Congress for a declaration of war against Spain, April 11, 1898.

114. *Scholastic* 37:18, Feb. 6, 1904, 307.

115. *Scholastic* 39:16, Feb. 3, 1906, 274–75.

116. *Dome* 1914, 244. "Meagher of the Sword" (1823–67) escaped a British death sentence for his Irish nationalism; in the United States he commanded the Irish Brigade during the Civil War, after which he served as acting governor of the Montana Territory.

117. *Scholastic* 52:14, Feb. 1, 1919, 225. The Irish War of Independence ended in a truce in 1921 that resulted in the island's political partition.

118. *South Bend Tribune*, Oct. 14, 1919, 1–2; *Dome* 1920, 261; *Scholastic* 53:5, Oct. 25, 1919, 71–72. Eamon de Valera (1882–1975) was chief minister (prime minister or president, but not head of state) from 1919 to 1921 of the new Assembly of Ireland formed by Irish members of Parliament. He visited the United States to gain support for Irish independence from Britain. He later played a significant role in writing the 1937 constitution that created a president as head of state, an office first filled by Douglas Hyde. Thus each man can be considered the first president of Ireland.

119. *Scholastic* 40:8, Nov. 3, 1906, 128. Fairbanks (1852–1918), after whom the Alaskan city is named, was U.S. senator from Indiana, 1897–1905, before becoming vice president under Teddy Roosevelt, 1905–9.

120. *Scholastic* 41:20, Feb. 15, 1908, 335. The great American orator William Jennings Bryan (1860–1925) ran for president as a Democrat unsuccessfully three times—in 1896, 1900, and 1908—and ultimately served as Wilson's secretary of state, 1913–15. Bryan is probably best remembered today for his Christian fundamentalism and opposition to Darwinism, as manifested in the 1925 Scopes trial in which he opposed Clarence Darrow, dramatically re-created in Jerome Lawrence and Robert Edwin Lee's *Inherit the Wind*, which initially ran on Broadway for over two years from 1955 to 1957, and was made into a successful film in 1960 and three made-for-television productions in 1965, 1988, and 1999.

121. *Scholastic* 47:25, April 25, 1914, 614–15. Benson, the son of the archbishop of Canterbury, had converted to Catholicism in 1903 and was ordained a priest a year later. The First Vatican Council proclaimed the doctrine of papal infallibility in 1870.

122. *Scholastic* 49:25, March 18, 1916, 406.

123. *Scholastic* 54:4, Oct. 16, 1920, 61.

124. *Scholastic* 41:11, Nov. 23, 1907, 174.

125. Also, Lincoln (1865), Garfield (1881), and Kennedy (1963). Both Lincoln (1865) and Garfield (1881) died when the first Washington Hall operated.

126. *Scholastic* 35:2, Sept. 21, 1901, 36–40.

127. *Dome* 1922, 210.

Chapter 7. The Ghost of Washington Hall, 1920–2004

1. Father Robert Austgen, C.S.C., interview with the author, Oct. 7, 2003.

2. *Scholastic* 8:13, Dec. 19, 1874, 171. Blacksmiths and wheelbarrow makers in the 1850s in both South Bend and California during the Gold Rush, the Studebaker brothers created the largest wagon manufacturing company in the world largely thanks to U.S. Army orders during the Civil War. They were the only horse-drawn vehicle makers successfully to shift to gasoline automobiles, with production centered in South Bend until 1963. See the Studebaker National Museum site at http://www.studebakermuseum.org/history.asp (accessed June 8, 2010).

3. *Scholastic* 54:12, Jan. 15, 1921, 212. Coincidentally, this club held a banquet at the Oliver Hotel (at Main and Washington Streets in South Bend where George Gipp lived) on Dec. 20, just a week after he died. A twenty-five-story hotel and office building occupies the site of the 1899 Oliver Hotel today. See http://downtownsouthbend.com/history.php (accessed June 8, 2010).

4. *Scholastic* 54:12, Jan. 15, 1921, 213.

5. Ibid., 216.

6. *Scholastic* 54:13, Jan. 22, 1921, 232.

7. Ibid.

8. *Scholastic* 54:14, Jan. 29, 1921, 243–44.

9. *Dome* 1921, 305.

10. The unofficial name for the garage, northeast of the Fire Department, just north of St. Edward's Hall, where the infirmary stands today; it had rooms for residents on its second level at this time.

11. *Dome* 1926, 342–43. Brother Maurilius (William J. DeGan), C.S.C. (1878–1947), was rector of Carroll Hall from 1928 to 1937. Joseph Casasanta ('23) (1901–68), may be the talented trumpeter associated with the original 1920–21 ghost hoax. Serving as assistant director of the band while still a student, after graduation he went on to become the distinguished director of the Notre Dame Band from 1923 to 1942, and,

in a very real sense, he never really left Washington Hall. See *The Band of the Fighting Irish: A Pictorial History of the Notre Dame Band* (Notre Dame, Ind.: Ave Maria Press, 2002), 1:12–13, 144–45. A talented composer, Casasanta is perhaps best known for the melody to "Notre Dame, Our Mother," with words by Charles L. O'Donnell (1931), which became the university's alma mater, and for his popular arrangement of the "Notre Dame Victory March."

12. Burns, *Being Catholic, Being American: The Notre Dame Story, 1842–1934,* 1:213–17. Interestingly, Burns also finds no evidence to support Gipp's ever being referred to as "the Gipper" when he lived (1:219–22).

13. *Scholastic* 67:12, Jan. 15, 1932, 17.

14. *Notre Dame Alumnus* 10:4, Jan. 1932, 114.

15. *Scholastic* 71:12, Dec. 17, 1937, 7, 22. Demosthenes, Cicero, and Washington refer of course to the Gregori/Rusca murals.

16. *Scholastic* 74:4, Oct. 11, 1940, 9.

17. *Scholastic* 76:8, Aug. 7, 1942, 7, 26.

18. *Scholastic* 87:3, April 5, 1946, 10, 32.

19. *Scholastic* 89:6, Oct. 31, 1947, 12–13. While as many as eight students lived in Washington Hall in 1920–21, by the late 1940s the number had declined to three or fewer.

20. *Dome* 1948, 409; *Scholastic* 90:5, Oct. 22, 1948, 10. This medieval interpretation of the Annunciation combined the musical efforts of both the Notre Dame and the Saint Mary's College Glee Clubs.

21. Daniel M. Boland, Ph.D., e-mail to author, Aug. 7, 2008.

22. *Scholastic* 107:22, May 13, 1966, 14.

23. *Observer* 3:16, Oct. 4, 1968, 2.

24. *Notre Dame Magazine* 3:4, Oct. 1974, 12. Reprinted from the *South Bend Tribune. Notre Dame Magazine* 3:5, Dec. 1974, 3.

25. *Scholastic* 117:4, Oct. 24, 1975, 24–27.

26. *Scholastic* 118:11, May 2, 1977, 8–9. *Notre Dame Magazine* 7:1, Feb. 1978, 64.

27. *South Bend Tribune,* Oct. 23, 1977, 8–9.

28. Jinny Porcari Keough, letter to the author, Nov. 1, 2006.

29. "The Ghost of Washington Hall," *Observer* 13:119, April 23, 1979, 7. No byline exists for part 1, but since Phil Hicks authored parts 2 and 3, he likely also wrote part 1. Brother Cajetan (Austin Gallagher), 1855–1927, worked at Notre Dame from 1883 until his death, and lived in nearby St. Edward's Hall where he served as prefect for the minims for forty-five years.

30. "Untimely Deaths on N. D. & S. M. C. Campuses 1840s–1990s," Dorothy Corson Papers (hereafter referred to as CORS), UNDA. Drownings in the lakes were the chief causes of untimely deaths.

31. *Scholastic* 14:38, June 11, 1881, 612. The Reverend Dr. Louis Neyron was professor of physiology from 1863 to 1871, at which time he also acquired an M.D. He continued on the faculty of science (human anatomy and physiology) through 1886–87.

32. Phil Hicks, "The Ghost of Washington Hall," *Observer* 13:121, April 25, 1979, 6.

33. Phil Hicks, "The Ghost of Washington Hall," *Observer* 13:122, April 26, 1979, 6–7.

34. Toni Rutherford, "The Ghost in Washington Hall," *Observer* 17:110, March 4, 1983, 8–9.

35. Paul Whitfield, "N. D. Theater Combines Change, Tradition," *South Bend Tribune,* Aug. 18, 1985, 18.

36. *Dome* 1986, 274.

37. *South Bend Tribune,* March 11, 1990, D1–D2; *Scholastic* 139:1, Summer 1997, 14; *Scholastic* 140:5, Oct. 29, 1998, 14–15; Christina Ries, e-mail to author, Aug. 12, 2008; *South Bend Tribune,* Oct. 23, 2005, A1, A10.

Chapter 8. More Than the Home of the Lecture, 1922–1956

1. University of Notre Dame Commencement Exercises Program, Friday, June 8, Saturday, June 9, and Sunday, June 10, 1923. William Farmer private collection. The opera singers and musicians were Kathryn Browne, mezzo-soprano, William Rogerson, tenor, of the Chicago Grand Opera Association, and Adalbert Huguelet.

2. *Dome* 1923, 202.

3. Zarrilli, et al., discuss "Media and Theatre: Niche Marketing," in *Theatre Histories: An Introduction* (New York: Routledge, 2006), 446–49. For niche theory, see J. W. Dimmick, *Media Competition and Coexistence: The Theory of the Niche* (Mahwah, N.J.: Lawrence Erlbaum, 2003).

4. *Scholastic* 66:1, Sept. 23, 1932, 15. The ground floor of Washington Hall was often described as the basement.

5. *Notre Dame Alumnus* 11:4, Jan. 1933, 111. "Rockefeller Hall" was the informally and unofficially named collection of buildings and additions east of Washington Hall which had originally housed the water closets serving surrounding buildings.

6. Stritch, *My Notre Dame,* 123.

7. *Scholastic* 66:13, Jan. 20, 1933, 17.

8. Stritch, *My Notre Dame,* 121, 123.

9. M. Clay Adams, e-mail to author, April 25, 2005.

10. *New York Times,* June 15, 1936, 1, 21.

11. *Scholastic* 66:12, Jan. 13, 1933, 14.

12. *New York Times,* Oct. 15, 1933, 34. Although he had an Italian father, Marconi's mother was Irish. Guglielmo Marconi (1874–1937) was probably best known for his invention of the wireless telegraph (1896), which became radio. In 1909 he received the Nobel Prize for Physics.

13. *Scholastic* 67:5, Oct. 20, 1933, 3, 10. The Reverend Charles Christopher Miltner, C.S.C., Ph.D. (1886–1966), was a professor of philosophy from 1917 to 1940. He was appointed the first head of the Philosophy Department in 1920 and also served as dean of the College of Arts and Letters. He was president of the University of Portland from 1940 to 1946.

14. *Scholastic* 70:6, Oct. 30, 1936, 3, 23.

15. *New York Times,* Oct. 26, 1936, 18.

16. *Scholastic* 70:6, Oct. 30, 1936, 1, 23.

17. *Dome* 1937, 252, 352; *Scholastic* 70:8, Nov. 20, 1936, 12. The Most Reverend Fulton John Sheen (1895–1979) successfully used radio (1930–50) and television (1950–57, 1961–68) to preach and reaffirm the faith. His cause for canonization was opened in 2002, and he is today a Servant of God.

18. *Scholastic* 97:19, March 23, 1956, 32. The work of Thomas Anthony Dooley III (1927–61) in southeast Asia inspired President Kennedy to create the Peace Corps.

19. *Dome* 1932, 245, 276–83, 288–89, 293–94.

20. *Scholastic* 73:18, March 8, 1940, 21–22. With funding from Lord Carnarvon, English Egyptologist Howard Carter (1874–1939) began looking for the tomb of King Tutankhamen in 1914, "discovered" it in February 1923, and worked there until 1933.

21. *Scholastic* 73:13, Jan. 12, 1940, 20; *Scholastic* 73:21, April 12, 1940, 9. This was at the very end of the career of Anthony Frederick Sarg (1880–1942), America's Puppet Master. In 1928 Sarg introduced "upside-down" marionettes, the giant helium-filled character-inspired balloons that traverse the parade route on behalf of Macy's on Thanksgiving Day, and in 1935 he was the creative force behind Macy's animated seasonal window decorations. His touring puppet theatre productions included *Treasure Island, Rip Van Winkle,* and *Robin Hood,* mentioned here. Sarg's *Alice in Wonderland* received special acclaim due to the alternating substitution of the Alice marionette with a live actress; the Huber marionettes paid homage to Sarg's creativity in the film *Being John Malkovich* (1999). Sarg's protégé, Bill Baird (1904–87), went on to train Jim Henson

(1936–90). For this 1940 performance, celebrating twenty-one years on the road, David Pritchard headed the troupe.

22. *Scholastic* 67 [65]:14, Feb. 5, 1932, 5, 10; 66:2, Sept. 30, 1932, 29. [The 1931–32 *Scholastic* was chronologically vol. 65 but was printed as vol. 67.] Other ads for "8-tube" radios were as much as $45, just over $700 in 2009 dollars. The $200–$700 range, however, is in line with amounts students spend in 2009 on electronic communication devices such as cell phones and laptop computers. To compare buying power since 1914, see the consumer price index inflation calculator at http://www.bls.gov/data/inflation_calculator.htm (accessed June 8, 2010).

23. See *Bulletin* 20:4, 1924–25, 87–94.

24. *Bulletin* 19:5, 1923–24, 108–10.

25. Ibid., 72.

26. *Scholastic* 54:15, Jan. 28, 1927, 460, 462; 68:19, March 8, 1935, 6.

27. *Notre Dame Alumnus* 10:4, Jan. 1932, 105. Charles Phillips was professor of English at Notre Dame from 1924 until his death in late December 1933.

28. *Dome* 1927, 217.

29. Program, premiere season of the University Theatre, Dec. 17, 1926, unpaginated eight-page program, William Farmer private collection. The historical pageant seems never to have been done.

30. Commencement program, Friday, June 3, 1927, William Farmer private collection.

31. Congress proposed the Nineteenth Amendment to the Constitution in June 1919, and it was ratified in August 1920.

32. The production was done in both March and May with the same cast. *Julius Caesar* program, March 17 and May 31, 1929, William Farmer private collection.

33. *The Taming of the Shrew* program, Dec. 16, 1929, William Farmer private collection.

34. *Scholastic* 68:19, March 8, 1935, 6. *Turn to the Right* was "the first dramatic effort of the year by the University Theatre group" which was unusually late. See *Scholastic* 68:21, March 22, 1935, 7. Distractions emanating from below in Brownson Recreation Hall during lectures in Washington Hall included "blaring radios, pounding pianos, and yelling pool-players," not to mention the noisy ventilators and lack of heat, according to *Scholastic* 68:23, April 12, 1935, 9. *Shades of Notre Dame* was the June 2, 1935, commencement play (*Dome* 1935, 139).

35. *Scholastic* 69:6, Nov. 1, 1935, 7. John Francis Cardinal O'Hara, C.S.C. (1888–1960), was president from 1934 to 1940.

36. *Scholastic* 69:20, March 20, 1936, 9.

37. *Scholastic* 72:6, Oct. 28, 1938, 9.

38. *South Bend Tribune*, Nov. 12, 1938. *Room Service* (1937), by John Murray and Allen Boretz, had been on Broadway for nearly a year, and there was a film version with the Marx brothers, Lucille Ball, and Ann Miller (1938).

39. *Scholastic* 72:10, Dec. 2, 1938, 6, 19. This revival of males playing females related to "legitimate" theatre; before, during, and after this period men played female roles in parodic/satiric skits and revues.

40. Ibid., 11. The curtain call occurred historically when the applause did not stop.

41. *Dome* 1940, 133.

42. *Dome* 1923, 196.

43. The Monogram Club first appears in the *Dome* 1922 (235), although the Monogram Men have a page as early as the *Dome* 1915 (118). The Monogram Club's own history claims its origins as the Varsity Club in 1898; see http://und.cstv.com/sports/monogramclub/spec-rel/monogram-club-history.html (accessed Aug. 15, 2009). The *Scholastic* 49:27, April 1, 1916, 437, says, "Wearers of the monogram have organized under the name of the Notre Dame Monogram Men's Club."

44. *Dome* 1924, 208–10. Eddie Cantor (1892–1964) began in vaudeville. Known as Banjo Eyes, he performed in blackface into the 1940s. It is a supreme irony that these same students allied with local Polish and Hungarian immigrants (who were as despised by the Klan as the Irish Catholics at Notre Dame) to humiliate the local Ku Klux Klan in the May 1924 riots in the streets of South Bend. Both Director of Athletics Rockne and President Walsh spoke in Washington Hall at that time to persuade the students to sign a pledge declaring "to refrain from further rioting" (*Chicago Daily Tribune*, May 21, 1924, 4). As a direct result of the Klan riots, aggravated by so many students living off campus and thus in the midst of the turmoil, the university immediately began to build more dormitories, with the goal of physically separating gown from town. See Burns, *Being Catholic, Being American: The Notre Dame Story, 1842–1934*, 1:305–22, and Todd Tucker, *Notre Dame vs. the Klan: How the Fighting Irish Defeated the Ku Klux Klan* (Chicago: Loyola Press, 2004).

45. *Scholastic* 68:24, May 4, 1934, 6. Father Charles McAllister, C.S.C., founded the Linnets and supervised this event. The group takes its name from a finch that sings beautifully.

46. *Dome* 1934, 286–87.

47. *Scholastic* 72:7, Nov. 4, 1938, 18; 72:8, Nov. 18, 1938, 7. Eva Jessye (1895–1992), music director for George Gershwin's *Porgy and Bess* on Broadway in 1935, had a long and distinguished career as a choral conductor.

48. *Scholastic* 73:2, Sept. 29, 1939, 6. Walter O'Keefe (1900–1983) went on to be a Broadway composer and television personality. Charles Butterworth (1896–1946) had a successful film career in musical comedy. Both have stars on the Hollywood Walk of Fame.

49. *Scholastic* 73:12, Dec. 15, 1939, 7.

50. *Dome* 1938, 210. *Scholastic* 74:9, Nov. 29, 1940, 5; 74:11, Dec. 13, 1940, 5, 9.

51. *Scholastic* 73:17, Feb. 23, 1940, 7.

52. *Scholastic* 99:8, Nov. 22, 1957, 26.

53. *Scholastic* 87:1, March 22, 1946, 15.

54. *Scholastic* 89:12, Dec. 19, 1947, 11.

55. *Scholastic* 87:4, April 12, 1946, 16. The first black student, Edward B. Williams, arrived in 1944. See Biographical Files, Notre Dame Information Services (hereafter referred to as UDIS) 137/30, UNDA; and First Black Students and Graduates, PNDP B1-1, UNDA.

56. *Scholastic* 70:7, Nov. 13, 1936, 12.

57. *Dome* 1938, 208.

58. Also see *Scholastic* 75:11, Dec. 12, 1941, 11.

59. Gilbert and Sullivan flourished from 1871 to 1896; the members of their D'Oyly Carte Opera Company performed at the Savoy Theatre in London and thus became known as "Savoyards."

60. *Scholastic* 78:10, April 23, 1943, 17, 22.

61. It was usual during World War II to stay at Notre Dame only until one could qualify for a commission and deployment. Thousands of men came and went during the 1942–45 period, only to return later to complete their degrees. For those doing "regular college" the degree programs were accelerated during this time by adding a full summer semester and thus a four-year eight-semester program shortened to two and two-thirds years with the concept of annually designated "classes" and spring commencement no longer relevant.

62. *Scholastic* 80:8, Jan. 14, 1944, 10. The V-12 Navy College Training Program (1943–46) flourished at over a hundred colleges and universities and provided thousands of additional commissioned officers for the Navy and Marine Corps during the Second World War.

63. *Scholastic* 80:10, Jan. 28, 1944, 10.

64. *Scholastic* 88:16, Feb. 21, 1947, 9, 29; 88:17, Feb. 28, 1947, 7, 19. Schlereth points out that Vetville "housed married students and their

families until 1961, when its buildings were bulldozed and burned to make way for the Memorial [now Hesburgh] Library" (*The University of Notre Dame*, 192).

65. *Dome* 1948, 429. Upon graduation, Cashman worked on Tin Pan Alley and Broadway before becoming a producer on the Texaco Star Theater (with Milton Berle).

66. *Scholastic* 90:3, Oct. 8, 1948, 9.

67. *Scholastic* 92:21, April 13, 1951, 34.

68. *Scholastic* 93:10, Nov. 16, 1951, 33.

69. *Scholastic* 93:3, Sept. 28, 1951, 12. Joseph H. Huebner returned to Notre Dame in 1963 and served more than thirty years as a faculty librarian; his invaluable collection of professional costume renderings graces the walls of the DeBartolo Center for the Performing Arts today. At Notre Dame he was instrumental in the significant advances made in the acquisition of fine and performing arts materials, including support for the academic study of film, television, and theatre through his early recognition of the importance of video recordings and other nonmonograph resources in the modern research library.

70. *Scholastic* 93:4, Oct. 5, 1951, 15.

71. Sommer also rehearsed scenes out of order, perceived at the time to be avant-garde. See *Scholastic* 93:7, Oct. 26, 1951, 12.

72. *Scholastic* 93:7, Oct. 26, 1951, 16.

73. Players Incorporated, an international repertory company from Washington, D.C., was composed of Catholic University graduates.

74. *Scholastic* 93:10, Nov. 16, 1951, 13, 16; 93:11, Nov. 16, 1951, 6, 11.

75. *Scholastic* 93:13, Dec. 14, 1951, 16.

76. *Scholastic* 93:25, May 2, 1952, 12.

77. *Scholastic* 93:23, April 4, 1952, 17–19; 93:26, May 9, 1952, 20–21.

78. *Notre Dame Alumnus* 30:5, Oct. 5, 1952, 1; *South Bend Tribune*, Sept. 28, 1952, 11; also see *Dome* 1953, 351–53.

79. *South Bend Tribune,* March 6, 1953; program, UDIS 55/8, UNDA.

80. See *Scholastic* 94:24, May 8, 1953, 24; Musicals Written and Performed by Students 1940s–1950s, PNDP 76-Mu-1, UNDA, which contains an informative and accurate "History of N. D. Student Musicals." Don Rathgeb, associated with Saint Michael's Playhouse at Saint Michael's College, has had a distinguished career in the professional theatre.

81. *Scholastic* 95:9, Nov. 20, 1953, 11, 15; interview with the author, March 30, 2004. Father Eugene Francis Gorski, C.S.C., returned as a faculty member in the philosophy department and has had a long career of inspired teaching. Joe Huebner was "in charge of costumes" for this production.

82. Within ten years of graduation from Notre Dame, Phil Donahue would originate the tabloid talk show on television, characterized by Christine A. Becker as "presenting a revolutionary blend of the personal and the political" (e-mail to the author, July 3, 2009).

83. Reginald F. Bain, "A Remembrance of Father Arthur S. Harvey, C.S.C., 1911–2008," eulogy, Feb. 10, 2008.

84. Thomas J. Barry press release, UDIS 49/05, UNDA; *South Bend Tribune,* July 18, 1940, 1, 18. *Twelfth Night* was performed outdoors on the south side of the Commerce Building (now Hurley Hall) and not in Washington Hall, but I include it here because it is the beginning of a movement unique in the history of Notre Dame. Sister Kathleen Cannon, O.P., advised me that while "technically, nuns refers to cloistered women and sisters refers to those who have some active ministry or apostolate . . . in general usage, I think most people just refer to both groups as 'the nuns'" (e-mail to the author, April 30, 2008).

85. *South Bend Tribune,* July 19, 1953, 11. Also see "Twelve nuns attending Summer Session to present a Play . . . ," PNDP PR 53/155 UNDA, and "Theater—Summer School Nuns Rehearsing for 'A Soul in Fine Array,'" Notre Dame Information Services (hereafter referred to as GDIS) 35/07, UNDA. Internal evidence strongly suggests that Casey wrote the play quickly in 1953, the first summer it was produced, and not 1951 as the archives date suggests.

86. Notre Dame press release 54/137, UDIS 55/7, 1937–58, UNDA.

87. *South Bend Tribune,* July 25, 1954, 7. John Kovach, archivist at Saint Mary's College, confirmed that Natalie E. White "was listed as a visiting lecturer for the 1953–54 and 1954–55 academic years," and he shared the article in *The Sunday Visitor,* Sept. 13, 1953, n.p., which said Natalie White of "Hollywood, Calif." had joined the Speech Department as a new faculty member (e-mail to the author, April 1, 2008). In a *South Bend Tribune* interview (Dec. 20, 1953), White characterized her work at Saint Mary's as being "more strenuous" than her years in the professional theatre, and she mentions both the Pasadena Playhouse, "where she taught, acted, and directed," and the Ten O'Clock Theater in Hollywood (20). Penn Genthner, archivist at Pasadena Playhouse (now the State Theatre of California), confirmed that "Jane White" graduated from the Pasadena Playhouse School of Theatre Arts in 1948, and acted and directed there rather consistently between July 1947 and March 1949. After a nine-year hiatus, she returned in May 1958 and worked on four productions (two as actor and two as director) between May 1958 and March 1960 (e-mail to the author, April 29, 2008). If Jane and Natalie

White were one and the same, it was during this hiatus that she wrote and directed musical farces for the nuns in Notre Dame's Summer Theatre Program.

88. *Summer Session Calendar 1954,* Saint Mary's College, July 25, 26, 1954, n.p.

89. *Notre Dame Alumnus* 32, Nov.–Dec. 1954, 9. White's dissertation was "Shakespeare on the New York Stage, 1891–1941" (Yale University, 1946), and her M.A. thesis was "Hamlet on the New York Stage, 1900–1910" (George Washington University, 1941). She also went on to write a sequel, *Seven Nuns South of the Border* (Dramatist Play Service, 1962), the copy of which in the Catholic University Library includes her suggested changes of December 1963.

90. Catholic Theatre Conference program, June 12–15, 1955, UDIS 7/08, UNDA.

91. "Nuns in a Musical Frolic," *Life* 41:6, Aug. 6, 1956, 115–16. Also see "Sister Act," *Time,* July 30, 1956.

92. *Notre Dame Alumnus* 34:5, Oct. 1956, 3.

93. *Indiana Catholic,* July 29, 1960. UDIS 025/12, UNDA.

94. *Sunday Visitor,* Huntington, Ind., Oct. 10, 1954. Father Arthur S. Harvey, C.S.C. (1911–2008), was born in Washington, D.C., and attended the University of Notre Dame (A. B., 1947), Holy Cross College in Washington, D.C., and the Catholic University of America (M.A., 1953). He was ordained in 1951 and joined the Notre Dame faculty where he was director of the University Theatre from 1954 to 1969, after which he served as an assistant to Executive Vice President Father Edmund P. "Ned" Joyce, C.S.C.

95. *Scholastic* 96:1, Oct. 1, 1954, 14, 33.

96. *South Bend Tribune,* Nov. 15, 1956, 42.

97. Professor Jerome J. Green (1866–1943) was professor of electrical engineering at Notre Dame from 1895 to 1915; his seminal wireless telegraphy (Morse code) experiment in the United States occurred in April 1899 at Notre Dame after a series of trials involving shorter distances. See *Scholastic* 32:28, April 22, 1899, 494, and *American Electrician,* July 1899, 344–46.

98. WNDU-TV dedication program, Sept. 30–Oct. 2, 1955, n.p., PNDP 1302-1955, UNDA.

99. For the sake of comparison, the 2007–8 Broadway theatre season sold just over twelve million tickets (all the performances for all the plays for a year), while a single episode of a popular television show like *American Idol* drew over thirty million viewers.

100. *Scholastic* 97:22, May 4, 1956, 10; 97:23, May 11, 1956, 20.

101. Supplement No. 1 to Appraisal of Property Belonging to University of Notre Dame, March 17, 1955, 78, Notre Dame Controller/Comptroller (hereafter referred to as UCMP), UNDA.

102. At halftime during a scoreless game with Army in 1928, Rockne is apocryphally credited with asking the team to "win one for the Gipper," keeping a promise that he said he had made to Gipp on his deathbed, after which Notre Dame rallied to beat Army 12−6. Although it is highly unlikely that George Gipp made such a request, the story nevertheless became forever burned into the national imagination when Ronald Reagan as Gipp spoke the lines in the 1940 film to Pat O'Brien's Rockne.

103. John A. Gueguen, manuscript journal, Sept. 15, 1953, 1−2. John C. Lujack, Jr., quarterback and Heisman Trophy winner (born in 1925), graduated from Notre Dame in 1947, the year he won the Heisman, and played for the Chicago Bears 1948−51.

104. *Scholastic* 95:2, Oct. 2, 1953, 15.

105. *Scholastic* 88:1, Sept. 20, 1946, 10.

106. *Scholastic* 54:7, Nov. 5, 1926, 200; 54:8, Nov. 12, 1926, 233. See Donald Crafton, *The Talkies: American Cinema's Transition to Sound, 1926–1931* (New York: Charles Scribner's Sons, 1997), 70–88, 225, for a complete discussion of Vitaphone technology. Father William Arthur Carey, C.S.C., was professor of classics from 1918 until his death in 1947 and held many administrative positions including registrar from 1920 to 1929.

107. *Scholastic* 64:1, Sept. 26, 1930, 8, 26. Motiograph manufactured and sold projectors and sound amplifiers.

108. *Scholastic* 67:13, Jan. 22, 1932, 17.

109. *Scholastic* 67:1, Sept. 25, 1931, 7.

110. *Scholastic* 74:2, Sept. 27, 1940, 1; 74:3, Oct. 4, 1940, 7.

111. *Scholastic* 74:2, Sept. 27, 1940, 1; 74:3, Oct. 4, 1940, 7. Ronald Reagan (1911–2004) returned to Notre Dame in May 1976, and later as president at the May 1981 commencement, at which he received an honorary degree, and in March 1988 for the Knute Rockne commemorative stamp dedication.

112. *Scholastic* 67:13, Jan. 22, 1932, 17.

113. *Scholastic* 68:17, March 2, 1934, 7.

114. *Scholastic* 67:3, Oct. 6, 1933, 1.

115. *Scholastic* 75:15, Feb. 20, 1942, 12.

116. *Scholastic* 86:1, Nov. 16, 1945, 8.

117. *Notre Dame Alumnus* 24:2, April 1946, 30. Brother Canute (Jeremiah Lardner), C.S.C., was born December 21, 1871, in Chicago and died in Washington Hall, February 2, 1946.

118. *Scholastic* 89:10, Dec. 10, 1947, 34; 89:12, Dec. 19, 1947, 4.

119. *Scholastic* 93:7, Oct. 26, 1951, 30. The Engineering Auditorium, built in 1932, seated 480 and was used for classes through December 1999.

120. *Scholastic* 93:10, Nov. 16, 1951, 16. Students typically knew Brother Robert as "Brother Movie," since it was common in those days to give a job-related nickname to a working brother. Brother Robert (Francis Thomas O'Brien), C.S.C. (1885–1973), is buried in the Community Cemetery at Notre Dame. "Good taste and propriety" of course relate to the Legion of Decency established in 1934 by U.S. Catholic bishops (see *HarperCollins Encyclopedia of Catholicism,* 763), about the same time as the Motion Picture Production Code also went into effect.

121. *Scholastic* 73:13, Jan. 12, 1940, 18.

122. *Scholastic* 86:5, Dec. 14, 1945, 8.

123. *Scholastic* 86:7, Jan. 11, 1946, 4.

124. *Bulletin of Information* 58:1, 1961–62, 62.

125. Ibid.; Edward Fischer, *Notre Dame Remembered: An Autobiography* (Notre Dame, Ind.: University of Notre Dame Press, 1987), 108.

126. *Dome* 1956, 9.

127. Ibid., 18–31. Also see *South Bend Tribune,* May 19, 1956; *Scholastic* 97:24, May 18, 1956, 14; and David Vaughan, *Merce Cunningham: Fifty Years,* ed. Melissa Hart (New York: Aperture, n.d. [1997]), 88–89.

Chapter 9. Modernization, 1956–1984

1. E-mail to the author, Aug. 7, 2008.

2. *Notre Dame Alumnus* 34:4, Aug. 1956, 15. Lightolier is a lighting equipment company founded in 1904 which by the 1920s was associated with style as well as function and thus also became a generic term. It was a major innovator in "mood" recessed and track lighting in the 1950s.

3. E-mail to the author, June 10, 2009.

4. *Scholastic* 96:16, March 2, 1956, 16–17.

5. Stritch, *My Notre Dame,* 62.

6. I first worked with Father Art Harvey when I invited him to return to direct *Death of a Salesman* on the Washington Hall stage for the 1987–88 season (for which I served as producer and assisted in locating period properties). Father Art insisted on complete historical accuracy:

the audience never knew that a small bottle containing saccharin tablets sitting on a shelf in the Loman kitchen was indeed from the late 1940s. I keep that bottle to this day in my office as a memento of the production and as an example of a director's insistence on detail.

7. Before *The Lion King* opened in Los Angeles in 2000, for example, Pantages Theatre underwent a multi-million-dollar renovation so the production could be a clone of the Broadway show.

8. "Pin-point blocking" does not always produce good results. The *Scholastic* 106:7, Nov. 20, 1964, 21, said his blocking for *King Lear* "seemed uninformed."

9. Father Harvey's seven-week rehearsal period much more consistently followed the useful guide of one hour of rehearsal time for every one minute of playing time, meaning that a 2-hour play demands 120 hours of rehearsal. Some of his predecessors had often significantly under-rehearsed their shows with only a couple of weeks of rehearsal, that is, no more than fifty hours.

10. *Observer* 37:42, Nov. 1, 2002, http://www.nd.edu/~observer/11012002/News/2.html (accessed May 20, 2010).

11. Barbara Benford Trafficanda, letter to the author, Aug. 14, 2009.

12. *The Voice* 2:4, Oct. 16, 1963, 2; 2:12, Jan. 15, 1964, 2.

13. Alumnus Tony Bill ('62) related that his experience in the audience at *The Boy Friend* convinced him to be an actor. He promptly auditioned for *Murder in the Cathedral* but was not cast. Instead of accepting the offer to work backstage, he auditioned successfully at Saint Mary's College where he performed regularly over the next four years. Within months of graduation, Tony Bill created the role of Frank Sinatra's brother, Buddy, in *Come Blow Your Horn* (1963) and would go on to have a distinguished career as a producer (e.g., *The Sting,* 1973) and director (e.g., *My Bodyguard,* 1980). Interview with the author, Nov. 3, 2006.

14. E-mail to the author, June 15, 2009.

15. *Dome* 1957, 32–33.

16. While students from the Harvey era onward might have perceived that Notre Dame had a "theatre department," and there was a major in theatre, to this day at Notre Dame students who wish to study theatre academically do so as a concentration within the larger departmental major of film, television, and theatre.

17. *Dome* 1957, 335.

18. Frederic W. Syburg, "University Theatre Celebrates 10th Anniversary," *Notre Dame* 16:4, Winter 1963, 9–13.

19. *South Bend Tribune,* Nov. 9, 1962, 43.

20. Kavanaugh's *New York Times* obituary, Aug. 9, 1988, described the forty-seven-year old stage actor as one "who made his Broadway debut portraying the fly-eating lunatic in 'Dracula'" and who for almost two decades "was associated with the Trinity Repertory Theater of Providence." Father David Garrick, C.S.C., offered a memorial mass on the Washington Hall stage for his former classmate, a rare time when the secular space became sacred. The superbly talented David Clennon (born in 1943) has had a very successful professional career in film and television, beginning with the 1979 film *Being There*. He perhaps remains best known for the character Miles Drentell in both *Thirtysomething* (1987–91) and *Once and Again* (1999–2002).

21. *Scholastic,* Dec. 11, 1964, 11.

22. See Minutes of the Local Council, April 17, 1865, f 107r, IPAC; *Scholastic* 15:4, Oct. 1, 1881, 50; *Scholastic* 35:2, Sept. 21, 1901, 36–40.

23. Fred Syburg, letter to the author, Dec. 29, 2005; *South Bend Tribune,* May 7, 1964. Student David A. Garrick, Jr., played Colonel Pickering and later returned as a theatre faculty member from 1992 to 1998. David Clennon played Henry Higgins.

24. *Scholastic* 108:5, Oct. 28, 1966, 14; *The Potting Shed,* program, PNDP 76-Un-03, UNDA. Also see the *Dome* 1967, 256.

25. I am indebted to Father Paul Doyle, C.S.C., whose insight into the period and Father Harvey greatly helped me with context (interview with the author, Jan. 24, 2007). As a student, Father Doyle lived on the third floor of Washington Hall for two years (1963–65), where he fondly recalled that his duties included pulling the curtain and locking up the building at night. Students resided in Washington Hall at least through 1977–78 when the *Scholastic* described Tim Ambrose's living there to help with Indiana insurance laws which "state that an inhabited building is less of a risk than an uninhabited one." The insurance issue is part of folklore I cannot confirm. See *Scholastic* 119:3, Oct. 7, 1977, 24–25.

26. E-mail to the author, Feb. 3, 2004.

27. Reginald Bain, e-mails to the author, Feb. 3, 2004, May 29, 2009. Father Don Dilg, C.S.C., today is sacramental minister at Our Lady of the Woods Catholic Church in Colorado Springs, Colorado. Also see Harry J. Priebe death notice, UDIS 29/20, UNDA. Other memorial masses on the stage of Washington Hall occurred in 1988 for Richard Kavanaugh ('63) and in 2003 for Aubrey Pane ('74).

28. Linda DeCicco, *SLF Album: An Informal History of Notre Dame's Sophomore Literary Festival, 1967–1996* (Notre Dame, Ind.: University of Notre Dame Press, 1997), xxii.

29. *Scholastic* 109:11, Jan. 12, 1968, 26–27.

30. *Scholastic* 109:18, March 29, 1968, 17.

31. James McKenzie (Ph.D., '71), "The Literary World," *Notre Dame Magazine* 39:2, Summer 2010, 4.

32. *Dome* 1969, 33; *Scholastic* 111:8, Nov. 24, 1969, 17; *New York Times,* Feb. 8, 1969, 63.

33. James H. Roberts III, e-mail to the author, June 16, 2006.

34. *Scholastic* 120:9, March 2, 1979, 7–8.

35. *Scholastic* 121:6, Feb. 22, 1980, 2.

36. *Scholastic* 112:16, March 5, 1971, 8–9.

37. *Scholastic* 109:21, May 10, 1968, 6–7.

38. Ibid., 11.

39. Ibid., 10.

40. *Scholastic* 110:19, March 25, 1969, 10.

41. *Scholastic* 111:4, Oct. 10, 1969, 9.

42. Reg Bain, e-mail to the author, Feb. 22, 2008.

43. *Scholastic* 118:11, May 2, 1977, 8–9.

44. "Exorcising the Ghosts of Washington Hall," *Notre Dame Magazine* 7:1, Feb. 1978, 64. Notre Dame typically begins construction projects only when donors are fully committed and a large proportion of the money is actually in hand.

45. *Scholastic* 120:11, April 20, 1979, 13.

46. Program courtesy of Frederic Syburg.

47. Reg Bain, e-mail to the author, Feb. 22, 2008. Through no fault of the building, Bain adds, "*Hamlet* also did not complete its run. Lance Davis totally lost his voice after the Friday, Oct. 12, performance and the Saturday performance had to be cancelled. The cast was most upset, but they all gathered on the stage that night at performance time and we partied on the set!"

48. Interview with the author, March 26, 2004; also see *Monk's Notre Dame* (Notre Dame, Ind.: University of Notre Dame Press, 2005), 134.

49. *Scholastic* 93:11, Nov. 30, 1961, 12.

50. *Scholastic* 28:25, March 16, 1895, 402.

51. *Scholastic* 48:16, Jan. 23, 1915, 266.

52. William Krier, e-mail to the author, June 9, 2009. A student at Notre Dame 1961–65, he returned as a professor in 1969.

53. Don Costello, interview with the author, Aug. 5, 2004.

54. *Scholastic* 106:1, Oct. 2, 1964, 11.

55. *Scholastic* 106:2, Oct. 9, 1964, 11.

56. On May 23, 1978, the U.S. Department of the Interior had placed the main and south quadrangles of the university on the National Reg-

ister of Historic Places (in cooperation with the Indiana Department of Natural Resources Division of Historic Preservation), with the practical consequence of making immutable both the exterior elevation and the ground-plan footprint of Washington Hall. I am indebted to Michael Garvey (in an e-mail to the author, Feb. 16, 2009), for clarification on this designation of historic status.

57. *Scholastic* 120:8, Feb. 16, 1979, 6. For the classification as an academic building see *Notre Dame Report* 8, 1978/79, 230.

58. *Scholastic* 120:8, Feb. 16, 1979, 6.

59. *Scholastic* 121:7, March 21, 1980, 14–15.

Chapter 10. Renovation and Revitalization, 1984–2004

1. Washington Hall in 2009 seats 571, lowered from over 800 in the 1950s. The Carey Auditorium in the Hesburgh Library (1963) seats 306. The largest classroom/auditorium room in the DeBartolo Classroom Building (1995) seats 450, while the Jordan Auditorium in Mendoza College of Business (1996) accommodates 300. Stepan Center (1962) can seat up to 2,500 in an informal but flexible space. The Annenberg Auditorium in the Snite Museum (1980) seats 304. The McKenna Hall Auditorium in the Center for Continuing Education (1966) seats 370. The Engineering Auditorium (1932, and closed in 1999) seated 480, and for many years served as a primary venue for film screenings. The Athletic and Convocation Center, dedicated in 1969, was renamed in honor of the Reverend Edmund P. Joyce, C.S.C., in 1987. The renovation of the south dome in 2009, renamed the Purcell Pavilion, decreased seating from 11,418 to 9,800.

2. *New York Times,* Sept. 14, 1984, A1, A22. The Supreme Court had decided *Roe v. Wade* on January 22, 1973. Notre Dame had previously sponsored an "Abortion Parley," Oct. 15–17, 1979, which took place not in Washington Hall but in the auditorium of the Center for Continuing Education (built in 1965).

3. The *Observer,* Dec. 8, 1981, 1, reported that the controversial priest spoke "to a capacity crowd at Washington Hall" and "was applauded when he commented on the issues of priestly celibacy, women's ordinations, and remarriage after divorce. . . . He calls for the practicing of true Christianity instead of the falseness of decrees."

4. Governor Cuomo's complete 1984 speech is available at http:// classic.archives.nd.edu/episodes/visitors/cuomo/cuomo.html (accessed Aug. 13, 2009).

5. My directorial debut at Notre Dame occurred in 1984–85 in O'Laughlin Auditorium with the final production of the season, Dario Fo's *We Won't Pay! We Won't Pay!*, but I directed ten mainstage productions on the Washington Hall stage from *The Tempest* in 1985–86 through *Antigone* in 2001–2.

6. Tom Barkes, e-mail to the author, Jan. 12, 2007, forwarded from Karen Morris. Those of us who worked in the building at night dealt with the bats who resided in the attic of the auditorium but who had great curiosity with regard to rehearsals and performances, always to the immediate consternation of actors and audience members.

7. E-mail from the author to Arts and Letters Dean Harry Attridge, Sept. 24, 1996, compliments of Registrar Harold Pace.

8. See *South Bend Tribune*, "N. D. Theater Combines Change, Tradition," Aug. 18, 1985, 18–19: "When Notre Dame hired Mark Pilkinton to head their theater department a little less than a year ago, they gave him a simple directive that really was more of a license for change. He was told to 'revitalize' N. D. theater."

9. Theatres especially require a huge effort to keep them cool. With audiences of several hundred and high-wattage stage lighting instruments, coupled with the custom of closing and cloaking doors and windows to keep out exterior sound and light, theatres become uncomfortably hot almost immediately in the absence of a dedicated cooling system. It is therefore not surprising that with the inauguration of the Summer Drama Project in 1940 under the direction of Robert W. Speaight, *Twelfth Night* took place outside on the south side of the Commerce Building (now Hurley Hall) precisely to escape the heat.

10. *Scholastic* 35:1, Aug. 1, 1901, 16.

11. Carla Johnson, *South Bend Tribune*, Nov. 11, 1988, B9.

12. *Observer*, Nov. 10, 1988, 9.

13. Stritch, *My Notre Dame*, 132.

14. *The Good Woman of Setzuan*, program, University of Notre Dame, April 1991. Also see http://archives.nd.edu/theatre/plays121.htm (accessed Aug. 13, 2009).

15. *The Love of the Nightingale*, program, University of Notre Dame, April 2000. Also see http://archives.nd.edu/theatre/plays130.htm (accessed Aug. 13, 2009).

16. *Scholastic* 27:39, June 30, 1894, 684.

WORKS CONSULTED

Archives

Archives of the University of Notre Dame (cited as UNDA):

Arthur Harvey Papers (GHRV)

Bagby Negatives (GBBY)

Dorothy Corson Papers (CORS)

Early Notre Dame Student, Class, and Financial Record Books (ULDG)

Early Notre Dame Students, 1849–1912
http://archives.nd.edu/search/students.htm

Early Teachers and Administrators at Notre Dame, 1850–1950
http://archives.nd.edu/search/faculty.htm

Francis P. Clark Collection (GFCL)

Notre Dame Architectural Drawings, Plans, and Views (UNDD)

Notre Dame Controller/Comptroller (UCMP)

Notre Dame Copy Negatives Collection (GNEG)

Notre Dame Glass Plate Negative Contact Sheets Collection (GGPP)

Notre Dame Information Services (UDIS or GDIS)

Notre Dame Life Photograph Collection (GNDL)

Notre Dame Miscellaneous University Records (UNDR)

Notre Dame Portraits Collection (GPOR)

Notre Dame Printed and Reference Material Dropfiles (PNDP)

Notre Dame Saint Cecilia Philomathean Society (UCPS)

Notre Dame University Photographer (GPHR)

Theatre Chronology, 1845–2009
http://archives.nd.edu/search/theatre.htm

Thomas Ewing Family Papers (CEWI)

Thomas J. Schlereth Photographs (GTJS)

Indiana Province Archives Center (cited as IPAC):

Archives of the Minor Chapter, 1847–1854, 1970/15.

Brother Gatian, "Journal Kept by the Secretary to Serve in the Composition of the Chronicle," February 8, 1847–January 10, 1849, 1970/02.

Council of Professors, II, July 1, 1846, 1970/15.

"Draft for Prospectus for Notre Dame. August 15, 1868." Edward Sorin, C.S.C., Collection, 1868, 1970/01.

La Matricule de la Congrégation de Sainte-Croix [Matricule Générale or General Matricule], 1860–1937 (GM).

Local Council of the Trades 1845–1846, Archives of N. D. No 28. Council of Trades. Sept. 7, 1845–Nov. 21, 1846 [later pencil hand]. 1845 and 1846, 1970/15.

Local Council Minute Book (1865–1875), May 22, 1865–Sept. 10, 1875, 1970/15.

Local Council Minute Book (1875–1883), Sept 17, 1875–Jan. 1, 1883 [1884], 1970/15.

Local Council Minute Book (1884–1890), 1970/15.

Local Council Minutes [Transcriptions], March 1846–Aug. 27, 1857, 1970/15.

Local Council Minutes [Transcriptions], Aug. 27, 1857–Jan. 2, 1866, 1970/15.

Local Council Minutes [Transcriptions], Jan. 2, 1866–Dec. 29, 1876, 1970/15.

Local Council Minutes [Transcriptions], Dec. 29, 1876–Dec. 20, 1889, 1970/15.

Minutes of the Local Council (Minor Chapter) 1855–1865, 1970/15.

Provincial Council Minutes, 1870–1880, 1973/03.

Published Works

Althusser, Louis. "Ideology and Ideological State Apparatuses." In *Lenin and Philosophy and Other Essays.* New York: Monthly Review Press, 1971.

American National Biography Online (cited as *ANB*). http://www.anb.org (accessed Aug. 17, 2008).

Auden, W. H. "The Poet & the City." In *The Dyer's Hand and Other Essays.* New York: Random House, 1962.

Biographical Dictionary of Kansas Artists (Active before 1945). Compiled by Susan V. Craig, 2006. http://kuscholarworks.ku.edu/dspace/bitstream/1808/1028/1/BDKAversion1.pdf.

A Brief History of the University of Notre Dame du Lac, Indiana, from 1842 to 1892, Prepared for the Golden Jubilee to be Celebrated June 11, 12 and 13, 1895. Chicago: Werner, 1895.

Brockett, Oscar G., and Franklin Hildy. *History of the Theatre.* 9th ed. Boston: Allyn & Bacon, 2003.

Bulletin of the University of Notre Dame 13:3. Notre Dame, Ind.: The University Press, 1918.

Burns, Robert T. *Being Catholic, Being American: The Notre Dame Story, 1842–1934.* Vol. 1. Notre Dame, Ind.: University of Notre Dame Press, 1999.

———. *Being Catholic, Being American: The Notre Dame Story, 1934–1952.* Vol. 2. Notre Dame, Ind.: University of Notre Dame Press, 2000.

Carroll, Patrick J., C.S.C. *William P. Breen: In Memoriam.* Notre Dame, Ind.: University of Notre Dame du Lac, 1931.

Casey, Michael. *A Soul in Fine Array: A One-Act Play for Nine Females.* New York: Samuel French, 1954.

Collins, Jim. *Uncommon Cultures: Popular Culture and Post-Modernism.* New York: Routledge, 1989.

Crabtree, Susan, and Peter Beudert. *Scenic Art for the Theatre: History, Tools, and Techniques.* St. Louis: Butterworth-Heinemann/Focal Press, 1998.

Crafton, Donald. *The Talkies: American Cinema's Transition to Sound, 1926–1931.* New York: Charles Scribner's Sons, 1997.

DeCicco, Linda. *SLF Album: An Informal History of Notre Dame's Sophomore Literary Festival, 1967–1996.* Notre Dame, Ind.: University of Notre Dame Press, 1997.

Dimmick, J.W. *Media Competition and Coexistence: The Theory of the Niche.* Mahwah, N.J.: Lawrence Erlbaum, 2003.

The Dome. Notre Dame, Ind.: University of Notre Dame, 1906–2004.

Dwyer, Larry, and Kenneth Dye, eds. *The Band of the Fighting Irish: A Pictorial History of the Notre Dame Band.* Vol. 1. Notre Dame, Ind.: Ave Maria Press, 2002.

Ellis, Joseph J. *His Excellency: George Washington.* New York: Knopf, 2004.

Farmer, William. Private collection.

Fischer, Edward. *Notre Dame Remembered: An Autobiography.* Notre Dame, Ind.: University of Notre Dame Press, 1978.

Graham, Frank D., and Thomas J. Emery. *Audel's Carpenters and Builders Guide #2.* New York: Theo. Audel, 1923.

Griffith, Allen Ayrault. *A Drill Book for Practice of the Principles of Vocal Physiology, and Acquiring the Art of Elocution and Oratory.* Chicago: Adams, Blackmer, and Lyon, 1868.

———. *Lessons in Elocution with Numerous Selections, Analyzed for Practice.* 2nd ed. Chicago: Adams, Blackmer, and Lyon, 1865.

A Guide to the University of Notre Dame, and the Academy of St. Mary of the Immaculate Conception, Near South Bend, Indiana. Philadelphia: J. B. Chandler, 1865.

Haid, P. Leo, O.S.B. *Major John Andre: An Historical Drama in Five Acts.* New York: Catholic Publication Society, 1876. Promptbook.

The HarperCollins Encyclopedia of Catholicism. Edited by Richard P. McBrien. New York: HarperCollins, 1995.

Hay, Samuel A. *African American Theatre: An Historical and Critical Analysis.* New York: Cambridge University Press, 1994.

Hope, Arthur J., C.S.C. *Notre Dame: One Hundred Years.* Notre Dame, Ind.: University Press, 1943.

Howard, Timothy Edward. *A History of St. Joseph County Indiana.* 2 vols. Chicago: Lewis, 1907.

Jackson, Donald, ed. *The Diaries of George Washington.* Vol. 1. *1748–1765.* Charlottesville: University Press of Virginia, 1976.

Jackson, Donald, and Dorothy Twohig, eds. *The Diaries of George Washington.* Vol. 6. *January 1790–December 1799.* Charlottesville: University Press of Virginia, 1979.

Jameson, Fredric. "Reification and Utopia in Mass Culture." *Social Text* 1 (Winter 1979): 130–48.

Jolly, Ellen Ryan. *Nuns of the Battlefield.* Providence, R. I.: Providence Visitor Press, 1927.

Lyons, Joseph A., A.M. *The American Elocutionist and Dramatic Reader for the Use of Colleges, Academies, and Schools.* 3rd ed., rev. Philadelphia: J. H. Butler, 1874.

———. *The Silver Jubilee of the University of Notre Dame, June 23rd, 1869.* Chicago: E. B. Myers, 1869.

Malloy, Edward A., C.S.C. *Monk's Notre Dame.* Notre Dame, Ind.: University of Notre Dame Press, 2005.

McAvoy, Thomas T., and Lawrence J. Bradley. *Guide to the Microfilm Edition of the Thomas Ewing, Sr., Papers.* Notre Dame, Ind.: University of Notre Dame Archives Publications, 1967.

———. *Guide to the Microfilm Edition of the William Tecumseh Sherman Family Papers (1808–1891).* Notre Dame, Ind.: University of Notre Dame Archives Publications, 1967.

McGreevy, John T. *Catholicism and American Freedom: A History.* New York: Norton, 2003.

McKenzie, James. "The Literary World." *Notre Dame Magazine,* Summer 2010, 4.

Miscamble, Wilson D., ed. *Go Forth and Do Good: Memorable Notre Dame Commencement Addresses.* Notre Dame, Ind.: University of Notre Dame Press, 2003.

Morrissey, John P. "Exorcising the Ghosts of Washington Hall." *Notre Dame Magazine,* February 1978, 64.

O'Connell, Marvin R. *Edward Sorin.* Notre Dame, Ind.: University of Notre Dame Press, 2001.

Officer, Lawrence H., and Samuel H. Williamson. "Purchasing Power of Money in the United States from 1774 to 2008." *MeasuringWorth,* 2009. http://www.measuringworth.com/ppowerus/ (accessed July 27, 2009).

O'Sullivan, John Louis. "The Great Nation of Futurity." *The United States Magazine, and Democratic Review,* Nov. 6, 1839, 426–30.

Oxford Dictionary of National Biography Online (cited as *ODNB*).

Oxford English Dictionary Online (cited as *OED*).

"The Papers of George Washington." http://gwpapers.virginia.edu/project/faq/index.html (accessed Aug. 15, 2008).

Pilkinton, Mark C., ed. *Records of Early English Drama: Bristol.* Toronto: University of Toronto Press, 1997.

Robertson, Pamela. *Guilty Pleasures: Feminist Camp from Mae West to Madonna.* Durham, N.C.: Duke University Press, 1996.

Rockne, Knute K. *The Autobiography of Knute K. Rockne.* Edited by Bonnie Skiles Rockne. Introduction by John Cavanaugh, C.S.C. Indianapolis: Bobbs-Merrill, 1930.

Saylor, Henry H. *Dictionary of Architecture.* New York: Science Editions, 1963.

Schlereth, Thomas J. *The University of Notre Dame: A Portrait of Its History and Campus.* Notre Dame, Ind.: University of Notre Dame Press, 1976.

Scholastic 1–146. Notre Dame, Ind.: University of Notre Dame, 1867–2004.

Sorin, Edward, C.S.C. *The Chronicles of Notre Dame du Lac.* Translated by John M. Toohey, C.S.C. Edited and annotated by James T. Connelly, C.S.C. Notre Dame, Ind.: University of Notre Dame Press, 1992.

Stritch, Thomas. *My Notre Dame: Memories and Reflections of Sixty Years.* Notre Dame, Ind.: University of Notre Dame Press, 1991.

Syburg, Frederic W. "University Theatre Celebrates 10th Anniversary." *Notre Dame* 16:4 (Winter 1963): 9–13.

Thirty-Eighth Annual Catalogue of the Officers, Faculty and Students of the University of Notre Dame, Indiana, for the Academic Year 1881–82. Notre Dame, Ind.: Scholastic Press, 1882.

Tittler, Robert. *Architecture and Power: The Town Hall and the English Urban Community c. 1500–1640.* Oxford: Clarendon Press, 1991.

Tucker, Todd. *Notre Dame vs. the Klan: How the Fighting Irish Defeated the Ku Klux Klan*. Chicago: Loyola Press, 2004.

Twenty-First Annual Catalogue of the Officers and Students of the University of Notre Dame, Indiana, for the Academic Year 1864–65. Notre Dame, Ind.: Printed at the Office of the "Ave Maria," 1865.

Vaughan, David. *Merce Cunningham: Fifty Years*. Edited by Melissa Hart. New York: Aperture, n.d. [1997].

White, Natalie E. *The Billion Dollar Saint: A Farce in Three Acts*. Notre Dame, Ind.: Genesian Press, 1955; New York: Dramatists Play Service, 1955.

———. *The Complaining Angel: A Farce with Music*. New York: Samuel French, 1957.

———. "Hamlet on the New York Stage, 1900–1910." M.A. thesis, George Washington University, 1941.

———. *Seven Nuns at Las Vegas: A Farce in Two Acts*. Notre Dame, Ind.: Genesian Press, 1954; New York: Dramatists Play Service, 1954.

———. *Seven Nuns South of the Border*. New York: Dramatists Play Service, 1962.

———. "Shakespeare on the New York Stage, 1891–1941." Ph.D. diss., Yale University, 1946.

Wittke, Carl, F. *Tambo and Bones: A History of the American Minstrel Stage*. Durham, N.C.: Duke University Press, 1930.

Zarrilli, Phillip B., Bruce McConachie, Gary Jay Williams, and Carol Fisher Sorgenfrei. *Theatre Histories: An Introduction*. New York: Routledge, 2006.

Abbey Players, 227

Academy of Music (1879–1882)
architecture, 79–80, 83, 88, 89fig4.5
beginnings, 73
completion, 90, 94, 96–97
construction, 81, 83–85, 88–89, 91, 104, 219
construction costs, 104, 345n18, 348n1
dedication, 99, 101–6
electrification, 93
funding, 80–81, 84
renaming as WH, 2, 107

Ackermann, Francis Xavier, 356n122, 360n35

Ackermann, Jacob
career, 46, 94, 347n62, 356n122
mentioned, 96, 108
set design, 100, 110, 111–13, 114–15fig5.3, 129, 139, 152, 171, 172fig6.5, 359n35

acoustics, 266

Actors from the London Stage (AFTLS), 306, 308

Adams, M. Clay, 229

Adolphus, Brother (Patrick Walsh), 44, 338n27

air-conditioning, xxv, 277, 295fig10.1, 304, 315

Aitken, H. E., 190

alcohol consumed onstage, 23, 183

Allardt, Charles, 191

Althusser, Louis, 5, 141, 147, 266

Amadeus, 308

Ambrose, Tim, 381n25

American flag, 161–65, 358n12

"The Anchor" (Ford), 136

André (Dunlap), 342n91

André, John, 342n91

Andrew, Dudley, 288

Annenberg Auditorium, 383n1

Anniversary of the College Dedication celebrations, 55

Annunciation Day, 96

Anselm, Brother (Léopold Nobels), 109, 112, 127, 349n10

Anthony, Brother (Henry Reissacher), 46, 338n34

Antigone, 127–28, 311

Arbuckle, Maclyn, 192, 366n96

Arbuckle, Roscoe "Fatty," 366n96

Arcadia, 311

architectural lag concept, 59, 139

architecture
audience sight lines, 256–57
canine newel posts, 122
costume shop, 248–49
dimensions
—Academy of Music, 79, 83, 344n12
—first WH, 37, 44, 344n12

architecture (*cont.*)
—gymnasium, 111fig5.2,
349n19
—Music Hall/Junior Recreation
Hall, 44
illustrations/photographs
—first WH, 27fig2.4, 32fig3.1,
33fig3.1, 34fig3.2, 35fig3.3,
36fig3.4, 38fig3.5, 45fig3.6
—gymnasium, 111fig5.2
—Main Building I, 15fig2.1,
21fig2.2
—Music Hall/Junior Recreation
Hall, 35fig3.3
—new WH, 89fig4.5, 100fig5.1,
118fig5.5, 119fig5.6,
120fig5.7, 121fig5.8
—1956 modernization,
267fig9.1
—Notre Dame, 22fig2.3
—set design, 172fig6.5,
177fig6.6
—three original buildings,
3fig1.2
—WH close up, 4fig1.2
noise problems, 257
north entrance, 99, 122
orchestra brass rail, 151
orientation, 31, 44–45
praised, 105
programmatic plans, 79–80
radio studios, 260–61
reading rooms, 107
stage, 37
stairs
—east wing entrance steps,
150–51, 168
—north, 99, 121
—south (interior stairs
replaced the exterior stairs
in 1933), 100fig5.1, 107,
120fig5.7, 122, 224, 225fig8.1,
226–27, 226fig8.2, 228fig8.3

style, 83
tower, 117, 118fig5.5, 119fig5.6,
120fig5.7
windows, 26
See also Edbrooke, Willoughby;
interiors; seating capacity
architecture, changes to the
for acoustics, 266
for film equipment, 266
for heating and ventilation, 266
lighting
—electrification, 102, 104–5,
109, 113, 125, 144
—gas, 144
—Harvey era, 266
—stage, 68–69, 100, 108–10,
144, 268
for offices and dressing rooms,
268–69
orchestra pit, 61
plumbing
—interior, 157
—shower addition, 169, 269
—toilet facilities, 110, 111fig5.2,
168–69, 170fig6.4, 171fig6.4,
269
for a projection booth, 192–93
for rehearsal space, 17
for set design, 100, 111–13,
114–15fig5.3, 129, 151–53,
359n35
for sound equipment, 257
stage, 61, 68–69, 100, 108–10,
144, 268
for storage
—illustrations, 169fig6.3,
170fig6.4, 171fig6.4
—for instruments, 41, 46
—for sets, 153–54, 157,
167–68, 169fig6.3, 170fig6.4,
171fig6.4
See also interiors
armory, 22, 90

Arms and the Man, 312
Armstrong, L. O., 201
Arnold, Benedict, 342n91
Arnold, William H., 104, 124, 125, 128
art films, 258
Arts and Letters College Seminar, 195
Astaire, Fred, 239
As You Like It (Shakespeare), 181, 306
Athletic and Convocation Center, 383n1
Athletic Association, 198
athletic fields for communal assembly, 5
Auden, W. H., 5
audiences
    behavior of the, 58, 258–60, 287–90
    interactions, 68–69
    at the movies, 159fig6.2, 258–60, 287, 289–90
    niche, rise of, 290
    overcrowding problems, 172
    as performers as well, 58–59
    photographs of, 158fig6.1, 159fig6.2, 172–73
    technology, effect on, 157
    traditionally, 8
audio recordings, 260
Augustin Daly's Company of Comedians, 361n50, 361n51
Austgen, Father Robert J., C.S.C., 205
Ave Maria Press, 340n59

Babes in Arms, 276
Badin Hall, 226
Badin Hall ghost, 205, 206
Bailey, Professor, 130
Bailey, W., 104

Bain, Reginald
    professor
    —*As You Like It,* 306
    —*Camelot,* 277
    —*Electra,* 299
    —*Guys and Dolls,* 277
    —*Hamlet,* 286, 305
    —innovative work of, 245, 264, 275, 280–81
    —*The Love of the Nightingale,* 310
    —*The Madwoman of Chaillot,* 310
    —*Oliver,* 277
    —popularity of, 276, 280–81
    —Priebe memorial mass, 281
    —on renovation of WH, 285
    —retirement, 310–11
    —*Rhinoceros,* 280–81
    student
    —backstage, 247
    —*The Billion Dollar Saint,* 251
    —*Death of a Salesman,* 253, 277
    —*Detective Story,* 253
Baird, Bill, 371n21
Balfe, Michael William, 146, 148, 149fig5.14, 268
Bancrofts and Booth, 152–53
Band Annex (original "Huddle"), 141, 268, 302, 313
Band Building, 313
Barkes, Tom, 220–21, 266, 303–5, 307–8, 350n20, 352n46
the barn, 18
Barnes, H., 135, 191
Basil, Brother (John Magus), 28, 331n5, 336n49
Basilica of the Sacred Heart, 3fig1.2, 5, 11, 17–18, 254
Becker, Christine A., 376n82
Becker, John J., 235
Beckett, Samuel, 308
Beecher, Philemon, 335n37

Beethoven, 145, 147, 267
Bell, Alexander Graham, 67
Bellamy, Francis, 358n12
Belloc, Hilaire, 227
Benson, Monsignor Robert Hugh, 200–1
Bent, 300
Berlin, Irving, 239
Best, Louis E., 361n50
Beyer, Paul, 366n111
Bill, Tony, 380n13
The Billion Dollar Saint, 251
Bill's Barber Shop, 223, 226–27, 226fig8.2
Birder, Cecil, 179, 180fig6.7, 181, 183, 241, 364n69
The Birth of a Nation (film), 7, 189, 190–91, 193
blackface and minstrel shows, 61, 156, 178–79, 183, 184fig6.9, 237–40
Blackfriars Guild, 253
Black Orpheus (film), 289–90
Blakey, Jack, 309fig10.2
Blithe Spirit, 251
Bob Martin, Substitute Half-Back, 181
Boland, Daniel, 216, 264
Bolger, William J., C.S.C., 167
Booth, John Wilkes, 42
Born to Good Luck, or An Irishman's Fortune, 50
Bow, Clara, 259
The Boy Friend, 276
Boyle, Maria Wills, 335n37
Breen, William P., 160, 162, 358n10
Breen Medal in Oratory, 194, 195, 358n10
Breen-Phillips dormitory, 358n10
Brown, Judge, 16
Browne, Kathryn, 370n1
Brownson (Senior) Recreation Room, 344n13

Brownson, Orestes, 350n22
Brownson Glee Club, 196
Brownson Hall/College (seniors/collegiate), 211, 226, 334n30, 350n22
Brownson Recreation Hall, 107–8, 233, 257, 269, 298, 350n22
Brute Farce, 246
Brutz, Jim, 239
Bryan, Charles M. B., 163
Bryan, William Jennings, 157, 199–200, 295, 297, 367n120
Buckley, John, 206, 208, 209, 212, 214
Burke, Father Eugene, 259, 360n37
Burke, Reverend Joseph, C.S.C., 172
Burns, M. T., 104
Burns, Mr., 44
Burns, Reverend James A., C.S.C., 155, 158–59, 167, 212
Butterworth, Charley, 240

Cadillac Hall, 210
The Caine Mutiny Court Martial, 253
Camelot, 277
campus clothing store, 226
"Canadian Rockies" (Armstrong), 201
Canfield, Emily, 188
Cannon, Sister Kathleen, O.P., 376n84
Cantor, Eddie, 238, 373n44
Canute, Brother (Jeremiah Lardner), 259, 379n117
Carey, Bill, 244
Carey, Father William Arthur, C.S.C., 257, 287, 378n106
Carey, Helen Kuhn, 195
Carey, William T., 195
Carey Auditorium, 383n1
Carmody, Professor, 178, 361n50
Carnarvon, Lord, 231

Carrier, Father, 42
Carroll, Archbishop John, 136,
    355n95
Carroll Hall/College (juniors/
    preps), 50, 150, 188, 334n30,
    350n22, 368n11
Carter, Howard, 231, 371n20
Casasanta, Joseph J., 212–13, 219,
    235, 237, 368n11
Casey, Daniel Vincent, 162
Casey, Michael, 246, 249, 253
Cashman, Edward, 243, 375n65
Catholic-American tensions, 165
Catholic Art Association of
    America, 193
Catholicism-patriotism
    philosophy, 6, 20, 29, 65
Catholic Players, 245
Catholic Theatre Conference,
    251–52
Catholic Total Abstinence Union
    (C.A.T.U.), 122, 198
Catholic University of America,
    136, 278, 280
Cavalli, Dr., 317
Cavanaugh, Father John William,
    C.S.C., 155, 158fig6.1, 165,
    173, 183, 185, 200, 360n39
Cavanaugh, John Joseph, 219
Cavanaugh, Mr., 84
The Celebrated Case, 178
Center for Continuing Education,
    282, 383n1
A Center of Theatre Education and
    Research (ACTER), 308
Chantard, Francis S., 103
Cherry Bounce, 134
Chesterton, G. K., 6, 227, 229, 230
choir, 40, 50, 331n5, 340n59
Choral Union, 53
Christmas, 13, 53–54
Christmas Exercises, 128–29, 131,
    134

Christ's Passion, 310
Cibber, Colley, 355n100
Cicero, 147, 148, 213, 267, 268
Cinema 61, 288
Citizens for Decent Literature,
    282
Civil War era, 39–40
Clair, René, 258
Clarence Cramer's Opera Festival,
    262
Clarke, T. F., 104
Cleary, Reverend James, 198
Cleary, W., 104
Clennon, David, 278, 381n20,
    381n23
Cleveland, Grover, 163
The Clod, 188
Clooney, Rosemary, 239
Cluchey, Rick, 308
Coccia, Regis, 220
Cochems, Eddie, 363n67
coeducational summer school, 158,
    166
Cointet, Father François (Francis),
    C.S.C., 15, 331n4
Cole, Ken, 312
College Band, 28
college football, 156
College of Arts and Letters, 303
Collins, Jim, 9
Collins, Walt, 244
Collmer, Irma, 361n50
Colovin, Father, 38fig3.5, 63, 64
Columbian Dramatic Club, 86
Columbian Literary and Debating
    Society, 96
Columbian quatercentenary,
    137–38, 141
Columbians (minims)
    The Celebrated Case, 178
    mentioned, 85
    purpose, 47
    Richard III, 115fig5.3

Columbians (minims) (*cont.*)
  *Robert Emmet: The Martyr of
    Irish Liberty* (1885), 112–13,
    114–15fig5.3
  Saint Patrick's Day celebrations,
    69, 112–13, 114–15fig5.3,
    138, 178
  Waiting for the Verdict, 174
Columbus, 42
The Comedy of Errors
  (Shakespeare), 236
commencement
  Academy of Music dedication,
    101–6
  Columbian quatercentenary, 138
  first WH, 39, 42–43, 51, 69,
    86–87, 91
  Golden Jubilee, 159–61
  growing pains (1895–1922), 10,
    159–61, 223
  interim years (1922–1956),
    223–224, 248fig8.5
  lack of space for, 252
  new WH, 101–6, 126–28, 140,
    141
  pre-WH, 13–14, 17–19, 23,
    317–18
commencement plays
  Columbus, 42
  Exhibition Hall opening, 24
  Henry IV, 39, 42
  The Recognition, 51
  The Rivals, 23
  Sacerdotal Golden Jubilee years,
    136
  William Tell, 42
Committee on Student
  Entertainment, 244
communal assembly
  cultural change affecting, 8
  decentering of, 8–11, 196, 223,
    280
  football and, 196, 255–56

pre-WH, 5–7, 13–14, 16–20,
  24–25
technology's effect on, 7–9,
  129–30, 156–57, 188, 201
television and, 254–55
communal assembly, at WH
  centrality to the campus, 1, 3–6,
    202–3
  for debate and oratory, 194–96
  demand for, 224, 269, 270–71,
    276, 290–91
  diminishment of, 264
  for indoor athletic festival, 198
  emotional appeal of, 224
  ending of, 10, 280
  film in fulfilling, 157, 159fig6.2,
    196, 224, 256–57, 290
  for football games, pre-radio,
    156–57, 201
  multipurpose nature of,
    173–74, 227
  for new-student orientation, 256
  for niche audiences, 224, 290
  praised as venue, 177
  primary for theatre, ending of,
    280
  space lacking for, 141, 223
  symbolic, 199
Communication and Theatre
  Department, 290–91, 298,
    301, 303–4
communication innovations, 7,
  65–67, 157
Comparet, Alex, 94
The Complaining Angel, 252
*The Compleat Works of William
  Shakespeare (Abridged)*, 306
Connell, "Doc," 211
Conscription Act of 1863, 39–40
Contemporary Arts Festival,
  283–84
Cooperative Department of Speech
  and Drama, 290

Coquillard, Alexander, 330n2
Coquillard, Alexis, 332n10
Corby, Father William E., C.S.C.,
    42, 49, 53, 75, 81–82, 84, 145
Corby, M. T., 39, 58
Corby Hall, 287
Corby Hall Glee Club, 179
Cornet Band
    Academy of Music dedication,
        103
    Christmas Exercises, 134
    Garfield memorial, 92
    Saint Patrick's Day celebrations,
        138
    Silver Jubilee year, 51
    St. Edward's Day celebrations,
        51, 52–53, 93, 124, 136
    venues off campus, 332n10
    Washington's Birthday
        celebrations, 50, 139
Corona, Joseph, 212
The Corsican Brothers, 86, 163,
    174
Corson, Dorothy, 218
cosmosphere, 130
Costanzi, Mark, 309fig10.2
Costello, Don, 288–89
Costello, Jerry, 246
Council of Professors, 15
Count De Moor, 53–54
"The County Chairman" (film),
    192
Courtney, J. S., 124
"Courtship and Marriage"
    (Hesburgh), 262
Cox, Mr., 179
Coyle, Father Matthew, 237, 241
Crafton, Donald, 378n106
Cramer, Clarence, 262
Crescent Club, 107
Crosby, Bing, 239
Crowley Hall, 141, 313
The Crucible, 251, 308

Crumley, Father Thomas Aloysius,
    C.S.C., 206, 219
Cunningham, Merce, 262
Cuomo, Mario, 6–7, 200, 294–98,
    295fig10.1
Cushing Engineering Auditorium,
    223, 256
Cushing Hall of Engineering,
    248–49, 331n6
Cyprian, Brother (James O'Hara),
    C.S.C., 179, 181, 183, 186,
    363n61

Daily, Daniel, 308, 309fig10.2
Daly, Augustin, 160, 361n50,
    361n51
"Damon and Pythias," 161
Daniel Sully Company, 361n52
David Garrick, 181
Davis, Charles, 217–18
Davis, Lance, 286, 305, 382n47
Death of a Salesman, 253–54, 272,
    277, 308, 309fig10.2
DeBartolo Classroom Building,
    300, 301, 359n34, 383n1
debate, 1, 4, 10, 13, 50, 56–58, 128,
    136–37, 148, 194–96, 224,
    231, 233, 270. *See also*
    University debating team
DeCicco, Linda, 281
Decio Mainstage Theatre, 141,
    331n6
declamatory, oratory, elocution
    triad, 57, 126, 137, 194, 195
DeFranco, Joe, 239
Demosthenes, 147, 148, 213, 267,
    268
Dennis, Chris, 352n46
Derrick, Professor, 183
Detective Story, 253
Detroit University three, 196
de Valera, Eamon, 157, 199, 227,
    367n118

The Dictator, 179

Dilg, Father Don, C.S.C., 281, 381n27

Doctor Faustus, 311

Domitille, 251

Donahue, Philip J., 247, 253–54, 277, 376n82

Donnelly, Richard E., 302, 308, 310

Dooley, Thomas Anthony III, 6, 229, 230–31, 371n18

Dorais, Charles E. "Gus," 181

dormitory, WH used as a, xxi, xxii, 39, 40, 42, 46, 76, 82, 83, 85

Dougherty, Daniel, 160

Dougherty, Mr., 135

Doyle, Albert L., 236

Doyle, Edward L., 253

Doyle, Father Paul, C.S.C., 381n25

Doyle, Joe, 216

drag routines, 239

Drama Club, 186

Dramatic Club, 173, 241

Dramatic Society, 23, 331n5

Dramatic Stock Company, 173

Dreyer, Kevin, 300

Drill Hall, 10, 141, 251–52, 254, 271, 313

Drury, John, 183, 364nn73–74

Dunlap, William, 342n91

Durkin, Rachel, 309fig10.2

Dvorak, Robin, 309fig10.2

Dwenger, Right Reverend, Bishop of Ft. Wayne, 103, 106

Dynamo Theatre, 308

Easter Monday, 181, 182fig6.8

Edbrooke, Willoughby, 76, 77fig4.4, 105

Edison, Thomas Alva, 67

Edison Phonograph Company, 67

Edwards, James Farnham, 86, 174, 345n35

Eichenlaub, Raymond, 364n67

Eisenhower, Dwight, 363n67

Electra, 299

electrification, 93–94, 102, 104–5, 109

Ellison, Ralph, 282

elocution classes, 57, 62, 126, 339n46, 347n55

Elsen, William J., 244, 245

Eltinge, Julian, 194

Emmet, Robert, 351n40

Engineering Auditorium, 260, 288, 379n119, 383n1

English Department, 260

environmental theatre movement, 245

Euglossians, 69, 86, 127, 131, 134, 347n55

Eva Jessye Choir, 238

Everyman, 251

"Evicting the Ghost of Washington Hall" (Morrissey), 217

Ewing, Ellen Boyle (Mrs. William T. Sherman), 335n37

Ewing, Ellie, (Sherman niece), 43

Ewing, John G., 162, 202

Ewing, N., 104

Ewing, Philemon Beecher, 335n37

Ewing, Thomas W., 335n36, 335n37

Exhibition Hall (Academy of Music)

architecture, 88, 89fig4.5

completion, 96

construction, 81, 88, 89, 90

recreational space, 88–89, 89fig4.5

seating capacity, 97, 139

square footage, 344n12

exhibition halls

central functions of university, 156

obsolescence of, 8–10

pre-WH, 1–2, 20–24, 21fig2.2, 153

role in college life, 7

"Exorcising the Ghosts of
Washington Hall"
(Morrissey), 217
experimental theatre, 245
The Expiation, 93

Fairbanks, Charles Warren, 199,
367n119
Fairbanks, Douglas, 193
"Faith" (Bryan), 199–200, 297
Fallon, Jerome, 261
"Falsely Accused, a Domestic
Drama in three Acts," 129
Famous Players Company, 192
The Fantasticks, 276
Farnum, Dustin, 192
Faulkner Symposium, 281
Faust, 244, 245
female theatrical roles
eliminated or replaced, 60–61,
179, 361n50
played by men, 156, 179–86,
180fig6.7, 182fig6.8, 194, 236
played by women, 235–37, 274,
275fig9.2, 279–81, 279fig9.3,
361n50, 361n52
shift in gender depiction,
174–76, 178
Festival of Saint Aloysius
celebrations, 55
Festival of Saint Edward, 123–24
Festival of the Arts, 283
Field Band, 44, 56
Field Clubs, 107
Fieldhouse, 10, 141, 223, 286, 313
Filipino Club, 206
film, 4, 7, 9, 129, 130, 157, 214,
255–61, 287–91
African Americans in, 239–40
art-films, 258
audiences, 157, 159fig6.2,
258–60, 287, 289–90, 290
benefactors, 191
biopics, 188–89

Catholic themes and characters,
193
communal assembly function
of, 159fig6.2, 196, 256–57
conflicting schedules, 245–46
female impersonators in, 194
impact on WH, 187
as lecture, 188–89
Marconi on silent vs. talking,
230
minstrel numbers in, 179, 239,
362nn59
motion pictures, 157, 186–91
movies, 190, 193, 203, 230
moving pictures, 187, 189
photo-drama, 190
photo-play, 192, 193, 194
plays filmed, 278
popularity of, 260
projection booth, 192–93
screening paradigm, 7
selection process, 288–89
sound equipment installed, 257
See also specific films
film (photography)
exposure speed, 152
ghost caught on, 215, 220
Film, Television, and Theatre,
Department of, 312, 314,
339n46
film studies, 261, 288, 290
film/television production facility,
298
Fine Arts Quartet, 247
Finian's Rainbow, 255, 276
fire extinguishers, 113, 117
first WH (1864–1882)
beginnings, 23–25
curriculum, 50, 57, 62, 65–66,
194
dedication, xxi, 13, 27–28
demolished, 2, 78, 88, 97, 99,
106–7
described, 31, 34, 37, 87, 95

first WH (1864–1882) (*cont.*)
  events
  —last, 97
  —numbers participating in,
    57–59
  —ticketing for, 61–62
  —variety in, 63, 68
  funding, 2, 24, 25
  gymnasium conversion
    proposal, 78, 89–90, 96, 97
  naming of, 6
  obsolescence of, 11
  purposes served, 11, 36, 85
  rectors, 46
  Scholastic history of, 47–48
Fischer, Ed, 261, 288
Fisher, Eddie, 254
Fisher, Greta, 352n46
Fisk Jubilee Singers, 240
Fitzgerald, Robert S., 283
Fitzgibbon, James R., 137
Florman, Mr., 104
Foik, Father Paul, C.S.C., 345n35
Foley, J. S., 138
football games
  half-time minstrel shows, 240
  Notre Dame-College of the
    Pacific, 258
  Notre Dame-Purdue, 201
  televised, 254
  in WH, pre-radio, 156–57, 201
football program, 156–57
football stadium, 11, 141
football team, 196, 227, 255–58.
    See also Gipp, George;
    Rockne, Knute
Ford, W., 136
Forget-Me-Nots, 174
Foskett, Donald A., 213
Foster, Thomas J., 332n12
Founder's Day celebrations. *See*
    St. Edward's Day celebrations
the Four Horsemen, 227

Fourth of July celebrations, 16–17,
    167
Frederick, Brother (Edmund
    Kräling), 94, 100, 108,
    111–12, 114–15fig5.3, 347n62
Frenay, Mr., 27
French, Father James J., C.S.C.,
    357n9
French Club, 258
Furnished Apartments, 28

Gabriel, Brother (Bernard Smyth/
    Smith), 24, 39, 335n31
Gaddis, William, 283
Gaelic League, 199
Galaxy, Lavish Escapade (Merce
    Cunningham Dancers), 262
Galileo, 306
Galileo and the Church
    Conference, 311
Gallagher, Tom, 239
The Galloper, 179, 180fig6.7
Garfield, James A., 91–92, 278
Garrick, Father David, C.S.C., 220,
    381n20, 381n23
Gatian, Brother, 16, 18, 331n7,
    332n8
George, Zelma Watson, 262
The Ghost, 53
ghost of Washington Hall
  Brother Cajetan as, 218
  construction worker as, 217
  earliest published reports, 205,
    206–7
  George Gipp as the, 157, 186,
    206, 210–14, 216–21
  perpetrating the hoax, 208–10,
    217–18
  photographs, 209fig7.1,
    215fig7.2, 220
  sightings, 211, 216–17, 220
  steeplejack version, 90, 217,
    218–19, 220

theater student version, 220
tradition of, 3, 221
"Ghost of Washington Hall"
    (*Scholastic*), 207–8
ghosts of Notre Dame
    Badin Hall, 205, 206–7
    Music Hall, 206
    Studebaker Factory, 205–6
Gibbons, P. J., 309fig10.2
Gilbert, L., 124
Gillespie, John Purcell, 335n37
Gillespie, Maria Rebecca, 335n37
Gillespie, Mother Mary Angela,
    C.S.C., 330n2, 335n37
Gillespie, Reverend Cornelius
    "Neal" H., 19–20, 54–55,
    62–63, 175, 330n2, 335n37,
    340n59
Gillespie Choral Union, 62, 340n59
Gilson, Etienne, 227
Ginsberg, Allen, 282, 283
Gipp, George
    football career, 185–86, 255,
    258
    the ghost of Washington Hall,
    157, 186, 206, 210–14,
    216–21
    mentioned, 227
    nickname, 369n12
    residence, 368n3
    "win one for the Gipper,"
    378n102
Girac, Max
    career, 334n20
    choir founding, 331n5
    music lost in Great Fire, 72
    pedestal in WH, 146, 149,
    149fig5.14, 267, 268,
    356n115
    Silver Jubilee music, 53
    Washington's Birthday
    celebrations music, 20, 50
The Girl of the Golden West, 183

Glee Club
    1888 fundraising Exhibition,
    134–35
    beginnings, 62–63, 196
    Golden Jubilee, 161
    Kate Smith radio show, 258
    mentioned, 303, 314
    new venues for, 264
    Saint Patrick's Day celebrations,
    86
    Washington's Birthday
    celebrations, 161, 167
    WWI hiatus, 197
Gold and Blue Serenaders,
    182fig6.8, 183
Golden Jubilee, 155, 159–63
Goldstein, Al, 282
Goodell, Charles, 284–85
Good News, 274, 275fig9.2, 276,
    277
The Good Woman of Setzuan, 309
Gorski, Father Eugene Francis,
    C.S.C., 246–47, 253, 375n81
Gouesse, Father, 53
Gounod, Charles François, 146,
    148, 149fig5.13, 268
Grace, S. P., 227
grade school (minims), 158.
    See also St. Edward's Hall
    (minims)
Grand Chorus of the Alumni, 159
Grand Jubilee Ode Chorus, 160
Granger, Father Alexis, C.S.C., 63,
    142, 332n12
Granger, Indiana, 332n12
Gray, Isaac P., 160
Great Fire of 1879
    damages, 2, 71–72, 75fig4.3
    insurance coverage, 78
    photographs, 73fig4.1
    rebuilding project, 74–76, 138,
    218–19
Green, Jerome J., 254, 377n97

Gregori, Luigi
  career, 348n5
  as costume designer, 102, 104,
    109, 127
  mentioned, 108
  portraiture by, 130–31,
    132–33fig5.9, 136
  WH interior redo, 112, 113,
    116fig5.4, 126, 142–50,
    143fig5.10, 143fig5.11,
    148fig5.12, 149fig5.13,
    150fig5.15
  WH interior undone, 101,
    142–44, 266–68
Griffith, Allen A., 50–51, 57,
  147–48, 339n46, 347n55
Griffith, D.W., 190
Grisoli, Ron, 352n46
Gueguen, John, 256
Guilty Pleasures, 176
Guiteau, Charles J., 91
Guys and Dolls, 277
gymnasium
  communal assembly functions,
    10, 141, 254, 313
  completion, 108
  construction, 46–47, 218
  dimensions, 111fig5.2, 349n19
  first plans, 78, 89–90, 96, 97
gyroscope, 201

H. & C. Studebaker, 353n63,
  368n2
Hacket, Mr., 135
Haid, Father, 342n91
"Hail Columbia," 54
Haller, George Dewey, 167
Hamlet (Shakespeare), 131, 263,
  278, 286, 305–6, 306
Hardtke, Father, 253, 269
Hare, David, 283
Harper, Jesse C., 364n67
Harvey, 244

Harvey, Father Arthur S., C.S.C.
  biographical details, 377n94
  modernization of WH, 142,
    144, 263–64
  photograph of, 309fig10.2
  productions
    —*Babes in Arms*, 276
    —*The Boy Friend*, 276
    —Broadway hits, 246, 276–79
    —*The Caine Mutiny Court
     Martial*, 253
    —*Camelot*, 277
    —*Death of a Salesman*, 253–54,
     272
    —*Detective Story*, 253
    —*The Fantasticks*, 276
    —*Finian's Rainbow*, 255, 276
    —*Good News*, 274, 275fig9.2, 276
    —*Guys and Dolls*, 277
    —*Hamlet*, 278
    —*How to Succeed in Business
     Without Really Trying*, 277
    —*King Lear*, 278, 305
    —*Macbeth*, 278
    —*The Medium*, 276
    —*The Most Happy Fella*, 276
    —*My Fair Lady*, 272, 276, 278,
     279fig9.3
    —*Oklahoma*, 276
    —*Othello*, 278
    —*The Playboy of the Western
     World*, 280
    —*The Potting Shed*, 280
    —*Seventeen*, 254, 276
    —*Shadow and Substance*, 308
    —*South Pacific*, 276
    —*The Threepenny Opera*, 276
  return to WH, 308
  theatre program under, 244,
    246, 247, 252–55
  University Theatre creation
    assumed by, 269–70
  See also University Theatre

Harvey, Tad, 239

Haydn, Franz Joseph, 146, 148, 149fig5.13, 268

Hedda Gabler, 247, 249

Hellenists, 101–4, 108, 109, 112

Heller, Joseph, 282, 284

Henehan, Tom, 283

Henry IV (Shakespeare), 16, 39, 42

Henson, Jim, 371n21

Hering, Frank Earle, 164

Hesburgh, Father Theodore M., C.S.C.

  on Americanization of Father Sorin, 20

  "Courtship and Marriage" lecture, 262

  favorite musical, 276

  ghost of Washington Hall and, 3, 205

  Kennedy assassination, 278

  move to coeducation, 274

  on television and the university, 254

  on WH purpose, 4

Hesburgh Library, 383n1

Hickey, William M., 242fig8.4

Hicks, Granville, 281

Hicks, Phil, 218–19

The Hidden Gem, 67–68

high school plays, 251

A History of St. Joseph County Indiana (Howard), 42

Hoch, Theodor, 352n40

Holderith, Father George, 258

Holiday Inn (film), 239

Holland, Peter, 306

Holslag, Frank W., 191

Holy Cross House, 287

Hope, Arthur J., C.S.C., 19

"The Horn Blows at Midnight" (Walker), 214

Hotel Universe, 251

The House of Blue Leaves, 277

Howard, E., 135

Howard, Professor, 28, 336n49

Howard, Timothy Edward, 39, 42, 131, 195

Howard Hall, 258

Howells, William Dean, 187

How to Succeed in Business Without Really Trying, 277

Hoynes, Colonel William, 202, 227

Hubbard, Lucius, 125

Hudson, Mr., 23

Hudson, Reverend D. E., 92

Huebner, Joseph H., 245, 375n69, 375n81

Huguelet, Adalbert, 370n1

Hyde, Douglas, 199, 367n118

Hynes, Jack, 246

ideomotor theory, 206

If I Were King, 53

Impersonal Pronoun Productions (IPP), 284

"Informal Senior Night," 223–24

The Inspector General, 286

interiors

  Ackerman/Frederick, 114–15fig5.3, 144, 153–54

  expenses, 144

  gallery railing, 108

  Gregori/Rusca redo, 112, 113, 116fig5.4, 126, 142–50, 143fig5.10, 143fig5.11, 148fig5.12, 150fig5.15, 153–54, 155

  Gregori/Rusca redo undone, 101, 142–44

  new seating, 44–45

  orchestra brass rail, 151

  Sosman & Landis, 116fig5.4, 152, 153–54, 155

In the Zone, 188

Ireland, Bishop, 160

Ireland, Reverend John, 198

Irish folklore lecture (Hyde), 199
Irish Renaissance, 229
"Irish Renaissance" (Yeats), 229
"Irish Wit and Humor"
    (McManus), 198–99
Irving, Henry, 68, 360n41
Isidore, Brother (Patrick Crowley),
    24, 46, 334n31, 339n34
It Ain't Hay, 244

Jazz Band, 303
Jellison, Pauline, 361n50
Jewett, Mr., 135
John Adams High School, 258
Johnson, Carla, 305–6
Jolly, Ellen Ryan, 167
Jones, LeRoi (Amiri Baraka), 284
Jordan Auditorium, 383n1
Joyce, Reverend Edmund P.,
    C.S.C., 383n1
Joyce Athletic and Convocation
    Center, 10, 141, 293, 313,
    330n11
Juilliard School Drama Division,
    308
Juilliard String Quartet, 262
Julius Caesar (film), 189
Julius Caesar (Shakespeare),
    124–26, 131, 137–39, 175,
    235, 306
Junior Band, 41, 56
Junior Play Room (Junior
    Recreation Hall). *See* Music
    Hall/Junior Recreation Hall

Kabel, Mr., 15
Karr, Frederick, 195, 366n104
Kavanaugh, Richard, 278, 381n20,
    381n27
Kaye, Danny, 239
Kean, Charles, 358n15
Keane, Bishop John J., 160
Keenan Hall, 220

Kehoe, Father, 259
Kelly, Francis "Frank" William, 135,
    173, 232–35, 245, 269–70,
    274, 361n50
Kendall, George Samuel, 231
Kennedy, John F., 278, 329n6,
    371n18
Kennedy, Kevin, 309fig10.2
Kennedy, Robert, 285
Kenvin, Roger, 277
Keough, Jinny Porcari, 218
Kertez, Katy, 312fig10.3
King, Martin Luther, Jr., 282
King Lear (Shakespeare), 278, 305,
    306
Kiss Me Kate, 246–47, 310
Kleine, George, 189, 365n89
Knights of Columbus
    Council meeting on ghost, 206,
        210
    Crumley talk on ghosts, 219
    "under God" in Pledge of
        Allegiance, 358n12
    vaudeville shows sponsored,
        185, 213, 238–39, 240
Knute Rockne All American (film),
    255–56, 257–58
Koehler, Charlemagne, 181
Kolars, Frank, 212
Krapp's Last Tape (San Quentin
    Players), 307–8
Krier, William, 288
Ku Klux Klan, 191, 373n44
Küng, Father Hans, 296
Kuntz, Peter, 174, 175
Kunz, Harvey, 191

Laboratory "black-box" Theatre
    Bent, 300
    created, 298, 300
    Macbeth, 306
    Night of the Assassins, 300
    Othello, 306

La Chassaigne, M., 28, 336n49
The Lady's Not for Burning, 247, 251
LaFortune Student Center, 303
Lahey, Mr., 135
La Madre, 251, 252
Lane, Kathleen, 352n46
Law Auditorium, 233, 236
Law Debating Society, 194
law library, 218
Law Society, 194
Lawton, Tony, 306, 311, 312fig10.3
Leahy, Frank, 255
lecturers and guests, notable. *See specific names*
Legion of Decency, 379n120
Le Million (film), 258
Lemonnier, Father Augustus
    band and choir role, 40, 41, 56
    biographical details, 340n58
    death of, 62–63
    Philomathean Constitution approved, 54
    photograph of, 27fig2.4
    responsibilities, 58
    scene design, 96
Lemonnier Circulating Library, 340n58, 359n24
Lenihan, Emmett George, 165, 183, 186, 364n73, 364n75
Lessons in Elocution with Numerous Selections (Griffith), 339n46
Leszczynski, Marion, 247
Let's Get Going, 241–42, 244
The Life of Galileo, 311, 312fig10.3
Lifton, Mitchell, 286, 290–91, 298
lighting
    electrification, 102, 104–5, 109, 113, 125, 144
    gas, 144
    Harvey era, 266
    stage, 68–69, 100, 108–10, 144, 268

Lilly, Father Edward, C.S.C., 146, 148–49, 149fig5.14, 267, 268, 356n115
Lincoln, Abraham, 42, 43, 278
Linnets, 238, 373n45
Liscombe, Frederick J., 135, 136–37, 355n96
literary societies founding, 331n5
Little Theatre, 233, 269
Little Theatre movement, 252
Livingston, Leon, 226
Local Council of Holy Cross
    amphitheatre construction instructions, 15
    commencement location decision, 18
    Exhibition Hall decisions, 23–24, 24, 26, 27, 61–62
    fire extinguisher decision, 113, 117
    fire repairs decision, 19
    gymnasium authorization, 46–47
    Junior Play Room construction, 43–44
    on Lincoln assassination, 42
    musical instruments funded, 22
    Music Hall rectors assigned, 46
    music program, direction of, 17, 40–41, 43–44
    Science Hall authorized, 108
    ticketing decision, 61–62
    Washington Hall decisions, 40, 46, 59–60
Lockman the illusionist, 231
Lockwood, Harold, 192
Log Chapel, 331n4
Lord Byron, 234, 235
"The Lost Confessional" (Nugent), 197–98
Loux, Michael J., 303, 305
The Love of the Nightingale, 310
Lujack, John C., Jr., 256, 378n103

Lyman, Walter C., 137
Lyons, Joseph A.
    ability of, 62–64, 90, 340n59
    elocution lessons, 126
    injury, 125–26
    Major John Andre, 90
    mentioned, 147–48
    oratory and elocution courses, 57
    photograph of, 115fig5.3
    Pius IX's Golden Episcopal
        Jubilee, 64
    play production, 97, 126, 131,
        175
    Silver Jubilee, 60
    St. Cecilia Philomathean
        Society advisor, 54–55, 56,
        58, 68
    St. Edward's Day celebrations,
        124
    Washington Day celebrations, 63

Macbeth (Shakespeare), 131, 277,
    278, 305, 306
MacLaughlin, Professor, 177fig6.6
The Madwoman of Chaillot, 310
The Magnificent Ambersons, 186
Maguire, Mrs. Antoine, 131
Mailer, Norman, 282
Main Building
    architecture, 76
    commencement events, 91, 127
    completion, 108, 117
    electrification, 93–94, 113
    music department housed in, 81
    purposes served, 3, 11
    rebuilding post-fire, 74–75
    rotunda, 84, 346n49
Main Building I
    commencement function,
        13–14, 18, 317–18
    exhibition hall space, 153
    expansion of, 20–22
    portico, 19

Main Building II
    beginnings, 43
    Great Fire of 1879 and, 46
    orientation, 45–46
    performance space, 49
Main Quad, 3fig1.2
Major John Andre, 64, 65, 90
Malloy, Father Edward "Monk,"
    C.S.C., 287, 313–14
Mamet, David, 283
Mangan, John, 212
Manier, Ted, 309fig10.2
Manion, Clarence "Pat," 218
The Man on the Flying Trapeze
    (Tony Sarg Marionettes), 232
Manual Labor School, 32fig3.1
The Man Who Came to Dinner, 244
Marconi, Guglielmo, 229–30, 254,
    371n12
Marie P. DeBartolo Center for the
    Performing Arts, 5, 10, 141,
    270, 294, 311–13
Marmon, Joseph A., 161, 357n9
Marrivault, Father, 317
Marshall, Dick, 244
Mary Agnes, Sister, 250
Mary Frances Jerome, Sister,
    359n23
Mary Francis, Sister, P. C., 251
Mary Lucretia, Sister, 359n23
Maurilius, Brother (William J.
    DeGan), C.S.C., 212, 213,
    219, 368n11
Maximus, Brother (Eugene Petit),
    24, 335n31
McAllister, Father Charles, C.S.C.,
    373n45
McAvoy, Father Thomas T., 346n35
McBrien, Father Richard P., 296
McCue, M. J., 227
McDonald Studio, 152, 356n121
McGath, J. J., 124
McGean, Mr., 19

McGuire, Randy, 39
McKenna Hall Auditorium, 383n1
McKenzie, James, 282
McKinley, William, 155, 202, 278, 367n113
McKowen, Doris, 235
McManus, Seumas, 198–99
McMeel Family Chair in Shakespeare Studies, 306
McMullin, Ernan, 311
McMurtry, Larry, 283
McNally, E. A., A.M., 49
Meagher, Thomas Francis, 199
The Medium, 276
Meet the Missus, 244
Melady, Mr., 135
Memorial Library auditorium, 264
memorial services
    Garfield, James A., 91–92, 278
    Kennedy, John F., 278
    Lincoln, Abraham, 278
    McKinley, William, 278
Mendoza College of Business, 383n1
Merce Cunningham Dancers, 262
The Merchant of Venice (Shakespeare), 131
The Merry Wives of Windsor (Shakespeare), 241, 242fig8.4, 311
A Midsummer Night's Dream (Shakespeare), 306
Mignon Club, 96–97
Mills, Thomas E., 236, 241
Miltner, Reverend Charles Christopher, C.S.C., 230, 371n13
Mi-na-gi-shig, chief of the Otchipwe, 63
Minavi, Jim, 213
minims, 334n30. *See also* St. Edward's Hall (minims)
minstrel numbers in the movies, 239, 362nn59

minstrel shows, 7, 61, 156, 178–79, 183, 184fig6.9, 237–40, 362nn58–59
Mishawaka Band, 19
Misiewicz, Kassie, 309fig10.2
The Mistake, 52
Mister Roberts (cancelled), 247, 253
Modern Languages Departments, 260
Mohun, M., 137
Molière, 60, 61, 62, 145, 147, 178, 245, 267, 314, 335n100
Moloney, Father, 174, 179, 181, 358n15
Monday Night Movies, 290
Monogram Absurdities, 239
Monogram Club, 234, 237, 240, 373n43
Monogram Minstrels, 237
Montenegro, Pio, 206, 210, 211, 212, 213, 214
Mooney, Charles P., 187
Moot Court, 53–54
Moreau Center for the Arts (SMC), 263–64, 269, 294
Morley, Hilda, 283
Morris, Karen, 300
Morris Inn, 254
Morrissey, J. P., 217, 285–86
Morrissey, Reverend Andrew, C.S.C., 145, 162, 202, 357n9
Morse, Mr., 65
Morton, Mr., 135
Moses, Thomas Gibbs, 357n122
The Most Happy Fella, 276
Mozart, 145, 267
Mr. and Mrs. Broadway, 244, 246
Mr. Noisy, 52
Murdock, Samuel T., 161–62
Murphy, Chris, 283
Murphy, Michael, 309fig10.2
museum, Main Building 1, 22

music
  accompanying oratorical
    contests, 195
  commencement events, 14,
    18–19, 27, 42, 127–28, 223
  Golden Jubilee, 159–60
  holiday celebrations, 19–20
  Independence Day exercises, 167
  McKinley memorial, 202
  niche audiences served, 157
  Silver Jubilee, 51–52
  St. Edward's Day celebrations,
    51–52, 136
  technology's effect on
    communal nature of, 8–9,
    66–67
  Washington Hall dedication, 28
  Washington's Birthday
    celebration, 161–62, 164, 167
musicals, student-written, 241,
  244, 246
Music Department
  Crowley Hall acquired, 141
  established, 41
  faculty, 26, 40, 41, 44–45, 88
  present-day, 314
  University Theatre influence, 235
  vocal department established, 47
  in WH, limitations of, 233,
    270–71, 294
  WH departed by, 301–3
Music Hall (Academy of Music),
  74, 81, 83–86, 88, 90, 94,
  96–97
Music Hall ghost, 206
Music Hall/Junior Recreation Hall
  architecture, 44
  construction, 31, 40, 41, 42,
    43–44, 85
  described, 122
  Great Fire of 1879 and, 2, 46,
    72, 73fig4.1, 74fig4.2, 76, 79
  location, 344n13

mentioned, 34
  rectors, 46
music program, 16, 17, 20–22,
  40–41
music saloon, Main Building,
  13–14, 18
My Fair Lady, 272, 276, 278,
  279fig9.3
My Notre Dame (Stritch), 157

"Napoleon and France" (film), 189
Nash, Matt, 309fig10.2
National Congress of Religious of
  the United States, 249
National Players of Catholic
  University, 278, 280, 306
National Theatre of the Deaf, 307
Navy Drill Hall, 223, 269
"Navy's 'Passage to Freedom'"
  (Dooley), 231
Nelis, Jim, 309fig10.2
Neuert, Willard, 298, 308,
  309fig10.2
Newman, H. H., 227
New Orleans' Exposition and
  World's Fair, 129–30
New Playwrights Workshop, 300
new WH (1882–1895)
  Academy of Music renamed as,
    xxii, 2, 106–7
  completion, 99, 108, 117,
    120–22, 153–54
  construction costs, 122
  described, 103, 105–6, 124–25,
    145–47, 155
  events
    —debate and elocution,
      136–37
    —described, 124–25
    —pre-filmic productions,
      129–30, 188
  first reference to, 107
  praised, 104–5

purposes served, 101
See also Academy of Music
    (1879–1882); Washington
    Hall
New Year's night, 53–54
Neyron, Reverend Louis, M.D.,
    90, 346n45
Nightingale, Wm., 18
A Night Off, 178
Night of the Assassins, 300
"Nights and Daze," 243
Niles Band, 19
Nims, John Frederick, 283
Nobles, Mr., 104
Notre Dame
    academic reorganization
        (1920), 232–233
    Americanization of, 20, 29
    black students matriculate, 240
    central core of buildings, 17–18
    coeducation at, 248, 274
    curriculum reform, 156
    electrification, 93–94, 102,
        104–5, 109, 113
    endowment, 158
    films about, 255, 257–58
    fire (1974) and renovation
        post-, 285–86
    Golden Jubilee celebration, 142
    graduate school formation,
        158–59
    honorary degrees, special
        convocation, 230, 254
    Irish connection, 198–99
    patriotism and, 163–64
    telegraphy and telephonics,
        65–67, 157
    traditions, 162
"Notre Dame, Our Mother,"
    369n11
Notre Dame Band
    beginnings, 68, 331n7
    Christmas Exercises, 129

commencement events, 106,
    128, 330n1
director appointed, 40
Exhibition events, 49–50
founding, 331n5
Golden Jubilee, 160
instrument storage, 41
Kate Smith radio show, 258
McKinley memorial, 202
Music Hall wing, 86
Saint Patrick's Day celebrations,
    178
Washington's Birthday
    celebrations, 19–20, 50,
    125, 164
Notre Dame Monogram Men's
    Club, 373n43
Notre Dame Players, 181, 186.
    See also Players Club;
    University Players
Notre Dame Radio Club, 260–61
Notre Dame/Saint Mary's
    Savoyards, 241
"Notre Dame Victory March,"
    369n11
Nugent, Reverend F. J., 197–98
Nuns of the Battlefield (Jolly), 167
nuns' summer school play. *See*
    summer school nuns' play

Oberkoetter, Robert, 279fig9.3
O'Brien, James, 24, 334n31
O'Connor, Nancy, 309fig10.2
O'Connor, W., 104, 175
O'Dea, Michael, 147, 356n114
O'Donnell, Charles L., C.S.C., 219,
    230, 369n11
O'Donnell, J.V., 103
O'Donnell, Reverend J. Hugh,
    C.S.C., 234
Oedipus Rex, 101–4, 126, 263, 306
Oedipus Tyrannus, 175, 176,
    177fig6.6

Office of Student Activities, 312
Office of Student Affairs, 260
The Office Seekers, 102, 103
"Oh, Columbia, Beloved!" 137
Ohala, John, 288
O'Hara, John F., 236, 237
Ohmer, Susan, 195
O'Keefe, Walter, 240, 374n48
Oklahoma, 276
O'Laughlin Auditorium, 263, 269, 305
Old Heidelberg, 245–46
Oliver, 277
Oliver Hotel, 188, 368n3
Oliver Opera House, 190, 191
O'Mahony, Professor, 62, 63
O'Malley, Austin, 202
O'Malley, Frank Ward, 227
O'Malley, Raymond G., 164, 177fig6.6
O'Meara, Timothy, 303, 308, 311
Onahan, William J., 198
One-Act Play Festival, 247
O'Neil, J., 44–45
orchestra
  Columbian quatercentenary, 137
  commencement events, 91
  Exhibition Day, 336n49
  Golden Jubilee, 160–61
  instrument funding, 16
  Music Hall wing, 86
  St. Edward's Day celebrations, 53, 136
  Washington's Birthday celebrations, 50, 125, 139, 161, 167
O'Rourke, William, 281
Orpheonics, 125, 127, 128
Orpheus Mandolin Orchestra, 160, 161, 178
O'Shaughnessy Hall, 247, 254, 298
O'Sullivan, John Louis, 357n3

Othello (Shakespeare), 278, 306
Our Pastor (Daniel Sully Company), 361n52
The Outcast, 102, 103
Overmayer, Mr., 41

Pacelli, Eugenio Cardinal (Pius XII), 6, 229, 230
Pane, Aubrey, 381n27
papal infallibility lecture (Benson), 200–1
Parade at the Devil's Bridge, 251
Paul, Professor, 62, 131, 139
Paulding, Dr. Frederick, 186, 365n81
Paulist Choir, 227
Payne, F., 227
Peking Opera Troupe of Shanghai, 308
performing arts center, need for, 16–17, 293, 313
Peter, Brother (Felix Whaller), 24, 334n31
Peterson, Professor, 196–97
"Phantom at Notre Dame" (Davis), 217
Phelan, Mary Madeline Miers Gillespie (Mrs. William), 19, 24, 25, 39, 330n2, 335n37
Phelan, William T., 19, 330n2, 335n37
Phelan family, 1–2
Phelan Hall, 107, 349n18
Phelan Science Hall, 93
phenakistoscope, 130
Philbin Studio Theatre, 141
Philharmonic Association, 49, 53
Phillips, Charles, 234–35, 372n27
Phillips, Frank B., 358n10
Philodemic Literary and Debating Association, 136–37, 194
Philopatrian Society (preps), 28, 56, 69, 181, 194

Philopatrians of Carroll Hall
(preps), 360n42
Philopatrians of St. Edwards Hall
(minims), 360n42
phonograph, 67
photography, 152
Piatt, Donn, 101, 348n2
Pickford, Mary, 259
Piepul, "Moose," 239
Pierre Patelin, 251
Pius IX, 6, 63–65, 342n90
Pius VI, 136, 355n95
Pizarro, 28, 101, 102
The Playboy of the Western World,
280
Players Club, 173, 187, 188, 208,
234. *See also* Notre Dame
Players; University Players
Players Incorporated, 375n73
playwriting course, 235
Pledge of Allegiance, 156, 358n12
plumbing
interior, 157
shower addition, 169, 269
toilet facilities, 110, 111fig5.2,
168–69, 170fig6.4, 171fig6.4,
269
Poligano, Mr., 146–47
Pornography (and Censorship)
Conference, 282
Porterfield, J. D., 227
The Potting Shed, 280
"The Pound of Flesh," 85
The Prayer (Augustin Daly), 361n50
Preservation Hall Jazz, 308
President's Day, 173, 179, 360n39,
363n74
Preston, Professor, 164, 178, 195
Priebe, Harry, 281
*The Prince of Portage Prairie, or
The Burning of Bertrand,*
53–54
The Princess Marries a Page, 251

Pritchard, David, 371n21
The Prodigal Law Student, 52, 53
Purcell, Bishop, 18
Purcell Pavilion, 383n1

Qi Shu Fang's Peking Opera
Troupe of Shanghai, 308
Quadrangle, 224
Quinn, F. A., 124, 181
Quo Vadis (film), 189–90, 193

A Race for a Dinner, 54
Radio & Television Production
Procedures, 261
radio lectures, 232
radio studios, 260
Ramsay, W. E., 131
Rathgeb, Donald, 246
Rea, Mrs., 90
reading rooms, 107
Reagan, Ronald, 258, 378n102,
378n111
Rebeck, Theresa, 286
The Recognition, 51, 129
recreational space
Academy of Music, 88–90,
89fig4.5, 122
billiard room, 26, 34
bowling alley, 34
destroyed in the fire, 88
first WH, 88
Main Building I, 21, 21fig2.2
reading rooms, 107
of WH, replaced, 141
See also Music Hall/Junior
Recreation Hall
Reed, Ishmael, 283
Regan, Martin J., C.S.C., 115fig5.3,
163
Rehan, Ada, 160, 361n50
Reynolds, Marjorie, 239
Rhinoceros, 280–81
Rhodius, G., 103

Ricci Band Rehearsal Hall, 141, 302

Rice, Thomas Dartmouth, 346n46

Richard III (Shakespeare), 115fig5.3, 127, 131, 134, 136, 138, 175

Richardson, William, 257

Richelieu, 52–53, 172, 174

Ries, Christina, 221

The Rightful Heir, 178

The Rise of Peter McCabe, 179

The Rivals, 23

Roach, William, 226

Robert Emmet: The Martyr of Irish Liberty, 112–13, 114–15fig5.3

Robert Francis, Brother (Thomas O'Brien) "Brother Movie", 260, 287, 379n120

Roberts, James, 282

Robertson, Pamela. See *Guilty Pleasures*

Robin Hood (Tony Sarg Marionettes), 232

Rockefeller, Nelson, 285

Rockefeller Hall, 226, 302, 303, 370n5

Rockne, Knute
  biographical details, 156–57, 363n63
  celebrity, 180fig6.7, 363n66
  commemorative stamp, 378n111
  at Notre Dame
  —athletic career, 156–57, 181, 363n67, 364n69
  —as coach, 185
  —fims about career, 255–57
  —Klan riots, 373n44
  —roles played, 227
  —scholarship, 185, 337n16
  —on stage and in the orchestra, 179, 181, 182fig6.8, 183, 185–86, 364n69
  "win one for the Gipper," 378n102

Rockne Memorial, 218

Rockne Week festivities, 258

Rogerson, William, 370n1

Romance of the Willow Pattern, 251

Room Service, 236–37, 251

The Rosary, 183

Rosencrantz & Gildenstern Are Dead, 306

Rossini, Gioachino, 146, 148, 149fig5.14, 268

Ruddiman, Mr., 66

rugby football association, 134–35

Rusca, Louis
  biographical details, 112, 356n113
  WH interior redo, 108, 113, 114–15fig5.3, 116fig5.4, 142–50, 143fig5.10, 143fig5.11, 148fig5.12, 149fig5.13, 150fig5.15, 266–68
  WH interior undone, 101, 266–68

Rutherford, Toni, 220

Saint Mary's Academy, 330n2, 335n37

Saint Mary's College
  faculty-written plays, 249–51
  mentioned, 43
  ND/SMC cooperative theatre program, 279–81, 291, 308
  Pacelli convocation, 230
  performing arts center, 255
  Washington's Birthday celebrations, 165–66
  wireless message from Sacred Heart, 254
  women onstage policy, 274, 275fig9.2, 279fig9.3

Saint Patrick's Day celebrations
  The Ballroom, 176
  Columbian quatercentenary, 138

The Corsican Brothers, 86
female theatrical roles, 176
Macbeth, 176
mentioned, 6, 13, 63
minstrel shows, 178
new WH, 112–13, 114–15fig5.3, 138
preparations for, 69
Robert Emmet: The Martyr of Irish Liberty, 112–13, 114–15fig5.3
San Quentin Players, 307–8
Sarg, Anthony Frederick, 371n21
Sarnoff, David, 254
Saturday Night Movie, 288–89
Savage, Henry, 192
Scheppers, Madame, 125
Schmidt, Eddie, 209
The School for Scandal, 186
school of fine arts, 232–33
Schubert, Charlie, 246
Schumacher, Matthew, 177fig6.6
Schwartz, Maurice, 300–1
science and technology demonstrations, 201
Science Hall, 108, 110, 113, 211, 303
Scientific Association, 130
Scott, Joseph, 227
Scott, Siiri, 306, 308, 309fig10.2
The Screen Arts, 261
Seamon, Mark, 306
seating capacity
    Academy of Music, 97, 139
    first WH, 34, 37, 61
    Harvey era, 265
    new WH, 97, 103, 105, 117, 122, 139, 141
    present-day, xxv, 355n107
self-serve laundry, 302
semi-annual Exhibition, 49–50
Senior Orchestra, 68
senior play room, 344n13

Senior Recreation Hall (containing Washington Hall)
    completion, 28, 43
    construction, 23
    dancing floor created, 47
    demolished, 99, 107
    Great Fire of 1879 and, 73fig4.1, 78
Seniors' Day 1908, 169, 171
Seniors' Play Room, 36fig3.4
September 11, 2001, terrorist attacks, 311
Seven Nuns at Las Vegas, 249–51
Seven Nuns South of the Border, 377n89
Seventeen, 254, 276
Shadow and Substance, 308
Shaefer, C., 24
Shaeffer, Mr., 104
Shake Down the Thunder (film), 261
Shakespeare, William, 278, 306. *See also specific plays by*
Shakespeare night, 131
Shakespeare portrait by Gregori, 130–31, 132–33fig5.9
Shakespeare Studies, 306
Shaw, Father, 331n5
Shaw, Reverend Mr. (of Vincennes), 318
Shea, Laurie, 309fig10.2
the shed, 16–17
Sheen, Reverend Monsignor Fulton J., 229, 230, 371n17
Sheridan, Benny, 239
Sherman, William Tecumseh, 42–43, 335n37
She Stoops to Conquer, 237
shoe-shine stand, 226
Shortis, Richard A., 330n2
Showboat, 277
Silver Jubilee, 49, 51–53
Silver Jubilee (Lyons), 60
Silver Jubilee Club, 51, 52

Simon, Nick, 309fig10.2
singing, pedagogical value of, 62
Sinnott, Joe, 216–17
The Skin of Our Teeth, 277
Smith, Father John Talbert, 238
Smith, Kate, 258
Smith, Mr., 135
Snavely, Luther, 299
Snite Museum, 383n1
Society for Psychical Research, 208
Soldani, Charles, 364n72
Sommer, Leonard, 245
Sophomore Literary Festival,
    281–83
Sorin, Edward F., C.S.C.
    Americanization of, 167
    biographical details, 340n58
    commencement location
        decision, 18
    construction of the barn,
        332n13
    correspondence, 25, 39, 94
    death of, 142
    first mass thirty-ninth
        anniversary celebration, 91
    Founder's Day celebrations, 13,
        51–52, 55, 68, 82, 83–84, 93,
        123–24
    Great Fire of 1879 rebuilding, 84
    mentioned, 78
    Music Hall plans, 79
    naming of WH, 6
    patriotism of, 20, 29, 65
    performing arts center vision,
        314
    Philomathean Constitution
        approved, 54
    on rebuilding, 75–76
    Sacerdotal Golden Jubilee,
        135–36
    Silver Jubilee year celebrations,
        51–53
    Summer Entertainment
        attended, 63

Washington Hall
    —dedication, 2, 13, 28
    —fundraising, 25
    —praised, 37
Sorin Hall Brigade, 138
Sorin Literary and Dramatic
    Association, 130
Sosman & Landis, 152, 153–54,
    356n122
A Soul in Fine Array, 249, 250fig8.6
South Bend, 46
South Bend Band, 14, 16, 19, 318
South Pacific, 276
Spalding, Bishop, 160
Spalding, John Lancaster, 160
Spanish-American War, 155, 164
Speaight, Robert W., 331n6
Speech and Drama, Department
    of, 233, 284
Speech Department courses, 241,
    261
Spencer, Terrence, 278
The Spirit of Notre Dame, 255–56,
    257
Stace, Arthur J., 52, 60, 80, 178,
    344n16
St. Aloysius Literary and Historical
    Society, 341n64
St. Aloysius Literary Society, 194
St. Aloysius Philodemic Society
    (Literary Association), 53,
    57, 340n59
Stansel, G. C. L., 191
Stanton, Mr., 24
Starr, Eliza Allen, 198, 366n111
Stay Tuned for Addleman, 246
St. Cecilia Day celebrations, 55, 56,
    93
St. Cecilia Philomathean Society
    beginnings, 54, 340n59
    changes concerning, 173
    Christmas Exercises, 128–29
    commencement, 55
    commencement plays, 51

constitution, 54–55

A Cure for Dumbness or Doctor Nolens, 62

debate and elocution, 57

The Execution of Major John Andre, 342n91

faculty officers, 54–55

festival days, 55

first WH departed, 95, 97

The Hidden Gem, 67–68

influence of, 233

"Le Bourgeois Gentilhomme," or "The Upstart," 60

mentioned, 156

The Miser, 62

The Office Seekers, 101, 102, 103

The Outcast, 101, 102, 103

Pius IX's Golden Episcopal Jubilee, 64

The Prodigal Law Student, 52, 53

purpose and history of, 47, 54, 56

The Recognition, 51

Silver Jubilee, 52, 53

St. Edward's Day celebrations, 69, 86

Summer Entertainment, 63

The White Knight, 58

St. Cecilia Philopatrian Association, 90, 97

St. Edward's College, 136

St. Edward's Day celebrations, 13, 51–52, 55, 68–69, 82–84, 86, 93, 123–24, 136

St. Edward's Hall (minims), 91, 113, 188, 334n30

St. Edward's Literary Association, 57

St. Edward Societies, 53

St. Edward's Society, 57

steeplejack ghost, 90, 217, 218–19, 220

Stepan Center, 141, 282, 313, 383n1

stereopticon exhibitions, 129–30, 188

Stevenson, Harry, 206, 209, 210–11, 213, 219

Stewart, Ann-Marie, 312

St. James's Quartette, 131

St. John's Orphan Asylum, 318

St. Joseph Company, 334n20

St. Joseph County sheriff, 282

St. Joseph Farm, 332n12

St. Joseph's Novitiate, 66

St. Louis University, 39

St. Mar, Mr., 16, 17

St. Michael's Laundry, 302

Stoffel, Reverend Nicholas, C.S.C., 104, 126, 127, 348n5

storage
  illustrations, 169fig6.3, 170fig6.4, 171fig6.4
  for instruments, 41, 46
  for sets, 153–54, 157, 167–68, 169fig6.3, 170fig6.4, 171fig6.4

Stormont, Robert, 305

The Story of the Irish Race (McManus), 198

Strategic Moment, 304

Stritch, Thomas, 157, 227, 229, 271, 308

Studebaker, Clement, 126, 353n63, 368n2

Studebaker, Henry, 353n63, 368n2

Studebaker Factory ghost, 205–6

Student-Faculty Film Society, 288–89

Students' Army Training Corps (SATC), 166

Student Welfare, Department of, 234, 244

student-written musicals, 241, 244, 246

Suite for Five (in Time and Space) (Merce Cunningham Dancers), 262

Sullivan, Joseph J., 202

Sullivan, Mary E., 166

Sullivan, Daniel, 188
Sully, Daniel, 361n52
Summer Drama Project, 249, 331n6
Summer Entertainment, 60, 63
Summers, H. G., 190
summer school, coeducational,
    158, 166
summer school nuns' play, 247–52,
    248fig8.5, 250fig8.6
Summer Shakespeare, 306, 331n6
Summertree, 277
Sweatnam, Willis P., 192
Syburg, Frederic
    Amadeus, 308
    The Billion Dollar Saint, 251
    Detective Story, 253
    The Good Woman of Setzuan,
        309
    Macbeth, 277, 278
    Othello, 278
    Priebe, Harry, 281
    retirement, 308–9, 311
    return to WH, 310
    University Theatre role, 264,
        268, 269, 276–78

Tabor Opera House, 347n61
A Tailor-Made Man, 241
The Taming of the Shrew
    (Shakespeare), 235, 306
Tartuffe, 310
Taylor, Mr., 23
technology
    communal assembly, effect on,
        7–9, 254–55
    for communication, advances
        in, 7, 65–67, 157, 201
    lectures and demonstrations of,
        201
    radio lectures, 232
Telecommunication Arts, 261
the telegraph and the telephone, 7,
    65–67, 157, 201

telegraph office, 226, 226fig8.2
television, 230, 254–55, 298
temperance movement, 198
The Tempest (Shakespeare), 305
Tenth Biennial National
    Convention of the Catholic
    Theatre Conference, 249
Teschke, Holger, 311, 312fig10.3
Tharp, Twyla, 284
Theater Grottesco, 308
theatre
    film and television overtaking
        of, 264
    focus on, costs to other
        performing arts, 270–71,
        273–74, 276
    as freestanding art form, 174
    ND/SMC cooperative program,
        279–81, 291, 308
    revitalization of, 233, 255,
        303–5
    Shakespeare productions as
        traditional, 305
    See also University Theatre
Theatre Department, 46, 152–53,
    268–69, 303–5
Theobald Matthew, Father, 353n56
Thespian Society
    Academy of Music dedication,
        101, 102
    advisors, 357n9
    beginnings, 54, 340n59
    changes concerning, 173
    Christmas entertainment, 62
    Columbian quatercentenary, 137
    commencement, 69
    "Falsely Accused, a Domestic
        Drama in three Acts," 129
    The Ghost, 53
    Golden Jubilee, 161
    Henry IV, 39
    Julius Caesar, 139
    mentioned, 156, 233

"Oh, Columbia, Beloved!" 137
Pizarro, 28, 101, 102
post-fire, 85
purpose, 60
Richelieu, 52–53
Silver Jubilee Club, 51
Silver Jubilee year productions, 52–53
St. Edward's Day celebrations, 52
Washington's Birthday celebrations, 69, 129, 139, 161
WH departed by, 96
WH painting funded, 38–39
Thorpe, Jim, 363n67
Three Men on a Horse, 247
The Threepenny Opera, 276
ticketing for performances, 61–62, 172, 229
Tittler, Robert, 5
Tony Sarg Marionettes, 232
Toohey, Father John M., 114fig5.3
torpedo demonstration, 201
Tracey, Marty, 309fig10.2
Tracy, Diane, 309fig10.2
Tumpane, John, 245, 246, 247, 252, 253, 254
Turn to the Right, 236
Twelfth Night (Shakespeare), 171–72, 172fig6.5, 175, 186, 305–6
Twining, Mr., 179
Twyla Tharp Dance Company, 284

"The Undead Flit About Tonight" (Wilcox), 214
Under Cover, 186
United States population, 330n11
University debating team, 195
University Dramatic Club, 179, 189, 233
University Players, 245–46. *See also* Notre Dame Players; Players Club

University Stock Company, 152, 156, 173–74, 181
University Theatre
   Elsen years, 244–46
   faculty-written plays, 249–52
   Harvey era (1954–1969)
   —new staging model, 275–76
   —role redefined, 244, 247, 252–55, 271–73, 276, 277–78
   —student-written musicals ended, 253
   —women onstage, 274, 275fig9.2, 279–81
   Kelly, Francis "Frank" William and the, 173, 232–35, 269–70
   seating capacity, 265
   See also specific productions
"Untimely Deaths on N.D. & S.M.C. Campuses 1840s–1990s" (Corson), 218
"The Upstart," 124
U.S.S. *Maine,* 164

V-12 Navy College Training Program, 243
Vacation, 174
Vargyas, Hildegarde, 253
variety shows, 237, 243
Varsity Club, 373n43
vaudeville, 185, 186, 213, 237–38, 240
Vaudeville Show (1911), 179
"The Victim" (film), 193
Vigeant, Gregory, 105
Vile Bodies, 246
"The Virginian" (film), 192
Virgin Mary statue, Golden Dome, 3fig1.2
Von Weller, Prof., 51

Wagner, Richard, 360n41
Waide, John, 39
Waiting for the Verdict, 174

Walker, Johnny, 214
Walsh, Dr. James J., 227
Walsh, J., 104
Walsh, Reverend J. J., 246
Walsh, Reverend T. E.
    Christmas Exercises, 128–29,
        134
    commencement events, 128, 223
    death of, 142
    Garfield memorial, 92
    Klan riots, 373n44
    The Outcast translated by, 102
    photograph of, 114–15fig5.3,
        133fig5.9
    Shakespeare night, 131
    St. Edward's Day celebrations,
        124
Walsh Hall Little Theatre, 233
Washington, George, 136, 146, 147,
    150fig5.15, 267, 268
Washington Hall
    expansion, need for, 37, 59–60,
        86, 87, 138–42, 172, 245
    future of, 314–15
    location, symbolism of, 11
    obsolescence of, 4–5, 96, 157,
        261, 300–1, 312
    one hundredth anniversary, 286
    as performance venue
    —1926–1927 program, 234–35
    —1955–1956 program, 261–62
    —1997–1998 calendar, 306–7
    —conflicting schedules, 245–46
    —demand for, 243–44
    professional management, 303–5
    purposes served, 6–7, 11
    timeline, xiii, xxi–xxv
    See also Academy of Music
        (1879–1882); first WH
        (1864–1882); new WH
        (1882–1895)
"The Washington Hall Ghost"
    (*Dome*), 209fig7.1

Washington's Birthday celebrations
    attendance, 60
    Catholic-American tensions, 165
    first WH, 2, 50–51, 53–54, 60,
        63, 69, 86
    flag ceremony, 156, 163–65,
        166–67, 358n12
    Golden Jubilee, 161
    mentioned, 6, 13
    music, 161–62, 164
    new WH, 124–26, 129, 139
    performances
    —*Bob Martin, Substitute
        Half-Back,* 181
    —*Julius Caesar,* 358n10
    —*A Night Off,* 175
    post-Great Fire, 86
    pre-WH, 19–20
    in the rotunda, 164–65
    Saint Mary's College women
        join in, 165–66
    WH dedication, 28
Watterson, Henry, 160
Watterson, Reverend John A.,
    103, 128
Waugh, Evelyn, 246
Weber, Georgia Ann (Mrs.
    Reginald Bain), 253–54
Welsh Singers, 227
Western Union Office, 223, 226,
    226fig8.2
Where's Charley, 247
White, Natalie E., 249–51, 252,
    376n87, 377n89
White, Orrin A., 361n50
White Christmas (film), 239
The White Knight, 58
The Widow's Might (film), 194
Wilcox, Joe, 214
Williams, A. A., 137
Williams, Edward B., 364n70,
    374n55
William Tell, 42, 91

Wiskirchen, Father George, C.S.C., 299
Wister, Owen, 192
WNDU-TV, 254–55, 278
Woelfle, Jack, 213
A Woman's Won't (Augustin Daly), 361n50
women onstage
 beginnings, 235–37
 Harvey era, 274, 279–81
 photographs of, 275fig9.2, 279fig9.3
 Summer School Nuns' Play, 247–52, 248fig8.5, 250fig8.6
 in touring companies, 361n50, 361n52

"The Wonders of the Ancient World" (Kendall), 231–32
Woodworth, George, 20, 334n20
World War I, 155, 165–66, 186
WSBT-TV, 254

"The Year of the Bard," 306
Yeats, W. B., 227, 229

Zahm, A. A., 104, 124
Zahm, Albert Francis, 220, 347n58
Zahm, Reverend John Augustine, C.S.C., 93, 105, 113, 129–30, 188, 195, 347n58
Zurhellen, Joan, 39

MARK C. PILKINTON

is professor of film, television, and theatre
at the University of Notre Dame.